KAZAAAM! SPLAT! PLOOF!

KAZAAAM! SPLAT! PLOOF!

The American Impact on European Popular Culture since 1945

Edited by
Sabrina P. Ramet
and
Gordana P. Crnković

ROWMAN & LITTLEFIELD PUBLISHERS, INC.
Lanham • Boulder • New York • Oxford

For Marijan Gubić
and
Andrea Feldman

ROWMAN & LITTLEFIELD PUBLISHERS, INC.

Published in the United States of America
by Rowman & Littlefield Publishers, Inc.
A Member of the Rowman & Littlefield Publishing Group
4720 Boston Way, Lanham, Maryland 20706
www.rowmanlittlefield.com

P.O. Box 317, Oxford OX2 9RU, United Kingdom

Copyright © 2003 by Rowman & Littlefield Publishers, Inc.

British Library Cataloguing in Publication Information Available

Library of Congress Cataloging-in-Publication Data

Kazaaam! splat! ploof! : the American impact on European popular culture since 1945 /
edited by Sabrina P. Ramet and Gordana P. Crnković
    p. cm.
    Includes bibliographical references and index.
    ISBN 0-7425-0000-4 (alk. paper) — ISBN 0-7425-0001-2 (pbk. : alk. paper)
    1. Europe—Civilization—American influences. 2. Ethnic attitudes—Europe. 3.
Popular culture—Europe—History—20th century. 4. National characteristics, European.
5. National characteristics, American. 6. United States—Relations—Europe. 7. Europe—
Relations—United States. I. Ramet, Sabrina P., 1949–   II. Crnković, Gordana.

D1055 .K39 2003
303.48'24073—dc21

                                                                2002031707

∞™ The paper used in this publication meets the minimum requirements of American
National Standard for Information Sciences—Permanence of Paper for Printed Library
Materials, ANSI/NISO Z39.48–1992.

Contents

Preface and Acknowledgments

THIS IS THE SECOND VOLUME in a two-volume set dealing with U.S.-European Interactions in the postwar era. Volume 1 (*Coming in from the Cold War*) was published in December 2001, with a copyright date of 2002.

In an effort to ensure that the chapters would be of the highest quality and that the chapter authors would have the occasion to read each other's chapters, discuss them, and exchange ideas, and in the process obtain a clearer sense of the direction and spirit of the project as a whole, the series editors considered that it would be well advised to endeavor to bring the contributors together for an intense period of mutual consultation and interaction. This was accomplished at the University of Washington, 16–17 April 1999, thanks to the generosity of the Henry M. Jackson School of International Studies, the International Studies Center, the Center for West European Studies, the Russian, East European, and Central Asian Studies Program, and the European Union Center. The chapters by Debouzy, Giffard, Poiger, Stark, and Holmgren were originally presented and discussed in the course of this event. We would also like to thank Jere Bacharach, Reşat Kasaba, John Keeler, and James West for their support and Katherine Kittel, Phil Sheckleton, Melinda Rice, Kurt Engelmann, Jane Meyerding, Phil Lyon, and Vjeran Pavlaković for their hard work, contributing to the success of the period of intense interactive mutual consultation. We are also deeply grateful to David Hahn for critical assistance at the final stages of the preparation of this manuscript.

Chapters 6, 11, and 14 were originally published in the *Journal of Popular Culture*. We are deeply grateful to the authors of these articles and to the editors of the journal for permission to reprint these articles here. The chapter on UFOs (chap. 14) appears here in a revised and updated form. Chapter 13 was first published in *East European Politics and Societies* in 1988 and reissued in a revised form in *Rocking the State: Rock Music and Politics in Eastern Europe and Russia,* edited by Sabrina P. Ramet (Westview, 1994). We are grateful to the University of California Press, copyright holder for *East European Politics and Societies,* and Westview Press for permission to reuse this article here. Chapter 13 appears here in a revised and updated form.

I
INTRODUCTION

1

Americanization, Anti-Americanism, and Commercial Aggression against Culture: An Introduction

Sabrina P. Ramet

A TELEVISION COMMERCIAL shown on American television in July 1999 showed the Eiffel Tower sailing into New York harbor on a barge, the Statue of Liberty, an earlier French import, having been fully assimilated. The viewer was thereby invited to muse that America would soon obtain a taste of Paris, as it were. But at another level, one saw Paris reduced to its best-known symbol, even to kitsch, and one wondered whether Paris itself could be made as "American" as the Statue of Liberty. Not all of Europe reaches America as kitsch, just as America does not have to be reduced to kitsch in order to make its presence felt in European culture. But in cultural interactions, there are always processes of transformation—whether of adaptation to local milieux, simplification, syncretic mixing, creative modification, or just plain "kitschification."

In the case of American ingestion of European cultural artifacts and commodities, the most potent vehicle for cultural transformation is commercialization, which exaggerates whatever is seen as potentially profitable and minimizes or eliminates everything which cannot be translated into profits. But when Disneyland, Starbucks, McDonald's, and Pizza Hut open franchises in Europe, the products they offer, although of European inspiration and derivation, are so distorted as to be incomprehensible except either as "American" or as "vulgarizations" of "authentic" European artifacts. This, in turn, accounts, at least in part, for the ferocious resistance against American cultural imports as manifested, for example, in violent attacks on McDonald's franchises in the 1990s, in Antwerp, Athens, Copenhagen, London, St. Petersburg, and Millau, a town in France. The last of the aforementioned cases elevated José Bove, a French sheep farmer, to hero status in France, after he led a group which demolished a McDonald's still under construction and delivered speeches denouncing "lousy food."[1] The same anger at perceived American cultural vulgarity emerged also in the French debate about Euro-Disney, as Marianne Debouzy documents in her chapter. This anger also appears as the apparent anti-Americanism in the semifictional works of Dubravka Ugrešić, as Gordana Crnković explains in her contribution to this book. The relationship may also be reversed, as illustrated by the so-called "spaghetti westerns" of Italian manufacture, in which Clint Eastwood and others, under Italian direction, offer a simplified, even cardboard, portrayal of heroics in the Old West.

Some influences are transitory—such as the coonskin cap craze in England in the 1950s (associated with Fess Parker's "Davy Crockett" films)—while others show signs of greater durability—such as the long fixation on Levi's throughout Europe (and perhaps especially in Eastern Europe) or the proliferation of cheese shops and coffeehouses in fin de siècle America.

It has become commonplace to speak of the emergence of a global culture and to highlight the role presumably played by American television, American films, and the allegedly resplendent Internet in fostering this anticipated result. What is important to realize is that this global culture cannot be expected to displace pre-existing cultures, only, at the most, to coexist alongside them. Moreover, to the extent that the new "global culture" is porous with those cultures which most actively contribute to it, those cultures will, by the same virtue, remain the most receptive to "foreign" artifacts already assimilated into "global culture." Perhaps the chief impact of the globalization of culture is to accelerate the transformation of and cross-cultural penetration of diverse cultures and cultural mediums.

Indeed, when speaking of globalization, one needs to avoid exaggeration. As Mel van Elteren has argued, "the idea of a global cultural homogenization under the hegemony of American popular culture . . . is untenable."[2] Not that European governments from the French[3] to the Soviet[4] to the Bulgarian[5] have not worried about American cultural or ideological influences which might be purveyed via certain cultural artifacts. But the entire process of cultural diffusion is reciprocal, selective, mediated, translated, and sometimes reinterpreted (whether through conscious adaptation or unconscious assimilation of unintended possible or alternative meanings) and undergoes ongoing processes of hybridization and "creolization," so that the contents may change, even where the "vessel" may appear to be the same.[6] Coca-Cola bottled in Germany, for example, even tastes different from the home brew.[7] On the other hand, at least some American cultural artifacts may function as conduits for direct cultural influence. Mattel's Barbie doll, for example, may well be the vehicle for promoting the American "gospel of 'conspicuous consumption'" in which even her assigned "mate," Ken, is no more than an "accessory."[8]

Between 1951 and 1975, the number of U.S.-foreign joint ventures increased by 64 percent annually, on the average,[9] producing a quantum increase in the number of contact points at which reciprocal influence and reciprocal artifact assimilation could occur. Ironically, though not surprisingly (given the more powerful marketing of American cultural artifacts, the larger home market for American artifacts, the increasing dominance of English as the global lingua franca, and the lack of interest in many European societies in the products of other European societies), American popular culture has "conquered" Europe in a way in which no local European popular culture could have done. Thus, the films of George Lukas and Steven Spielberg or, in an earlier era, of Alfred Hitchcock have commanded audiences across the European continent in a way with which no European directors can compete. The result, as Christine Ockrent has said, albeit with *some* exaggeration, is that "The only truly pan-European culture is the American culture."[10]

Europeans have always been ambivalent about American culture, including popular culture. That ambivalence is only reinforced by an element of fear, prompted by the suspicion that America may be charting the future for the rest of the world, or at least for Europe. Ironically, where American pop cultural artifacts and advertising alike celebrate the "brave new future" being fashioned in hyper-individualistic America, the European response has ranged from "anticipation of progress" (embodying also a sense of marvel at America's prodigious output of commodities and fashions) to "cultural pessimism" (as Europeans face their fears of cultural homogenization and effacement).[11]

The absorption of cultural products or symbols may, of course, involve very deliberate irony. Former Soviet president Mikhail Gorbachev's appearance in a 1997 Pizza Hut commercial intended for the Russian market[12] is an example of such "strategic irony." Another such example comes from Seattle, Washington, where a mammoth statue of Lenin, standing amid flames, symbolizing the destruction he had wrought on capitalism, now stands in front of a local Mexican fast-food restaurant. In this way, Lenin, the archenemy of capitalism, is recast as guardian of a local capitalist outlet, possibly even as a (would-have-been) fan of American fast food. The statue was brought to Seattle from Bratislava by a local enthusiast.

When absorption is completely successful, of course, it ceases to be seen any longer as "foreign." It comes to be seen, understood, and experienced as a completely indigenous cultural artifact—at least by the younger generation. Comic books are a case in point. Take, for instance, the Norwegian translation of the comic book adventures of "Blå Tonya" (Blue Tanya). In the fifty-three pages of a recent Blå Tonya adventure (no. 3, 2001), some forty-six sound-bite splash words were used, including "SHRAKKOOM," "FWUMPH!" "PROOMP!" "SHKLKK," and "BLADDAM!" Comics have their own universal jargon. But there is always some room for local innovation; hence, in the course of Blå Tonya's triumph over a menacing Goliath-like Viking villain, the Norwegian translator (Jens E. Røsåsen) pens in the splash word "RØSK!"

This volume brings together essays on American cultural impact on and influence in both Western and Eastern Europe, with individual chapters devoted to cultural contexts and genres in France, Germany, Britain, Italy, Norway, Poland, Hungary, Yugoslavia and the Yugoslav successor states, and Russia. The division of the book into distinct sections on Western and Eastern Europe reflects profound differences in their experience of American influence. Western Europe was clearly in the American sphere of influence in the years after 1945, with the transfusion of funds via the Marshall Plan and the stationing of American troops across the western half of the continent only facilitating American cultural inroads. In Eastern Europe, by contrast, the early communist years saw the region effectively sealed off from American influence and subjected to systematic sovietization. Already by the 1960s, however, a shift was under way, as Western Europe became ever more concerned about American cultural inroads, while ordinary Eastern Europeans, fed up with Soviet political and cultural hegemony, increasingly looked to the United States with admiration, interest, and genuine, if not always well-informed, attraction. Thus, in some regards, the ways in which Western and Eastern Europe have reacted to American cultural exports have been entirely opposite to each other. Only now, in the years since 1989, with processes of "mellowing" in Western Europe and increasing exposure to diverse influences in Eastern Europe, is the old divide gradually being overcome. No doubt some differences will remain, but with the end of the continent's political division, these differences are ever less likely to be defined by region and cultural polarization as such is increasingly a thing of the past.

Some chapters look at the formative role of American policies (such as the chapter by Uta Poiger on postwar Germany), while others focus on the reception of American culture by Europeans (such as the chapters by Marianne Debouzy, C. Anthony Giffard, Steinar Bryn, Herbert Eagle, and Beverly James) or the interaction of European and American popular culture (such as the chapter by Cooper and Cooper on popular music in Britain and the United States). Debouzy cites Emmanuel de Roux's characterization of Disneyland as "the slaughterhouse of dreams," underlines the passivity reportedly induced in park visitors by the highly mechanized rides, and concludes with a warning that American mass culture is tending "to weaken, homogenize, and even eradicate [Europe's] original cultures, impoverishing the cultural heritage of nations." Giffard examines another arena of American cultural penetration of Europe: television programming and films. He charts European efforts to restrict the importation of American films and television programs and to encourage local film industries and television program development, tying the ensuing Euro-American debate to broader issues connected with the World Trade Organization.

Chapters by Steinar Bryn and Herbert Eagle analyze the marketing of Coca-Cola in Norway and the emergence of gangster films in Poland and Russia, respectively. Eagle analyzes the action in the Polish film *Dogs* (1992) and the Russian film *Brother* (1997) and argues that "the American gangster film and its recent transformations in Russian and Polish contexts provide an illuminating example of the flexibility of a genre's textual structures and their adaptability in the service of different kinds of messages." As Eagle notes, the ambivalence in American gangster films has been carried over to Poland and Russia, so that film gangsters are simultaneously censured and admired within the context of the films. Beverly James, for her part, reports the results of interview research in Hungary, noting that Hungarian responses to American cultural artifacts such as Dairy Queen have been characterized by ambivalence (liking the physical plant but remaining critical about the food quality, in this example). Her Hungarian interviewees also criticized American films for presenting a false and oversimplified image of American life but expressed admiration for American "determination." My chapter on Yugoslav rock bands shows that while the earlier Yugoslav rockers aspired to nothing more than to mimic and replicate the top English and American hits, the Yugoslav rock scene gradually acquired its own voice, emerging from its American cocoon, as it were, and drawing its inspiration increasingly from local idioms, though not without taking note of new ideas coming from the United States. My other chapter, on UFOs over Russia and Eastern Europe, treats reports of UFOs and visiting extraterrestrials as a cultural phenomenon, tracing similarities between reports in Central and Eastern Europe and those in the United States and suggesting that this may constitute evidence of the diffusion of popular culture concerning the extraterrestrial. Rodney Stark, in his chapter on American missionaries in Europe, shows how religious entrepreneurs based in the United States are challenging the religious balance in Europe, citing recent actions taken against American-based groups by the German and French governments in support of his contention that the challenge is a serious one.

Finally, chapters by Giulia Guarnieri, Gordana Crnković, and Beth Holmgren on literary influences round out the book. As Guarnieri notes in her analysis of the "American myth" in postwar Italian literature, America is simultaneously supremely attractive and supremely repugnant for many European intellectuals. America is, in the eyes of Italian writers such as Umberto Eco, the quintessential embodiment of "the postmodern opposition of truth and fakeness, vacuity and values, superficiality and culture." America is the most paradoxical and inscrutable of all countries, at least to Europeans. The only country in the world which has been symbolized by an amusement park (Disneyland) or by vacant land ("the Frontier"), the only Western country to attempt to ban sales of alcohol in the twentieth century, and the only country where students can graduate from high school (and, for that matter, also from the university) without knowing a foreign language, the United States remains a source of endless fascination for Europeans, who marvel at the ingenuity of Americans, at the barbarity of American streets and manners, at the extremes of egregious wealth and dire poverty, at the proliferation of guns in American society, and at the contradiction between the postmodern sophistication of Americans (especially in technological skills) and the ahistoric, one might say, lack of familiarity, among the largest sector of Americans, with such basic European, and one would like to suppose also global, cultural artifacts such as Plato's *Republic* (scarcely read in America's schools any longer), Beethoven's symphonies (aside from the final movement of his *Symphony No. 9*), and Goethe's *Faust*. After all, Europeans might well ask themselves, if Americans are, on the whole, oblivious to the greatest achievements of 2,500 years of European cultural history, does that tell us anything about the intellectual depth of at least some of the more pop-oriented artifacts to come out of America's 250 years of cultural history?

The argument should not be carried too far. In the twentieth century alone, after all, America gave the world Martha Graham and Merce Cunningham, Fred Astaire and Ginger Rogers, Leonard Bernstein and Aaron Copland, Irving Berlin and Cole

Porter, Charles Ives and John Cage, Bing Crosby and Ethel Merman, Robert Frost
and Muriel Rukeyser, Glenn Miller and Artie Shaw, Frank Lloyd Wright and Andy
Warhol, Philip Glass and Lou Harrison, the Marx Brothers and *Saturday Night Live*,
Ernest Hemingway and Gertrude Stein, Joseph Heller and Kurt Vonnegut, Edward
Albee and Robert Lowell, *The Lucy Show* and *Hogan's Heroes*, *Casablanca* and *Gone
with the Wind*, 3-D photography and holograms. But to the extent that the producers of *pop* culture are in ignorance of the higher achievements of world culture, including of past pop culture, and, more to the point, to the extent that they prostitute themselves to produce products considered marketable by the corporations
which control most of the market, they communicate in a sparser, poorer, and ultimately less creative language, in which the patterns of postcommercial success are
digested, assimilated, and regurgitated without reflection. In this way, commercial
pop culture ceases to be culture at all, becoming a mere manufactured commodity,
and the globalization of American corporate-produced "culture" may be understood as a form of commercial aggression against authentic popular culture.

Notes

1. Eric Schlosser, *Fast Food Nation: What the All-American Meal Is Doing to the World*
(London: Penguin, 2001), 244.

2. Mel van Elteren, "Conceptualizing the Impact of US Popular Culture Globally," *Journal of Popular Culture* 30, no. 1 (Summer 1996): 65.

3. See Jill Forbes, "Winning Hearts and Minds: The American Cinema in France
1945–49," *French Cultural Studies* 8 (1997): 30–31.

4. See Sabrina Petra Ramet, Sergei Zamascikov, and Robert Bird, "The Soviet Rock
Scene," in *Rocking the State: Rock Music and Politics in Eastern Europe and Russia*, ed. Sabrina Petra Ramet (Boulder, Colo.: Westview, 1994), 186–90.

5. See Stephen Ashley, "The Bulgarian Rock Scene under Communism (1962–1990),"
in *Rocking the State*, ed. Ramet, 147–49.

6. van Elteren, "Conceptualizing the Impact," 62; and John Dean, "The Diffusion of
American Culture in Western Europe since World War Two: A Crosscultural Survey," in
Journal of American Culture 20, no. 4 (Winter 1997): 11.

7. On Coca-Cola in Europe, see Magnus Pyke, "The Influence of American Foods and
Food Technology in Europe," in *Superculture: American Popular Culture in Europe*, ed. C. W. E.
Bigsby (Bowling Green, Ohio: Bowling Green University Popular Press, 1975), 87–88.

8. Marianne Debouzy, "The Barbie Doll," in *European Readings of American Popular
Culture*, ed. John Dean and Jean-Paul Gabilliet (Westport, Conn.: Greenwood, 1996), 143.

9. Dean, "Diffusion of American Culture," 20.

10. Christine Ockrent, quoted in the *Star Tribune* (Minneapolis), 31 December 1990,
3D, as cited in van Elteren, "Conceptualizing the Impact," 77. See also Uta G. Poiger, *Jazz,
Rock, and Rebels: Cold War Politics and American Culture in a Divided Germany* (Berkeley:
University of California Press, 2000).

11. See Rob Kroes, *If You've Seen One, You've Seen the Mall: Europeans and American
Mass Culture* (Urbana: University of Illinois Press, 1996), 17–18.

12. Schlosser, *Fast Food Nation*, 237.

2

"American" Utility vs. "Useless" Reflection
On Possible Futures on Both Sides of the Atlantic

Gordana P. Crnković

THE CURRENT VOLUME HAS no single overarching theoretical meta-narrative of, say, either the all-consuming "Americanization" of Europe or the more "feel-good" theories of hybridization or almost equal interaction between imported American and local European cultures, as discussed by author Rob Kroes[1] and mentioned in chapter 1 by Sabrina P. Ramet. Each of the chapters has not only a distinct subject reflecting the specific disciplinary and intellectual imprint of the given author, but also very different implications for possible theoretical generalizations on the whole issue of the American cultural impact on Europe, stemming from specific insights derived from studying of a specific subject. Thus, for example, Marianne Debouzy, looking at various cultural aspects of French Euro-Disney, can say persuasively that while "it would be a consoling thought to speak of mutual assimilation or reciprocity . . . as Benjamin Barber rightly warns us, the reciprocity between American mass culture and other national cultures is 'the reciprocity of the python who swallows the hare.'" Giulia Guarnieri, on the other hand, looking at Italian writers such as Eco, Calvino, and Vattimo, can rightly conclude that this part of Italian culture has a much more ambivalent and active attitude toward American culture than that exhibited by visitors to French Euro-Disney.

The Italian writers discussed by Guarnieri, unlike the voiceless visitors to French Euro-Disney, do indeed have different takes on "America." These writers are participating in the long and vital tradition of European intellectuals and writers reflecting on America; their worthy predecessors include George Orwell, Albert Camus, Simone de Beauvoir, Jean-Paul Sartre, Johan Huizinga, Federico García Lorca, Tadeusz Borowski, and many others. The reaction of the European intellectual sphere, as one may call it, to the impact of Americanization is very different from that of the mass entertainment sphere of Euro-Disney. The intellectual, reflexive, or critical parts of European cultures draw on their own strong histories and sources in a way in which the popular parts of these cultures cannot relate to their own traditions given the drastic changes of social life in the second half of the last century; one may still read certain books, but one may not find so easily available traditional features of popular culture such as local fairs or town carnivals or even relaxed evening strolls through one's own city.[2]

Different theoretical implications developed by various chapters in this book also relate to the use of one or the other of the different currently employed concepts of culture in the first place. While some chapters employ a more narrow definition of popular culture as cultural artifacts (e.g., films, literature, or popular music, as in the chapters on popular music interchanges between the United States and Great Britain or gangster films in Poland and Russia), other chapters take these same cultural artifacts out of the "cultural" arena and critical discourse on culture, and discuss them as global market commodities (as in C. Anthony Giffard's chapter) that constitute one of the few areas of U.S. trade surplus with Europe, a surplus that American media companies are determined to keep and enlarge, using free-trade laws, and that European states are determined to counter and diminish. The clash itself between the "American" view of mass media products as being first and foremost commodities such as cars or clothes, and "European" perceptions of these products as cultural elements and thus subject to considerations other than only economic or trade ones, as discussed by Giffard, is a very telling one.

Still other contributions discuss culture in the broader sense of the term than that focusing on cultural artifacts, the sense that includes patterns of behavior and ways of accepted "formatting" of any part of one's life and world. Thus, Rodney Stark's intriguing chapter examines religion as an important part of such a broader concept of culture, looking at the work of American religious missionaries in Europe—an often overlooked subject in more standard treatments of American cultural influence in Europe. Or again, Debouzy's chapter provides fascinating insights into the tense relationship between the "American" (or rather the Disney corporation's) work practices and the traditional French work culture (as exhibited in the strained history of labor practices in Euro-Disney) and into the uneasy dynamics of replacing the more traditional ways of spending one's free time (more active and participatory, subject-oriented and social) with Disney ways (seen as passive, consumerist, and antisocial). For Beth Holmgren, on the other hand, it is precisely in an American context that transplanted Russian artists find their own language, free of ideological blinders.

Two issues emerge repeatedly throughout this volume. The first one concerns the question of how much any aspect of the "Americanization" of Europe is really that (direct influence) and how much it is a result of imminent development of European postindustrial societies that are in some areas reaching the points that the United States has simply reached first and are now merely adopting the existing forms (which happen to be "made in the United States") that fit those points. To give a rather prosaic example, a European immigrant may find abhorrent the amount of time that Americans spend in front of their television sets, not to mention the low quality of the programming on the main networks. But after living in the United States for some time and really engaging with American culture and society, this same European immigrant may appreciate how, say, the huge amount of work and overwork, ever-present anxiety over downsizing and job loss, nonexistence of a serious social safety network, breaking of family and social ties due to mobility in pursuit of work, precariousness of social amenities such as health and education, weakness or nonexistence of any kind of a more permanent community, and so forth, can all produce "Americans" who can be so tired, lonely, and fed up with it all that "vegging out" in front of the TV becomes a viable option. What follows is that, if Europe is going the way of the United States, with an ever-increasing participation in global markets and increasing pressure to perform, then Europeans themselves may perhaps at some point become similarly tired, anxious, and displaced, opting for Hollywood soaps or Disneyworlds.

If American culture or ways of life are imminent or at least a possible future for European societies, and of the developed world more broadly, then we are not talking so much about two places as about two points in time within the same historical narrative, modifications or variations notwithstanding. The American—or "already there"—impacts or encounters Europe (as the "not yet there"), but Europe has the chance of responding to this impact and its own potential future, perhaps changing that future in the process. The response, it seems, is more important than the impact itself, because it activates the openness of time and practice where things are not fully determined and can be changed. And what is being shaped in this response is a destiny for all of us, where the distinction between the United States and Europe almost loses its significance. While the United States has the advantage of primacy in this relationship, Europe has the opportunity to reflect on this impact and on possible ways of dealing with it. The goal of the current volume is to participate in that work of reflection on the American cultural impact on Europe and on possible collective histories on both sides of the Atlantic.

If we talk about the somewhat unified history where the United States is ahead and Europe is following, then many differences outlined in the following chapters (and in other books on the subject) are relating not only to the distinctions between the United States and Europe but also to those between what we are all becoming and the ways we remember (rightly or wrongly) ourselves to have been in the past. "Europe," then, is a metaphor for what we still remember or may even still have but are afraid of losing—know we'll lose—and the "United States" becomes a metaphor for the ways we have to adopt and accept in order to survive. Reflections on the relations between the United States and Europe become reflections on who we are, where we are going, and where we would like to go (or not). In that sense, it may actually help to put in quotation marks national denominations and distinctions ("American," "European") that frame this book and see the following chapters as (also) participating in a more global discussion about our common destinies.[3]

Consequently, the second point that may emerge from the reflections on this volume is that, if we actually discard its national framing, we can look at many observations of U.S. cultural impact on Europe as being to an extent reflections on the current historical tendencies that concern us all. What one seems to want to preserve, paradoxically enough (but also predictably), is the very opposite of the victorious "American" world, which seems to be advancing globally and which is "increasingly organized around the tenets of rationality, utility, mechanization, and instrumentality";[4] it is the other world that "pays tribute to what is useless and unproductive," the sphere of "silence and reflexiveness."[5]

But if reflection that is "useless and unproductive" when seen through the eyes of the market and its demand for instantaneous gratification and justification is indeed valuable and needs to be preserved, then scholars might do well to reconsider their own increasingly "Americanized" discourse of constant proving that what they do is indeed "useful" and productive and has to be supported as such. The justification in terms of usefulness may eventually be self-defeating because the very concept of usefulness has itself been "Americanized" and seen in terms of some more or less direct market value: universities should produce an employable workforce, and disciplines such as Slavic studies should justify their funding by arguing that Russia and Eastern Europe are full of potentials for economic investment and trade. Instead of accepting the terms of usefulness (and profitability) handed down to them by the increasingly "Americanized" society at large (regardless of whether that society happens to be in the United States or in Europe), scholars should perhaps—as some already do—focus on the work of producing alternative conceptualizations and imaginations of possible worlds. Aside from, and through, discussing specific instances of American cultural impact on Europe, this book hopes to participate in that kind of reconceptualizing work as well.

Notes

1. Rob Kroes, *If You've Seen One, You've Seen the Mall: Europeans and American Mass Culture* (Urbana: University of Illinois Press, 1996).

2. The specific intellectual traditions, in their turn, naturally shape to an extent the current European intellectuals' attitudes toward America; Crnković's chapter on Croatian writer Dubravka Ugrešić, for example, discusses how the attitude toward the American culture present in one of her books has as much (or more) to do with literary and aesthetic conventions of her writing as with any American "realities."

3. Americans themselves, after all, are the first ones who had to be "Americanized," the ones who are still interacting with their own "Americanization" in numerous precarious ways, the ones who have been immersed in it for a longer time and more thoroughly than the others, and the ones who—the point often missed by Europeans—are aware of it and reflecting about it and trying to shape it or struggle against it. As Kroes writes, "In general it is safe to say that Americans are second to none in their anti-Americanism. It is almost a constant of American culture, although this tends to escape European critics." See *If You've Seen One*, 20–21.

4. Kroes, *If You've Seen One*, 19.

5. Kroes, *If You've Seen One*, 19.

II

WESTERN EUROPE

3

Does Mickey Mouse Threaten French Culture?

The French Debate about EuroDisneyland

Marianne Debouzy

IN A WORLD FULL OF SOUND AND FURY, the creation of a theme park may appear to be a minor event. But in the mid-1980s, the opening of EuroDisneyland near Paris became a major event on the French political scene. Crucial issues were at stake: in particular, the promise of jobs at a time when the unemployment rate was reaching new heights, and the integrity of national culture at a time when the preserving of national identity was made into a clarion call for some political forces.

In this chapter, I shall look at the many dimensions of the original Disneyland project and the controversies it entailed. We shall see how the theme park has operated and why the Disney company's social policy and management style generated numerous conflicts from the start. Disneyland not only marked a break with traditional French work culture but was also considered a threat to French national culture. I shall analyze the lively debate French intellectuals engaged over the significance of Disneyland for French culture and culture in general. Finally, given the ambivalent feelings of the French toward the American model, I shall try to evaluate the impact of Disneyland in terms of the Americanization of French life.

The Disneyland Project and French Politics

Legend has it that a former representative of the National Front, the extreme right-wing group which later claimed to be fiercely hostile to Disneyland, introduced French Socialist officials to Disney people for the first time in 1984. The ascertained facts are that talks began in 1985; the initial letter of intent was signed by Laurent Fabius, the Socialist prime minister, and Michael Eisner, chairman of

Disney, in December 1985; negotiations went on after the change of government; and the final contract was signed by Jacques Chirac, conservative prime minister, and Eisner in March 1987.

The Disney project was very ambitious.[1] The theme park, covering one hundred acres, was only a tiny part of a giant resort complex (six hotels with over five thousand rooms, a golf course, etc.), a large-scale real estate operation covering five thousand acres (ample office space, apartment buildings, convention center, shops, mall, etc.), and a whole new city outside Paris. The project was to be the biggest construction site in Europe after the Channel Tunnel and would be carried out in three phases. The French administration, at the national and regional levels, not only supported the enterprise but even participated in its realization. EuroDisney was really a state matter (*une affaire d'Etat*).[2] It became the center of the urban development to the east of Paris.

Disney's strategy was based on the promise of jobs and the threat of choosing another location (most likely Spain) if the company's demands were not met. "The basic ploy used by the Disneys who were determined to establish their European Disneyland near Paris was to get Paris to beg them to come."[3] The Disneys managed to treat the French state as they would any business partner and to obtain all sorts of advantages[4] in exchange for what was most valuable to politicians at the time: the promise of jobs. At the same time, they did their best to assuage fears concerning French culture. Robert Fitzpatrick, chairman of EuroDisney and heading up the theme park project, was a former professor of French literature, was married to a French woman, could quote DuBellay, and thus was the company's "cultural guardian."

Disney proved to be deserving of its business reputation: tough and efficient.[5] The negotiations were long and difficult. But in the end most of Disney's requests were met. Thus, the demand that contractual disputes be resolved by international arbitration first met with staunch refusal and an indignant comment by a French official who thundered, "France is not a banana republic," before being finally accepted. The firm was granted all sorts of privileges. The French government agreed to pay for about a quarter of the cost of the enterprise through a variety of grants, handouts, and tax breaks. It covered the construction costs for rail and highway networks linking the site to Paris—a TGV stop, motorway access, and extension of the subway line. One could list an impressive number of gifts from the state which have been analyzed at length by observers.[6]

The project fueled a lively debate, and for a while opponents were very vocal. Some political groups were particularly active. The environmentalists protested against the "sacrifice" of thousands of acres of excellent farming land for unskilled, dead-end jobs. They claimed the whole project was a front for a large-scale real estate operation.[7] In a lengthy report, Alain Lipietz, an economist and environmentalist, criticized the project's cost and its allegedly beneficial employment spin-offs. The environmentalists also denounced the lack of transparency and democracy in the negotiations. They formed local associations such as SOS—Environment and

ACID (Association des Citoyens contre le Développement d'EuroDisneyland) to fight against the project.

The Communists joined the environmentalists to protest the secrecy of the negotiations, but their main target was the tremendous amount of public money spent for the sake of Disney and its profits.[8] Squandering taxpayers' money to secure preferential loans to Disney was all the more scandalous as the social needs of so many citizens were not met. It was outrageous, said the Communists, that the government should trust a private corporation—and foreign to boot—to build a whole new city[9] and subsidize an imported substandard culture. They also criticized the lack of local control over a project which was a source of concern to elected officials and area residents as it was certain to change their lives.[10] The Socialists were divided. Those in government backed the project whatever their misgivings. But a few Socialist personalities, such as Jean-Pierre Chevènement, voiced their opposition. Some Gaullists were quite incensed, as was the archconservative Philippe de Villiers. As for extreme right-wing politicians of the Jean-Marie Le Pen stripe, they opposed the project mainly for cultural reasons, claiming that Disney was an attack on national culture.

Apart from politicians, two groups expressed their open hostility to the project: farmers and intellectuals. Disneyland was to be located in La Brie, an area which had some of the best farmland in the country. Farmers were to be expropriated and were soon identified as "the Indians of the Brie."[11] The intellectuals voiced their fears concerning the downgrading of French culture, the theme park's "operation of cretinization." One of them wondered how much money parties and politicians had received from Disney.[12]

This opposition should not mask the political consensus around the project's desirability. Succeeding Socialist and conservative governments backed it and were both ready to grant the Disney company highly preferential treatment. Some politicians claimed Disneyland would be a place where people would "become familiar with new technologies and training would be associated with entertainment."[13] But the main argument was that jobs and economic activities would be generated both from the park and the influx of tourists. The entire venture was stated as an economic, touristic, and urban challenge.

The theme park was to be a replica of America's Disneyland. From Main Street the Magic Kingdom is divided into four areas: *Frontierland,* with the Big Thunder Mountain, including the Phantom House and Thunder Mesa Riverboat Landing around the Frontierland Lake; *Adventureland,* where visitors can explore Adventure Island and an abandoned gold mine and encounter the Pirates of the Caribbean; *Fantasyland,* the world of fairy tales, with Sleeping Beauty's Castle, Alice's Curious Labyrinth, and It's a Small World; and *Discoveryland,* which replaces the American Tomorrowland and includes the Visionarium presenting films on the future seen through the eyes of great visionaries.

From the outset, the promise of jobs was a matter of controversy. How many would there be? What kind? For whom? On what contractual terms?

Disney Jobs and Social Conflicts

One chief French negotiator, Jean-René Bernard, claimed there would be over thirty thousand jobs to start with.[14] However, the contract signed in 1987 provided for the employment of 10,375 people—6,550 full-time, 2,400 part-time, and 2,025 seasonal. Half of those would be employed in hotels and the park, the rest in shops, restaurants, the golf course and camping site.[15] The figures most often quoted by newspapers approximated thirteen thousand jobs of which ten thousand were full-time, two thousand part-time, and one thousand seasonal.[16] In January 1992, Robert Fitzpatrick himself spoke of nine thousand hires, of whom four thousand already worked on the site, the rest would be hired gradually.[17] Rumor spread that Disney had trouble hiring French people because of strict work standards and low wages. The firm advertised for jobs in areas where the unemployment rate was very high, as in Brittany. The firm's hiring policy was a hot news item and the job applicant questionnaire created a stir with such questions as "Do you belong to one or several associations? Which ones?" or "Do you have other nonprofessional activities?" which violated French labor law. Disney claimed such questions enabled applicants to enhance their skills. Nobody believed them. An early version of the questionnaire was even more outrageous in the eyes of the French: applicants were asked whether they were available on weekends, in the daytime and at night; they were also asked to name their bosses in their three previous jobs and why they had left.[18] They had to promise to respect the firm's bylaws.

The dress code created an uproar. Applicants could not be overweight. Men were not to have beards or moustaches, and they had to wear black shoes and socks. Women had to have a "classical" haircut and appropriate underwear, their nails had to be a given length and not colored, and jeans and high heels were prohibited. They were not allowed to wear more than one ring, and their makeup had to be "natural." The use of deodorant was compulsory for all "cast members." This code sounded grotesque and humiliating to French ears, and it was declared illegal by a court ruling.[19] It took a long time for this ruling to be enforced, and from the testimonies of union representatives one may wonder whether it really is today. The weekly *Le Canard Enchaîné* made fun of another questionnaire put out by the so-called Disney University which asked applicants to check such sentences as "I am often sad or depressed," "I take interest in few things," "My sleep is agitated," and "I have the blues."

In his first report to shareholders (4 June 1992), Robert Fitzpatrick prided himself on having hired sixteen thousand people, full-time and seasonal, belonging to eighty-six nationalities and speaking thirty-four languages. According to *Le Monde* (8 July 1992), 65 percent of the hotel staff were French, 11 percent British, 4 percent Dutch, 3 percent Irish, and 3 percent German. The Disney Internet site (4 April 1998) gave the following information: 55 percent of cast members were men; 68 percent were single. Their average age was twenty-seven, and they belonged to eighty-three nationalities. Of course, Disney did not mention working conditions. What do we know about them?

From the testimonies of employees, tough working conditions resulted in an initially high rate of resignations in the beginning—eight per day. Employees complained about low wages, heavy workloads, flexible schedules, authoritarian bosses, and racism.[20] They also complained about constant surveillance. A squad of one hundred to two hundred foremen called "The Foxes" watch over employees at work, and there are security guards (everybody calls them "The Mickey police"), mostly former police officers and gendarmes, who are supposedly there to deal with visitors but obviously control the staff as well.

Social conflicts started to break out even before the opening. Cleaning women were the first to protest. Because they were so-called "cast members," they could be made to work at night, sometimes seven nights on end. Their workload was very heavy though earning the minimum wage. Because they protested, some of these Cinderellas were laid off.[21] After the opening, some cleaning women in the Santa Fe hotel complained about unpaid overtime: they were obliged to work nearly every Sunday and holiday with no extra pay. Bosses promised to meet with them but then managed to isolate seven women considered to be the leaders. They were locked in a room, ordered to give back their uniforms, and fired. The women called the CGT (Confédération Générale du Travail) union for help and were reinstated.

Every day complaints were made about illegal firings, overexploitation, intimidation, and racism. At night, only blacks worked. Even though there were over eighty nationalities on the site, not one black or North African employee was given a post of responsibility. They were concentrated in the cleaning department.[22]

Another grievance was housing. People had to pay outrageous rents to be packed in small lodgings, three or four in one room. They also complained about the Disney police's constant searching for drugs and alcohol and breaking into apartments while people were at work.

For all these reasons, people started to organize clandestinely, which brought *Le Canard Enchaîné* to write, "Mickey, the Yankee mouse stirring class war in France and regenerating Marxist unionism, this is truly magic."[23] Before the opening two unions were represented: the CSL (Confédération des Syndicats Libres), a kind of company union with a rather bad reputation, and the CGC (Confédération Générale des Cadres), a union for supervisory personnel and middle management. In July 1992, according to labor law, representative elections of "Délégués du Personnel" had to be called. The CFDT (Confédération Française Démocratique du Travail) and the CGT were gaining ground.

The same month, a strike broke against low wages, work schedules, illegal firings, and attacks on human dignity.[24] Workers objected to both exploitation and infantilization: "When we do our work properly we are given chocolate bars"; "When they feel we won't take it any more, they want to smooth things over and give us a free breakfast"; "When they are not satisfied with an employee's work, he is punished. He is sent to the food or spare parts stockrooms where work is hard and done at night." Employees could not stand the constant surveillance both on and off the job. There were repeated violations of labor law: employees would not be given a standard paycheck in due time; they would be cheated of overtime; they would not be granted sick leaves.[25] Once again *Le Canard Enchaîné* marveled at Disney magic: "Mickey invents the exploitation of man by the mouse."[26] From April to August 1992, there were 1,700 resignations.

When people started to organize, Disney responded with homegrown union busting. It tried to prevent employees from voting in representative elections through intimidation or by giving a day off, then persecuted union delegates. This strategy helped to dampen participation of voters: only 20 percent of the 11,440 employees voted.[27] The results were nevertheless significant: the CSL obtained 38 percent of the votes, the CGT 32 percent, and the CFDT 18 percent.

Later, several strikes took place against layoffs: two thousand permanent employees were laid off in five months in 1993 during Disney's most serious financial troubles. The company tried to settle each case individually so as to avoid having to pay legal severance pay for downsizing (*licenciement économique*). The turnover must have been very high, since in one year 6,646 employees had "disappeared" from the rolls.[28] Then musicians struck in the fall because Disney had violated labor law and job categories when selectively laying off people. The strikers won and had to be reinstated. The firm's hiring policy became quite clear: more and more part-time people were being taken on as permanent employees were being laid off. Complaints were rampant as employees resented being brainwashed, informed upon at all levels, constantly harassed, and generally considered to be available at all times regardless of their personal and family needs. In a word, some Disney employees were getting fed up with the Disney culture.

In June 1994, some cleaning people, later joined by restaurant workers, went on strike to demand a wage increase, the reevaluation of night overtime, and recognition of their skills. When strikers were harassed by guards, they scattered little pieces of paper all over the place which executives were made to pick up. A group of women was particularly active in fighting labor law violations of pregnancy leaves.[29] None of this prevented Disney from claiming the company wanted to be "the social showcase of Europe."[30] In November 1994, cleaning people once more went on strike to protest against subcontracting and threats to job security.[31] The personnel manager repressed the strike in a way which later—even at Disney—led to his dismissal. Two guards who were accused of misdemeanors were identified by anonymous witnesses sitting behind an opaque window.[32] In May 1995, a strike closed down one attraction (the steam railroad), and in August of the same year even the CSL, of all unions, called out the hotel employees and people in charge of rides, gardens, and park repairs. About three hundred employees asked for a nighttime bonus. On New Year's Eve (31 December 1995), the CGT, Force-Ouvrière (FO), and Confédération Française des Travailleurs (CFT) called a strike. Dozens of employees demonstrated with banners in spite of the fact that the strike was prohibited. They demanded higher wages, a shorter workday, paid night overtime, and an end to racist practices. "The workers concerned had actually declared a day's strike, but management had changed the rotas to give all those suspected of involvement a compulsory day off. Instead striking workers had to demonstrate, but they were prevented from doing so."[33]

Is there a link between these conflicts and the fact that in 1997 the CGT won the top union spot with over 27 percent of the votes, while the CSL is now the weakest organization? It is difficult to say. In 1997, technicians went on strike once more against night schedules, while, in July 1998, the musicians waged the then-longest strike ever.[34] According to the CFDT union, 150 of the 220 costumed cast members went on strike to obtain recognition of their status as actors. They were joined by technicians, electricians, and restaurant employees. On their banners one could read, "On stage you dream, in the wings you die for the minimum wage; So I am on strike" and "Yesterday we survived to dream, today we dream to survive." When the company refused their wage demands, they asked for recognition of the collective agreement which is applicable to all theme parks in France.[35] In September, it was the turn of telephone operators to strike for a wage increase and new job categories which recognize their skills. Reservations were blocked for several days.

Of course, all these strikes were difficult to organize and involved only a small fraction of the workers. There are eighty-six trades on the site, part-time, full-time, and seasonal workers. Employees are divided by the hierarchy and the racialization of tasks, not only from one sector to another (guest relations, shops, cleaning, hotel services) but inside every sector.[36] So solidarity is hard to build, all the more so as the company's repressive strategy is very tough. Still, the June 1998 strike mobilized between two hundred and five hundred cast members and lasted from 24 June to 11 July, but management made very few concessions. In December, though, a court ordered Disney to enforce the national theme parks' collective agreement. Of course, Disney appealed the decision.

All these events reflecting Disney's employment policies and management style confirmed many of the fears about the kind of jobs the firm would provide. They were emblematic of the celebrated flexibility that breaks with the so-called rigidities associated with archaisms of the French conception of work. Flexibility is characteristic of the new kind of employment which Disney symbolizes. As a German journalist pointed out, there is a striking coincidence between the opening of Disneyland and the closing of the famous Renault factory in Billancourt.[37] Even though factory work is certainly no ideal (especially for young people), Renault stood for French industrial prestige and for stable employment, and its closing came as a shock to many especially when it was replaced by the Disney type of jobs. The euphemizing Disneyspeak—calling its workforce "cast members" (a name they dared not translate into French), waiters and waitresses "quality hosts," cleaning people "custodial hosts," and the Disney police who visited the lodgings of employees when they were out "investigators"—did not conceal the brutal methods of this new corporate culture. And this was only part of the story: not only did Disney make a clean break with the French work culture; it also signified, for many people, an attack on French culture in general. This was the focus of the debate among intellectuals who were not quite unanimous in their views.

The Intellectual Debate

Contrary to common wisdom, not all intellectuals were opposed to Disneyland. Among those who accepted it, some claimed that Disney was part of "their" culture. As children, they had enjoyed Mickey cartoons and had read *Le Journal de Mickey*. Two early defenders of the project, M. Cantal-Dupart and C. Bayle, were an architect and an urban planner, respectively. They saw Disneyland as the hub of a new city with leisure and tourism at the center. A major enterprise like Disney would strengthen the new urban area. One should therefore not take refuge in a "timorous conservatism."[38] Others argued that American culture was already omnipresent in France through films, music, and many other cultural products and had not destroyed—so they said—French culture. Why be afraid of Disneyland? It was only a theme park.

The debate became more intense with the park's inauguration. The well-known philosopher and journalist Jean-François Revel asserted that American influence should not be feared. He claimed the term "cultural Chernobyl" used by Ariane Mnouchkine, the famous theater producer, was totally inadequate. It ignores the European inspiration of Disney themes and the "unpredictable paths followed by folklore." Cultural history, he said, must be perceived as a constant "circulation and interpenetration so as to stimulate invention"; cultural interaction is sometimes paradoxical. As for mass culture, French intellectuals should recognize that Americans have been more successful than Europeans in translating the old recipes of melodrama, fairy tale, mystery, and violence into media language. Finally, if we think the taste of the public is bad, we should educate it but not try to prevent the public from enjoying American mass culture. He expressed his strong opposition to any form of "cultural protectionism"—but so did those who opposed the park. The fact that Disney had used European tales and myths and was bringing them back to Europe was repeatedly mentioned by those who spoke for Disney. And no one recalled it more often than Robert Fitzpatrick himself.[39]

But intellectuals who opposed Disneyland were not convinced. On this last point, they tended to agree with the well-known journalist Dominique Jamet, who wrote, "As for the characters from Grimm and Perrault tales, they have come back to their place of birth in a grotesque, unrecognizable shape, as though they had been transformed by the distorting mirror of business, as though they had overeaten ice-cream, corn flakes and popcorn."[40]

The fear of an American invasion of French culture had been quite strong from the beginning and intensified with the opening in 1992. The fear was not entertained just by Communists and left-wingers but widely shared by conservatives as well. An early expression was the call launched by a number of "progressive" intellectuals—among them Guillevic (a poet), Gilles Perrault (a journalist), Robert Escarpit (an academic), Antoine Vitez (a theater producer)—and by architects, engineers, researchers, and union leaders. Their protest was cultural and political. "EuroDisneyland is a multinational which has the means to advance its world cultural project." They claimed that "our national identity should be protected and promoted, which does not mean being hostile to other cultures but creating the conditions to develop our own national imagination." They criticized the project's cost and the state for investing so much for the sake of a private enterprise, while so many national economic, social, and cultural needs were being ignored.[41] In *Le Monde* Paul-Marie Couteaux, a Gaullist and a high civil servant of the Commissariat Général de la Langue Française, was quite vehement. He warned that the French were being asked to forsake their own myths and adopt as their own "the mythological heroes of the master of the world." He argued that "all dominated peoples long for their children to share the imaginary world of their master." Soon French children will know the history of the West in the nineteenth century and that of rockets and missiles better than their own— all this in the name of modernity. Besides, Couteaux added, "Mickey is totally phony, and Uncle Scrooge has nothing to say to us." His conclusion was that "French politicians have a slave mentality" and their capitulation has brought about "a cultural Waterloo."[42]

The threat of America's colonization of French culture was depicted as quite real by the Commissariat Général de la Langue Française which sent the prime minister a comprehensive report. They protested against the fact that wide sectors of French culture had been handed over to foreigners: Television Channel Five had been conceded to Italian Silvio Berlusconi ("spaghetti-cola television") and a theme park to Disney. All this was an infringement on the national cultural heritage and identity. Disneyland was referred to as "a counter-cultural monster" and an "anti-French cultural monster." The central argument of the report was that "every cultural model is an element of economic and political influence and even of domination in some ways."[43] Disney was a political and an economic error. It would compete with French cultural enterprises like the Cité des Sciences (Science and Industry Museum) and would try to eliminate them. Signing the contract would be a cultural disaster. American cultural imperialism would lead to the loss of French cultural identity, one fundamental aspect of which was the language. The Commissariat initiated a major battle for the use of French in the park. They demanded that sign posting and the name of attractions be in French.

A few media pundits joined in the fray. The popular anchorman Yves Mourousi said that it was a pity that we should look to other countries for inspiration while we have plenty of material to exploit. "We have myths which are much more inspiring than that of Mickey and would allow us to do better than just buy a packaged product."[44] The journalist Dominique Jamet also felt that American cultural imperialism was at bay, and he criticized both the right and the left for failing to resist. Pessimistic about the future of culture, he wrote, "At the present moment no barrier can contain the monstrous surge of the wave which, coming from the other side of the Atlantic, is sweeping over the whole world." The balance of power was also unequal. "Of what weight are the Academy and French literature compared to these nightmarish creatures which people the dreams of our children?" Jamet asked. He deplored the fact that France's historical heroes—Jeanne d'Arc, Bayard, Louis XIV, Napoléon—were retreating before an American mouse. There is, unfortunately, not much to be done to stop the uniformization of the world, "under the crushing pressure of the dollar." He concluded, "We have sold a part of our cultural identity for a handful of dollars."[45] Jean-Marie Rouart, the literary critic of the conservative paper, *Le Figaro*, was adamant: "Euro-Disney is the very symbol of the process by which people's cultural standards are lowered and money becomes all-conquering." He added, "France should never have backed such a project. This country must stand for universal cultural values, not universal nonvalues. I believe every Frenchman carries in him a notion of the dignity of France and of its past achievements, and that is part of the reason Euro-Disney is less popular than expected. I would be ashamed to go there."[46] The Gaullist Philippe de Saint-Robert decried the alienation of French imaginative power and the renunciation of the French language.[47] Once the contract was signed, the fight over half a dozen words to be used in the park for signalling seemed somewhat disproportionate to what was at stake.[48] The French government and the Disney people tried to allay these fears. The French negotiator, Jean-René Bernard, asserted that "French will be predominant" and that "France had obtained concessions including the depiction of scenes from French history."[49] But his claims proved illusory.

The Disney people thought this whole argument about American cultural imperialism was irrelevant. Michael Eisner exclaimed, "Stop demonizing American culture,"[50] and did not hesitate to assert that "American imperialism is dead."[51] But when asked to comment on "Disney as the spearhead of a new offensive," Jack Lang, former Socialist minister of culture, pointed out the difference between "the American culture of the daring, the inventive, of idea" and "the culture of standardization, the culture of the lowest common denominator. This is not so much American as a marketing culture."[52] He also said it was a pity that Disneyland did not give more space to the different national cultures of Europe. The Disney people promised they would have more French executives on their staff. A year after opening the new French director, M. Bourguignon, reasserted that EuroDisney would take into account the specific tastes of the European visitors.[53] This contradicted what Robert Fitzpatrick had often repeated: They had intended to make EuroDisney more French, but a study including interviews of thirty thousand Europeans showed that "almost all of them wanted Disney to be the same as in the U.S." He claimed to have adapted the park to the European mentalities and to have kept French as the official language.

In reality, they made few concessions. Originally they had two creations for France. One is a Renault-sponsored Visionarium which projects a 360-degree film. The world of the future is seen through the eyes of Leonardo da Vinci; Jules Verne, played by Michel Piccoli; and H. G. Wells, played by Jeremy Irons. The other "European" attraction is Alice in her curious labyrinth. An attraction called "Space Mountain," inspired by a Jules Verne's novel *From the Earth to the Moon*, was created in 1995. It can launch 2,600 visitors per hour into space.[54] Indeed, the main concession is that since June 1993 alcohol can be served in hotels and restaurants. Finally, "food plays a much more prominent role here."[55] To quote a British journalist, Disney's attempts to Europeanize the park were "half-hearted," and "the changes are at best cosmetic."[56]

Intellectuals also looked at the park itself and at the kind of entertainment it provides. What did they see? There is an impressive unanimity in their descriptions of its general atmosphere: "*sucrerie bariolée*" (P. M. Couteaux), "*mièvrerie planifiée*" (*L'Idiot International*), "*fadeur surgelée*" (Marc Fumaroli), and "*usine à débiter de la pseudo-féerie*" (Jean-Yves Guiomar). What strikes them all is the "phoniness" (*ringardise*). Two of them have visited the park and observed everything carefully. Marc Augé, an anthropologist, and Jean-Yves Guiomar, a historian, both have similar feelings. The former writes, "One experiences pure freedom, without an object, without reason, without anything at stake. . . . We experience emptiness and freedom."[57] The latter goes so far as to describe the park as "the conservatory of nothingness." He describes very precisely the way space is occupied. The "30 shops and 29 restaurants occupy far more space than the 33 attractions," which are the bait for consumers. Guiomar distinguishes three kinds of attractions: The first entails those in which you board a barge or a small vehicle like a train which moves you along a closed circuit. You are carried past animated characters in Disney film settings. The ride lasts eight minutes. There are also two big Mississippi-style boats which take you about the lake of Frontierland for twenty minutes and a little train which takes you for five minutes through an abandoned mine (it is a scenic railway with scenery). The second kind of attraction includes places where you can walk— an island and a castle in the basement of which a mechanical dragon spits smoke at regular intervals. In the third kind, you are invited to watch something from a fixed place—a 360-degree film or a three-dimensional film (ten minutes each). Of these three kinds of attractions, one resembles what you have in ordinary fairs (films and scenic railway, even if their settings are a little more sophisticated). The other is peculiar to Disneyland: to this group belong attractions in which you wander about and explore a site including rides—by boat or train—which take you past animated scenes, hardly seen because of the speed and pretty mediocre anyway. None of the attractions is of a high technical quality, according to Guiomar. Apart from the three-dimensional film, nothing is exceptionally modern. The whole place is terribly phony and so is The Big Parade which, in the eyes of Guiomar, is appallingly poor.[58] What struck him most was that children allegedly did not show any outward sign of their having fun. They were too busy getting in line and getting moved around. Like Marc Augé, he had the feeling that the children serve as "pretexts" for adults who make up a large majority (three out of four visitors in 1993).[59]

So what comes out in the end is the utter passivity of visitors, observed by Umberto Eco, Louis Marin, and others.[60] This passivity, partly caused by exhaustion, is willed both by the company which wants to control the crowd and by the visitors who crave for complete safety in their leisure. In this sense, the park infantilizes adults and ends up being "the slaughter-house of dreams." As emphasized by Emmanuel de Roux, nothing is left to chance; the unexpected is carefully avoided. Everything is under control.[61] Many observers think that the real function of the park is to incite people to consume, to buy things, and to turn buying them into a form of existential entertainment.[62] Shops and restaurants are decorated so as to look like attractions, and contiguous to the park lies a vast space called "Entertainment Area" which is really a mall. Entertainment is, of course, the key word. As Neil Postman explains so well, in a nation of consumers rather than citizens, entertainment must be geared to consumption.[63] That is what the Disney model is all about.

So what did the opening of EuroDisney signify for culture? On this point, intellectuals had diverging views. For some, as Disneyland was typically American, it was the Magic Kingdom's "exoticism" which appealed to people. For others, Disney's European expansionism was a symptom of deeper trends that characterized the evolution of Western societies, in terms of consumption and leisure, merchandized culture, standardized taste, and lost individual creativity.[64] Was it one more sign of the "Americanization" of French society? But then what does "Americanization" mean? Is it only the imitation and adoption of what America does, of American style and values? Or does it mark the parallel evolution of modern societies along the American model due to objective factors such as deindustrialization, expansion of services, media power, increased leisure, changes in family life, and so forth, with its similar patterns? Probably both. America is a model, and similar changes produce somewhat comparable effects.

An opinion widely shared by American commentators before EuroDisneyland was that "Today the only paneuropean culture is American culture."[65] American mass culture has become the link between European countries: "With the collapse of communism, one can see a new Europe emerging which is federated by music, images and a lifestyle originating in the U.S.," says Ben Wattenberg from the American Enterprise Institute. Indeed, American mass culture is "the new world culture."[66] Some go even further to say that American mass culture has lost its national distinctiveness to become universal. "Things with names like Coca-Cola are no longer American. Those icons have become global."[67]

The cultural significance of Disneyland instigated a large debate. Intellectuals wondered whether it was creating a new kind of culture. Some, of course, denied it, inasmuch as Disneyland was only a subculture—certainly not American culture of the kind French intellectuals admire and celebrate. They objected to this subculture being presented as a model for mass culture everywhere. For them, it was a negative model to be avoided. Thus, the academician Marc Fumaroli feared its diffusion would bring about "a taylorization of leisure time" and the "disneyfication" of all kinds of French historical sites and monuments.[68]

Others thought a cultural turn linked to technological and social changes had occurred and altered our vision of reality. Michel Maffesoli, a philosopher, believed that Disney contributed to the movement toward the proliferation of images. More and more the world was being turned into a show. This evolution had already been analyzed at length by Guy Debord in *La Société du spectacle* in the sixties. According to Alain Finkielkraut, with mass tourism, media power, and theme parks, the whole world has been turned into a tourist attraction. For Michel Maffesoli, Disneyland was "the paroxysm of the world become a show" (*le devenir spectacle du monde*).[69] The new culture brings people together so they can look at images. Isn't that what the cinema has been doing for a century, one may ask? But some intellectuals point to two dangers arising from the proliferation of images in Disney's artificial world: it contributes to the process of "de-realizing reality" which is at play more generally due to the omnipresence of media and computers; besides, won't people suffer from an overdose of images? Alain Finkielkraut speaks of images "blocking" imaginative powers, and Danièle Sallenave of "the reign of images saturating imaginative capabilities." For these reasons, some intellectuals believe that Disney has a pernicious effect on children. Besides, this new culture creates a new kind of socialization and of togetherness. It is identified as a culture of communion by Danièle Sallenave, for whom culture should not be a "fusion" process but a constructive process. Culture should contribute to the construction of the subject, expressing the will of the subject to be free and autonomous. The new culture was not doing that.[70]

But did not French intellectuals bear a responsibility for this situation? Danièle Sallenave asked, What have we done to resist mass culture? Have intellectuals been incapable of creating new cultural models? This is precisely what some American observers claimed: "European intellectuals have themselves to blame for lack of an indigenous popular culture."[71] Though they may not like to hear of their failures in American media, French intellectuals have recognized their inability to renew European popular culture. They admit having accepted the diffusion of a "machine-oriented subculture" (Danièle Sallenave), a form of "technosentimentalism" (Alain Finkielkraut). The sentimentality dripping from every detail in Disneyland is what they dislike the most, this attempt to reconcile men with the world, by eliminating what is cruel, what is at odds with happy feelings. As some observers have remarked, in Disney's world skunks do not stink. The image of lost Paradise, symbolized by an idealized nineteenth-century western town, is typical.[72] Everything has to be rosy, edulcorated because Disney's gospel is to purge human existence of all that is undesirable in it (Alain Finkielkraut).

Two things have especially bothered French intellectuals. One is that mass culture seeks to appropriate the vocabulary and concepts of culture. Thus, the word *university* is used as in the "Disney University" to describe what is in fact the very negation of what the university stands for, as the Disney university is nothing but a place where the firm trains, indoctrinates, and disciplines its future employees to turn them into "the loyal soldiers of the Disney enterprise."[73] When Robert Fitzpatrick speaks of what the company does, he always identifies it with "culture." He claims that "entertainment is also a form of culture"[74] and explains the company's goal as offering to a vast audience "a high quality product which, before, was reserved for an elite."[75]

The other is that French people are told by the media and many politicians that they should welcome this new form of entertainment because it is "modern." The fact that theme parks have not been popular with them until recently is interpreted as one more sign of the French being archaic.[76] Disneyland is supposed to be a desirable archetype of modernity. But why?

Theme parks are seen by many intellectuals as an end to more collective, grassroots forms of fun. For Alain Finkielkraut, there was a time when a sense of wonder could be fed by very simple things, like a walk in the countryside. This more natural sense of wonder is being obliterated in the totally antiecological world of Disney. Nature's wonderland has been lost and replaced by a "technocosmos." Others are sensitive to the fact that theme parks have suppressed the active participation of people in traditional types of festivals: active togetherness has given way to a system of built-in passivity and strictly disciplined forms of fun.[77] The more spontaneous kinds of popular culture rooted in nature and living traditions have been replaced by the products of "cultural marketing" and "cultural engineering."[78] These traditions have withered as have the myths exploited by Disney. They have been emptied of their meaning; "they have become mercantile objects, cut off from any social roots." Even though these myths are moribund, Disney can use them because they still have a nostalgic value for people.[79]

Resistance to Disneyland?

Was the opposition to Disneyland then only a backlash of "grumpy intellectuals"? In spite of a massive advertising campaign and favorable coverage of the event by most media, French people did not rush to the park on its opening day. Thirty-thousand visitors were expected, and warnings about massive traffic jams were repeatedly issued. But they failed to materialize, and there was a relatively low turnout at the park—about ten thousand people, according to police estimates. Then in the first six months French people seemed to shy away from the Magic Kingdom: they represented only 29 percent of visitors (10.5 million in 1991–1992). The main reasons may have been the steep price for tickets (two hundred francs), which was lowered later, and the prohibition of picnics and alcoholic beverages. Sociologist Alain Touraine spoke of the "passive resistance" of the French who refused this internationalization of culture.[80] Another hypothesis was that Disney has two major traits which contradict the grain of Gallic humor: "the arrogance of the savior and the prudishness of his sanitized world."[81] Whatever the reasons, the numbers of visitors plunged in 1993 (9.8 million) and 1994 (8.8 million), years in which Disneyland was experiencing deep financial trouble.[82] From then on figures went up. By 1998, there were 12.5 million visitors, with the proportion of French visitors reaching 38 percent. But the company still had trouble attracting people from the Paris region: only 20 percent came from Ile-de-France.[83]

So has Disney adapted to the French? Will it be "gallicized"? It is often recalled that France is the world's biggest consumer of Disney products after the United States. This was supposedly one of the criteria of Disney's choice of Paris and its expectation of success. The Disney magic did not work quite as well as expected. The American-style free enterprise model did not fit. Obviously the Disney management arrogance had to be toned down. As an American journalist remarked, French staff is less tractable than its American counterpart. Disney's attempt to create a union-free zone failed. Employees have not been tamed to the point of giving up the defense of their rights as workers. In general, Disneyland never became quite legitimate in the eyes of most intellectuals and of the cultural establishment, though it has obviously attracted a great number of French visitors. Even the Communist Party has come to accept it and organizes visits of disadvantaged children to Disneyland at holiday time (so does the charity organization *Secours Populaire Français,* which is close to the party). The party's daily, *L'Humanité,* was chided by one of its readers for portraying Disneyland too favorably.[84]

The fiercest battle waged against the theme park had been a battle of words. Few opponents did take action. Thus, demonstrators denouncing American cultural imperialism pelted Michael Eisner with Brie farm produce the day EuroDisney floated shares on the Paris Stock Exchange. On opening day, a group of poets and writers close to the Communist Party gathered in front of the replica of the Statue of Liberty near the Seine. They celebrated true democratic American culture by reciting Walt Whitman's "Ode to France." They denounced the hijacking of fairy tales and the colonization of French myths, imagination, and language. On the same day, a group of young people, also linked to the Communist Party, showed up at the gate of Disneyland, with placards reading "Mickey, you are only a rat," "The Earth to Farmers not to Speculators," and "Mickey the Hustler." Meanwhile, residents in the park vicinity demonstrated by driving at a snail's pace and blocking traffic to protest against the nuisances of the park.[85]

But political demonstrations against Disneyland were few, and to a large extent Disneyland has become part of the French landscape, including the French political landscape. It has adopted Mickey and Disneyland as pet targets often presented in political cartoons of satirical papers like *Le Canard Enchaîné* and *Charlie-Hebdo,* and as a symbolic place it has been occasionally used for political demonstrations to attract media attention. In June 1992, farmers who opposed a reform of European community agricultural policy protested against subsidy cuts and demonstrated at Disneyland's gate. The farmers' organizations leaders explained that Disney "is for farmers the symbol of American presence on French national territory while the United States wants to kick Europeans out of world markets." The farmers' choice of Disneyland expressed their refusal of the American diktats that shaped European agricultural policy reform.[86] It has even found a place in French "cultural" life: the quintessentially French cycling race, the Tour de France, passed through Disneyland in 1994 and ended there in 1997 with all the decorum that marked its final day.[87] The race's director explained that the race had to be "modernized" and therefore "a little americanized."

What about Americanization?

Were French intellectuals then justified in fearing Disneyland's impact on French culture? In recent years, scholars have been debating the influence of American mass culture on people and its americanizing force around the world. The debate has centered on the "passivity" of audiences or their role as active participants in the consumption of mass culture. Some scholars, including Richard Pells, criticize the assumption that "people were little more than receptacles";[88] few scholars (if any) today would entertain such an idea. But as T. Jackson Lears makes clear, to say that audiences are "active participants" is not enough, for it simplifies a complex and somewhat obscure reality. The kind of activity involved remains to be analyzed.[89] How is this activity expressed in concrete, definable terms? What is its intent and meaning? Is it the kind of activity advertised by Disney in its press releases suggesting, for example, that in Hotel Cheyenne's Red Garter Saloon, "guests will be able to see themselves as heroes in a western"?[90] It is often claimed that people "appropriate" mass culture products, even "subvert" them, and that foreign countries "transform" and "adapt" American mass culture to their needs. Of course, there may be some truth in this, within limits. As we have seen, minor "adaptations" have been made to French taste in Disneyland. But does the fact that one can drink wine in Disneyland-Paris restaurants change the whole project and its impact? The natives are not always taken in by such changes, as suggested by this anecdote concerning another aspect of American mass culture in France: In September 1999, the French peasants campaigning against the American embargo on foie gras and roquefort targeted a McDonald's restaurant as a symbol of U.S. domination and "*mal bouffe*" (unhealthy food). At the newly rebuilt restaurant's inauguration, in order to pacify them, the manager announced that he would serve French roquefort cheese on the menu. The response of one peasant to this concession was "Serving roquefort in a McDonald's is like sprinkling holy water in a sex shop."[91]

We have also mentioned the resistance to Disneyland since the beginning: the park had a slow start, and some employees tried to oppose the company's management style. But one should not overestimate "resistance" to the park itself, which is now a commercial success, nor should one ever lose sight of the Disney giant's overwhelming power, though be it not "all-powerful." The view that "ordinary people have little more control over the mass cultural products presented to them than they do over the categories constructed by opinion pollsters" seems to me full of sense.[92] The omnipresence of Disney products is a clear enough sign of the power of their producers. What the Austrian scholar Reinhold Wagnleitner pointed out for Austria is certainly just as true for France: "Disney is simply everywhere, and we are bombarded with messages on TV, in cinemas, videos, tapes, journals, advertisements, fast food chains, and any number of stores, by Disney publishing, Walt Disney Home Video, Walt Disney Pictures, Walt Disney Records, The Disney Store, The Disney Channel, Walt Disney Television, Disneyland, Walt Disney World, EuroDisney, Disney Interactive, and the Disney Home Page."[93]

Does Disneyland's success then mean the French are being americanized? In my opinion, yes. By Americanization, we certainly do not mean that France has been turned into a "miniature version of the United States," to use Richard Pells's phrase, or a copycat "remake" of American society. Americanization is not about cloning. While the language of propaganda and polemical talk of intellectuals and politicians—be they Communist, Gaullist, or the radical right—may have suggested at times that France was an American colony or that American cultural imperialism amounted to "ethnocide," no serious scholar believes that people are chameleons or that the French can be changed into Americans under the influence of American mass culture and economic power. Americanization, which implies some form of domination, means integrating into one's culture (i.e., way of life, patterns of behavior, social practices, tastes, artistic activities, etc.) elements that originally come from the United States and more particularly from American mass culture.[94] As indicated earlier, some of these elements are linked to objective factors which shape the evolution of modern societies. But obviously many are imported directly from the States, bringing about American-inspired changes in national habits and culture. In Disneyland many elements are "representations of American culture . . . explicitly modeled after stereotyped images already in wide circulation through the mass media and elsewhere: they offer ersatz images of recognizable icons."[95] How can we evaluate the americanizing force of Disneyland? We cannot. No scientific evidence is available, of course, to let us know whether people's experience at the park influences their idea of leisure, fun, or whatever, how it ties in with other encounters with American mass culture products (TV series, etc.).

We should resist any simplistic vision of Americanization, for it is a multilayered process. As emphasized by political scientist Pierre Hassner, there are different levels of perceptions of the United States, concerning foreign policy, economics, culture, and a lack of connection between these different levels: one may oppose American foreign policy and love American films and music. The fascination with America works in different ways at different times, with different social classes and age groups. Americanization is not a static phenomenon but a process that operates differently as generations go by and the world context changes. Surveys and opinion polls have made it clear that, for all sorts of political and cultural reasons, there has been an evolution of French perceptions of the United States over the past thirty years and that there has been "a swing back in favor of the Americans" from the 1970s on.[96] Older and younger generations do not have the same familiarity with American mass culture. Young people live in a world where it is (and has always been) omnipresent and appeals especially to them. You cannot be a child today and not be familiar with Disney. If you were born fifty years ago, you may have been told Grimm's and Perrault's tales. Today most children only know Disney's version of them.

The company's will to win over young people (and have them visit Disneyland) is reflected in its steady marketing campaign in French schools. Disney has developed a sophisticated type of culturally oriented advertising to persuade teachers that taking their pupils to Disneyland will be educational. "Thanks to Space Mountain they will discover the work of Jules Verne. . . . On Main Street they will improve their English." The company tells teachers they will be able to conduct their classes in the park. The scheme seems to have been successful since, according to *Capital*, a business review, six hundred thousand children go with their school to Disneyland every year.[97]

Altogether, the attitude of French intellectuals toward American mass culture is quite out of step with that of young people who do not seem to care so much for "high culture" and have been raised on mass culture. Young people are americanized, not in the sense that they have lost all Frenchness but that this culture has been profoundly altered. One anecdote will illustrate what I mean. My grandson, about seven, wanted to go up Notre Dame tower, so we went. As we got to the top, I pointed to a gargoyle and was about to explain what it was. Hardly casting a glance at it, he said to me in a very blasé tone: "I know about them; I got a plastic one at McDonald's." That was the week when McDonald's was promoting Disney's film *Notre-Dame de Paris* (with no mention of Victor Hugo).

American mass culture does have a peculiar aura in the eyes of many young people, as is revealed by this other anecdote. On 30 November 1998, a radio journalist interviewed passersby on the street, asking them what birthday gift they would have given to President Chirac on that day of his sixty-sixth birthday. A young man said he would have offered him "*une journée de folie*"(a day of extravaganza): lunch at McDonald's, a visit to Disneyland, and the evening out in a nightclub.

In spite of all the talk about "cultural exchanges," the "europeanization of the United States," "cross-fertilization," and the like, the pervasiveness of American mass culture in France is an undeniable reality. It would be a consoling thought to speak of "mutual assimilation" or reciprocity, but, as Benjamin Barber rightly warns us, the reciprocity between American mass culture and other national cultures is "the reciprocity of the python who swallows the hare."[98]

At a time when American "diversity" is all the rage and "multiculturalism" abundantly celebrated, it is ironic to see that the "soft hegemony" of American mass culture—be it through drinking Coca-Cola, collecting Barbie dolls, or cloning Disneyland in local theme parks, to name a few—tends to weaken, homogenize, and even eradicate original cultures, impoverishing the cultural heritage of nations.

Notes

1. Marc-Ambroise Rendu, "Des parcs de loisir à l'aventure," *Le Monde* (Paris), 27 July 1989, p. 10; and Charles Vial, "Eurodisneyland ou le divertissement prétexte," *Le Monde* (Paris), 27 July 1989, p. 11.

2. "Le projet Euro-Disneyland en France," Rapport du groupe no. 3 du séminaire "cycle international," Promotion Condorcet de l'Ecole Nationale d'Administration, November 1991, unpublished. See also Martha Zuber, "Mickey sur Marne: une culture conquérante," *French Society and Politics* 10, no. 3 (Summer 1992): 63–80.

3. Patrick Marnham, "Wake Me Up When Mickey Mouse Arrives in Paris," *The Independent* (London), 25 March 1987, p. 12.

4. *International Herald Tribune* (Paris), 15 March 1986, pp. 1, 7.

5. Marie-Christine Robert, "La signature du contrat d'Euro-Disneyland," *Le Monde*, 24 March 1987, p. 40.

6. See *Business Week,* 12 March 1989, p. 38: "A Government Contract Protects Disney from Competition in a 12,000 Acre Area"; David Lawday, "Where All the Dwarfs Are Grumpy," *U.S. News and World Report,* 28 May 1990, pp. 50–51.

7. F. M., "Mickey a aussi des détracteurs," *Le Matin,* supplément économique, 18 December 1986, p. VII.

8. Gérard Le Pull, "Risques sans assurance," *L'Humanité,* 10 July 1986, p. 2.

9. An idea shared by ENA students, Rapport ENA, p. 22.

10. "Le Disneyland français inquiète les élus locaux," *Le Monde,* 24 December 1985, p. 13.

11. *Le Quotidien de Paris,* 29 September 1989, p. 23; *Le Quotidien de Paris,* 25 November 1992, p. 11; *L'Humanité,* 29 September 1989, p. 19; and *L'Humanité,* 7 April 1990, p. 4. The expropriation of farmers and their struggle against the project are told in a TV documentary, "Les paysans du Disneyland," A2 Channel, 8 June 1992.

12. Jean-Edern Hallier, *Le Figaro,* 28 March 1987.

13. Michel Giraud, president of the regional council of Ile de France, *Le Monde,* 14 January 1986, p. 2.

14. *Le Monde,* 4 November 1986, p. 12.

15. Gilles Smadja, *Mickey l'Arnaque* (Paris: Messidor, 1988), p. 99; and *Le Monde,* 4 September 1991, p. 20.

16. Gilles Smadja, "Picsou bien plus que Mickey," *L'Humanité,* 15 January 1992, p. 17.

17. *Le Quotidien de Paris,* 27 January 1992, p. 24.

18. Gérard Petitjean, "La souris et le fromage," *Le Nouvel Observateur,* 14–20 February 1991, p. 97.

19. *Le Monde,* 4 December 1991, p. 22.

20. *Libération,* 8–9 August 1992, p. 6.

21. Lucien Degoy, "Les Cendrillons osent parler," *L'Humanité,* 3 March 1992, p. 17.

22. Anne Cicco, "Les masques tombent," *L'Humanite,* 4 July 1992, p. 12.

23. *Le Canard Enchaîné,* 19 August 1992, p. 4.

24. Sandrine Burnacci, "La souris fait la tête," *L'Humanite,* 1 August 1992, p. 11.

25. *L'Evénement du Jeudi,* 7 January 1993, p. 115.

26. *Le Canard Enchaîné,* 19 August 1992, p. 4.

27. *L'Humanité,* 4 February 1993, p. 17, and 1 April 1993, p. 7.

28. *L'Humanite,* 13 August 1993, p. 6.

29. *L'Humanite,* 20 June 1994, p. 13, and 21 June 1994, p. 15; Jean-Michel Normand, "Eurodisney tente d'atténuer les effets de son plan social," *Le Monde,* 21 June 1994, p. 22.

30. *L'Humanité,* 5 September 1994, p. 8.

31. *L'Humanité,* 30 November 1994, p. 24.

32. Loic Grasset, "Disneyland Paris, Mickey n'est pas tiré d'affaire," *Capital* (February 1995): 40.

33. Mary Dejevsky, "Strikers Take the Mickey Out of Disney," *The Independent* (London), 4 January 1996, p. 13; Jérome Canard, "Nouvelle attraction anti-grévistes à EuroDisney," *Le Canard Enchaîné,* 7 February 1996, p. 4; *L'Humanité,* 17 February 1996, p. 4; and *L'Humanité* 25 March 1996, p. 8.

34. *Le Monde,* 1 July 1998, p. 18.

35. Tiphaine Clotault, "La petite sirène en a assez d'avoir le cul dans l'eau," *Libération,* 4–5 July 1998, p. 19.

36. Philippe Bataille, *Le racisme au travail* (Paris: La Découverte, 1997), 66–68.

37. Ludwig Siegele, "EuroDisney ouvre, Billancourt ferme," *Le Courrier International,* 9–15 April 1992, pp. 25–26.

38. M. Cantal-Dupart et C. Bayle, "Ma culture, c'est Mickey," *Le Monde,* 10 July 1986, p. 2.

39. Interview in *Projet* 229 (Spring 1992): 93–102.

40. Dominique Jamet, "Dollars et bords de Marne," *Le Quotidien de Paris,* 25 March 1987, p. 18.

41. Quoted in Smadja, *Mickey L'Arnaque,* 185–86.

42. Paul-Marie Couteaux, "L'imaginaire du maître," *Le Monde,* 10 July 1986, p. 2.

43. *Le Quotidien de Paris,* 13 June 1986, p. 17.

44. Quoted in Smadja, *Mickey l'Arnaque,* 181.

45. Dominique Jamet, "Dollars et bords de Marne," *Le Quotidien de Paris,* 25 March 1987, p. 18.

46. Quoted in Roger Cohen, "A Not So Magic Kingdom," *International Herald Tribune,* 19 July 1993, p. 12.

47. Philippe de Saint Robert, *Le Quotidien de Paris,* 10 December 1991, p. 17.

48. Robert Melcher, "Disneyland Discord," *The European* (London), 1–3 March 1991.

49. Quoted in *International Herald Tribune,* 23 March 1987, p. 7.

50. *L'Express,* 19 March 1992, p. 79.

51. *Le Monde,* 14 April 1992, p. 2; also Scott Sullivan, "We're Not So Different," *Newsweek,* 13 April 1992, p. 19.

52. Quoted in *Newsweek,* 13 April 1992, p. 12. See Pierre Guerlain, "Qui diabolise Mickey? (EuroDisney et les malentendus franco-américains)," *Esprit* (June 1992): 160–69.

53. Christophe de Chenay, "Disney à la mode de chez nous," *Le Monde,* 13 April 1993, p. 19.

54. "La lune; nouvel astre de la galaxie Disney," *Le Monde,* 15 September 1995, p. 22.

55. Martha Zuber, "Mickey sur Marne: une culture conquérante," *French Politics and Society* 10, no. 3 (Summer 1992): 74.

56. *The Independent,* 2 November 1991, p. 45.

57. Marc Augé, "Un ethnologue à Euro Disneyland," *Le Monde Diplomatique* (Paris) (August 1992): 18–19.

58. Jean-Yves Guiomar, "Le conservatoire du néant," *Le Débat* 73 (January–February 1993): 152–61.

59. Agathe Logeart, "Euro-Disney: le rêve en moins," *Le Monde*, 23 December 1993, p. 19.

60. Umberto Eco, *La guerre du faux* (Paris: Grasset, 1985); Louis Marin, *Utopiques, jeux d'espaces* (Paris: Editions de Minuit, 1973); Jean Baudrillard, *Simulacres et simulation* (Paris: Galilée, 1981).

61. Emmanuel de Roux, "L'Ouverture d'EuroDisney à Marne La Vallée," *Le Monde*, 12–13 April 1992, p. 9.

62. Nicole Pénicaud, "Mickey contre les portefeuilles, tout contre . . . ," *Libération*, 11–12 April 1992, 6–7.

63. Neil Postman, "They Came, We Saw, They Conquered," *The Times*, 27 December 1985, p. 12.

64. Christian Mellon, "Loisir, l'autre temps," *Projet* 229 (Spring 1992): 4.

65. *Los Angeles Times* as quoted in Jean-Sébastien Stehli, "La culture cartoon," *Le Point*, 21 March 1992, p. 74.

66. Ben Wattenberg quoted in Pascal Privat with Fiona Gleizes, "Empire of the Fun," *Newsweek*, 13 April 1992, p. 10.

67. Marshall Blonsky quoted in *Newsweek*, 13 April 1992, p. 10.

68. Marc Fumaroli, "Le défi américain," *Le Nouvel Observateur*, 9–15 April 1992, p. 92.

69. Emission de France-Culture, 11 April 1992.

70. Emission de France-Culture, 18 April 1992.

71. "Empire of the Fun," *Newsweek*, 13 April 1992, p. 10.

72. A French journalist speaks of the Disney "tendency to turn the past into a sanitized, prettified tourist attraction." Isabelle Lefort, "La doctrine Mickey," *Challenges* (July–August 1989): 26–27.

73. Alain Finkielkraut, emission de France-Culture, 11 April 1992.

74. Quoted in Emmanuel de Roux, "L'ouverture d'Euro-Disney à Marne la Vallée," *Le Monde*, 12–13 April 1992, p. 9.

75. "Eurodisney, le rêve pour tous, Entretien," *Projet* 229 (Spring 1992): 94.

76. *Le Monde*, 27 July 1989, p. 11.

77. Denis Lacorne, emission de France-Culture, 11 April 1992. See also his article, "Disneyland et EuroDisneyland," *Esprit* (June 1986): 105–13.

78. Jean Hurstel, emission de France-Culture, 11 April 1992.

79. Willy Bakeroot, "Des mythes devenus objets," *Projet* 229 (Spring 1992): 86, 88.

80. Quoted in Laurence Beauvais, "A Disneyland, les français résistent aux 'barbares colonisateurs,'" *Le Quotidien de Paris*, 15–16 August 1992, p. 7.

81. Paul Vacca, "Eurodisney et le syndrome d'Astérix," *Le Quotidien de Paris*, 19 May 1992, p. 16.

82. Philippe Baverel, "Disneyland Paris adoucit l'arrogance américaine," *Le Monde*, 20 May 1998, p. 11. Needless to say, many articles deal with the financial problems of Disneyland, but, due to considerations of space, I chose not to cover this aspect.

83. *Le Monde*, 29 January 1998, p. 16.

84. Fernand Nouvel, "Les surprises de Mickey," *L'Humanité*, 21 August 1992, p. 11.

85. *L'Humanité*, 14 April 1992, p. 23.

86. "Les agriculteurs prennent Mickey en otage," *Le Quotidien de Paris,* 27–28 June 1992, p. 9; *L'Humanité* (Paris), 27 June 1992, p. 6.

87. Mary Dejevsky, "Mickey Finds a Place in French Life," *The Independent* (London), 30 October 1996, p. 19.

88. Richard Pells, *Not Like Us: How Europeans Have Loved, Hated and Transformed American Culture since World War II* (New York: Basic Books, 1997), 279. See Lawrence Levine, "The Folklore of Industrial Society: Popular Culture and Its Audiences," *American Historical Review* 97 (December 1992): 1369–99. See also Marianne Debouzy, "De la production à la réception de la culture de masse," *Le Mouvement Social* 152 (July–September 1990): 31–47.

89. T. Jackson Lears, "Making Fun of Popular Culture," *American Historical Review* 97 (December 1992): 1417, 1426; see also Michael Kammen, *American Culture, American Tastes: Social Change and the Twentieth Century* (New York: Knopf, 1999), chap. 8, "Mass Culture in More Recent Times: Passive and/or Participatory."

90. Quoted in Shanny Peers, "Marketing Mickey: Disney Goes to France," *Tocqueville Review* 13, no. 2 (1992): 133.

91. *Le Monde,* 22 September 1999, p. 22.

92. Lears, "Making Fun of Popular Culture," 1424.

94. Reinhold Wagnleitner, "Where's the Coke? There's the Coke!" in *Living with America, 1946–1996,* ed. Cristina Giorcelli and Rob Kroes (Amsterdam: VU University Press, 1997), 69.

94. On Americanization, see *Le Messager Européen* 2 (1988); Alain Finkielkraut, "Eurodisneyland," *Le Messager Européen* 6 (1992): 197.

95. Shanny Peers, "Marketing Mickey," *The Tocqueville Review* 13, no. 2 (1992): 134.

96. Denis Lacorne, Jacques Rupnik, and Marie-France Toinet, eds., *The Rise and Fall of Anti-Americanism: A Century of French Perception* (London: Macmillan, 1990), 80, 7 (French ed., 1986). See also Richard Kuisel, *Seducing the French: The Dilemma of Americanization* (Berkeley: University of California Press, 1993).

97. Ivan Letessier, "Comment les marques font leur pub à l'école," *Capital* (September 1999): 98, 100.

98. Benjamin Barber, "Disneyfication That Impoverishes Us All," *The Independent, Week End Review,* 29 August 1998, p. 7. See also Alan Bryman, "The Disneyization of Society," *Sociological Review* 47 (February 1999): 25–47.

4

Culture versus Commerce

Europe Strives to Keep Hollywood at Bay

C. Anthony Giffard

EUROPEANS HAVE LONG SOUGHT to protect their unique cultures against the subversive onslaught of Walt Disney and McDonald's. In an age when watching television is the most popular—and perhaps the most influential—leisure-time activity, they want to ensure that the images and ideas transmitted to their living rooms reflect European cultural values. For some on the other side of the Atlantic, the source of much of the television programming shown in Europe, the issue is quite different. Europeans, they charge, are less interested in promoting their indigenous cultures than in thwarting efforts by the United States to expand its markets for audiovisual products—one of the few sectors in which it has a substantial trade surplus.

Trade disputes usually involve such protectionist measures as import tariffs, quotas, taxes, or subsidies on tangible things—vehicles, steel, agricultural products—the value of which can readily be calculated. The European Union (EU) and the United States already have locked horns in the General Agreement on Tariffs and Trade (GATT) and the World Trade Organization (WTO) over just such issues. Some trade disputes, however, involve not only economics but social issues like environmental concerns or food safety that are less susceptible to economic reasoning.[1] Television programs and movies are one such issue. The United States wants unlimited access to the burgeoning European audiovisual markets; Europeans want to encourage local production and limit imports from Hollywood.

To Americans, European attempts to stimulate endogenous production are simply a means of protecting domestic audiovisual industries from foreign competition. Europeans see these measures as essential for other reasons as well. They want to keep the lid on imports of American films and TV programs to give local products more space. But they also want to use the media to forge a sense of European unity: television is seen as the best way to help citizens acquire an awareness of the history and culture of their neighbors.

With this in mind, Western European nations have adopted legal frameworks which facilitate the exchange of information by encouraging a free flow of television programs among themselves but which limit imports from non-European countries. This has been done by coordinating national legislation governing broadcasts which cross frontiers. The regulations stipulate that parties to the agreements should guarantee free reception or retransmission in their territories of TV programs from other signatories. They govern the amount and kind of advertising permitted, protect minors against exposure to pornography or gratuitous violence, and provide for a right of reply for persons whose reputations are injured by an assertion of incorrect facts.

In addition, the regulations seek to promote endogenous production of television programs, in part by specifying that a majority should be made in Europe. This latter provision has angered American exporters of television programs and movies, who argue that it restricts the free flow of information and abrogates free trade provisions of the WTO.

The regulations are found in equivalent formulations in two documents. One is the Television without Frontiers Directive adopted by the Council of the European Communities.[2] The council deals with media law insofar as it concerns establishing a common market for goods and services. The draft directive was first published in April 1986 and modified considerably in March 1988 to take account of amendments proposed by the European Parliament. The EC council approved the directive on 3 October 1989. Further revisions were adopted in June 1997.[3] The directive provides for coordination of laws and regulations concerning television broadcasting in the fifteen member states of the European Union. Each member state had to develop, adopt, and implement legislation, regulations, and administrative procedures to comply with its provisions by 3 October 1991.

The directive lays down minimum rules needed to ensure free transmission of programs across frontiers. Member states can keep their own ways of organizing and financing their national broadcasting systems. They are also free to set stricter rules than those in the directive for broadcasters under their jurisdiction.

A parallel agreement is the European Convention on Transfrontier Television, adopted in May 1989 by the Council of Europe, an organization of forty-one Western and Eastern European states that promotes democratic values and human rights.[4] The council takes an active role in development of media law and policy. The intention is to coordinate the approach of member states with respect to cultural, economic, and social aspects of the media.[5] The council's recommendations are not binding on members, but its Committee of Ministers draws up agreements or conventions which become binding on states that ratify them.

While the European Union's Declaration and the Council of Europe's convention differed significantly in early draft forms, the final texts cover essentially the same grounds and generally are phrased in similar language.[6] In 1998, the convention was amended to keep it congruent with the 1997 changes to the EU Declaration.[7] The regulations are spelled out in more detail in the declaration than in the convention. All fifteen members of the European Union also are members of the Council of Europe. The convention stipulates that in those nations EU rules take precedence (Article 27.1).

The reasons for the adoption of the regulations are to be found in the technological, economic, and political factors which have led to expansion and growing internationalization of European broadcasting.[8] Until recently most European TV networks were government monopolies, largely because the limited number of channels available required that the broadcast spectrum be used for public service broadcasting, rather than for the benefit of commercial interests. Rapid changes in communications technology have made this argument largely irrelevant. Cable systems are providing a variety of additional channels. Several direct broadcast satellites offer programs ranging from news and sports to movies and music TV that can be received simultaneously in several countries. New techniques for terrestrial broadcasting, such as low-power TV, have increased the number of local channels. The expansion is accelerating with the arrival of digital television. Digital compression typically allows between eight and twelve channels to occupy the same capacity required by a single analogue channel.[9]

As in the United States, the past few years in Europe have seen an increasing tendency toward deregulation and privatization in various sectors, including broadcasting. Most European countries now have dual systems, with private, commercial channels supplementing or competing with the national public service networks. Britain was the first European country to open television to the private sector in 1954. Deregulation took place in Italy in 1974; in France in 1982; in Germany in 1984; in Sweden, Belgium, and the Netherlands in 1987; in Spain and Ireland in 1988; in Greece in 1989; and in Portugal in 1990.[10]

The number of private channels now exceeds the number of public service channels, which usually are financed by viewer license fees, or a combination of license fees and advertising. Public broadcasting systems, unable to raise their license fees for political reasons and limited by regulation in the amount of advertising they can carry, cannot provide more services. A report by the Dublin-based research consultancy Norcontel forecasts that license fee income will continue to fall in real terms, reflecting Europe-wide constraints on public sector spending.[11] Only a handful of the new channels introduced in the past decade are public services. By far the majority are privately owned, commercial channels, funded by advertising, subscriptions, or pay-per-view.

As a result of these developments, the number of channels available in the EU nations increased significantly. In 1983, for example, there were thirty-seven

Western European TV channels. By mid-1989, there were ninety-one.[12] The 1990s saw even more rapid growth. In 2000, there were more than 580 channels broadcast in the EU by terrestrial, satellite, or cable. It is estimated that among them they provide about 3.5 million broadcast hours a year. About fifty of the channels target countries other than the country of origin, usually by satellite. The number of channels is increasing rapidly as more states introduce multi-channel digital services, as happened in the United Kingdom (1998), Sweden (1999), and Spain (2000).[13]

The striving for greater economic and political unity in Europe was a major catalyst for the new regulations that encourage broadcasting across frontiers and the retransmission of one nation's programs in another. The preamble to the Council of Europe's television convention notes that the council's aim is to "achieve greater unity between its members." The directive of the European Community states that its objectives include "establishing an even closer union among the people of Europe, fostering closer relations between the states belonging to the Community, ensuring the economic and social progress of its countries by common action to eliminate the barriers which divide Europe."

In addition, the preambles to both the directive and the convention note that broadcasting is one manifestation of a more general principle—the freedom of expression enshrined in Article 10(1) of the Convention for the Protection of Human Rights and Fundamental Freedoms, to which most European nations are signatories. The article states that everyone has the right to freedom of expression, which shall include freedom to hold opinions and to receive and impart information and ideas without interference by public authority and regardless of frontiers. It does not, however, prevent states from requiring licensing of broadcasting.

More specifically, the EU declaration derives from the Treaty of Rome, which established the European Community in 1957 and requires that obstacles to freedom of movement of goods and services among member states be abolished. Broadcasting is considered a service within the meaning of the treaty, and broadcasts across frontiers are one of the ways of pursuing EU objectives.

The Single European Act (SEA), which came into force in July 1987, amended the Treaty of Rome with a view to achieving by the end of 1992 a single internal market—an area without internal frontiers in which the free movement of goods, persons, and capital is ensured. The SEA operates on the principle of mutual recognition of standards. Since different states had different laws and regulations governing broadcasting, there was a need to harmonize national standards to facilitate the unimpeded flow of information mandated by the new treaties.[14] The intention of the directive is to create a common market in broadcasting. It applies Articles 55 and 62 of the Treaty of Rome to broadcasting, thus prohibiting any restrictions on the free flow of TV programs among the member states, which are not required to give up their own law in favor of an EU standard but must recognize the national standards of other states, provided that minimum EU standards are complied with.[15]

Under previous EC rules, any state could block incoming broadcasts, except in border regions where there is unavoidable overspill. Nor was there anything to prevent a state from restricting the sale of decoders or satellite dishes.[16] Now member states cannot object to programs from other EU countries being received and retransmitted in their own territory, provided these programs conform to the regulations. To facilitate this free flow, both the declaration and the convention propose common rules and standards for programs as well as advertising on television. These include the following:

- *Advertising and sponsorship.* The regulations limit the amount and kind of advertising. They require that advertising should be recognizable as such and prohibit subliminal and "surreptitious" advertising—defined as representing the name or trademark of a supplier of goods or services with the intention of advertising. Both sets of regulations specify that advertising spots should generally not interrupt programs. Instead, ads should be inserted between programs or, in the case of programs more than forty-five minutes long, they may be interrupted once for each complete period of forty-five minutes. There can be no commercial breaks in news and current affairs programs, documentaries, or children's programs if the program duration is less than thirty minutes. The total amount of advertising should not exceed 15 percent of daily transmission time or more than 20 percent in any given clock hour. Teleshopping windows on generalist channels may not number more than eight per day, and their total duration may not exceed three hours a day.

  Both the declaration and the convention impose a complete ban on advertising cigarettes or other tobacco products, and on drugs and medical treatment that are only available with a prescription in the country where the broadcast originates. Ads for alcoholic beverages cannot be aimed specifically at minors or give the impression that drinking leads to enhanced physical performance or to social or sexual success. Ads directed at children cannot encourage them to buy a product by exploiting their inexperience or credulity or directly encourage them to persuade their parents to buy the product advertised.

- *Sponsored programs.* Sponsors cannot influence the content and scheduling of programs in a way that will affect the editorial independence of broadcasters. Firms whose principal activity is the manufacture or sale of tobacco products may not sponsor programs.

- *Protection of minors.* Both documents further seek to protect the "physical, mental or moral development of minors" through a ban on programs that involve pornography or gratuitous violence at times when children are likely to watch them.

- *Right of reply.* TV broadcasters are required, in terms of both documents, to provide a right of reply, or equivalent remedies, to persons whose reputation and good name have been damaged by an assertion of incorrect facts in a broadcast.
- *Independent producers.* The EU stipulates that member states should ensure, where practicable, that broadcasters reserve at least 10 percent of their transmission time for European works created by independent producers. The intention here, according to the directive's preamble, is to stimulate new sources of TV production, especially the creation of small and medium-sized enterprises, and to offer new opportunities for employment in the cultural field. To prevent excessive repeats of golden oldies, an adequate proportion should be recent—"transmitted within five years of their production."[17]
- *Important events.* Member states may draw up a list of events that must be broadcast unencrypted even if pay-TV stations have bought exclusive rights. These events may be national, such as the Tour de France or Britain's Cup Final, or international, such as the Olympic Games, the European Football Championship, or the World Cup.
- *European content.* The regulations that have aroused the most controversy, however, are those requiring that a majority of the programs broadcast should be of European origin, rather than imports. Article 4 of the EU directive and Article 10 of the council's convention both require that member states shall "ensure where practicable and by appropriate means, that broadcasters reserve for European works a majority proportion of their transmission time, excluding the time appointed to news, sports events, games, advertising and teletext services."

  The convention defines European works as "creative works, the production or co-production of which is controlled by European natural or legal persons." The directive is more specific. European works are defined as works originating from EU member states or other European nations that are members of the Council of Europe. Productions that are not European works but are jointly produced by member states and third countries will be treated as European works if the major proportion of the costs is covered by EC coproducers, who also must control production.

The arguments for the European content regulations fall into two general categories: economic and cultural. The economic argument relates to the fact that the European Single Market will be one of the largest and richest in the world, with 340 million consumers—nearly as many as the United States and Japan combined—and a gross national product of more than $4.5 trillion. The Norcontel study forecasts that consumer expenditure on audiovisual services in Europe will double in real terms by 2005 as new pay-per-view and interactive services are launched on the new wave of multichannel digital television networks.[18] The study suggests that the total value of the audiovisual market in seven European countries—France, Germany, Italy, Spain, Great

Britain, Denmark, and Ireland—will reach 53.87 billion euros in 2005 (at 1995 prices), nearly 70 percent more than in 1995. At present, however, the market for television producers is fragmented and lacks the economies of scale. It is much cheaper for European nations, especially the smaller ones, to import programs from larger ones than to make their own. A program imported from the United States for showing in Europe often costs about one-tenth as much as a local production, because most of the American production costs are covered in the huge domestic market.

European broadcasters have become huge markets for imported movies and television programming, and Europe runs a large and growing trade deficit in audiovisual products. A recent study found that while TV fiction of national origin tended to prevail during prime time, Hollywood fiction tended to fill the other schedule slots. As a result, trade in TV rights with the United States in 1998 showed a deficit of about $2.9 billion, out of a total audiovisual deficit estimated at $6.6 billion. The trade imbalance continues.[19]

In addition, although there has been a revival in production of cinematic films in Europe (634 were produced in 1999, up from 456 in 1994), Hollywood movies still account for 71 percent of the box office. The five major U.S. studios shared 80.5 percent of the British market in 1999.[20] The share of American films on television in EU nations ranges from 23.9 percent in France to 74.1 percent in the Netherlands.[21] European producers argue that the money now paid for U.S. imports could be used instead to improve the amount and quality of locally produced programs, slowing the "brain drain" of talented producers and artists to Hollywood.

The cultural argument for favoring local European programs is made with equal force. The concern is that programs from the United States are invading Europe and threatening to submerge its traditional cultures. A 1984 green paper, "Television without Frontiers," which served as a working document for preparation of the EU directive, makes the point that "television will play an important role in developing and nurturing awareness of the rich variety of Europe's common cultural and historical heritage."[22] It also notes that most of the films shown in the European Community come from one single non-member country—the United States. As a result, there is already a certain uniformity in the range of films screened on television in the EC. Almost every television station in the member states carries programs such as *Dallas*. The creation of a common market for television products is "thus one essential step if the dominance of the big American media corporations is to be counterbalanced." As Jacques Delors, then president of the European Community, remarked, "I would simply like to pose a question to our American friends: Do we have the right to exist? Have we the right to preserve our tradition, our heritage, our languages? How will a country of 10 million inhabitants be able to maintain its language—the very linchpin of culture—faced with the universality that satellites offer?"[23]

Carol Tongue, a British member of the European Parliament, summed up the cultural and economic arguments for quotas in a letter to the London *Financial Times*:

> Let us create space for European programmes to circulate, enhancing our culture, increasing mutual understanding and creating thousands of jobs in our creative arts. Again, broadcast and investment quotas are ways to encourage this. They are needed for a transitional period of up to 10 years to provide a breathing space for the European industry to restructure and for investment to be stimulated. European industry might then be able to take on the might of the US companies, which are able to sell their films in a secondary market at a 10th of the cost it takes to produce quality European drama and documentaries. In a situation of imperfect market competition, special policies are required to ensure that all Europe's voices are heard and all Europe's stories are told, and that Europeans gain economically and culturally from an ever-growing industry.[24]

Yet another argument for limits on imports from the United States is their impact on Europe's traditional concept of public broadcasting, with its emphasis on information, culture, and education, rather than on commercial entertainment. The new commercial channels, both cable and satellite, tend to show a high proportion of American imports—because they are relatively cheap and appeal to large audiences—that can be sold to advertisers. The public service systems depend on listener license fees for their revenue. The concern is that if viewers were to abandon these channels in favor of commercial offerings, there would be political pressure to do away with TV license fees. The public service channels would either have to lower their standards to compete for mass audiences with the commercial services or dwindle into elitist media with limited support.[25]

The need then, as perceived by the EU directive and the Council of Europe's convention, is to encourage the development of European audiovisual production and distribution, particularly in countries with a low production capacity or restricted language areas. This is to be accomplished by promoting markets of sufficient size for television producers in the member states to recover their investments and by protecting them from outside competition. The effectiveness of the European content rule has been undermined, some critics charge, by a loophole in the regulations, which stipulates that member states shall ensure "where practicable and by appropriate means," that broadcasters reserve a majority proportion of their transmission time for European works. The clause was inserted in 1989 at the insistence of British prime minister Margaret Thatcher and was meant to protect Rupert Murdoch's commercial satellite channel BSkyB, which carried a high proportion of cheap American imports.[26] (Murdoch's four national newspapers in Britain supported Thatcher's Conservative Party government).

The quota issue surfaced again in 1995. Article 26 of the directive stipulated that it would be revisited five years after adoption and revised if necessary to adapt to changing circumstances. Any proposed revision had to survive a lengthy and complicated codecision procedure involving the European Commission, the European Parliament, and the council. Most of the amendments sought to clarify existing provisions. One major change was the addition of an article stipulating that a member state could designate events "which it considers to be of major importance for society" (mainly sports, such as the World Cup soccer games or the Tour de France) and ensure they be available on free-to-air television, even if pay-TV channels had previously bought exclusive rights. Each state would draw up a list of such events, which other states would have to respect.[27]

The most controversial issue in the directive again had to do with content quotas. In May 1995, the commission recommended to the council and the European Parliament that the words "where practicable" be dropped from the European content rule but that the quotas be phased out after ten years. This compromise deeply divided the twenty-member commission. The United States had warned that the exclusion of American companies from the European media market could damage trade relations,[28] and some feared it could start a transatlantic trade war because it was aimed at Hollywood. Stuart E. Eizenstat, the U.S. ambassador to the European Union, said the commission had missed "an historic opportunity to take a bold step towards a more open system."[29]

France led the fight for stricter enforcement of quotas. The French film producers association, Union des Productions des Films (UPF), complained that the commission's proposal would "rapidly put the European film and television industries under U.S. patronage." It called for France to exercise its veto to protect Europe from the "terrifying economic, sociological and cultural consequences of the measure."[30] Pascal Rogart of the Chambre Syndicale des Producteurs Français described the quotas as the "vitamins" needed to boost Europe's audiovisual industry, stating that "frantic lobbying" by the U.S. entertainment industry at the slightest hint of a change in the existing EU regime was "proof that the quotas were attacking the right target."[31] The French position drew support from Belgium, Spain, Portugal, Greece, and Socialist members of the European Parliament. Many member states, however, were indifferent or even hostile to the French position. Britain wanted to scrap the quotas altogether. Stephen Dorrell, the U.K. national heritage minister, said they create an "irreconcilable contradiction at the heart of the Directive. The best course would be to eliminate them or phase them out."[32]

Also opposed to quotas were the Netherlands, Denmark, Luxembourg, and Sweden. As one Netherlands official put it, the directive is a defensive measure; the Dutch government prefers positive measures such as subsidies for domestic production. "Quotas are for codfish," he said.[33] Sweden was concerned about freedom of expression and wanted to retain its links with other Scandinavian countries that were not members of the EU. Denmark said the quotas were not democratic. Luxembourg is the home of Astra, the biggest satellite operator in Europe and a platform for many commercial channels. German delegates argued that culture should remain the remit of national authorities and, in the German case, that the programming autonomy of the individual Länder (provinces) be respected.[34] The Länder were concerned that Brussels could dictate German broadcasting law, although Germany's Constitutional Court ruled in March 1995 that the Bonn government had no right to commit the Länder to EU broadcasting rules.

In any event, the proposal to drop the "where practicable" clause failed to survive the codecision procedure among parliament, the council, and the commission, nor did the proposal limit the application of quotas to ten years. Article 4 remained essentially unchanged when revisions to the directive were approved in July 1997. Jack Lang, the Socialist parliamentarian who, as France's cultural minister was the driving force behind the original 1989 quota provisions, deplored the result. "Washington can now rest assured that on questions of culture, the majority of Europeans will lie down as soon as the United States gives the order," he said.[35] Emmanuelle Machet of the European Institute for the Media commented that "the debates ended up with a rather unsatisfactory compromise for all the parties concerned. The revision of the Directive ended up with the status quo . . . it pleased everyone and no one at the same time." The French government was in favor of extending the scope of the directive and of reinforcing the quotas but considered that the revised directive was even more flexible than the original text. Other member states, on the contrary, regretted that the quota system could not be abolished.[36]

The directive and the convention set minimum standards that member states are expected to adhere to. But countries may apply stricter rules for domestic productions. The Netherlands, for example, expects the national public broadcaster, NOS, to acquire 25 percent of its programs from independent producers, rather than the 10 percent required by the directive.[37] In France, 60 percent of television programs must be European, including at least 40 percent made in France—although some stations fail to meet the targets. Switzerland, a member of the Council of Europe but not of the EU, requires satellite broadcasters serving Switzerland to broadcast at least an hour of Swiss programming a week and to contribute to a fund used to subsidize Swiss film production.[38]

Although there is no compulsion to adhere to the European content rule, broadcasters are subject to moral suasion. Every two years, member states are required to provide the European Commission with a report on application of the 51 percent rule, including "reasons, in each case, for the failure to attain that proportion and the measures adopted or envisaged in order to achieve it." The commission's fourth report on the application of the European content rule, adopted in 2000, noted that its objectives had largely been achieved. The average of European works broadcast by the major channels varied from about 53.3 percent to 81.7 percent—except for Portugal, where the figure was 43 percent. Overall, the report said, "the television channels' broadcasting of European works and independent productions satisfactorily complies with the rules contained in the Directive, and the aims of the Directive have been generally achieved." Some commercial satellite and recently launched channels were failing to broadcast a majority of European productions. These included so-called theme channels providing highly specialized programming which was not readily available from European producers. Examples are science fiction and subscription film channels.[39]

Viewer preference also appears to be playing a part in stimulating domestic production. Once the new private broadcasters become established and begin earning substantial amounts of money, they invest in local productions, especially soap operas, talk shows, magazines, sports, and sitcoms, that reflect the reality of viewers' lives. Pascal Albrechtskirchinger, head of the ZDF–German Television bureau in Brussels, notes that Europeans find a program like *Dallas* interesting for a short while, but they would happily watch *Coronation Street* or *Lindenstrasse* for years.[40] In one respect, however, the regulations have been less successful. They are intended to encourage a wider exchange of programs among European nations. But although domestic production has increased, the proportion of fiction programs of European origin imported by EU member states dropped by 40 percent between 1994 and 1996. In 1995, Europe's terrestrial TV channels carried a mix of national and U.S. programs, with only 8 percent of their programs from other European countries.[41]

American producers of movies and television programs see the European content rules as a threat. Despite the size of the U.S. domestic market, export earnings are often essential for Hollywood studios to break even. In recent years, more than half of the revenue from exhibition in motion picture theaters has come from outside the United States. Foreign markets generate about 40 percent of the revenue from television and video.[42] In addition, the sale of American films and TV programs abroad is the second largest export after defense and a major contributor to the U.S. trade balance. In the European market alone, the United States earns $5.6 billion more from sales of its films and TV programs than the European countries earn in the United States. American producers see the European market as having the greatest potential for growth in the coming decade, not only for exports but also for mergers and takeovers.[43] They are determined, therefore, to protect their interests.

In the broader sense of all intellectual property protected by copyright laws—motion pictures, television programs, and home videocassettes; computer business and entertainment software; music, records, CDs, and audiocassettes; and textbooks, trade books, reference, and professional publications and journals—the importance of this sector is even more striking. A report published by the International Intellectual Property Alliance (IIPA) in 2000 estimates that in 1999 industries that create copyrighted products contributed $457.2 billion to the U.S. economy, accounting for 4.94 percent of the U.S. gross domestic product (GDP). From 1977 to 1999, the value added to the GDP increased by 360 percent. In 1999, 4.3 million Americans worked in the core copyright industries—about 3.24 percent of the entire U.S. workforce. And in that year the core copyright industries achieved foreign sales and exports of $79.6 billion, surpassing every other export sector, including chemicals, electrical components, automotive, agriculture, and aircraft.[44] The IIPA's seven member associations—the Association of American Publishers, the American Film Marketing Association, the Business Software Alliance, the Interactive Digital Software Association, Motion Picture Association of America, the National Music Publishers' Association, and the Recording Industry Association of America—represent more than 1,350 U.S. companies producing and distributing works protected by copyright laws throughout the world. Although the IIPA's primary concern is to improve copyright protection and enforcement, it also seeks a market-oriented approach in the global information infrastructure and the dismantling of legal barriers that restrict the access of the U.S. creative industries to foreign markets. It believes the leading goal of U.S. policy should be "the broadest possible free flow of information across international borders."[45]

The most vocal opponent of European restrictions on media imports is the Motion Picture Association of America (MPAA) and its international counterpart, the Motion Picture Association (MPA).[46] These trade associations represent the seven major producers and distributors of films and television programs in the United States: Walt Disney, Sony Pictures, Metro-Goldwyn-Mayer, Paramount Pictures, Twentieth Century Fox, Universal Studios, and Warner Bros. The MPA represents these firms in 150 nations that screen U.S. films and in 125 international markets for U.S. television programs. The MPA was formed in 1945 to reestablish American films in the world market in the aftermath of World War II "and to respond to the rising tide of protectionism resulting in barriers aimed at restricting the importation of American films." The association works hand-in-hand with the U.S. government to open markets for American exports. Its web page notes that it is often referred to as "a little State Department," with a wide range of activities in the diplomatic, political, and economic arenas.

Adoption of the EU directive in 1989 raised fears that European quotas would limit American export earnings. As Jack Valenti, chairman of the MPA, argued in a letter to Congress, "The Directive will stifle growth in existing TV markets, and impose severe limits on emerging markets, including private TV and satellite broadcasters. The real impact may not be felt so much in existing markets as in markets just beginning to develop. One thing is certain. The quota will hurt us. Count on it."[47] Congress took up the issue when the

House Energy and Commerce Subcommittee on Telecommunications and Finance held hearings on the EC directive in July 1989. On 23 October 1989, the House unanimously passed a resolution denouncing the directive and deploring the damage that could be inflicted on the U.S. broadcasting and film industries.[48]

A common complaint voiced by congresspeople in the debate on the resolution was that the local content rules are not, as Europeans claim, a matter of cultural sovereignty but instead an attempt to protect European industries from foreign competition, particularly from the United States. Representative Sam Gibbons, chair of the House Ways and Means Committee, said that cultural protectionism was not the issue. "The issue is censorship; the issue is restrictive trade practices." Gibbons said he was worried about the whole principle of freedom. "We're talking about free trade, the free flow of products. And certainly you can't have a free flow of products if you're going to have control of intellectual material that flows across borders into the public." As Representative Bill Frenzel (D-Minn.) phrased it, "We should never let culture become the last refuge of trade scoundrels."[49] The larger concern is that a unified Europe will close its borders to American imports generally. Carla Hills, the U.S. trade representative, stated in a letter to the European Parliament that "this directive sends a message to Americans that the EC 1992 initiative is indeed being used to construct a fortress Europe."[50] Hills threatened to sue under the intellectual property provisions of the 1988 U.S. Trade Act and to demand compensation in the GATT.

In addition, there is concern that the European action could encourage other nations to restrict imports on the grounds of culture, health, or safety as a means of solving trade problems outside the multilateral discipline of GATT. Congressman Sam Gejdenson (D-Conn.) noted in the debate that "like the broadcasting Directive, we have the potential for walls to be put up for American auto parts." The House resolution maintained that the European quotas violated Articles I and III of GATT and called on the president to "take all appropriate and feasible action," including possible action under section 301 of the Trade Act of 1974, "to protect and maintain United States access to the EC broadcasting market." A more specific threat of retaliation was made by Representative Bill Richardson (D-N.M.), who announced that "as a result of this blatantly anti-U.S. action I am preparing legislation which would bar public television stations from purchasing television programming from any foreign country which limits U.S.-made programming. Any support from taxpayer-supported institutions in furthering the European entertainment industry is unacceptable as long as the European Community broadcast initiative is in effect."[51]

The issue is still very much alive and is certain to become a contentious topic in future debates of the WTO. The EU was granted a "cultural exemption" at the last round of multilateral trade talks in Uruguay in 1994. This exempted the audiovisual industry from the usual trade rules and allowed nations to protect their markets and subsidize local production.[52]

In 1998, scores of French writers, filmmakers, and composers joined forces in Paris to defend their government cultural subsidies against the threat posed by the Multilateral Agreement on Investment (MAI), an international accord designed to end discrimination against foreign investors that France feared would undermine its cultural identity. Lionel Jospin, the French prime minister, said France would not sign unless it was allowed to continue giving home-grown films, television programs, books, and "creators" subsidies and privileges.[53]

Leaders of forty-nine French-speaking nations declared at a 1999 meeting of the Francophonie organization that they were "convinced that cultural goods were in no way reducible to their economic dimension" and claimed a right of "freely defining their cultural policies and resorting to appropriate tools of [government] intervention."[54]

In October 1999, the EU agreed to a common position for the WTO's "Millennium Round" of talks in Seattle in November/December. The talks were intended to set the agenda for negotiations aimed at further liberalizing trade in agricultural products, services, intellectual property, and investment by 2002. The EU, urged by France, agreed to a common position that member states be permitted to develop their own cultural and audiovisual policies and preserve their cultural diversity.[55] Shortly before the talks were due to begin, Jacques Attali, founding president of the European Bank for Reconstruction and Development and a former aide to French president François Mitterrand, warned that if Europe did not guard against "America's dominance in the new telecommunications technologies and their virtual power over global images, icons and information, it would wreak havoc with Europe's interests."[56] The big American enterprises, Attali said, "had no choice but to enlarge their markets to remain profitable. It is therefore vital for them to penetrate Europe—the world's top market—in reality and virtually." The stakes were decidedly more far-reaching than a mere trade negotiation, Attali warned apocalyptically. "Unlike trade in manufacturing, the unlimited liberalization of services can mean the end of nations and democracy: indeed, it can mean the loss of European control over its own destiny."

In any event, the Seattle talks never got around to cultural issues. Clashes between police and demonstrators protesting the effects of globalization, between the EU and the United States over agricultural policies, and between rich and poor nations over labor practices, torpedoed the meeting, which was abandoned. There is no doubt, however, that culture will be high on the agenda when the talks resume. By then, there may be a new field of contention. There are indications that the Motion Picture Association is backing off attempts to reopen debate over restrictions on analogue television. "We have indicated that we do not want to go over the arguments of seven years ago," said Chris Marisch, managing director of the MPA.[57] However, Europeans are concerned that new technologies could be used by the United States to circumvent EU television quotas and deluge Europe with American films and programming over the Internet.

Meanwhile, Europeans are pressing ahead with measures to promote endogenous production. The European Investment Bank and the European Commission announced in May 2001 that they jointly would provide 1 billion euros worth of programs aimed at enhancing the competitiveness of the European film and audiovisual industry, promoting creation of European cinematographic and television works, and assisting the industry to adapt to technologies and digitalization of production. Introducing the measures, Viviane Reding, European commissioner responsible for cultural and audiovisual issues, stated that "I cannot accept that American films account for 75% of box-office takings in Europe while the EU produces more films than the United States. I will not sit back and watch our young artistic talents and audiovisual entrepreneurs disappear across the Atlantic."[58]

Article 25 of the directive stipulates that the regulations must be reexamined before 30 June 2000. In preparation for the review, the EU Commission has started several studies on different areas covered in the directive: the impact of its provisions on the production of European TV programs and independent production, recent market and technological developments in the sector, and the development of new advertising techniques. The commission will submit the review to the council and European Parliament toward the end of 2002.[59]

Notes

1. "At Daggers Drawn," *The Economist*, 8 May 1998, pp. 17–20.

2. Directive 89/552/European Economic Community, reprinted in *Official Journal of the European Communities*, L 298/23, 17 October 1989.

3. Directive 97/36/European Community, reprinted in *Official Journal of the European Communities*, L 202, 30 August 1997.

4. Council of Europe, "European Convention on Transfrontier Television," Strasbourg, No. 132, 5 May 1989.

5. Henry Olsson, "Council of Europe and Mass Media Law," *Media Law and Practice* (July 1986): 64.

6. Christoph Engel, "Aussenhandel mit Rundfunk: Rundfunkrichtlinie der Europäischen Gemeinschaft versus Fernsehkonvention des Europarats," *Rundfunk und Fernsehen* 37, no. 2–3 (1989): 203–214; and Mario Hirsch, "Convention over Directive," *Cable & Satellite Europe* 2 (1989): 18–20.

7. Council of Europe, "New Rules for Transfrontier Television in Europe," at culture.coe.fr/infocentre/press/eng/98/epress98.09.09.htm; accessed 17 July 2001.

8. Jurgen Wilke, "Regionalisierung und Internationalisierung des Mediensystems," *Auspolitik und Zeitgesichte* (June 1990).

9. "A World View," *The Economist,* 29 November 1997 (U.S. ed.).

10. Nelson Traquina, "Western European Broadcasting, Deregulation, and Public Television: The Portuguese Experience," *Journalism and Mass Communication Monographs* (September 1998): 9.

11. "Audiovisual Spending Expected to Soar," *Financial Times* (London). 17 June 1997, p. 4.

12. Martina Kessler and Klaus Schrape, "Fernsehmarkt Westeuropa," *Media Perspektiven* 1 (1990): 26.

13. Commission of the European Communities, *Third Report from the Commission to the Council, the European Parliament and the Economic and Social Committee on the Application of Directive 89/552/EEC "Television without Frontiers"* (Brussels: 15 January 2001).

14. The European Institute for the Media, "Europe 2000: What Kind of Television?" (Amsterdam: 1988), 68.

15. Michael Flint and Louise Hart, "1992: How Does it Plead?" *Cable & Satellite Europe* 2 (1989): 14–20.

16. Alastair Tempest, "Tempest over Strasbourg," *Cable & Satellite Europe* 3 (1988): 43.

17. "Smith Takes on Murdoch's Sky TV," *The Independent* (London), 8 June 1998, p. 4.

18. "Audiovisual Spending Expected to Soar," *Financial Times* (London), p. 4.

19. Commission of the European Communities, Third Report from the Commission.

20. Communication from the Commission to the European Parliament and Council of Ministers, "Audiovisual Policy: Next Steps" (Brussels: July 1998).

21. European Audiovisual Laboratory, "Focus 2000: World Film Market Trends," at www.obs.coe.int/online_publication/reports/focus2000.pdf.ed; accessed 29 July 2002.

22. Commission of the European Communities, *Television without Frontiers: Green Paper on the Establishment of the Common Market for Broadcasting, Especially by Satellite and Cable* (Luxembourg: ECC, 1984), 28.

23. Philip Schlesinger, "Europe's Contradictory Communicative Space," *Daedalus* 123, no. 2 (1994): 31.

24. "Europe Needs Special TV and Film Policies," *Financial Times* (London), 17 February 1995, p. 16.

25. Willard D. Rowland and Michael Tracey, "Worldwide Challenges to Public Service Broadcasting," *Journal of Communication* 40, no. 2 (Spring 1990): 8–27.

26. "A Plea to Europe, Save Us from Ourselves and Curb Murdoch at Last," *The Guardian* (London), 6 April 1998, p. 16.

27. Directive 97/36/European Community of the European Parliament and of the Council of 30 June 1997, amending Council Directive 89/552/EEC, Article 3.

28. "France Issues Call to Arms in European Culture Wars," *The Independent* (London), 2 February 1995, p. 11.

29. "New Curbs Proposed on Foreign TV Programs in Europe," *New York Times,* 23 March 1995, sect. D, p. 8.

30. "Battle Lines Drawn over EU's Controversial TV Policy," *Business Times* (Singapore), 4 April 1995, p. 17.

31. "Vision Fades for Fortress Europe," *Financial Times* (London), 18 February 1995, p. 7.

32. "France Fights off Hollywood in Europe," *The Herald* (Glasgow), 14 February 1995, p. 8.

33. Nol Reijnders, deputy head of media policy, Netherlands Ministry of Education, Culture and Science, interview, The Hague, 28 May 1999.

34. Heiko von Debschitz, ZDF director for international affairs, interview, Mainz, 8 June 1999.

35. "Parliament Fails to Tighten Broadcasting Quotas from U.S. Television Companies," *Television*, 25 November 1996.

36. Emmanuelle Machet, "A Decade of European Broadcast Regulation: The Directive 'Television without Frontiers'" (Dusseldorf: European Institute for the Media, 1999), 39.

37. Helga M. Zeinstra, legal adviser, Netherlands Ministry of Education, Culture, and Science, interview, Zoetemeer, 28 May 1999.

38. Peter Marti, section head, Abteilung Radio und Fernsehen, Bundesampt fuer Kommunikation, interview, Biel, Switzerland, 2 June 1999.

39. COM(2000) 442 final.

40. Pascal Albrechtskirchinger, head of ZDF-German Television bureau in Brussels, interview, Brussels, 28 May 1999.

41. "Vision Fades for Fortress Europe," *Financial Times* (London), 18 February 1995.

42. Bonnie J. K. Richardson, vice president, trade and federal affairs, MPA, "Intellectual Property Rights: The Film Industry Perspective," remarks before the House Committee on International Relations, Subcommittee on International Economic Policy and Trade, 21 May 1998, at www.mpaa.org/legislation/press/98/98_5_21a.htm; accessed 29 July 2002.

43. "Buddy, Can You Spare a Reel?" *The Economist*, 19 August 1989, pp. 56–57.

44. International Intellectual Property Alliance, "Copyright Industries in the U.S. Economy" (Washington, D.C.: 2000), at www.iipa.com/copyright_us_economy_html; accessed 17 July 2001.

45. International Intellectual Property Alliance, comments of the IIPA on a draft strategy paper, "A Framework for Global Electronic Commerce," 28 January 1997, at www.mpaa.org/legislation/press/97/97_1_28.htm; accessed 29 July 2002.

46. Motion Picture Association, "About MPAA," www.mpaa.org; accessed 29 July 2002.

47. Valenti's letter is reprinted in *Congressional Record*, H 7331.

48. *Congressional Record*, H 7326.

49. *Congressional Record*, H 7326.

50. W. Dawkins, "U.S. Threatens Europe in TV Broadcasts Dispute," *The Times* (London), 5 May 1989.

51. *Congressional Record*, H 7326.

52. European Information Service Report, "EU/WTO Still Split over Seattle Agenda," 16 October 1999.

53. "French Film-makers Say Accord Will Ruin European Cinema," *Daily Telegraph* (London), 17 February 1998.

54. "Francophone Nations Push for United Cultural Exemption Front against U.S.," Agence France Presse, 4 September 1999.

55. "EU Members Plan on Unity at WTO Talks," *Journal of Commerce*, 25 October 1999.

56. FT Asia Intelligence Wire, 21 November 1999, "US Trade Thrust Throws Europe into Identity Crisis."

57. *Screen Finance,* "GATT Talks Overshadowed by Internet Threat," 5 August 1999.

58. Joint press release, European Commission/European Investment Bank, Brussels, 18 May 2001.

59. EU Commission: "Television without Frontiers: Effective Regulation for the European Audiovisual Sector" (DN: IP/)1/52; 2001-01-16.

5

Fear and Fascination

American Popular Culture in a Divided Germany, 1945–1968

Uta G. Poiger

IN THE AFTERMATH OF NATIONAL SOCIALISM and in the face of the Cold War, German debates over American culture were contests over moral, cultural, and political authority on both sides of the iron curtain. American imports such as Hollywood movies, jazz, rock 'n' roll, or jeans were increasingly popular with East and West German adolescents, and as a result, they constituted some of the most controversial aspects of consumer culture in the two states. In spite of many differences, authorities in both states made their citizens' cultural consumption central to their political reconstruction efforts. For most East German party and state leaders of the 1950s and 1960s, this meant more or less consistent hostility toward American imports. Many West German politicians, Church leaders, and educators likewise attacked what they saw as cultural Americanization. By the late 1950s, however, the picture had changed: West German youth now danced to American music in government-sponsored clubs, while an emerging Cold War liberal consensus made consumption, including the consumption of American popular culture, increasingly part of a new, liberal West German identity.[1]

After 1945, with the Allied occupation and the opening of its market, West Germany experienced an unprecedented influx of American products, from nylon stockings to popular music. The impact of these imports was by no means restricted to West Germany; especially via Berlin, it reached well beyond the iron curtain. East German authorities severely restricted U.S. imports into their own territory and tried to prevent their population from consuming American movies, music, and fashions, but they could not control access. Until the construction of the wall in 1961, a constant stream of people flowed back and forth between East and West Berlin. Large numbers of East Berliners and East Germans came to shop and enjoy themselves in West Berlin. Sometimes whole East Berlin school classes would cross into the Western sectors to watch movies. Many East Berlin boys and girls frequented West Berlin music halls, and young people from all over the German Democratic Republic (GDR) would go to West Berlin to buy jeans, leather jackets, or records, in spite of prohibitive exchange rates. At home, some of them would tune into Western radio stations, including the American Forces Network (AFN) and Radio Luxembourg, to listen to the latest American hits. In the 1950s, the GDR press routinely reviewed U.S. films as soon as they opened in West Berlin and also regularly commented on American music and musicians. Even after the wall, Western radio, television, and visitors continued to bring American popular culture into East Germany. Thus, whenever American music and fashions hit West Germany and West Berlin, their impact was felt in both Germanys.

While the exposure to American products, especially for West Germans, increased after 1945, both fascination and fear concerning American cultural influences had a longer tradition in Germany. During the 1920s, Hollywood movies, jazz music, dances like the Charleston, and the American "girl" in short, loose dress and bob haircut all made a splash. Some commentators, among them modern artists and left-leaning educators, embraced such imports, because they seemed improvisational, spontaneous, and wild. The majority of commentators, however, worried about lascivious women, weak or aggressive men, and a general cultural decline that the consumption of American movies or music allegedly caused. Criticisms of America found adherents among all political groups, although conservatives and fascists were most vocal. Racist attacks on American culture were evident before 1933 but grew stronger once the National Socialists came to power. For example, the Nazis denounced jazz as degenerate, and in the 1940s, they prosecuted so-called swing youths, groups of young women and men who listened to jazz and wore distinctive clothes. Yet even the National Socialists, caught between their racist utopia and the need to accommodate the German population, continued to show some Hollywood movies and to play jazz on the airwaves.

West German Hostilities

Until the second half of the 1950s, hostility also dominated commentaries on American popular culture in East and West Germany. Similarities between reactions in the two Germanys were sometimes astounding: in vehement rejections of American imports, both sides conflated uncontrolled female sexuality, African American culture, and German lower-class culture, linking all three to the threat of fascism. West Germans, especially conservatives, among them intellectuals as well as Church leaders and politicians who were promoting a "Christian West," found themselves fighting on several fronts: against their fascist past, against the present Cold War enemy, and against the specter of an American-style consumer culture. For example, in the early 1950s, West German educators and state officials attacked American music like the boogie-woogie as part of their youth protection efforts. The supposed "primitivism" of faster-paced dances, like the boogie, constituted a threat to the proper gender roles so necessary to postwar West German identity. In West German discussions of dancing, concerns about premarital sex, especially by women, intersected with misgivings about working-class culture *and* with a hostility toward black culture. Contemporaries cast working-class girls who hung out in the streets and who danced to boogie-woogie as potential sexual delinquents. A connected attack was to point to the emasculating and feminizing effect of "sultry negro songs" for boys.

Such West German fears were exacerbated by the arrival of rock 'n' roll and by youth riots in the mid-1950s, when West Germans connected what they saw as adolescent misbehavior to American influences. In 1956, for example, the West German youth magazine *Bravo* reported about male rioters who had roamed the streets in Britain after showings of the Bill Haley movie *Rock around the Clock*. *Bravo* claimed that Haley's music was rooted in the "ritual music of Africa's negroes." Furthermore, the magazine maintained that the influence of rock 'n' roll had turned "cool Englishmen" into "white Negroes" who rioted. *Bravo* thus labeled rioting a typically black behavior and warned against rock 'n' roll in racist terms; it also urged its German audience not to behave like the English. When it became clear that rock 'n' roll had many admirers in Germany and that German adolescents too took to the streets after showings of *Rock around the Clock*, another West German commentator worried about what he called "wild barbarians in ecstasy."[2]

West and East German reactions to the marketing of Elvis Presley in Germany revealed similar hostilities, which centered on Presley's failure to be properly masculine. In fact, music industry and press commentary worked together to effectively feminize him. In 1956, Presley's U.S. label RCA/Victor decided to market Presley in Germany with the slogan "He walks like Marilyn Monroe but at home he is a model son."[3] Employing a double strategy, the company sought to make Presley outrageous by associating him with the hip-swinging Monroe in public performances, while portraying him as tame and even dutiful in his private life. West and East German papers picked up on press releases from RCA and Presley's West German record company Teldec.[4] However, the German commentators played with RCA's slogan to further underline Presley's outrageous gender ambiguity, and, not surprisingly, they dropped the line on the "private" model son altogether. An East German commentator quipped that Presley was trying to "compensate for his vocal shortcomings by wildly swinging his hips like Marilyn Monroe."[5] The close association with Monroe, who along with French actresses like Marina Vlady and Brigitte Bardot had become a symbol of female sensuality in Germany, marked Presley as unmanly.

As the popularity of stars like Haley and Presley reached its peak in the late 1950s, some West German conservatives demanded state interventions. In 1957, the state-sponsored West German movie rating board ordered that scenes which allegedly showed the "aggressive flirting" of girls be cut from another rock 'n' roll movie, because the film would otherwise foster the "materialist understanding of life" among adolescents.[6] Rock 'n' roll was so disturbing precisely because it seemed to undermine the ideal nuclear families of restrained male breadwinner protectors and asexual female caretakers. The various reactions to rock 'n' roll showed that many West Germans felt that American cultural influences led to transgressions of gender and indeed also of racial norms with potentially dire political consequences. Some conservatives tried to root out such problems by calling for increased regulation or even prohibition of rock 'n' roll concerts. In a 1958 article directed at youth officials in state bureaucracies and private organizations, one Christian Democrat member of parliament, Elisabeth Pitz-Savelsberg, denounced "rock 'n' roll orgies with Bill Haley or Elvis Presley" as belonging to the category of public events which posed dangers to the youth and which the youth protection law therefore regulated. According to Pitz-Savelsberg, authorities were not fulfilling their task to watch out for the common good when they allowed such rock 'n' roll events.[7] But in spite of such attempts, rock 'n' roll was never prohibited in West Germany.

East German Hostilities

In East Germany, by contrast, the repression of American influences was far more systematic. Beginning in the late 1940s, East Germans described allegedly "decadent" and "degenerate" imports, like boogie-woogie, jazz, westerns, and jeans as part of an "American cultural barbarism," which they saw at the root of American and West German imperialism. After the June 1953 uprising in East Germany, for example, the GDR press and politicians accused Americanized male adolescents in Texas pants and cowboy shirts of being responsible for instigating the revolt.[8]

Hostilities became also visible when rock 'n' roll music and dancing arrived in Germany in 1956 via American movies and numerous press reports about rock 'n' roll concerts. In December 1956, a cartoon in the East Berlin daily *Berliner Zeitung* showed a small, emaciated Elvis Presley performing under larger-than-life female legs in front of a crowd of girls much bigger than he was. The cartoon implied that female Presley fans were sexual aggressors who emasculated men: the girls were throwing off bras and garter belts and licking their lips in obvious sexual excitement. Their hairstyles marked some of these young women as possibly black (short curly dark hair) and others as white (blonde ponytails), but in portraying all of them with stereotypical "negroid" features (wide noses, thick lips), the cartoon labeled their behavior as typically black. The accompanying article claimed that young women were the main consumers of rock 'n' roll (described as American nonculture) and asserted that rock 'n' roll appealed to primitive humans. In such a depiction, allusions to gender upheaval and to alleged racial transgressions reinforced one another to portray rock as dangerous.[9]

In August 1957, one East German Culture Ministry official gave explicit orders to prevent the spread of rock 'n' roll since the music and dancing represented a "degeneration" inherent in the American way of life.[10] Some youth clubs and bars put up signs: "No jeans allowed" or "Dancing apart prohibited."[11] In the midst of efforts to accelerate East Germany's development toward socialism and in the face of mounting tensions in the Cold War in the late 1950s, East German defense minister Willi Stoph issued warnings echoed in many papers that "rock 'n' roll was a means of seduction to make the youth ripe for atomic war."[12]

As an alternative to U.S. imports, officials promoted their own fashion dance, the Lipsi, after 1958. The dance was a compromise. Its name with the ending *i* had a modern, American ring, and couples danced it to a faster rhythm, but they avoided any of the dangerous "openness" of dancing apart. In spite of enormous propaganda efforts, conducted by the Ministry of Culture, the Freie Deutsche Jugend (FDJ, or Free German Youth), the Association of German Composers and Musicologists (VdK), and the GDR radio stations, the dance had only limited appeal.[13]

East German adolescents encountered state sanctions for publicly expressing their preference for West European and American popular culture. In 1959, groups of adolescents in several East German cities gave their admiration of rock 'n' roll and Elvis Presley an explicitly political twist. In two Leipzig suburbs, for example, groups gathered in the streets shouting, "We want no Lipsi and we want no Ado [*sic*] Koll, instead we want Elvis Presley and his rock 'n' roll." (Alo Koll was a Leipzig bandleader heavily promoted by authorities.) Then they apparently marched downtown expressing their disdain for the East German leadership. One of them shouted "Long live Walter Ulbricht and the Eastern Zone [East Germany];" the chorus answered "*Pfui, pfui, pfui.*" This was followed by "Long live Elvis Presley"; this time the crowd responded with an enthusiastic "Yes, yes, yes." The Leipzig demonstration was no isolated incident. A similar demonstration took place in Dresden, and by the end of the year, internal reports spoke of Presley groups in at least thirteen GDR towns. Police and courts took strict measures against the demonstrators. Many were arrested, and several of them were convicted and sent to prison.[14]

The fact that many of the products of American culture were rooted in the culture of African Americans, whom communists recognized as an oppressed group, did not dissuade East German authorities from attacks on American music and dances and especially jazz, boogie, and rock 'n' roll. Race played a complicated role in these attacks. It would seem that the racism apparent in East German charges of "decadence" and "primitivism" against American popular culture were clearly at odds with East Germany's public stance against racism in the United States. After all, East German papers in the mid-1950s reported extensively on efforts to integrate schools and public accommodations in the American South. However, East German visions of racial equality relied on ideals of male restraint and female respectability, including female sexual passivity, across races. This insistence on specific norms of male and female respectability found one of its most powerful articulations in official rejections of jazz as a music associated with gangsters and prostitutes. With such condemnations of jazz, which they saw as a black music, East German officials reasserted racial hierarchies in the realm of culture. Attacks on rock 'n' roll reinforced this. Even though highlighting American racism was one way to fight the Cold War against the United States and West Germany, East German authorities could not relinquish their own association between female sexual passivity, "civilization," and "whiteness."

But throughout the 1950s, there were also voices in East Germany arguing that jazz was a protest music for African Americans (whom East German authorities recognized as an oppressed group); as such, jazz could be part of developing a new, "clean" German dance music. In brief periods of greater leniency, they had some success: after the June 1953 uprising and again after Khrushchev's 1956 speech against Stalinism, jazz fans were able to found jazz clubs all over the GDR, usually connected to the state youth organization FDJ.

Well aware of such arguments, East German authorities often walked a tightrope. When students at the Humboldt University tried to found a jazz club after the building of the Berlin wall in 1961, East German officials were clearly alarmed but tried to avoid any public debates over jazz and American music. They suggested that jazz fans pursue their interests in authentic folk music in existing, carefully supervised dance and music groups and urged local FDJ functionaries to be aware "of the political background of a strengthened jazz movement." Officials of the FDJ Central Committee claimed that such jazz associations were funded by West German agents. Present-day jazz, these officials said, was shaped by commercialism and imperialist ideas and was thus part of the "decadent trends of bourgeois ideology."[15] At the same time, the East German press and youth officials focused heavily on transforming the boys and girls who had frequented bars and dance halls in West Berlin and who had consumed, among other things, rock 'n' roll. Within a week of the wall, the East German press reported that state-run youth clubs had turned boys in blue jeans into respectable young men wearing suits and dancing with girls in fashionable dresses. The official attention to the more conservative fashions of suits and dresses which the allegedly transformed youths wore shows how important proper gender roles were to the socialist conversions.[16] Also, in the weeks after the building of the wall, East German newspapers rejoiced that the much-maligned West Berlin border movie theaters, which had catered to East Berlin adolescents since they had opened in the early 1950s, would finally have to close.[17] As throughout the 1950s, East German authorities viewed adolescent consumption of American-influenced popular culture as a potential political threat.

Authorities continued to waver in the 1960s and sometimes opened spaces where adolescents could consume American influences. In 1963, they released an American western, *The Magnificent Seven*. In 1964, even Sozialistische Einheitspartei Deutschlands (SED, or Socialist Unity Party of Germany) leader Walter Ulbricht promoted the twist, and throughout the 1960s authorities tried to channel adolescent energies into folk music, including some American compositions. However, the atmosphere remained mostly hostile: authorities railed against beat, arrested long-haired male beat fans, reported about cultural barbarism at West German rock concerts, and even blamed the Prague Spring of 1968 on such phenomena.[18]

In spite of many differences, West and East German authorities shared strong hostilities toward American popular culture. Both sides drew on a prewar tradition of cultural anti-Americanism which had links to eugenics, but the Cold War battle added a new dimension. East German authorities time and again used images of Americanization in their propaganda, both against their own population and against the Cold War enemy to the West. In 1953, the East German press reported, for example, that West Germans were enslaved by American movies.[19] Here and in many other instances, East German officials tried to exploit American cultural influences to attack West Germany's transformation into a capitalist liberal democracy and Bonn's growing military and political association with the United States. Sometimes they indeed managed to put West German conservatives, who wondered whether adolescents were better protected in the East, on the defensive.

Cold War Liberalism

As the West German political and intellectual climate changed, this curious consensus of cultural anti-Americanism in East and West largely disintegrated. After the mid-1950s, West German authorities began to transform such ideas about consumption and rebellious youths. By the end of the decade, West German Cold War liberals increasingly replaced the religiously inspired conservatives who had seen consumption as a terrible and indeed political threat. Ludwig Erhard's ascendancy to the chancellorship and the rejection by the Sozialdemokratische Partei Deutschlands (SPD, or Social Democratic Party of Germany) of Marxism were all part of this move toward Cold War liberalism. These developments culminated in the Great Coalition from 1966 to 1969.

The conservative vision of promoting a "Christian West" in rejection of American consumerism dominated West German cultural politics in the first half of the 1950s, but it was increasingly pushed back by a different, Cold War liberal understanding of culture and consumption. Conservative hostilities toward American culture persisted, yet they lost some of their power. Cold War liberals were a loose conglomeration of intellectuals and politicians who began to transform the cultural conservatism of the first half of the 1950s; among them were Erhard and social scientists like Helmut Schelsky and Curt Bondy. Cold War liberals widened the definitions of acceptable adolescent behavior; both male aggression and female sexual expressiveness became less threatening. For Cold War liberals, adolescent rebelliousness and the consumption of American popular culture were nonpolitical, psychological phenomena.

West German Cold War liberals took up American David Riesman's conclusion in *The Lonely Crowd* (1950) that increased automation and increased leisure time leveled class distinctions, and, though critical, they confirmed the basic stability of a consumption-oriented society which had emerged in West Germany by the mid-1950s. Schelsky and Erhard, for example, made consumption compatible with a new (West) German identity which they located beyond fascism and totalitarianism—indeed, beyond all ideologies. In the late 1950s, West European and American intellectuals, among them Daniel Bell, were of course likewise propagating "the end of ideology" in the West. For West German Cold War liberals, a lot was at stake: They sought to disconnect themselves from Weimar and Naziism by erasing differences between West Germany and other Western societies and by fully integrating themselves into the fight against communism. They abandoned the fight for a third German way between consumerism in the West and communism in the East.[20]

Social scientists tried to render the German youth culture of the 1950s into a "private" matter. They stressed that adolescent rebelliousness, including listening to jazz or rock 'n' roll, was neither a political challenge nor a precursor of political challenges to come. For example, psychologist Bondy and his team concluded that participants in rock 'n' roll riots were not politically motivated, not even when they were shouting "rock 'n' roll—Russians out," thus attacking the Cold War enemy. The West German press and West German state officials increasingly accepted these assessments, which seems particularly ironic given the outrage that the student rebellion stirred up after 1966.

As part of reframing the youth rebellion as nonpolitical and psychological, West German sociologists and officials still tried to alter the practices in which adolescents engaged. These efforts reveal the gendered meanings of depoliticization. Researchers described male aggression as a normal adolescent life stage. Consumer culture could play a useful psychological role here: normal male aggressions could be "released," for example, through the consumption of rock 'n' roll or westerns. According to researchers and the press, male rebelliousness disappeared altogether once boys became involved in stable, heterosexual relationships. With images of German male and female "teenagers," who danced rock 'n' roll together but were harmless, the West German entertainment industry also fostered this vision. Rock 'n' roll and riots were cultural styles whose threats could be resolved "privately."[21]

The systematic marketing of Peter Kraus and Conny Froboess as teenager stars also fostered such opinions. Initially, Kraus (who happened to be an Austrian citizen) was sold as the "German Elvis." Racial ambiguity was not part of his image, and nobody referred to his thick lips (which he did have). Although Kraus, too, encountered "hysterical teenagers," he was mostly portrayed as a nice German boy, much "more likable in voice and behavior" than the American original.[22] When he was joined by a female mate, "Conny," his domestication was almost complete. "Conny and Peter" made movies together and were celebrated as West German rock 'n' roll stars. On the one hand, the duo was part of a heterosocial teenage world where young men and women together challenged older standards of respectable dancing or clothing; on the other hand, they tried to steer away from open challenges to sexual mores.[23]

In West Germany, government officials adopted the psychological paradigms of U.S. and West German social scientists to take the edge off adolescent rebelliousness. In 1962, the West Berlin minister for youth affairs, Ella Kay, assessed the 1956 youth riots which East and West Germans had blamed on American popular culture. "It is not easy for adults," said Kay, "to accept that youngsters lean towards rebellion, and that is a step towards adulthood." Kay thus agreed with wider definitions of acceptable behavior, especially for young men. Such assessments rendered "normal" adolescent needs for adventure as well as more outrageous behavior, like rioting, as mere sociological and psychological, rather than political, phenomena. Kay went on to claim that the Berlin government had learned from the "incidents" and had started bikers' groups and craft shops. She now concluded that the rioters, who caused so many worries in the mid-1950s, had all been decent boys.[24]

Nevertheless, Cold War liberals had an ambivalent relationship with consumer culture. Cultural goods associated with high modernism, and "high" culture, could help in redirecting adolescent behavior. Conservatives hardly championed expressionism or jazz, but by the late 1950s, Cold War liberals made modern art, modern architecture, and even jazz central to state efforts to portray West Germany as at once respectable, modern, and different from East Germany. As jazz became more respectable, West German jazz promoters, the press, and West German politicians portrayed both jazz musicians and fans as restrained and respectable; they also "whitened" the music by stressing that jazz had transcended its African American origins and by ignoring the Jewish background of many musicians.[25] In 1958, a state-funded film, *Why Are They against Us?* which was made specifically for schools and youth groups, made use of the new respectability of modern art and jazz in addressing problems of male rebelliousness. The working-class male hero rejected a "bad" girl, who danced to rock 'n' roll at the local soda fountain and who "came on" to boys, for a "good," restrained, middle-class girl who went to modern art exhibits and attended jazz concerts. Like Erhard in his many public statements, the movie was critical of the middle-class father's prejudices against the working-class boy, but as part of legitimizing this critique, the moviemakers portrayed "working-class" cultural practices, "public" women, and the consumption of popular culture in negative terms. The working-class boy, the movie suggested, could raise his status by adopting a bourgeois style of cultural consumption. Thus, in this movie, liberalism with respect to class (promoted also by people like Schelsky and Erhard) rested explicitly on gender and cultural conservatism.[26]

This became also evident when West Berlin officials, after 1959, opened so-called jazz dance cafés in order to channel adolescent desires and successfully encouraged visitors to come in suits and skirts, rather than in jeans. As one social worker concluded, these clubs educated young people not with "the sledge-hammer, but with the jazz trumpet." Most visitors of the jazz cafés came because of the "hot rhythms," the social worker reported; in the clubs, they were able to "move freely" and were valuing this freedom highly, as they allegedly learned to obey "unwritten laws." Such dance cafés thus were part of West German efforts to defuse the 1950s youth rebellion, but they also provided adolescents with the opportunity to listen to "hot," if not too hot, American music in a safe environment. In West Germany, definitions of acceptable adolescent behavior had clearly widened.[27]

A 1960 West Berlin government report on the "situation" of youth located such efforts firmly in the liberal ideas of scholars like West German Helmut Schelsky and American David Riesman who had confirmed the basic stability of consumption-oriented societies. The report spoke of a "skeptical generation" growing up in an "other-directed" consumer society. Adolescents had been freed from the social constraints of the bourgeois production-oriented society. This transformation, however, left adolescents without firm rules of conduct. In strong contrast to the West German politicians and educators of the early 1950s who had firmly believed that nuclear families of female homeworkers and male breadwinners would prevent juvenile misbehavior, the report maintained that the family alone was unable to solve these problems. In this context, the report claimed, state youth agencies had to fulfill their prime task in the realm of leisure and consumption: to teach adolescents "how to evaluate critically the offerings of the consumer and entertainment industries and how to use them in a meaningful manner." Both the dance clubs and film clubs that the West Berlin government supported were attempts to fulfill these goals. In this vision, state youth officials, as agents of the expanding welfare state, were to educate adolescents into sensible consumers.[28]

With East German authorities on the defensive, West Germans increasingly used the affluence and style of Americanized West German youth as a way to define the boundary between East and West. As West German authorities "depoliticized" consumption, it increasingly became a Cold War weapon. For example, West German officials made efforts to draw East Germans into the movie theaters on the Kurfürstendamm in the center of West Berlin. Here East Germans were also exposed to West Berlin shop windows. And the jazz dance cafés fulfilled a dual function: they drew young people off the streets, and they displayed the openness of West German society—in pointed contrast to the ongoing repression of American cultural influences in East Germany. It would still be a few more years until West Berlin officially integrated rock 'n' roll into state-run youth programs, but in 1962 a review of an East German dictionary mocked the entry which described rock 'n' roll as a political threat.[29] For the West German authorities of the 1960s, leisure and pleasure were not what would destroy the West; in fact, enjoyed in good measure, they would actually be a key weapon against the East, exposing its economic inferiority and lack of democratic choice. East German officials repeatedly attacked the "depoliticization" of youth in West German sociological and political discourse, and in 1968 they even blamed the "depoliticization" for the

Prague Spring. But overall, West Germans successfully countered East German attacks which had mobilized the ambivalence and even hostility toward America which existed on both sides of the wall. In this climate, consumption in fact remained politicized, if on a different terrain.

This transformation laid one foundation for the anti-American and antiauthoritarian radical movements of the late 1960s. As in the United States, the 1950s youth cultures raised expectations for individual expression and sexual openness among many young men and women, and some of them expressed these expectations in explicitly political terms in the 1960s. Certainly, the rebellions of the late 1960s can be understood as a reaction against both their parents' conservatism and the Cold War liberal consensus which had emerged in the late 1950s and early 1960s in West Germany. Sixties' radicals rejected a society focused on consumption, claimed that the personal was political, and were often unaware how much their own expectations had been shaped by American-influenced consumer culture.[30]

Conclusion

The combination of fear and fascination which had long characterized German reactions to American culture entered a new configuration with the Cold War. In the conflicts over American imports, East and West Germany each tried to lay claim to a German identity. East German authorities remained mostly hostile toward American popular culture. By contrast, West Germans began to draw on American styles and American ideas, while trying to tame "excesses" of cultural Americanization.

Recognizing the complicated ways in which the cultural consumption of American imports occurred and affected the public sphere, we may examine the centrality of (re)constructions of personal identities to state politics. And it is here that we most clearly see differences between the two states. East German elites made many efforts to reject and punish adolescents who openly consumed American imports. Since there was no relative autonomy of state and economy, or of state and party, they had the power to curtail American music imports and to use party and cultural organizations affiliated with party and state to control what adolescents consumed. Yet the authorities were never completely successful—neither before nor after the wall. Even within the state-/party-run institutions, there were constantly adolescents and sometimes educators who sought to widen what was acceptable. In particular, much confusion existed over what constituted "authentic" and appropriate working-class culture, and at times this confusion provided openings for jazz, beat, or even American-influenced fashions. By the early 1970s, East German authorities would even allow home grown rock music in attempts to tie the youth to the state.[31] The East German regime was often chaotic and control never complete.

In West Germany, most of the time, what was considered "normal" could be renegotiated more easily than in East Germany. For example, there was a greater variety of expert opinions, which could be exchanged in public and which could change policy decisions. Such variety and change were institutionally anchored. The economy was relatively independent from state institutions. It created and appealed to consumer tastes, and adolescent rebelliousness, within limits, became something companies sold. It was important for Cold War liberal social scientists and politicians to assure themselves that adolescent rebels did not pose political challenges. But there was no order, as in East Germany, from a state culture ministry official to prevent the spread of rock 'n' roll. In the end, East German state socialism was considerably more repressive than the West German liberal democracy. With East German authorities on the defensive, West Germans increasingly used American influences to battle their East German opponents. This dynamic, which developed in the second half of the 1950s and which reveals the multivalent meanings of American cultural imports, would continue until the end of the Cold War.

Notes

1. On American popular culture in postwar Germany, see Heide Fehrenbach, *Cinema in Democratizing Germany: Reconstructing National Identity after Hitler* (Chapel Hill: University of North Carolina Press, 1995); Heide Fehrenbach and Uta G. Poiger, eds., *Transactions, Transgressions, Transformations: American Culture in Western Europe and Japan* (New York: Berghahn, 2000); Konrad Jarausch and Hannes Siegrist, eds., *Amerikanisierung und Sowjetisierung in Deutschland* (Frankfurt am Main: Campus, 1997); Alf Lüdtke, Inge Marßolek, and Adelheid von Saldern, eds., *Amerikanisierung: Traum und Alptraum im Deutschland des 20. Jahrhunderts* (Stuttgart: Steiner, 1996); Kaspar Maase, *Bravo Amerika: Erkundungen zur Jugendkultur der Bundesrepublik in den fünfziger Jahren* (Hamburg: Junius, 1992); Uta G. Poiger, *Jazz, Rock, and Rebels: Cold War Politics and American Culture in a Divided Germany* (Berkeley: University of California Press, 2000); Reiner Pommerin, *The American Impact on Postwar Germany* (Providence, R.I.: Berghahn, 1995); Michael Rauhut, *Beat in der Grauzone: DDR-Rock 1964 bis 1972—Politik und Alltag* (Berlin: Basisdruck, 1993); Timothy Ryback, *Rock around the Bloc: A History of Rock Music in Eastern Europe and the Soviet Union* (New York: Oxford University Press, 1990); and Alfred Sywottek, "The Americanization of Everyday Life? Early Trends in Consumer and Leisure-Time Behavior," in *America and the Shaping of German Society 1945–1955*, ed. Michael Ermarth (Providence, R.I.: Berg, 1993), 132–52.

2. "Die ganze Welt rockt und rollt," *Bravo,* 30 September 1956; and "Außer Rand und Band," *Beratungsdienst Jugend und Film* 1 (November 1956): BVII. See also Heinz-Hermann Krüger, ed., *"Die Elvistolle, die hatte ich mir unauffällig wachsen lassen": Lebensgeschichte und jugendliche Alltagskultur in den fünfziger Jahren* (Opladen: Leske & Budrich, 1985).

3. "Deutsche Pitch for Elvis," *Variety,* 24 October 1956; "Elvis, the Pelvis," *Der Spiegel,* 12 December 1956; and "Gold aus heißer Kehle," *Beratungsdienst Jugend und Film* (February 1958).

4. Rüdiger Bloemeke, *Roll over Beethoven: Wie der Rock 'n' Roll nach Deutschland kam* (Andrä-Wördern: Hannibal, 1996), 100.

5. Werner Micke, "Philosophie des Stumpfsinns," *Junge Welt,* 5 February 1957, quoted in Rauhut, *Beat,* 31.

6. Arbeitsausschuß der FSK, "Jugendprotokoll: Außer Rand und Band, II. Teil," Landesbildstelle Berlin, Pressearchiv.

7. Elisabeth Pitz-Savelsberg, "Das Wächteramt des Staates," *Ruf in Volk* 12 (1958): 89–91.

8. See Poiger, *Jazz, Rock, and Rebels,* chap. 1.

9. "Appell an den Urmenschen," *Berliner Zeitung,* 13 December 1956.

10. Dr. Uszukoreit to state concert agency (Deutsche Konzert- und Gastspieldirektion), 21 August 1957, in Bundesarchiv Potsdam DR1 No. 243.

11. "Erfahrungsaustausch," 1960, Jugendarchiv beim Institut für Zeitgeschichtliche Jugendforschung Berlin (JA-IzJ) A6724.

12. Stoph quoted in Helmut Lamprecht, *Teenager und Manager,* rev. ed. (Munich: Rütten & Loenig, 1965), 87. See also Zentralinstitut für Lehrerweiterbildung, "Anleitung der Zirkelleiter zum Thema 'Jugendschutz in der DDR,'" 6 September 1957, Landesarchiv Berlin, Außenstelle Breite Straße (LAB [STA]) LAB (STA) Rep. 119 No. 22; "Bill Haley und die NATO," "Orgie der amerikanischen Unkultur," *Neues Deutschland,* 31 October 1958; "Jugend wird systematisch vergiftet," *Neues Deutschland,* 2 November 1958; and "7000 Rowdys 'in Aktion,'" *B.Z. am Abend,* 28 October 1958.

13. See Poiger, *Jazz, Rock, and Rebels,* chap. 5.

14. "Leipziger Jugendliche riefen 'Pfui,'" *Die Welt* (Bonn), 3 November 1959; Abteilung Org. Instrukteure, "Vorlage an das Sekretariat" (4 December 1959), Stiftung Parteien und Massenorganisation beim Bundesarchiv, Berlin (Ba SAPMO) DY30/IV 2/16/230; and Poiger, *Jazz, Rock, and Rebels,* chap. 5.

15. See Abt. Agit.-Prop., "Einige Bemerkungen zur Frage des Jazz," Berlin, 29 November 1961; and "Unser Standpunkt zum Jazz," Berlin; 7 December 1961—both JA-IzJ AB547.

16. "Bericht über Jugendklubs," 11 November 1962, LAB (STA) Rep. 121 No. 62.

17. See "'Blutiger Kid' vor leerem Haus," *Neue Zeit,* 17 August 1961.

18. Dorothee Wierling, "Jugend als innerer Feind: Konflikte in der Erziehungsdiktatur der sechziger Jahre," in *Sozialgeschichte der DDR,* ed. Harmut Kaelble, Jürgen Kocka, and Hartmut Zwahr (Stuttgart: Klett-Cotta, 1994), 404–25; and Rauhut, *Beat,* 216–26.

19. "Westfilm in amerikanische Versklavung," *Der Morgen,* 30 May 1953.

20. Ludwig Erhard, *Wohlstand für alle* (Düsseldorf: Econ, 1957); Helmut Schelsky, *Die skeptische Generation: Eine Soziologie der deutschen Jugend* (Cologne: Diederichs, 1957).

21. See Curt Bondy et al., *Jugendliche stören die Ordnung: Bericht und Stellungnahme zu den Halbstarkenkrawallen* (Munich: Juventa, 1957); and Schelsky, *Die skeptische Generation,* passim.

22. Vom Spieltrieb besessen," *Telegraf,* 11 July 1957.

23. See Poiger, *Jazz, Rock, and Rebels,* chap. 5.

24. "Totenkopf bürgerlich," *Revue,* no. 19 (1962).

25. See Dietrich Schulz-Köhn, "Der Jazz—Marotte oder Musik," *Kölnische Rundschau,* 14 December 1958.

26. Siegfried Mohrhof, *Warum sind sie gegen uns?* (Seebruck am Chiemsee: Heering-Verlag, 1958). In 1963, for example, Erhard urged his fellow Germans that prosperity for all should not lead them to lose track of "Christian values." See "Politik der Mitte und der Verständigung" (18 October 1963), in *Ludwig Erhard: Gedanken aud fünf Jahrzehnten,* ed. Karl Hohmann (Düsseldorf: Econ, 1988), 814–46.

27. Herbert Rudershausen, "Jugendpflege in der Bar," *Der Rundbrief* 10, no. 9/10 (1960). See also *Abgeordnetenhaus von Berlin: Stenographische Berichte*, 61st session (4 May 1961), 123–24.

28. Senator für Jugend und Sport, "Bericht über die Situation der Berliner Jugend," *Der Rundbrief* 10, no. 11/12 (1960): 1–24, especially 5–10.

29. "'Krieg' mit Rock 'n' Roll," *Abend*, 16 August 1962.

30. See Richard McCormick, *Politics of the Self: Feminism and the Postmodern in West German Literature and Film* (Princeton, N.J.: Princeton University Press, 1991).

31. Rauhut, *Beat.*

6

The Pendulum of Cultural Imperialism

Popular Music Interchanges between the United States and Britain, 1943–1967

Laura E. Cooper and B. Lee Cooper

One unforeseen side-effect of the BBC's greater wartime use of records was growing public exposure to American popular music; few records were issued in Britain during the war because of the shortage in raw materials, so the BBC came to rely extensively on imported American discs. But American musical influence was most profoundly felt through the presence of U.S. troops in the country . . . and the programmes of the American Forces Network (AFN). Maurice Gorham recalled that when the AFN began in 1943, it was the preordained programme for the bobby-soxers, with its American comedy, American swing, and the entire freedom from restrictions. . . . Although Gorham, for one, thought that the popularity and influence of AFN were exaggerated, British popular culture as a whole did undergo an insidious "Americanization" as the war progressed.

—*Stephen Barnard,* On the Radio: Music Radio in Britain *(1989)*

POPULAR MUSIC SERVED AS A VEHICLE of cultural imperialism between the United States and Great Britain from 1943 until 1967. During this period, each country took a turn at dramatically influencing, if not dominating, the other's popular recording industry. From 1943 to 1963, British popular music culture was significantly altered by American business practices and artistic styles. This music-related hegemony was established through the U.S. wartime and postwar military presence in Europe, by American commercial activities in numerous English sea port cities, and because of Great Britain's inability to generate indigenous popular music innovations. In 1964, the American dominance was abruptly reversed as British recording artists exported their own "new" style, ironically derived from America's own rock 'n' roll roots. Each country so completely overwhelmed the other with its popular music artistry during the twenty-five-year period that few alternative domestic recording styles mounted viable commercial competition, thus creating the dual situation of Anglo-American cultural imperialism.

Setting the Stage, 1943–1953

Popular culture reflects the values and beliefs of a particular country at a particular time. American influence on Europe's popular culture was established as early as the 1920s and 1930s, and was considered synonymous with diversity, innovation, and vitality. American popular culture was admired and emulated by much of the British public because of its advanced style and technological capabilities in both film and music. One German film director characterized American overseas influence by noting, "The Americans colonized our subconscious."[1]

American and British popular cultures were forced together during World War Two. The presence of U.S. troops on British soil precipitated direct contact and interchange. Also, because the United States served as the chief funding resource for Britain's postwar economy, continuing U.S. involvement and influence was inevitable. Additionally, soldiers remaining in Britain under NATO agreements further contributed to the spread of American culture by importing pop records and other literary reminders of home. The easy availability of American cultural artifacts further stimulated their popularity.[2]

Great Britain had an advantage over the rest of Europe in the acquisition of American music because of its many port cities. Liverpool, for example, received a steady flow of new American recordings from both commercial traders and the numerous U.S. seamen who journeyed back and forth across the Atlantic. Liverpool also hosted an American air base at Burtonwood. The late Beatle John Lennon described his birthplace by saying, "It's where the sailors would come home with blues records from America in the ships. There is the biggest country and western following in England in Liverpool, besides London."[3] Obviously, port cities throughout the U.K. emerged as centers of Britain's growing popular music scenes.

The British airwaves, usually in a tightly controlled state of "institutional inflexibility," opened up during and after World War Two to broadcast many new programs featuring American music. Exposure to American recordings via the American Forces Network (AFN), Radio Luxembourg from the continent, and even through controlled exposure by the British Broadcasting Corporation (BBC) introduced U.K. listeners to the latest American musical trends. Although the presence of American cultural artifacts made it relatively easy for American musical styles to assert themselves, it was Great Britain's lack of innovative radio programming and the BBC's stodgy commitment to classical and dance band music which created a growing desire among young British listeners for more of the new, exciting American musical entertainment.[4]

Hearing the Piper, 1954–1963

During the mid-1950s, BBC administrators did not wish to allow rock 'n' roll recordings too much public airtime. Consequently, popular music was relegated to only twenty-two hours of weekly airplay. This limitation on public exposure created an underground music audience seeking access to more and more American music. Local dance clubs became showcases for both U.S. recordings and domestically produced American music. Disc jockeys and amateur local bands played many of the new American rock hits brought to Britain by the U.S. soldiers or by British seamen at local seaports.[5]

In January 1955, Bill Haley and His Comets burst onto the British music scene with "Rock around the Clock." This song was so popular that it remained on the British charts for nineteen weeks, and then returned again in 1956 for eleven more weeks.[6] The fact that this single American rock song could dominate the British charts for so long indicated the strong desire among young English record buyers for American rock 'n' roll. Accompanying the celebration of rock music was the emergence of the Teddy Boy. Teddy Boys were rebellious British teens who associated themselves directly with the new styles of American film and music. They were readily identified by their slicked hair, slim-legged pants, and full jackets. The favorite hangout of the typical Teddy Boy was the local coffee shop. They represented an overt form of protest against "older traditions." Not unexpectedly, they were viewed by much of adult British society as negative counterparts of the raucous American rock 'n' roll. Ironically, the Teddy Boy phenomenon receded with the growing acceptance of rock music in Great Britain.[7]

In January 1958, Elvis Presley reached number one on Great Britain's record charts with "Jailhouse Rock." The Presley style was viewed as the prime example of the fusion of rhythm and blues and country music. His success in Britain was attributed to his unique "Americanness." That is, Presley's "Latin good looks" and "cowboy speech and manner" typified the American diversity which so greatly appealed to British young people. Presley also set a visual standard for many British rock musicians.[8]

American rock became both an economic and an artistic force to be contended with. Great Britain, however, could find no reasonable domestic alternative to combat this new form of audio-cultural imperialism. Direct imitation emerged. Television shows and performers with looks similar to those in America presented subdued styles of rock music. Billy Fury, Marty Wilde, Johnny Gentle, Dickie Pride, and Tommy Steele were but a few of the British artists marketed in the Elvis mold.[9] It is particularly interesting to note how closely Tommy Steele's professional life mirrored Elvis Presley's. From his initial career in British rock music, he diversified to television performances and later into movie roles. His professional career was manipulated by his manager, John Kennedy. Unlike Presley, though, Steele never achieved international stardom. His performing zeal eventually faded as a result of his disillusionment with the overbearing manipulation of his strong-willed agent.[10]

Great Britain attempted to reduce the desire for American rock by creating new television programs which showcased the latest American hits performed by British bands. These shows included "Oh Boy," "Juke Box Jury," and "6.5 Special." They were extremely popular. In addition to these television shows, two new music-oriented British publications emerged. *Melody Maker* and *New Musical Express* were created.[11] But American music was an unstoppable force. It overwhelmed British popular culture. It embedded itself in the minds and hearts of British youth, who demanded even greater availability of American recorded products. By 1958, American rock 'n' roll had become an especially important element of British culture and music.

By the late 1950s and early 1960s, many British groups had internalized American popular music sounds and had begun to develop their own distinctive performing styles. Two groups, The Beatles and The Rolling Stones, emerged as highly successful bands which drew strongly from American rock, blues, and rhythm 'n' blues roots. The change in the British rock scene became apparent even in the early 1960s when Great Britain, the island which had seemingly been devoid of any indigenous music creativity, suddenly began generating its own domestic music culture. At the same time, America unexpectedly found itself unable to generate much original music product. The so-called "Golden Age of Rock" was dead, and for once American music seemed to lack vitality.[12] Rock music's initial heroes were fading: Buddy Holly was dead; Chuck Berry was in prison; Jerry Lee Lewis was struggling with huge public relations problems; Little Richard had gone into a religious mode; and Elvis Presley had joined the army. American music had become a "teenage wasteland" filled with plastic idols.[13] However, the early rock style which was dying in the United States was being adapted and internalized by the new British "beat" bands. This artistically dry period for American musicians proved to be a very creative time for working-class British youth, who were rapidly formulating their own images and sounds.

Pirate radio broadcasting also grew during the early 1960s, providing British youth with even more American music. Pirate stations like Radio Veronica and Radio Caroline served as alternatives to the conservative BBC and had their popularity reinforced by high commercial and private backing.[14]

In 1956, John Lennon and Paul McCartney began playing together in a group called The Quarrymen. By 1958, George Harrison had joined the group. These three Liverpool natives were significantly influenced by American music.[15] Their beat band went through various name and member changes before finally emerging as The Beatles. Their Liverpool setting provided ready access to American, German, and other international markets. This exposure to diverse cultures was a significant element in The Beatles' aesthetic inspiration. The melting pot of ideas, rhythms, and recorded performances was a gold mine to Lennon in particular, who consciously observed the cultural spectrum offered by the port city.[16]

Lennon and McCartney, who epitomized the rebellious Teddy Boy image in clothing style and grooming, performed covers of many popular American rock 'n' roll hits. Elvis Presley had become a primary figure in Britain when "Heartbreak Hotel" charted in 1956; other American artists, especially Little Richard, Buddy Holly, and Chuck Berry, also exerted significant musical influence on the two Beatles. The Quarrymen had distributed formal visiting cards describing themselves as "Country and Western, Rock 'n' Roll, and Skiffle Performers."[17] This wide variety of musical styles illustrated the diverse song experiences of the youthful Liverpool-based band.

The Beatles, in 1959 still called The Silver Beatles, frequented many of Liverpool's beat clubs, particularly The Cavern and The Crack. Their spirited performances in these two clubs had earned them a small cult following. Their faithful fans were impressed by the group's mastery of the singing styles of their American heroes, Elvis Presley and Little Richard. But 1960 marked a low point in the careers of these struggling young musicians, who found themselves without a drummer and dissatisfied with the Liverpool club scene. It was during this bleak time that the group became The Beatles, a name inspired by yet another of their American rock heroes—The Crickets, with Buddy Holly. They decided to depart for Hamburg, Germany. Reluctantly, John Lennon and Stu Sutcliffe left art school, Paul McCartney discontinued his teacher training, and George Harrison, who encountered no opposition from either family or friends, headed to Germany to seek a new audience. Their major problem, the lack of a drummer, was solved when Pete Best joined the group. The two-month Hamburg tour began with the band finally complete.[18]

The Kaiserkeller, a popular rock 'n' roll club in the German port city, was the site of the Beatles' Hamburg performances. The Beatles played American rock hits hour after hour. The Hamburg experience, while full of personal, legal, and financial adversity, aided immeasurably in the artistic development of The Beatles. The group's reflection on the Hamburg activities is captured in Paul McCartney's observation, "We had a long time to work it out and make all our mistakes in Hamburg with almost no one watching."[19] Their following grew and during 1961 they adopted their signature floppy, banged hairstyles at the suggestion of their future business manager, Brian Epstein. The final shift in the group's lineup was the dismissal of Pete Best and the addition of drummer Ringo Starr.

On 11 October 1962, "Love Me Do" by The Beatles appeared on the British pop record charts.[20] Within weeks the Liverpool beat group seized control of the British popular music scene, a prophetic trend which they would repeat in 1964 on the international musical stage. Lonnie Donegan, a British skiffle group leader, reacted to the quartet's blitzkrieg popularity by observing, "A strange bedlam was taking over which had nothing to do with anything we had previously known."[21] The idea of British rock had never been accepted in the U.S., especially during the early 1960s, when many Americans had become disillusioned with all rock 'n' roll music.[22] The irony of the 1964–1965 emergence of British rock in the States was the fact that rock 'n' roll music, a black-derived American art form, should be revived via four white performers from Great Britain. The Beatles exposed many teenage

Americans to an unknown subculture by reflecting American black music from across the Atlantic, thus providing many Americans with their initial exposure to rhythm 'n' blues.[23] Of course, black artists understood exactly what was happening. The 1953–1957 cover era was being repeated. The Beatles, along with other artists of the so-called British invasion, "sanitized" soul. They made rhythm 'n' blues music commercially acceptable.

Reversing the Trend, 1964–1967

Nineteen sixty-four proved to be a particularly advantageous time for the emergence of English beat music. Not only had the United States experienced a musical creativity dry spell, but America's youth culture had also lost a popular political idol, President John F. Kennedy. A new charismatic focus was needed. Also, by 1964, seventeen-year-olds constituted the largest single age group in the United States, a prime target for the commercial distribution of the new British rock product.[24] The emergent British music phenomenon was tagged "Beatlemania." Both British and American publications described the early 1960s beat music as "a weird new kind of music that makes rock 'n' roll seem tame by comparison."[25] One American critic accurately charged that The Beatles' "Mersey Sound" was "1956 American rock bouncing back at us."[26] Yet The Beatles successfully melded American sound with European fashion. It should not be forgotten that Tommy Steele, Lonnie Donegan, Bill Fury, and Cliff Richard had on previous occasions unsuccessfully attempted to produce an American impact. This faulty track record left many American record companies suspicious about the long-term financial success of "Beatlemania." Finally, the American music industry became convinced that The Beatles were truly marketable. An all-out advertising campaign was launched to literally force The Beatles on an unsuspecting American public.[27] By February 1964, The Beatles were scheduled to tour America, bringing their new music style to such diverse venues as Carnegie Hall and "The Ed Sullivan Show." Radio stations continuously plugged their imminent arrival. Capitol Records distributed newsletters, stickers, and open-ended audio interview tapes allowing U.S. disc jockeys to conduct seemingly "live" conversations with the Liverpool group. As a result of this no-holds-barred Beatles publicity barrage, their song, "I Want to Hold Your Hand," became the fastest-selling release in Capitol Records' history.[28]

British beat music infiltrated American popular culture in the form of four mop-headed boys from Liverpool who had been inspired by the American rhythm 'n' blues/rock 'n' roll subculture. Their dress and grooming challenged the clothing styles of conventional American males, just as their rhythm 'n' blues–based music differed greatly from the current pop styles of Frankie Avalon, Fabian, Bobby Vinton, and Bobby Vee. Achieving popularity in the United States was a dream come true for The Beatles. Their generation had grown up under

American influence after World War II; the presence of U.S. popular culture in Liverpool had created an irresistible mystique. America was the home of *their* heroes. The Beatles were so set on conquering the United States that anything less than *great* success would have been a letdown.[29]

The huge campaigns paid off. The Beatles achieved fan idolatry, sold-out concerts, an extremely successful Ed Sullivan performance, and domination of the *Billboard* singles chart. The Beatles occupied the top five positions on the singles chart in addition to the top two positions of the LP chart.[30] The Fab Four also enjoyed great financial success from sales of vast quantities of Beatles paraphernalia. The Beatles had successfully infiltrated American popular culture; in essence, they dramatically turned the tables on the United States, which had dominated both popular dress and the music of young people in Great Britain for two decades.[31]

While enjoying huge popularity, The Beatles also encountered some opposition. Conservative evangelist Billy Graham claimed that they were "symptoms of the uncertainty of [our] times—and only a passing phase."[32] Others contended that a conspiracy of rock music was being launched to destroy the country through the lyrical glorification of sex and delinquency. Another writer claimed that Beatlemania was a communist plot designed to make a generation of American young people mentally ill and psychologically unstable. The Beatles, displaying their usual cynical wit, responded to these charges by observing, "Us, communists? Why, we can't be communists. We're the world's number one capitalists."[33]

One California record store owner opposed the British rock 'n' rollers because they were only "imitating" American rhythm 'n' blues artists—and thus violating the artistic standards required for international work visas. He asserted that foreign performers must demonstrate works of distinguishable merit or unduplicated uniqueness. He also alleged that an influx of British performers would put small, independent American record labels and song publishers out of business. This same retailer noted that the British practice of limiting U.S. records in England so that British cover recordings could be released was inherently unfair.[34] These pleas for protectionism went unheeded. The pendulum had already swung too far. The British Invasion was just beginning.

In America, where music culture had become a way of life among young people, kids discarded Bermuda shorts and stopped going to the barber. After The Beatles' initial visit, record sales rose dramatically and radio stations featured more and more British rock music groups. American record companies reacted to Fab Four success by scouring Liverpool clubs and dance halls in search of new "Beatles" groups. The British bands that emerged after 1964 included Herman's Hermits, The Searchers, Gerry and the Pacemakers, and The Kinks. American groups were also influenced by the British Invasion. Great Britain ruled the American airwaves.[35] As one author noted in 1964, "[The] advent of The Beatles shattered the steady day-to-day domination of made-in-America music. From here on it's expected that a significant ration of U.S. best sellers will be of foreign origin."[36] Internationally, The Beatles gave rock music credibility. They also established writing and performing as interdependent art forms. This self-contained production approach, successfully practiced on a smaller scale by Carl Perkins, Chuck Berry, and Buddy Holly, deindustrialized the music industry by demonstrating that rock artists could compose their own songs without assistance from assembly line writers.[37] The greatest overall effect, though, was the diversity of British beat music and its cultural impact in the United States. One writer observed, "The Beatles set the stage for the British Invasion with their unprecedented record sales and media appeal. They laid the groundwork for the appearance of The Rolling Stones."[38] Mick Jagger and Keith Richards simply continued the irony of reinterpreting American culture for America.

The Rolling Stones, a London-based group, were influenced both by The Beatles and by black American artists such as Chuck Berry, Jimmy Reed, Slim Harpo, and Bo Diddley.[39] While both groups were individually important factors in the mid-1960s British Invasion, they projected very different images. The Rolling Stones were viewed as a raucous group of devils who struck fear into the hearts of adults. The Stones adamantly claimed they were *not* merely another beat music band, but rather a black-oriented rhythm 'n' blues band. Brian Jones elaborated: "We haven't adapted our music from a watered-down music like American rock 'n' roll. We've adapted our music directly from the early black blues forms."[40] Music rooted in social adversity and the virtually ignored black subculture clearly served as The Rolling Stones' inspiration. The Stones considered themselves "Rebels *with* a cause . . . the cause of rhythm and blues."[41] They were determined not to be sanitized or commercialized by any recording industry. These rebellious qualities were much admired by their young, antiestablishment audience. The Stones were the very antithesis of The Beatles, who had rapidly gained a significant level of parental approval throughout the United States. Either for publicity purposes or in reality, The Stones fostered and perpetuated an image as "outsiders." Their hair was long and shaggy; they were a white band that had mastered forbidden black-based rhythms. Their rebelliousness created a strong cult following: to be a Rolling Stone was to partake of a secret vice.

An early Rolling Stones American release was "King Bee," a tune originally recorded by American bluesman Slim Harpo. While The Beatles were politely singing, "I Want to Hold Your Hand," The Rolling Stones were suggestively singing, "I'm a king bee, baby, buzzing 'round your hive. . . . Let me come inside." *Vogue* magazine described The Rolling Stones as "more terrifying than The Beatles."[42] The Stones introduced their white audiences to blues music—a music many Americans had ignored when originally performed during the early 1950s by domestic black artists.[43] The Stones stunned "The Ed Sullivan Show" with their sensual, raw performances. They received as much negative publicity as The Beatles received positive publicity. This controversial British rock group further established the new British foothold on the international pop scene.

Conclusion

The Beatles and The Rolling Stones, while performing different types of music, both drew heavily on the songs and performing styles of American artists of the 1950s and early 1960s. They successfully integrated and adapted American aesthetic models to their own music.[44] The irony of the "British Invasion" of 1964 is that it simultaneously represented the triumph and demise of American dominance over England's popular music culture. The period of U.S. cultural imperialism (1943–63) had ended. An intervening time of adjustment (1964–66) permitted an inordinately large number of new British bands to test their commercial wings in the States. Yet the era of British dominance of American record charts was destined to be brief, though undeniably significant. The Beatles and The Rolling Stones, schooled by Chuck Berry, Buddy Holly, Howlin' Wolf, Marvin Gaye, Bo Diddley, Carl Perkins, and others, finally graduated into their own worlds of physical imagery, instrumental experimentation, lyric structuring, and rhythm manipulation. Many critics echoed in awe the observation of U.S. journalist Jeff Greenfield: "The Beatles were a powerful influence in music and popular culture. Their success resulted from [their] ever changing style; they were always moving."[45]

Great Britain was still not completely free of American musical influence, of course. By 1967, though, with the release of the *Sgt. Pepper's Lonely Hearts Club Band* album, the group which had won the hearts of both America and Great Britain had identified its own independent musical style. The album also permanently ended the era of rock music as a strictly adolescent phenomenon. The Beatles helped make rock the music of an international generation. One critic acknowledged the creative brilliance of the 1967 Beatles' album by saying, "*Sgt. Pepper* isn't in the line of continuous development; rather it is an astounding accomplishment for which no one could have been wholly prepared, and it therefore substantially enlarges and modifies all the work that preceded it."[46]

The Beatles no longer needed to borrow American rock styles. They, like many other British bands including The Rolling Stones and The Who, had developed into unique, viable artists. The American cultural imperialism which had begun in 1943 had ended. The rebounding British cultural imperialism of 1964 waned after *Sgt. Pepper.* Commercial resurgence by American recording companies (Motown, Stax, and Atlantic) and the explosion of soul music (Wilson Pickett, Aretha Franklin, Sam and Dave, Otis Redding, The Temptations, and hundreds of others) generated the pendulum swing back to the center. Although the future would bring many new "invading" artists from Ireland, Wales, England, and Australia, there would be no maximum chart dominance by either American or

British performers. The two nations found equilibrium in their popular music interchanges after 1967.

Notes

This chapter was originally published in *Journal of Popular Culture* 27, no. 3 (Winter 1993): 61–78. Reprinted by kind permission of B. Lee Cooper and Laura E. Cooper, and of the *Journal of Popular Culture.*

1. Quoted in Simon Frith, *Sound Effects: Youth, Leisure, and the Politics of Rock* (New York: Pantheon Books, 1981). For a more global perspective on cultural imperialism, see C. W. E. Bigsby (ed.), *Superculture: American Popular Culture and Europe* (Bowling Green, Ohio: Bowling Green State University Popular Press, 1975). The musical viewpoint on cultural imperialism has been detailed in Laura E. Cooper and B. Lee Cooper, "Exploring Cultural Imperialism: Bibliographic Resources for Teaching about American Domination, British Adaptation, and Rock Music Interchange, 1950–1967," in *International Journal of Instructional Media*, Vol. 27 (Spring 1990), pp. 167–177; and Humphrey A. Regis, "Calypso, Reggae, and Cultural Imperialism by Reexportation," in *Popular Music and Society*, Vol. 7 (Spring 1988), pp. 63–73.

2. Iain Chambers, *Urban Rhythms: Pop Music and Popular Culture* (New York: St. Martin's Press, 1985), pp. 18–49. For a general history of post-war England, see Arthur Marwick, *British Society since 1945* (New York: Penguin Books, 1982), pp. 1–113.

3. Quoted in Dave Harker, *One for the Money: Politics and Popular Song* (London: Hutchinson & Co., Ltd., 1980), p. 83. For a detailed analysis of British population distribution, trade arteries, and transportation facilities linking urban centers during the 1945–60 period, see Bernard Reines, "United Kingdom," in Louis Barron (ed.), *Europe—Worldmark Encyclopedia of the Nations* (New York: Harper & Row, 1963), pp. 305–28; and David Bacon and Norman Maslov, *The Beatles' England: There Are Places I'll Remember* (San Francisco: 910 P, 1982). More specific studies, both literary and photographic, about Liverpool, can be found in Edward Lucie-Smith (ed.), *The Liverpool Scene* (Garden City, N.Y.: Doubleday, 1967).

4. Chambers, *Urban Rhythms*, pp. 44–49; Asa Briggs, *The BBC: The First Fifty Years* (Oxford: Oxford University Press, 1985); Tom Burns, *The BBC: The British Connection* (New York: Holmes & Meier, 1977); Richard Nichols, *Radio Luxembourg: The Station of the Stars* (London: Comet Books, 1982); and Phil Silverman, "Irish Biographer Says U.S. Armed Forces Radio Sparked His Lifelong Obsession with Little Richard and Rock Music," in *Record Collector's Monthly*, No. 34 (February–March 1986), pp. 1, 10–12.

5. Harry Castleman and Walter J. Podrazik, "The Beatles from Others," in *All Together Now: The First Complete Beatles Discography, 1961–1975* (New York: Ballantine Books, 1975), pp. 227–233; Stephen Barnard, "Saturday Night Out," in *The History of Rock* (1982), No. 31, pp. 618–620; Erik Dundson, "Juke Box Memories," in *Now Dig This*, No. 77 (August 1989), pp. 14–15; Marcus Gray, *London's Rock Landmarks: The A–Z Guide to London's Rock Geography* (London: Omnibus Books, 1985); Alistair Griffin, *On the Scene at the Cavern* (London: Hamish Hamilton, 1964); Brian Innes, "Clubs and Coffee Bars: Where Britain's Teenagers Found the New Music," in *The History of Rock* (1982), No. 7, pp. 132–134; Spencer Leigh, *Let's Go Down to the Cavern: The Story of Liverpool's Merseybeat* (London: Vermilion Press, 1984); John Pidgeon, "Blues in the Basement," in *The History of Rock*

(1982), No. 30, pp. 598–600; Alan Thompson, "Hail! Hail! Rock 'n' Roll," in *Now Dig This*, No. 647 (October 1988), pp. 24–25; Jurgen Vollmer, *Rock 'n' Roll Times: The Style and Spirit of the Early Beatles and Their First Fans* (Woodstock, N.Y.: Overlook Press, 1983); and Chris Woodford, "Boppin' the Blues in Newcastle!" in *Now Dig This*, No. 77 (August 1989), p. 23.

6. Harker, *One for the Money*, pp. 68–69. See also Jo and Tim Rice, Paul Gambaccini, and Mike Read (comps.), *The Guinness Book of British Hit Singles*, 2nd ed. (Enfield, Middlesex: Guinness Superlatives, 1979), p. 104; and Clive Solomon (comp.), *Record Hits: The British Top 50 Charts, 1954–1976* (London: Omnibus Press, 1977), p. 71.

7. Chambers, *Urban Rhythms*, pp. 22–39; Michael Watts, "The Call and Response of Popular Music: The Impact of American Pop Music in Europe," in C. W. E. Bigsby (ed.), *Superculture* (Bowling Green, Ohio: Bowling Green State University Popular Press, 1975), pp. 123–139; Richard Barnes, Johnny Moke, and Jan McVeigh (comps.), *Mods!* (London: Eel Pie, 1979); Peter Everett, *You'll Never Be 16 Again: An Illustrated History of the British Teenager* (London: BBC Books, 1986); Robert Freeman, *Yesterday: The Beatles, 1963–1965* (New York: Holt, Rinehart, & Winston, 1983); Stuart Hall and Tony Jefferson (eds.), *Resistance through Rituals: Youth Subcultures in Post-War Britain* (London: Hutchinson Books, 1976); Grace Hechinger and Fred M. Hechinger, *Teenage Tyranny* (London: Duckworth Press, 1964); Dan O'Sullivan, *The Youth Culture* (London: Methuen Educational Press, 1974); Crispin Steele-Perkins and Richard Smith (comps.), *The Teds* (London: Traveling Light Photography, 1979); and David P. Szatmary, "The Mods vs. the Rockers and the British Invasion of America," in *Rockin' in Time: A Social History of Rock 'n' Roll* (Englewood Cliffs, N.J.: Prentice-Hall, 1987), pp. 78–106.

8. Chambers, *Urban Rhythms*, pp. 36–37; Rice et al., *British Hit Singles*, pp. 175–177; Clive Solomon (comp.), *Record Hits: The British Top 50 Charts, 1954–1976* (London: Omnibus Press, 1977), pp. 116–118; and John Townson (comp.), *Elvis U.K.: The Ultimate Guide to Elvis Presley's British Record Releases, 1956–1986* (Poole, Dorset, England: Blandford Press, 1987).

9. Watts, "The Call and Response," p. 130; Steve Aynsley, "British Rock 'n' Roll, 1956–1962," in *Now Dig This* (15 June 1984), pp. 15–17; Brian Bird, *Skiffle* (London: Robert Hale, 1958); Ashley Brown, "The U.S. Rocks—Rock 'n' Roll Hit the Shores of Great Britain Like a Tidal Wave: Music Was Never the Same Again," in *The History of Rock* (1982), No. 7, pp. 121–123; Bob Brunning, *Blues: The British Connection* (Poole, Dorset, England: Blandford Press, 1986); Stuart Colman, *They Kept on Rockin': The Giants of Rock 'n' Roll* (Poole, Dorset, England: Blandford Press, 1982); Karl Dallas, "Lonnie Donegan and Skiffle: Was Skiffle the Start of British Rock?" in *The History of Rock* (1982), No. 7, pp. 124–128; Pete Frame, "British Pop, 1955–1979," in *Trouser Press*, No. 10 (June 1982), pp. 30–31; and Dave Waite, "Lonnie Donegan," in *Record Collector*, No. 93 (May 1987).

10. Harker, *One for the Money*, pp. 70–71. For examinations of nonperforming rock managers in pre-Beatles Britain, see Spencer Leigh, "Larry Parnes," in *Record Collector*, No. 122 (October 1989), pp. 86–88; John Repsch, *The Legendary Joe Meek* (London: Woodfordhouse Publishing, 1989); and Chris Woodford, "The Passing of Parnes," in *Now Dig This*, No. 78 (September 1989), p. 30.

11. Chambers, *Urban Rhythms*, pp. 33–41; Kevin Howlett, *The Beatles at the Beeb, 1962–1965: The Story of Their Radio Career* (London: British Broadcasting Corporation, 1982).

12. Bob Kinder, "Teen Idols and Rock and Screamers (1959–1963)," in *The Best of the First: The Early Days of Rock and Roll* (Chicago: Adams Publishers, 1986); Jean-Charles

Marion, "Death Valley Days of Rock, 1959–1963," in *Record Exchanges* (1977), No. 5, p. 15; and Jeff Tamarkin, "In Defense of Rock's Wimp Years," in *Goldmine*, No. 81 (February 1983), p. 3.

13. Greg Shaw, "The Teen Idols," in Jim Miller (ed.), *The Rolling Stone Illustrated History of Rock and Roll*, rev. ed. (New York: Random House/Rolling Stone Books, 1980), pp. 96–100; and Ed Ward, Geoffrey Stokes, and Ken Tucker, *Rock of Ages: The Rolling Stone History of Rock and Roll* (New York: Rolling Stone Press/Summit Books, 1986), pp. 165–246.

14. Harker, *Urban Rhythms*, pp. 79–80; Paul Harris, *When Pirates Ruled the Waves* (Aberdeen, Scotland: Impulse Publishing, 1968); John Hind and Stephen Mosco, *Rebel Radio: The Full Story of British Pirate Radio* (London: Pluto Press, 1985); Stuart Henry and Mike Von Joel, *Pirate Radio: Then and Now* (Poole, Dorset, England: Blandford Press, 1984); and Steve Jones, "Making Waves: Pirate Radio and Popular Music," in *OneTwoThreeFour: A Rock 'n' Roll Quarterly*, No. 7 (Winter 1989), pp. 55–67.

15. Roy Carr and Tony Tyler, *The Beatles: An Illustrated Record*, rev. ed. (New York: Harmony Books, 1978); Howard DeWitt, *The Beatles: Untold Tales* (Fremont, Calif.: Horizon Books, 1985), pp. 227–249; Wilfrid Mellers, *The Music of The Beatles: Twilight of the Gods* (New York: Schirmer Books, 1975), pp. 23–43; Terence O'Grady, "Early Influences and Recordings," in *The Beatles: A Musical Evolution* (Boston: Twayne Publishers, 1983), pp. 7–20; and Tom Schultheiss (comp.), *The Beatles—A Day in the Life: The Day-by-Day Diary, 1960–1970* (New York: Quick Fox, 1981).

16. DeWitt, *The Music of the Beatles*, pp. 1–125; and Greil Marcus, "The Beatles," in Miller (ed.), *The Rolling Stone Illustrated History*, pp. 177–189.

17. Phillip Norman, *Shout! The True Story of The Beatles* (London: Elm Tree Books, 1982), p. 26.

18. Ibid., p. 7; DeWitt, *The Beatles: Untold Tales*, pp. 1–74; and Gareth L. Pawlowski, *How They Became The Beatles: A Definitive History of the Early Years, 1960–1964* (New York: E. P. Dutton, 1989).

19. Quoted in John Lahr, "The Beatles Considered," in *New Republic* (2 December 1981), p. 20.

20. Rice et al. (comps.), *British Hit Singles*, p. 21.

21. Quoted in Chambers, *Urban Rhythms*, p. 50.

22. Nicholas Schaffner, *The British Invasion* (New York: McGraw-Hill Book Co., 1983), p. 4.

23. Alan Fotherington, "Telling the Children How It Was," in *MacLean's*, No. 27 (27 February 1989), p. 27; Castleman and Podrazik, *All Together Now*, pp. 226–242; B. Lee Cooper, "The Black Roots of Popular Music," in *Images of American Society in Popular Music* (Chicago: Nelson-Hall, Inc., 1982), pp. 111–123.

24. Peter McCabe and Robert D. Schonfeld, *Apple to the Core: The Unmaking of The Beatles* (New York: Simon & Schuster, 1972), p. 48; Vance Packard, "Building the Beatle Image," in Charles P. Neises (ed.), *The Beatles Reader* (Ann Arbor, Mich.: Pierian Press, 1984), pp. 11–13; and Ray Coleman, *The Man Who Made The Beatles: An Intimate Biography of Brian Epstein* (New York: McGraw-Hill Book Co., 1989).

25. Ray Coleman, "1964: The Year of The Beatles," in *Melody Makers*, No. 39 (19 December 1964), pp. 2–3. See also Chambers, *Urban Rhythm*, pp. 50–83; Evan David, "The Psychological Characteristics of Beatlemania," in *Journal of the History of Ideas*, No. 30 (April–June 1969), pp. 273–280; June Price, "The Beatles' Arrival: Mania in the Media," in *Goldmine*, No. 224 (24 February 1989), pp. 8, 93; A. J. S. Rayl and Curt Gunther, *Beatles '64:*

A Hard Days Night in America (Garden City, N.Y.: Doubleday Books, 1989), pp. 1–233; Rich Sutton, "Beatlemania Revisited: A Look Back," in *Song Hits*, No. 220 (June 1984), pp. 18–19; and A. J. W. Taylor, "Beatlemania—A Study of Adolescent Enthusiasm," in *British Journal of Social and Clinical Psychology*, No. 5 (September 1966), pp. 81–88.

26. Alfred G. Aronowitz, "Yeah! Yeah! Yeah! Music's Gold Bugs: The Beatles," in *Saturday Evening Post*, No. 237 (21 March 1964), p. 30. See also Castleman and Podrazik, *All Together Now*, pp. 226–242; Harry Castleman and Walter J. Podrazik, *The Beatles Again!* (Ann Arbor, Mich.: Pierian Press, 1977), pp. 77–83; and B. Lee Cooper, "Popular Music and the Computer," in *Images of American Society*, pp. 88–96.

27. See Chambers, *Urban Rhythm*, pp. 50–83.

28. Schaffner, *The British Invasion*, pp. 4–5.

29. Paul Theroux, "Why We Loved The Beatles," in *Rolling Stone* (16 February 1984), p. 21.

30. Joel Whitburn, *The Top Singles, 1955–1990* (Menomonee Falls, Wisc.: Record Research, 1991), pp. 38–39.

31. Schaffner, *The British Invasion*, pp. 3–53; Jeff Augsburger, Mary Eck, and Rick Rann, *The Beatles Memorabilia Price Guide* (Elburn, Ill.: Branyan Press, 1988); and Jerry Osborne, Perry Cox, and Joe Lindsay, *Official Price Guide to Memorabilia of Elvis Presley and The Beatles* (New York: Ballantine Books, 1988). For surveys of the British invasion years, see Harold Bronson, *Rock Explosion: The British Invasion Photos, 1962–1967*, ed. by Michael Ochs (Santa Monica, Calif.: Rhino Press, 1984); Alan Clayson, *Call Up the Groups: The Golden Age of British Beat, 1962–1967* (Poole, Dorset, England: Blandford Press, 1985); Colin Cross, with Paul Kendall and Mick Farren (comps.), *Encyclopedia of British Beat Groups and Solo Artists of the Sixties* (London: Omnibus Press, 1980); Peter Doggett, "The British Invasion," in *Record Collector*, No. 114 (February 1989), pp. 19–22; and Charles Webb, "The British Invasion, 1964: A Chronology," in *Goldmine*, No. 98 (27 April 1984), pp. 36–44.

32. Quoted in Tony Palmer, *All You Need is Love: The Story of Popular Music*, ed. by Paul Medlicott (New York: Grossman Publishers, 1976).

33. Paul McCartney at a Beatles press conference, New York (23 August 1966), at members.tripod.com/~holysmOke/NY3.html [last accessed 15 November 2001]. The most interesting overview analysis of the rock conspiracy issue is provided in Linda Martin and Kerry Segrave, *Anti-Rock: The Opposition to Rock 'n' Roll* (Hamden, Conn.: Archon Books, 1988), pp. 111–184. For specific attacks, see Phillip Abbot Luce, "The Great Rock Conspiracy: Are The Beatles Termites?" in *National Review*, No. 21 (23 September 1969), pp. 959, 973; and David A. Noebel, *Communism, Hypnotism, and The Beatles: An Analysis of the Communist Use of Music, The Communist Master Music Plan* (Tulsa, Okla.: Christian Crusade Publishers, 1965), pp. 1–26.

34. "U.K. Rock 'n' Rollers Are Called Copycats," in *Billboard*, No. 77 (19 June 1965), p. 12; "Beatles' Success in U.S.A. Trend for the British?" in *Variety*, Vol. 233 (5 February 1964), p. 46; H. Schoenfeld, "Britannia Rules Airwaves: Beatles Stir Home Carbons," in *Variety*, Vol. 233 (12 February 1964), p. 63; "U.S. Rocks and Reels from Beatles' Invasion," in *Billboard*, No. 76 (15 February 1964), pp. 1ff; R. Watkins, "Rocking Redcoats Are Coming: Beatles Lead Massive Drive," in *Variety*, Vol. 233 (19 February 1964), pp. 1ff; and Ian Dove, "January 1–March 31, 1964: 90 Days That Shook the Industry," in *Billboard*, No. 81 (27 December 1969), p. 126.

35. Whitburn, *Top Pop Singles*, pp. 150–187.

36. Schoenfeld, "Britannia Rules," p. 63. For a thoughtful analysis of the internationalization of the recording industry, see Alan Wells, "The British Invasion of American Popular

Music: What Is It and Who Pays?" in *Popular Music and Society,* Vol. 11 (1987), pp. 65–78; also Dave Harker, *One for the Money: Politics and Popular Song* (London: Hutchinson & Co., Ltd., 1980), pp. 87–145.

37. Chris Difford, "To Be As Good," in *Rolling Stone* (16 February 1984), p. 59. Also see William J. Dowlding, *Beatlesongs* (New York: Simon & Schuster, 1989); William McKeen, *The Beatles: A Bio-bibliography* (Westport, Conn.: Greenwood Press, 1989); and Tim Riley, *Tell Me Why: A Beatles' Commentary* (New York: Alfred A. Knopf, 1988).

38. Dove, "January 1–March 31," p. 126. For an overview of the Mick Jagger and Keith Richards songwriting team, see David Dalton, *The Rolling Stones: The First Twenty Years* (New York: Alfred A. Knopf, 1981).

39. Chambers, *Urban Rhythms,* pp. 65–75; Alan Beckett, "The Stones," in *New Left Review,* No. 47 (January–February 1968), pp. 24–29; Carr and Tyler, *The Beatles,* pp. 18–19; David Dalton (ed.), *The Rolling Stones: An Unauthorized Biography in Words and Photographs* (New York: QuickFox, 1979), pp. 15–47; John M. Hellmann, Jr., "'I'm a Monkey': The Influence of the Black American Blues Argot on the Rolling Stones," in *Journal of American Folklore,* No. 86 (October–December 1973), pp. 367–373; and John D. Wells, "Me and the Devil Blues: A Study of Robert Johnson and the Music of the Rolling Stones," in *Popular Music and Society,* Vol. 9 (1983), pp. 18–24.

40. Quoted in Schaffner, *The British Invasion,* p. 56.

41. Frith, *Sound Effects,* pp. 70–71.

42. As cited in Norman, *Shout!* p. 106.

43. See Schaffner, *The British Invasion,* pp. 54–93; and Robert Christgau, "The Rolling Stones," in *The Rolling Stone Illustrated History,* pp. 190–200.

44. For an extended discussion of musical adaptation based on recorded songs, see David Hatch and Stephen Millward, *From Blues to Rock: An Analytical History of Pop Music* (Manchester, England: Manchester University Press, 1987), pp. 1–179.

45. Jeff Greenfield, "They Changed Rock, Which Changed the Culture, Which Changed Us," in *New York Times Magazine* (16 February 1975), p. 12.

46. Richard Poirier, "Learning from The Beatles," in *Partisan Review,* No. 34 (Fall 1967), p. 526. For commentaries on the *Sgt. Pepper* album, see Peter Doggett, "Sgt. Pepper—The Album," in *Record Collector,* No. 94 (June 1987), pp. 3–6; David R. Pichaske, "Sustained Performances: Sgt. Pepper's Lonely Hearts Club Band," in Neises (ed.), *The Beatles Reader,* pp. 59–62; Charles Reinhart, "Sgt. Pepper's Lonely Hearts Club Band: It's 20 Years Later Now . . . And Still a Landmark," in *Goldmine,* No. 182 (17 July 1987), pp. 18–20; and Derek Taylor, *It Was Twenty Years Ago Today* (New York: Simon & Schuster, 1987).

7

The Coca-Cola Co. and the Olympic Movement

Global or American?

Steinar Bryn

*T*HIS ESSAY WAS ORIGINALLY COMPOSED *in 1993. Although some information has been updated, the chapter is still a discussion derived from that period and would be different if it were written today. However, its basic argument remains the same, and its basic conclusions are still sound today.*

> I've been experimenting on a little preparation—a kind of decoction nine-tenths water and the other tenth drugs that don't cost more than a dollar a barrel. . . . The third year we could easily sell 1,000,000 bottles in the United States—profit at least $350,000—and then it would be time to turn our attention toward the real idea of the business. . . . Why, our headquarters would be in Constantinople and our hindquarters in Further India! . . . Annual income—well, God only knows how many millions and millions!
>
> —*Colonel Beriah Sellers, in Mark Twain's* The Gilded Age *(1873)*

The relationship under examination is that between globalization and Americanization. In an extreme form, a "global village" is envisioned as a continuation of the unified nation-state. Roland Robertson argues that nation-states do not simply interact; they constitute a context in which it becomes meaningful to talk about the world as a holistic unity, a global world.[1] Within this global world, certain processes take place that have a relative autonomy from interstate processes. The term *globalization* is therefore to be preferred to *internationalization* (literally inter-nation-state exchanges).

Such a global world presupposes an overstate unity, which is not very likely in the foreseeable future. But if we shift the focus to cultural processes, we can, on the other hand, identify certain globalizing processes—for example, "the increase in the numbers of international agencies and institutions, the increasing global forms of communication, the acceptance of unified global time, the development of global competitions and prizes, the development of standard notions of citizenship, rights and conception of humankind."[2] The teenage culture in particular is becoming global in scope, and the same stars and symbols inspire young people in the Ukraine, Norway, Kenya, and Hong Kong. While the symbols might have originated in the United States, the teenagers live in a global sphere. As the late CEO of Coca-Cola Robert Goizueta expressed it, "People around the world are today connected to each other by brand-name consumer products as much as by anything else."[3] A recent attempt to define the "global teenager" discovered that while only 40 percent correctly identified the United Nations logo, 82 percent knew Coke's symbol,[4] justifying Goizueta's assertion.

The argument in this chapter is that our perception of a Mythic America affects the process of globalization and gives it a specific direction. This might be illustrated by a case study of the Coca-Cola Co.'s (hereafter called Coca-Cola) involvement with the Olympic Games. This is an effort by Coca-Cola to establish itself not as an American but as a global company. The following discussion of Coca-Cola also throws light on other issues dealt with in the chapter, especially the role of the visual environment in communicating cultural values.

When Coca-Cola and the Lillehammer Olympic Organization Committee (LOOC) signed the sponsor contract in Albertville, France, in 1992, President Keogh of Coca-Cola claimed that his company and the Olympic movement shared an important heritage and the same cultural values.[5] This is a problematic statement. Coca-Cola is, much like the Statue of Liberty or Stars and Stripes, one of the most powerful symbols of the American way of life, while the Olympic movement is a global movement and organization somewhat independent of the United States.

What is the difference, if any, between global and American? Did Coca-Cola leave its American origins behind when it presented itself on the global scene? Even if the aim of Coca-Cola is to be a global company, its commercials are still perceived as symbols of the American way of life.[6] We can therefore ask whether their presence as a major sponsor of the Olympic Games accelerated the Americanization or the globalization of Lillehammer.[7] A study of the relationship between Coca-Cola and the Olympic movement might shed some light on the relationship between Americanization and globalization.

The public discourse in Lillehammer could be broken down into four arguments dealing primarily with Coca-Cola's commercial interests. These four arguments should be kept separate:

1. The aesthetic argument: the quality and the localization of commercial signs and how they fit into the cultural landscape
2. The juridical argument: Is this sign legal?
3. The democratic argument: Who has the power and the money to put up signs?
4. The philosophical argument: What is the meaning of the sign?

The first two have been discussed at length in Lillehammer, and I will only briefly comment on them here. The democratic argument is worth mentioning, but the relevant issue in this context is the philosophical argument, which is silently bypassed in Lillehammer.

The Aesthetic Argument

This is an ongoing debate which intensified in the Lillehammer region, particularly due to some negative international criticism of Albertville ("the games without a soul"[8]). A local newspaper described the Winter Games in Albertville as the Coca-Cola games, and the general attitude in Lillehammer was "We do not want 'Albertville-conditions' in Lillehammer" (i.e., signs everywhere with no respect for local traditions).

The debate in Lillehammer dealt primarily with the size, format, material, and placement of the sign. I see this debate as the result of a general change in awareness with regard to visual pollution affecting several Western countries. This discourse is not directly connected to either the Olympic games or Coca-Cola but rather to the increasing commercialization of the cultural landscape.[9] This has led to dramatic changes in several Norwegian communities, some of which had no connection to Lillehammer and the Olympic Games. While there is some uproar against the extensive use of American words and symbols, the main thrust of the argument against the commercialization is aesthetic, stressing the necessity of a visual environment more in harmony with Norwegian artistic, architectural, and cultural traditions.

In 1991, the American Congress discussed the Visual Pollution Control Act which alerted Coca-Cola to these kind of problems. When I visited the Coca-Cola headquarters in Atlanta, Georgia, in September 1992, it was a visual pleasure. Both the architectural design and the discreet use of the Coca-Cola symbol were a visual surprise. It was clear that Coca-Cola did apply a different standard in Norway from what it applied in Georgia.[10]

The Juridical Argument

Local municipality officials are changing the rules regulating the use of names, signs, and symbols. Coca-Cola has to adapt to the local rules with respect to the size, the format, the material, and the content of its commercial signs.[11] The company claims this causes a problem because it expects maximum visibility in return for sponsoring the Olympic Games. There is an ongoing debate between Coca-Cola, LOOC, the county, and the involved municipalities about this issue.

Several of the local municipalities began the process of rewriting their rules and regulations. Coca-Cola had a sponsorship contract with Albertville, France, and signed a sponsor contract with Lillehammer, Gjøvik, and Hamar as well.[12] It is therefore in Coca-Cola's interest to support strict regulations which are open to exceptions. It wants rules which can keep its competitors out, while it, as a major sponsor not only of the Olympic Games but also of the municipalities, will get the visibility it deserves.

An important part of Coca-Cola's commercial strategy is "the power of presence." In an internal memo from 1987, President Keogh stressed that the power of presence is the secret to their successful competition with Pepsi. "It is at the play, at the game, at the sorority and at the drugstore. . . . The name, Coca-Cola, is in front of every pair of eyes, every day, everywhere."[13] Through its exclusive presence at places like the Houston Astrodome, the San Diego Zoo, Madison Square Garden, Yankee Stadium, Disney World, and four hundred other prestigious U.S. locations, Coca-Cola is seen by over 280 million patrons a year. This marketing strategy is becoming increasingly visible in Europe. In 1992, Coca-Cola targeted the Olympic Games in Albertville and Barcelona, the World Expo in Seville, Tour de France, Wimbledon, and the European Soccer Championship in addition to the general presence in front of "every pair of eyes, everywhere" on roadside and city kiosks and billboards.

The Democratic Argument

Freedom of expression is most often associated with freedom of speech. In a visual culture, it becomes less important to be heard, more important to be seen. In Lillehammer, Volkswagen offered the county hospital nearly $100,000 for commercial use of a side of the building.[14] Coca-Cola immediately made the hospital a better offer. With a global marketing budget of $4 billion (in 1992), it had the power to outbid most others.

While Coca-Cola was denied access to the hospital wall by the local government, its attitude seemed to be that Lillehammer owed a lot of visibility to Coca-Cola as part of the "Olympic Package." Coca-Cola's own rhetoric exploited this, by claiming that local regulations undermined its fundamental reason for sponsoring the Olympic Games. It sponsored the Olympic Games with a large sum of money and therefore deserved visibility. If Lillehammer wanted to host the Olympic Games, obliging the sponsor Coca-Cola's demands was simply the price Lillehammer had to pay. Not much debate was expressed about the power given to Coca-Cola by allowing them to dominate the visual environment up to and during the Olympic Games.

The Philosophical Argument

Our visual environment plays an important role in the transmission of cultural values. We therefore need a public debate about which symbols we want to let dominate this environment. We cannot leave this cultural battlefield solely to the marketers of products. In this context it becomes important to ask, Why is it so important for Coca-Cola to sponsor the Olympic Games? Is it to increase its profits? Is it to build a more positive image? Or are there other, less obvious reasons? What is the meaning of a Coca-Cola sign combined with the five Olympic rings? What is the message Coca-Cola wants to communicate to the younger generation, and how is this message received?

Coca-Cola is very concerned about building a positive image, and it believes the reason for its success partly has to do with the fact that people are not only buying a product but also buying an image. Fiora Steinbach Palazzini explains why people tend to choose Coca-Cola:

> Is it perhaps because the rival products have been tried and comparisons made? In 99 percent of cases the answer of course, is no. People drink Coca-Cola because they identify perfectly with the image Coca-Cola projects to its consumers. They choose to drink Coca-Cola not only for the intrinsic quality of the product, but beyond that, for the image the drink creates.[15]

The American advertising executive James Ogilvy argues that in building an image, every statement must carry the same message. That is, the advertising of a product must constantly project the same image, year after year. While most companies these days are concerned with changing and improving their advertising image, Coca-Cola is remarkably constant. The significant change is between the $46 spent in 1886 and the $4 billion spent in 1992.

The Coca-Cola Co.—From American to Global

Coca-Cola started out in 1886 with the catchwords *delicious* and *refreshing*, and consumers still reach for a Coke because it is delicious and refreshing. But slowly, over the years, Coca-Cola has built an image which goes far beyond the drink itself. Starting early, using newspaper and radio, blinking billboards from the town square to Piccadilly Circus, television commercials, and an increasing number of signs telling consumers about the availability of the soft drink, Coca-Cola has become the most recognized trademark in the world.

In *For God, Country, and Coca-Cola,* Mark Pendergrast describes the development of Coca-Cola in almost religious terms. The first long-term president of the company, Asa Candler, sent out his salesmen with missionary zeal, and they believed they were bringing something good to the United States. At the turn of the twentieth century, Coca-Cola spent almost $85,000 on advertising; by 1912, that figure was over a million dollars a year, and Coca-Cola had become the single best-advertised product in the United States. By 1914, the company had over five million square feet of painted walls.[16] In 1907, an ad showed Uncle Sam as a soda jerk filling up a glass of Coca-Cola in front of the White House. The accompanying text called Coca-Cola "The Great American Beverage" for "All Classes, Ages, and Sexes."[17]

Coca-Cola was originally developed by the pharmacist John Pemberton and marketed for its medicinal qualities, but when its active ingredient, cocaine, was taken out of the formula and Coca-Cola's ideology for the twentieth century was shaped, it became advertised for pleasure, not as a remedy. While most other advertisers were exploiting the fear of appearing a misfit unless their particular product were used, Coca-Cola did not play on consumer anxieties but instead stressed delicious refreshment for everybody. Coca-Cola was becoming emblematic of the United States attempt to package pleasure.

Some of the country's best artists were hired to make Coca-Cola commercials, including N. C. Wyeth, McClelland Barclay, Fred Mizen, Haddon Sundblom, Hayden Hayden, and Norman Rockwell. In a stressful world, Coca-Cola became "The Pause That Refreshes." As the United States was becoming increasingly industrialized, Rockwell painted ads with freckle-faced boys at the old fishing hole, complete with dog and Coca-Cola bottle. This clever appeal to a nostalgic time of peace back on the farm has continued to produce some of Coca-Cola's most famous advertising, among them the "Homecoming" commercial from 1974.

Within the company, there was a taboo on direct advertising toward children under twelve. But as children became a more important consumer group, they were integrated into Coke commercials. In 1931, Haddon Sundblom created the classic Coca-Cola Santa Claus. While Coca-Cola has influenced the world in many subtle ways, these commercials have directly shaped the way Americans (and some Norwegians) think about Santa.

These earlier commercials have become part of a cultural heritage. In 1934, the advertising department was ordered to "play up the soda fountain as an institution, a gathering place,"[18] and it did so successfully, to the point where the soda fountain has become a warm memory for many Americans. When veteran editor William Allen White was featured in *Life* magazine on his seventieth birthday in 1938, he insisted on having his picture taken sipping a Coke at a soda fountain in Emporia, Kansas.[19] Just afterward, he wrote the often quoted line "Coca-Cola is . . . a sublimated essence of all America stands for, a decent thing honestly made, universally distributed, conscientiously improved with the years."[20] President Woodruff of Coca-Cola added, "Coca-Cola is the essence of capitalism."[21] Not only was Coca-Cola an American icon; it was the most American thing about America.

In 1929, the company wrote:

Few Americans realize that Coca-Cola is now found within the bull fight arenas of sunny Spain and Mexico, at the Olympic Games Stadium below the dykes of Holland, atop the Eiffel Tower above "Gay Paree," on the holy pagoda in distant Burma, and beside the Coliseum of historic Rome. For many years Coca-Cola has been a national institution of the United States with widespread popularity throughout Canada and Cuba. But during the past three years it has extended beyond national borders and its sales are now international in scope. At present Coca-Cola is sold in seventy-eight countries.[22]

While the global export was still small scale, Coca-Cola missionaries had installed bottlers throughout the world. A journalist asks in 1932, "BY WHAT MAGIC does Coca-Cola make its universal appeal?"[23] At the fiftieth anniversary in Atlanta, in 1936, Harrison Jones delivered an apocalyptic speech titled "Tomorrow":

> There will be trials and tribulations. Men will be sorely vexed and their souls will be tried. . . . There may be war. We can stand that. There may be revolutions. We will survive. Taxes may bear down to the breaking point. We can take it. The four horsemen of the Apocalypse may charge over the earth and back again—and Coca-Cola will remain.[24]

The motto, as Jones concluded, was that Coca-Cola is not yesterday; Coca-Cola is tomorrow, and that might be part of the answer to that question about Coca-Cola's magic. Coca-Cola represents the modern, even when packaged as tradition.

When the United States entered World War II, Coca-Cola had reached a powerful position as a symbol of United States. In 1942, an ad for the United States Rubber Company asserted that among "the homely fragments of daily life" American soldiers were fighting for were "the bottles of Coke they'll soon be sipping in the corner drug store."[25] But there was no need to win the war in order to sip a Coke. Woodruff thought Coca-Cola could help the soldiers win the war. He therefore said, in a tremendous marketing maneuver, "We will see that every man in uniform gets a bottle of Coca-Cola for five cents, wherever he is and whatever it costs our company."[26]

One officer stressed "the great part Coca-Cola plays in the building and the maintenance of morale among military personnel," and he classified Coca-Cola as "one of the essential morale-building products for the boys in the Service."[27] Colonel Robert L. Scott wrote in his best-seller, *God Is My Co-Pilot,* that his motivation to "shoot down my first Jap" stemmed from thoughts of "America, Democracy, Coca-Colas."[28] A Kansas editor wrote that the sugar shortage really brought home the seriousness of the war. The general public's supply of Coca-Cola was severely rationed in the United States. This caused a problem, since a psychological addiction had been building up among Americans. George Brennan, a corporal, wrote that his wartime experience had given him a new appreciation for Coca-Cola: "You have to experience the scarcity of Coca-Cola or suffer its absence to acquire a full appreciation of what it means to us as Americans."[29] Pendergrast argues that Coca-Cola developed a psychological significance akin to an icon or rare religious relic.[30]

During the war, 248 Coca-Cola employees served the American soldiers ten billion servings of Coke. Sixty-four bottling plants were built overseas, largely at the U.S. government's expense, to make Coca-Cola more easily available to the soldiers.[31] Coca-Cola was also capable of exploiting the war in its home front commercials. One showed United States sailors at a bar with the caption "Wherever a

United States battleship may be, the American Way of life goes along. . . . So, naturally, Coca-Cola is there, too." Abroad, advertising agents continually emphasized the drink's status as an American icon. "Yes, around the Globe, Coca-Cola stands for the pause that refreshes—it has become a symbol of our way of living."[32]

The GIs were heroes, and in *The Americanization of Germany, 1945–49,* Ralph Willett writes about these American soldiers in the American occupation zone with endless supplies of chocolate bars, chewing gum, cigarettes, and Coca-Colas in the midst of a bombed-out world. Willett claims, "In Europe, . . . Coca-Cola has come to symbolize America and American culture: indeed the identification was so strong by 1948 that when non-Americans thought of democracy, it was claimed they instantly called to mind Coca-Cola."[33]

Willett argues that as a symbolic artifact, Coca-Cola remains powerfully resonant, "implying a culture in which certain values and attitudes predominate and in which there is a clear conception of the ideal society." In his analysis of the Americanization of Germany, he sees Coca-Cola in the forefront of the cultural "occupation" and the principal commercial symbol of a thoroughly propagandized American way of life.

The filmmaker Wim Wenders saw Germans living in a spiritual and cultural vacuum which needed to be filled. In his films, this process has been explored as the colonization of the German consciousness, and Germans were receptive to this process particularly because of their difficulties with their own past. "One way of forgetting it," he claimed, "was to accept the American imperialism."[34]

During World War II, the United States had a clean image, and Coca-Cola would use the slogan "Universal Symbol of the American Way of Life" (1943). At the 1948 international Coca-Cola conference in Atlantic City, Coca-Cola's advertising slogans revealed a Cold War ideology: "Coca-Cola helps show the world the friendliness of American Ways," "As American as Independence Day," and "When you have a Coke, listen, listen to the Voice of America." At the same convention, another placard read, "When we think of the communists, we think of the Iron Curtain. . . . But when they think of democracy, they think of Coca-Cola."[35] The world was open for Coca-Cola, and Coca-Cola representatives travelled around the world and established contact with potential bottlers, who all became "linked by a common faith in Coca-Cola, their belief in the honesty of the product and its value to mankind."[36]

Richard F. Kuisel[37] argues that the United States government saw Coca-Cola as the foremost propagandizer for the American way of life, while James Farley, Coca-Cola's traveling diplomat, claimed that the soft drink was effective in influencing favorable attitudes toward America and would eventually embrace all nations in a brotherhood of peace and progress.[38] When *Time* magazine featured Coca-Cola (15 May 1950), they wanted a picture of Woodruff on the cover. He refused, and *Time* instead commissioned a painting in which Coca-Cola feeds a thirsty globe.

As Coca-Cola started to expand in the global market, the company got the first warnings that its strong attachment to the United States was a double-edged sword. The Cold War, the Chinese revolution, and the increasing fear of Americanization in certain European countries forced Coca-Cola to rethink its strategy. When a conflict over Coca-Cola occurred in France in 1949–1950, the French National Assembly voted to ban the production of Coca-Cola in France, and the U.S. government got involved in order to strengthen the position of Coca-Cola in Europe. Both the U.S. government and *Le Monde* knew what was at stake. An editorial in *Le Monde* (23 November 1949) stated:

> Conquerors who have tried to assimilate other peoples have generally attacked their languages, their schools, and their religions. They were mistaken. The most vulnerable point is the national beverage. Wine is the most ancient feature of France. It precedes religion and language; it has survived all kinds of regimes. It has unified the nation.

The debate, on the surface, dealt with the ingredients of Coca-Cola, which caused Americans to remark that Coca-Cola was healthy enough for the American soldiers liberating France from the Nazis. However, the issue obviously struck deeper chords and symbolized a strong French desire for cultural independence. This made Alexander Makinsky comment that "the best barometer of the relationship of the United States and any country is the way Coca-Cola is treated."[39]

While as an American symbol Coca-Cola retained a magical power throughout the 1950s, the turmoils of the 1960s made it more difficult for Coca-Cola to play on its United States origin. As Thomas Oliver argues:

> Coke had grown up with twentieth-century America, where rites of passage are marked by moving from sipping Coke as a soda pop to mixing it with rum as an adult's elixir. And that famous Coca-Cola logo appears on signs and billboards in virtually every other country as well, linking America to the rest of the world and looming as large as a symbol of the United States as the Statue of Liberty. Coke is so strongly identified with the United States that when countries fall out with us politically, Coke's exile sometimes closely follows the expulsion of our ambassador. Antiwestern insurgents often identify Coca-Cola as the most visible example of capitalism in their countries and have blown up or taken over more than one Coca-Cola bottling plant in retaliation for some alleged grievance.[40]

As the world grew more global and also more troubled in the early 1970s, it became more treacherous for Coca-Cola to exploit its United States origin commercially. It made no sense to simply claim that "things go better with Coca-Cola," while the Vietnam War, international terrorism, and increasing racial tension were changing the human landscape.

In retrospect, a very important commercial was made in 1971, the so-called Hilltop commercial. Over two hundred people from thirty different nations, dressed in national costumes, stood together on a hilltop in Italy singing "I'd like to teach the world to sing." This was the first global Coca-Cola commercial, broadcast in several countries, and it is the most well-known Coke commercial (among those old enough to remember it).[41] It was a clean, wholesome, and appealing commercial in troubled times.

"I'd Like to Buy the World a Coke"

I'd like to buy the world a home
and furnish it with love
Grow apple trees and honeybees
and snow white turtle doves.
I'd like to teach the world to sing
in perfect harmony
I'd like to buy the world a Coke
and keep it company
[Refrain]
That's the real thing
What the world wants today
It's the real thing
Coke is what the world wants today
Coca-Cola—it's the real thing

(Lyrics and music by Backer,
Davis, Cook, and Greenaway)

The vision was a world without frontiers. Not for six lines was Coca-Cola mentioned. The song reached the hit parade, and the royalties were donated to UNICEF. This was a major groundbreaking commercial because it established Coca-Cola's universal appeal and charisma.

This commercial also clearly marked an ideological shift in the company. Seven years earlier, Coca-Cola had been threatened by CORE (Congress of Racial Equality) with a boycott if it didn't start to integrate black people into its commercials. This global message about peace and a more harmonious tomorrow has become increasingly visible over the past twenty years. Gone is the time when similar ads were made with only whites for a white audience and only blacks for a black audience. The text in a later commercial, "General Assembly," is very telling about the "One World—One Coke" theme. The commercial is run with singing children from different parts of the world.

"General Assembly"

I am the future of the world
I am the hope of my nation
I am tomorrow's people.
I am the new inspiration
and we've got a song to sing to you
We've got a message to bring to you
Please let there be—
for you and for me—a tomorrow, tomorrow.
If we all can agree

there'll be sweet harmony tomorrow, tomorrow
and we all will be there,
Coca-Cola to share—feelings so real and so true.
Coca-Cola to share
feelings so real and so true
Promise us tomorrow
and we'll build a better world for you.
Build a better world for you.

(Lyrics by Terry Boyle and Ginny Redington)

Coca-Cola wants to market itself not only as a global drink with universal appeal but also as the one thing we all have in common. While ethnic, racial, and economic conflicts may dominate in the world, Coca-Cola offers a unifying message of a more harmonious tomorrow. Pendergrast argues that Coca-Cola has achieved the status of a "substitute modern religion which promotes a particular, satisfying, all inclusive world view espousing perennial values such as love, peace and universal brotherhood."[42]

This message sounds rather silly coming from the producer of a soda pop. But unless Coca-Cola could connect itself to a global movement working toward the same goal, it risked the danger of falling flat. Fortunately, it did not have to search far for such a movement. As part of its scheme to market itself globally, Coca-Cola had been a major sponsor of the Olympic Games since 1928. It could now exploit the ideological dimension of this connection, since the Olympic movement shared the same vague humanitarian vision. In the *Olympic Charter '87*, the aims of the Olympic movement are described as follows:

- to promote the development of those physical and moral qualities which are the basis of sport,
- to educate young people through sport in a spirit of better understanding between each other and of friendship, thereby helping to build a better and more peaceful world,
- to spread the Olympic principles throughout the world, thereby creating international goodwill,
- to bring together the athletes of the world in the great four-yearly sport festival, the Olympic Games.

The Coca-Cola executives who made the first sponsorship contract with the Olympic Games in 1928 were probably unaware of the great ideological potential in this deal. As the Olympic movement has become more commercialized under Juan Samaranch, Coca-Cola has exploited this connection to the fullest.[43]

While the original sponsorship was part of a global marketing strategy, Coca-Cola itself wasn't yet really "it"—the company then marketed only a "delicious" and "refreshing" drink. The ideological shift which took place with the Hilltop commercial in 1971 created a situation in which Coca-Cola could combine the global marketing of a product with the global marketing of an image and a message ("we got a message to bring to you"). This image has a resemblance to the humanistic religion expressed by Pierre Coubertin, the founding father of the modern Olympics. Coubertin also wanted to unite people around something in which they could believe. The Olympic Charter talks about "the sacred Olympic fire which shall not be extinguished until the close of the Olympic Games", and most religious rituals also have their sacred drink.[44] To become recognized as the major sponsor of the Olympic Games and eventually as the Olympic drink was a major goal for the Coca-Cola Co., be it sacred or not.

Global Marketing

While Pepsi focused on beating Coca-Cola in the United States, Coca-Cola focused on the global market by searching for the most effective way to sell its products throughout the world.[45] A good example of this was the way it gave away the American Super Bowl to Pepsi in 1992 and instead focused on an increased marketing campaign during the Olympic Games. This decision was the result of its global marketing strategy.[46] The clearest result of such marketing occurred 24 January 1992. Melissa Turner wrote in the *Atlanta Constitution* the same day:

> The first worldwide telecast of an advertising message flashed on Cable News Network (CNN). Naturally it was a pitch for Coca-Cola, the best known brand on the planet. The same commercial was telecast simultaneously in about 130 different countries, including such exotic locales as North Korea and Mongolia, where television viewers were seeing a Coke commercial for the first time.

Coca-Cola had aired television commercials around the world for decades, and in recent years it had aired global spots using the same visuals but dubbed into local languages. Other big companies have also run ads in different countries, but the ads have never run simultaneously. Peter Sealy, Coca-Cola's senior vice president and director of global marketing, said about this occasion, "We have never created before in our history an ad designed explicitly to air in every country of the world."[47] The spot, titled "Hellos," marked the formal launching of Coca-Cola's 1992 worldwide Olympic advertising campaign. It was filmed in Paris, Corsica, Thailand, and Morocco, and the lyrics to the music incorporated twelve different languages.

At the time, this kind of global marketing was only in an experimental stage. But it was the result of the global approach which literally sees the world as one marketplace. Imagine how much Coca-Cola could save on marketing, while at the same time expanding its market, if simultaneous global marketing became a success.

During the 1992 Olympic Games, Coca-Cola featured Coke commercials in the United States from other countries. The ads, with the slogan "Shared around the World," were chosen for their universal themes: a little boy in Japan tasting his first Coca-Cola, a Brazilian schoolboy daydreaming about his pretty chemistry teacher. Ferrari, Coca-Cola's senior marketing vice president, claimed that viewers "watch the Olympic games with an openness about internationalism and brotherhood et cetera" and that they will be intrigued to realize that "we're selling this unique American thing all over the world." He further claimed that "participating in the Olympic games gives us the look of a leader. . . . An important part of our imagery and status is to maintain that leadership." The Olympic Games provide Coca-Cola with a unique ability to combine the global marketing of a product with the global marketing of an image. Ferrari said, "We could not not be there." Coca-Cola's goal was simply "that 100 percent of the consumers walk away knowing Coca-Cola is a sponsor."[48] Coca-Cola went into both Albertville and Barcelona with the order "Paint it red!"

Global or American?

The problem with global marketing is that Coca-Cola is such a fundamental symbol of the United States. If that is not the case within the modern United States any longer, it is still the case abroad. This was confirmed on 23 November 1992 when three hundred French farmers occupied a Coca-Cola plant in Grigny outside Paris to protest a possible trade agreement between the European Community and the United States. The plant had nothing to do with the controversy, except that it was a symbol of the United States. About the same time, the labor union in Bolivia initiated an international boycott of Coca-Cola as a protest against U.S. customs' confiscation of a shipment of Coca-tea. From a marketing point of view, therefore, Coca-Cola wants to move away from its tight association with the United States. This was clear in one of its 1992 commercials, "Coke—The Soft Drink of Europe," which ends, "One Europe—One Coke."[49]

Europe is an important market for Coca-Cola. Its earnings are already three times higher in Europe than in the United States. But, more important, the potential for increasing the profit is much higher in Europe, since Europeans drink much less Coke per capita than the Americans. With the breakdown of communism in Eastern Europe, a whole new market has opened up.[50] It is in this context that Lillehammer became particularly interesting. Coca-Cola claimed it was doing Lillehammer a favor by using the Lillehammer name on its Coke cans in 170 countries. But this argument was reversing the issue. The Lillehammer games were important to Coca-Cola as a part of its global strategy. It never considered not becoming a major sponsor. Rather, the company could not afford "not to be there."

Coca-Cola could create a few alternative, locally adapted signs which are less offensive to Norwegians, however unrecognizable to foreigners, in order to create local goodwill.[51] But Coca-Cola does not sponsor the Olympic Games to get local acceptance. Neither does it base its global marketing on television coverage of the Olympics. The company uses the five Olympic rings on its product line and in its own Olympic commercials worldwide. Since the Olympic symbol is one of the few symbols recognizable the world over, the rings become an important part of Coca-Cola's global marketing strategy.

The distinction between globalization and Americanization is a difficult one. The question is not whether Coca-Cola is an American or an international company. In the beginning of the 1990s, Coca-Cola was already earning most of its profits in Japan and Europe, and the headquarters in Atlanta is run by a very international group of people. Former CEO Roberto Goizueta was from Cuba. The company then rehired the Mexican Sergio Zyman, responsible for New Coke, as marketing director. Argentinean Brian Dyson and Moroccan Sam Ayoub also had leading positions during the 1980s.

Thomas Oliver has argued that when Coca-Cola introduced the New Coke in 1985, it was due to a global leadership out of touch with the American people.[52] It claimed it had found a better taste, and it probably had. But the American people did not want a better taste. The consumer revolt that followed, demanding the old Coke back, is strong evidence of the solid position Coca-Cola had acquired as part of the American tradition. While there may be other reasons which could explain the New Coke marketing failure, the presence of the global leadership might help to explain the increasingly global focus within the company.

When Lillehammer signed the sponsor contract with Coca-Cola in Albertville in 1992, the IOC president at the time, Juan Samaranch, said that without the support from Coca-Cola, the Olympic Games would not have reached its current position. Gerhard Heiberg, the president of LOOC in Lillehammer, was also grateful for the confidence Coca-Cola showed Lillehammer by sponsoring the Olympics. He added that LOOC would benefit from Coca-Cola's competence and experience.[53] When Atlanta won the bid to host the summer games in 1996, Lillehammer cheered in part because it knew that the Lillehammer–Atlanta package meant more profitable deals with sponsors than would a potential Lillehammer–Athens package.

The main advertisement dominating Lillehammer and its surrounding region of Gudbrandsdalen was the Coca-Cola logo and the Olympic rings with the text "Sammen for seier" (Together for victory) (see figure 7.1). Victory for whom? We know that Coca-Cola earned a profit in 1994 higher than the entire cost of the Olympics Games of 1994. Atlanta hosted the summer games in 1996. The late Goizueta was known as the most powerful man in Atlanta. Lillehammer and Atlanta were Olympics twins in the same way as Albertville and Barcelona. When Atlanta received the 1996 games, defeating Athens's bid, Melina Mercouri stated that Coca-Cola defeated the Parthenon. Coca-Cola responded with a global ad which replaced one of the Parthenon's columns with a Coca-Cola bottle. Its text read, "Some things are better classic," to honor Coca-Cola Classic.

FIGURE 7.1.
Coca-Cola's dominating advertisement during the Lillehammer Olympic Games in 1994.
Photo by Steinar Bryn. Used with permission.

Coca-Cola claims that it had little or nothing to do with Atlanta's successful bid and that Atlanta won because it had a better-organized city and was a more reliable host. It even ran a full-page ad in fifteen newspapers in Greece where it "clarified absolutely that it played no role whatsoever in the decision concerning which city would host the Olympics Games of 1996." The director of Coca-Cola, Greece, Anthony Papadatos, said the company donated $90,000 to the Greek campaign to host the Olympics and splashed the slogan "Greece can do it" on soft drink cans, in magazine ads, and on promotional materials.

Apart from the fact that $90,000 is just a token sum for Coca-Cola, there was no need to play any role in the decision-making process. Atlanta was seen as a much safer bet than Athens as an Olympic host city by the IOC members, since it was the hometown of Coca-Cola. Coca-Cola guaranteed, by its mere presence and profit-making ability, that Atlanta would host a successful centennial for the Olympic Games with Coca-Cola as the major sponsor.

Atlanta is also the hometown of CNN, then owned by Ted Turner. Ted Turner initiated the Goodwill Games in 1980 when the United States boycotted the Moscow Olympics. CNN was already widely recognized as one of the most influential interpreters of world events. The coming together of the Olympics Games, Coca-Cola, and CNN in Atlanta in 1996, the unification of three major globalizing forces, made Atlanta the focus of attention for students of globalization processes.

The Olympic movement claims to be a global movement, but when the European press wrote about the "Coca-Cola Olympics" in Albertville, the critique was directed toward the commercialization of the games and the visual pollution caused by companies such as Coca-Cola. In France, as in the rest of Europe, Coca-Cola is still an American symbol. To speak of the "Coca-Cola Games" is therefore an accusation against the Olympic Games of going American.

Coca-Cola will, of course, argue that this is not the American way. Their message is an emotional one: family, friends, and good times. They see themselves as representing the good things in life and that there is a thirst out there among everyone to have a good time. But we can always discuss whether this is an American or a global rhetoric.

When the Berlin wall fell in 1989, Coca-Cola greeted the East Germans with free Coca-Cola. It knew very well that the drink symbolized Mythic America. The company's breakthrough in Europe was directly related to the wartime effort by the United States Army and Coca-Cola's solid position as an important symbol of the American way of life. Coca-Cola's breakthrough in Eastern Europe forty-five years later is related to this solid position as the symbol of the American way as well.

The story of Coca-Cola illustrates its need to move away from its American origins and to think globally when necessary, but it also describes the company's ability to fully exploit its American origin when that approach is advantageous. The recent success by Coca-Cola in Eastern Europe demonstrates that Mythic America is very much alive. Coca-Cola has a unique ability to speak both an American and a global language. This is a great asset to the company, and its ability to know exactly when to emphasize the American and when to emphasize the global language is the secret to Coca-Cola's commercial success.[54]

Notes

1. See Roland Robertson, *Globalization: Social Theory and Global Culture* (London: Sage, 1992).

2. Mike Featherstone, ed., *Global Culture: Nationalism, Globalization, and Modernity* (London: Sage, 1990).

3. Mark Pendergrast, *For God, Country, and Coca-Cola: The Definitive History of the Great American Soft Drink and the Company That Makes It* (New York: Basic Books, 1993), 406.

4. In "World Youth," *Richmond Times-Dispatch*, 19 August 1990.

5. From an internal memo mailed to me, sender unknown.

6. In my association test among Norwegian students, in which they were asked to write down associations to America, almost everybody noted "Coca-Cola."

7. The presence of Coca-Cola created a debate in Lillehammer, a debate in which I admittedly played a central role. See Steinar Bryn, "The Americanization of the Global World: A Case Study of Norway," in *Networks of Americanization: Aspects of the American Influence in Sweden,* ed. Rolf Lundén and Erik Åsard (Stockholm: Actas Universitatis Upsaliensis, 1992). I am thereby directly affecting the data of my research, and I am fully aware of the limitations such an involvement puts on my comments. I am caught, however, between being a scholar and an active citizen in a community. I must be an active participant in civic dialogue while trying at the same time to observe certain processes in this community from an academic point of view without directly interfering with the same processes.

8. *Stern* (Hamburg), 20 February 1992.

9. But as the Olympic Games have become commercialized, this debate has intensified in the wake of the Olympic Games, a global mega-event. The games in Los Angeles in 1984 were the first successful venture into cooperation among the business community, the organizing committee, and international sponsors. It proved the Olympic Games could be a profitable event for the host city and the IOC. Juan Samaranch, the former president of the IOC, further exploited this. V. Simson and A. Jennings write in their highly critical book *Lord of the Rings: Power, Money and Drugs in the Modern Olympics* (London: Simon & Schuster, 1992):

> The five linked rings are now one of the world's more valuable commodities—in monetary terms. Just a quarter of a century ago they had a much rarer value. They could not be bought. IOC president Avery Brundage dispatched constant circulars from Lausanne denying competitors and federations the right to carry commercial logos on their clothing. He even set up a Commission for the Protection of the Olympic Emblems to prevent the rings being exploited by advertisers. It has been replaced under Samaranch by the Commission for New Sources of Financing, which is charged with selling off the emblem for the best price the market will bear. (128)

10. During a lecture at Emory University, Atlanta, I showed slides of Coke commercials in the Lillehammer region, and the students laughingly commented that those Coke commercials seemed museum-like.

11. For example, neon and plastic signs are forbidden on Main Street of Lillehammer.

12. These sponsor contracts are either tied to particular projects, such as "the Beautification of Gjøvik," or a general economic support to pay for commercial use. Coca-Cola will then be allowed to put up pop machines, garbage cans, and commercial signs carrying its logo and the Olympic rings.

13. Pendergrast, *For God, Country, and Coca-Cola,* 387.

14. The hospital is the only tall building in Lillehammer. Commercial exposure on the wall facing the town during the Olympic Games would be a coup for any business.

15. Fiora Steinbach Palazzini, *Coca Cola Superstar* (New York: Barron's, 1988), 112–13.

16. Pendergrast, *For God, Country, and Coca-Cola,* 91–93.

17. Pendergrast, *For God, Country, and Coca-Cola,* 100.

18. Pendergrast, *For God, Country, and Coca-Cola,* 178.

19. William Allen White, featured in *Life* magazine, 28 February 1938, pp. 9–13.

20. Thomas Oliver, *The Real Coke: The Real Story* (New York: Penguin, 1986), 4.

21. Pendergrast, *For God, Country, and Coca-Cola,* 4.

22. Pendergrast, *For God, Country, and Coca-Cola,* 173.

23. Pendergrast, *For God, Country, and Coca-Cola,* 176.

24. Pendergrast, *For God, Country, and Coca-Cola,* 178.

25. Pendergrast, *For God, Country, and Coca-Cola,* 199.

26. Coca-Cola Co., *An Illustrated Profile* (Atlanta: 1974), 77.

27. Pendergrast, *For God, Country, and Coca-Cola,* 200.

28. Pendergrast, *For God, Country, and Coca-Cola,* 211.

29. Pendergrast, *For God, Country, and Coca-Cola,* 211.

30. Excerpts from letters home in Pendergrast, *For God, Country, and Coca-Cola* (210–12), create clear associations to a sacred drink.

31. These bottling plants in France, Italy, Germany, and Australia were given away to Europeans to jump start the Coke production in Europe after World War II.

32. Pendergrast, *For God, Country, and Coca-Cola,* 207.

33. Ralph Willett, *The Americanization of Germany, 1945–49* (New York: Routledge, 1989), 99.

34. Willett, *The Americanization of Germany,* 4–5.

35. E. J. Kahn Jr., *The Big Drink: The Story of Coca-Cola* (New York: Random House, 1960), 164. This strong anticommunist stand within the Coca-Cola Company gave PepsiCo a great advantage in Eastern Europe during the 1960s.

36. Quoted in Pendergrast, *For God, Country, and Coca-Cola,* 238, from *CC Overseas* (December 1952): 1.

37. See Richard F. Kuisel, "Coca-Cola and the Cold War: The French Face Americanization," *French Historical Studies* 1 (1991): 95–116; and Richard F. Kuisel, *Seducing the French: The Dilemma of Americanization* (Berkeley: University of California Press, 1993).

38. An interesting foresight of the Hilltop commercial in 1971 which featured peace and the universal brother- and sisterhood theme.

39. Kahn, *The Big Drink,* 65.

40. Oliver, *The Real Coke,* 2.

41. The commercial was so successful that Coca-Cola twenty years later decided to remake the commercial. It became a reunion commercial on the same hilltop, and the singers brought their children.

42. Pendergrast, *For God, Country, and Coca-Cola,* 400.

43. During the 1988 Olympics, Coca-Cola paid for the Coca-Cola World Chorus, a hundred-voice choir selected from participating countries. For the opening ceremonies in Calgary and Seoul, the chorus debuted the official song of the event, "Can't You Feel It"? The lyrics didn't mention Coca-Cola, but the resemblance to "Can't beat the feeling" is obvious to the ear. To Coca-Cola, a commercialized Olympic Games was a hot marketing opportunity, and it was determined to leverage Olympic symbols to promote sales. In Lillehammer, Coca-Cola used the Coke trademark and the Olympic rings on murals, billboards, and its products. It was estimated that Coca-Cola spent $100 million on the Lillehammer Olympics alone.

44. I. Eidsvåg, "Olympsike leker—før og nå," *På Norske Vinger* 8 (1990): 34–39.

45. This is only partly true. Pepsi had a solid position in Russia and Eastern Europe, particularly due to Richard Nixon, who after his 1962 defeat for the California governorship joined Pepsi's law firm at a comfortable $250,000 yearly salary. Nixon circled the globe six times between 1962 and 1968 as Pepsi's ambassador abroad. While opening doors for Pepsi, this also gave Nixon international experience and helps explain why, when Coca-Cola in 1972 finally overcame its communist phobia and was willing to enter Russia, Pepsi had already struck a deal with the Kosygin regime.

46. The company's chief marketing officer Ira C. Herbert defines global marketing as a basic marketing strategy applied worldwide and claims that global marketing is the most effective way to penetrate the world. See "How Coke Markets to the World: An Interview with Marketing Executive Ira C. Herbert," *Journal of Business Strategy* (September–October 1988): 4–7.

47. Quoted in the *Atlanta Constitution,* 24 January 1992.

48. *USA Today,* 25 July 1992.

49. This commercial, which ended with the Coke symbol and the European flag, was wisely enough not shown in Norway, due to the Norwegian resistance to joining the European Community.

50. Ted Gest, "Global Goliath: Coke Conquers the World," *US News & World Report,* 13 August 1990; and John Marcom, "Cola Attack," *Forbes,* 26 November 1990. As of today, Coca-Cola is the second largest investor in Poland after Fiat. In East Germany, it has invested $450 million. Ringnes, the main bottler of Coca-Cola in Norway, has invested millions in Eastern Europe in a coventure with Coca-Cola. I assume it is a coincidence that the administrative leader of LOOC, Henrik Andenæs, was recruited from Ringnes.

51. In Lillehammer, Coca-Cola put up several signs carved out of wood. One sign is made with a chain saw and includes the Coca-Cola logo and a Norwegian Viking.

52. Oliver, *The Real Coke.*

53. From an internal memo mailed to me, sender unknown.

54. It has struck me that maybe Coca-Cola is right—maybe it is the real thing. Coca-Cola is the one representing warmth, friends, family. Coca-Cola wants to furnish our hospital with what it needs. Coca-Cola supports the "beautification" of Gjøvik. Coca-Cola keeps the local sports team alive. In our troubled world, Coca-Cola has become "it," that which helps us to keep going when everybody else fails, that which makes things happen.

8

The Impact of the American Myth in Postwar Italian Literature

Modernization, Postmodernity, or Homologation?

Giulia Guarnieri

UMBERTO ECO'S ESSAY "Travels in Hyperreality" focuses on the postmodern approach to the American myth stressing the problematic of the representation of reality which has been a crucial issue for many Italian writers, from the neo-realists to contemporary Italian writers such as Italo Calvino and Eco himself:

> Holography could only prosper in America, a country obsessed with realism, where, if reconstruction is to be credible, it must be absolutely iconic, a "perfect likeness," a "real" copy of the reality being represented . . . to speak of things that one wants to connote as real, these things must seem real. The "completely real" becomes identified with the "complete fake." Absolute reality is offered as real presence. . . . We can identify it through two typical slogans that pervade American advertisement. The first, widely used by Coca-Cola but also frequent as a hyperbolic formula in everyday speech, is "the real thing."[1]

Writers like Calvino and Eco define postmodernism as playing with discontinuous and ironic literary forms which uphold a fragmented, multiple-sided image of objectivity and truth. Postmodern narratives are centered on the idea that reality is subjective and points to many directions or signifiers, no universal or stable truths are being emphasized. Postmodernism affected contemporary literature in manifesting experimentation with innovative literary forms that accompanied a radical mutation of postwar Italian society, exhibiting an inclination toward modernization.[2] Taking America as an emblem of the postmodern opposition of truth and fakeness, vacuity and values, superficiality and culture, examining its museums, art galleries, and amusement parks, Eco perceives America as a contradictory and incoherent container of reality. The Italian contemporary philosopher Gianni Vattimo, for his part, has strived to underline the negative notion of our current era which he labels the end of modernity. The lack of a center and direction due to the endless possibilities offered by the modern world have caused Italian writers to develop an ambivalent attitude toward modernization, experiencing a sense of disorientation or attraction. This chapter does not attempt to provide a complete analysis of the American myth in Italian literature; it endeavors, rather, to represent a postmodern reading of the American myth and show its impact on Italian writers in the twentieth century.

After World War II, Italy, along with other European countries, became economically dependent on America; Italy underwent its so-called Americanization. The negative connotation assigned to this term dates back to the Fascist period. As documented in Emilio Gentile's essay "Impending Modernity: Fascism and the Ambivalent Image of the United States," the view of America as both fascinating and threatening was very present during the twenty years of the Fascist regime since America also became in the Fascist period a metaphor of modernity. At the same time, however, the opposition of the Fascist regime to America can be summed up by its fear of modernity. America was berated for its lack of cultural traditions and as "a society of machines and dehumanizing technology,"[3] and anti-Americanism became a metaphor for antimaterialism, antitechnology, and antimodernism. This aspect can also be detected in the writing of neorealist authors even though highly problematized. A similar approach was shared by neorealist writers such as Elio Vittorini and Cesare Pavese, who, on one hand, were fascinated by this economic and social phenomenon but, on the other hand, experienced this as illusory and dangerous to believe, as the protagonists of their novels happen to discover. Yet America was also a symbol of chance, possible worlds, and opportunities, a promised land since, during the 1950s, Italy and Europe underwent a massive invasion of American goods such as jeans, Coca-Cola, automobiles, records, and television. This peaceful invasion was seen partly as the "American Dream" of possible prosperity, the myth of the self-made man, consumerism, and economic growth. America became in those years a model of growth and prosperity for all European countries. The American propaganda set forth with the Marshall Plan used this same principle: "You too can be like us."[4] On the other hand, other neorealist writers began to incorporate in their writings both the fascination and sense of the danger of this corrupted sense of modernity.

The fifties proved to be a turning point for Calvino, who was deeply aware of the transformation of society and felt a need to reach out to the world of possibilities. The economic boom made him realize that the neorealist poetics was inadequate to confront these changing scenarios. He began to detach from neorealist themes in favor of a literature which would have an active role in society. In 1960, Calvino, thanks to a grant awarded to him by the Ford Institute, was able to spend six months in the United States examining and writing about American society. And it is here that we see his attraction to America as a container of possibilities and dreams but also that he perceived them to be vain and illusory. The confrontation with reality and historical change was always perceived by Calvino as something which had a deep impact for writers:

> The true topic of a novel should be a definition of our times, not the story of Naples or Florence, it should reveal an image that describes how we fit in the world . . . the writer should aim toward the becoming of history always starting from the reality of the country that one knows and loves more: historians have taught us that history is always contemporary history, it is active intervention in future history.[5]

Calvino demonstrates an openness to the adaptation to the new, to progress; it shows his reaching out to possibilities. At the same time, he seems reluctant to abandon his cultural and ideological formation when dealing with the new (the American myth) when he says "pur sempre partendo dalla realtà del paese che più ama e conosce" (always starting from the reality that one knows and loves more). It is in his discovery of literature as *ars combinatoria* that Calvino becomes a post-modern writer. He becomes interested in playing with literary forms and structures. The combination of a solid structure and spatiality in Calvino's literature recalls the structure and essence of New York's skyscrapers and bridges. For Calvino, the reality of American buildings is that they were designed to be highly functional, safe, and spectacular, springing up from the skies as reaching unlimited space and time. The windows were said to produce only pale reflections of the lives inside them since they cannot be penetrated with curious gazes from outside. Skyscrapers are also containers of hidden realities and possibilities, and this hypothetical parallel of Calvino's fascination with them seems, therefore, pertinent to the topic of his conceptualization of America. Calvino reveals his attraction to New York City's verticality, which is best identified with skyscrapers:

> The boredom of the trip is paid off by the sensations evoked upon arrival in New York, the most spectacular vision on earth. Little by little one distinguishes the colors, different from the ones we had once imagined, it is a complicated pattern of shapes. . . . Every time I go I find it more beautiful, closer to the ideal city. It is obviously a geometric city, crystalline. . . . New York, a city which is not all America or Europe, but which conveys an extraordinary energy that you immediately feel in your hands like you always lived there.[6]

What captures Calvino's perception of America's immensity is America as a container. He falls in love with its eccentric forms and geometrical shapes. In "Diario americano," this passion for structure is evident in the description of cars: "A study of the American soul can be done by looking at the back of cars and the great variety and joy of tail light shapes that seem to express all of American myths. . . . There are all kinds of shapes: missiles, skyscraper's spires, movie star eyes and the more complete catalogue of Freudian symbolism."[7] Calvino goes on to describe every shape of America, starting with the motels, the United Nations building, the IBM firm, museums, and supermarkets. But through his observations in search for meaning, Calvino reflects about America's magnetism and asks himself what lies behind the facade. In his typically ironic descriptions, he reflects about the reality behind the mask and discovers America's essence. Outside the skyscrapers and every shiny container, Calvino perceives the void, the emptiness, the squalor, the danger. In a 1962 essay, "I Beatniks e il 'sistema,'" he attacks the mass production society:

> It is useless to try to identify the barbarians as part of some kind of human category. This time these barbarians are not people but things. They are the objects that we believed we once possessed and that now possess us; they are the productive development which had to accommodate us but to which we became slaves instead, they are the means of communications of our thought that try to prevent us from thinking, they are the abundance of goods which do not convey the comforts of well-being, but instead portray the anxiety of forced consumerism. They are the madness of construction which impose upon us horrendous views of dear places; they are the fullness of our days in which friendships, affections and love wither like plants with no air [and] in which all conversation with others and ourselves perishes.[8]

In commenting on this phenomenon, Calvino sees the dangers of mobilizing the intellect in favor of some sort of cultural consumerism. His accusation against materialism reveals America as a metaphor; he likes America, the container, but finds the inside to be rather problematic. America is never directly addressed in his novels but its presence can be perceived in Calvino's stories written in the 1950s and early 1960s. More than any other works, *Italian Folktales* (1957–1958) and *Marcolvaldo, or The Seasons in the City* (1963) deal with modern urban paradoxes. These works are important because they choose to comment on the society of modernization. The myth is removed far from the "dream" and the ideal. This procedure resembles a similar literary *escamotage* accomplished by other neorealist writers, who describe America as a stage of possibility. The stage is perceived as a tabula rasa in which universal truths are assigned. With "Diario americano," Calvino did not intend to create a postmodern work, although he leveled the ground for the splitting up of the perception of the American myth and the subsequent creation of subjective "American" realities. The impact of America's modernization presented in his novels creates a floating image of America or modernity where universal truth can no longer be fixed reality. Realities become individualized with a sense of loss for metaphysical truth. In *Mythologies*, Roland Barthes specifically refers to the negation of universal myths and comments that our era is undergoing a process of creating a surplus of myths, an unthinkable concept for the neorealists who instead portrayed the American myth as something intangible and abstract.[9]

In his novels, Calvino writes of the meaningless universe, the frantic life, nervousness, consumerism, firms, publicity, the smog of contemporary society. However, he never clearly defines America as the target of his sarcastic criticism. The only time he does expose his favorite American city to some criticism is in *The*

Cosmicomics. The short story "Le figlie della luna" (Daughters of Moon, not present in the English translation) is a perfect example of Calvino's duality in dealing with the American myth. The story recounts a paradoxical capitalist society which tries to control economically (in terms of the production of new goods and elimination of old ones) even one of the most natural and mythological elements in nature: the moon. The story takes place in New York, Calvino's postmodern city par excellence. He criticizes the exasperation of technology and the fast pace at which things are being produced, which does not allow time for meditation and enjoyment:

> Earth had entered that phase in which all automobiles wear out more rapidly than shoe soles, [which] human beings, nearly human, produced bought and sold; the cities covered the continents with a luminous pigmentation. . . . There was also a New York in some ways similar to our familiar New York, but newer, outpouring new products, like a new toothbrush, a New York with its long Manhattan and its skyscrapers all lined up, bright as the nylon's bristles of a new toothbrush. In this world in which every object, attempting to break or getting old, at first stain or dent, was immediately thrown out and substituted with a new and impeccable one. There was only a downside, a shadow to all this: the moon, wandering in the sky naked, gnawed, gray, more and more foreign to the down below world residue, at this point of an incongruous way of being.[10]

Umberto Eco proposes a different analysis of the myth of America than the one described by Calvino. In his essay "Travels in Hyperreality," Eco approaches America with the eyes of a semiotician. He looks for signs which communicate the essence of what America is all about, and he comes out with an iconographic repertory for understanding the American myth and its impact in European culture. Eco defines America with a powerful image; it is seen as the "Fortress of Solitude" in which he claims to read America's social essence (also as a reproduction of reality):

> And yet in America there are many Fortresses of Solitude, with their wax statues, their automata, their collections of inconsequential wonders. You have only to go beyond the Museum of Modern Art and the art galleries, and you enter another universe, the preserve of the average family, the tourist, the politician.[11]

Eco's choice to investigate the reality that lies beyond the "glass-and steel sky-scrapers," museums, and art galleries could not have been more appropriate. Popular art can be perceived as a representation of reality which could be historical, social, sexual, ecological, idealistic, political, economical, and so on. Popular art is the icon of a nation's truth and it is the metaphor of a country's sense of its essence. Eco himself substitutes the word mausoleum with emptiness, fakeness, levity, lack of historization, as he comments:

> The most amazing Fortress of Solitude was erected in Austin, Texas by President Lyndon Johnson, during his own lifetime, as monument, pyramid, personal mausoleum. I'm not referring to the immense imperial-modern-style construction or to the forty-

thousand red containers that hold all the documents of his political life. . . . The Lyndon B. Johnson Library is a true Fortress of Solitude . . . it suggests that there is a constant in the average American imagination and taste, for which the past must be preserved and celebrated in full-scale authentic copy; a philosophy of immortality as duplication. It dominates the relation with the self, with the past, not infrequently with the present, always with History and, even, with the European tradition.[12]

Eco analyzes the paradox that surrounds America in which everything must be a reproduction of a past event, as if to preserve the idea of it, as if to stop the flow of history: "The past must be preserved and celebrated in full-scale authentic copy; a philosophy of immortality as duplication."[13] Art according to Eco becomes a text which can be read according to the individual. The artwork speaks to one's deconstruction of universal truths, as to create one's own hyperreality. For example: If one goes to visit some paintings in a church in Rome, one is not surprised if they are hard to see, without any videotape or recording explaining the painters' lives and the historical context; these paintings represent just what they are: old paintings. Copies of these same paintings can be seen all over the world, and perhaps the copy may even be understood as an improvement over the original. The real breaks the myth of the real, which is why it is feared. In the celebration of the myth of the real, the individual negates the outside reality and creates one of his or her own, a more idealized version of the real. The philosophy behind this, says Eco, is that "[t]hey are not giving you the reproduction so that you will want the original, but rather 'we are giving the reproduction so you won't feel any need for the original.'"[14]

Eco gives many examples of how "the almost real" is achieved in America. He talks about the New Orleans wax museums, the J. Paul Getty museum, Disneyland, and Hearst Castle to explain that this frantic search for the *other than the real* in America is nothing more than a neurotic reaction to the vacuum of memories. The absolute fake is an offspring of the unhappiness of a present without a past. Eco also brings the effect of America's ambiguity, uncertainty, vagueness into literature. In another work entitled *Six Walks in Fictional Woods,* Eco says that in literature there's a tendency to mix fiction and reality and that sometimes it is not easy to tell them apart. This confusion is the result of the modern society in which we live: "However, for all concerning Silvia's story, the ambiguous game between life, dream, past and present, is more similar to the uncertainty that dominates our everyday lives than the one in which Rossella [i.e., Scarlett] O'Hara knew that tomorrow is another day."[15]

Fiction, Eco continues, is more consolatory for readers who do not feel the need to pursue truth. He then gives examples using Gadda and Orson Welles to show how easy it is to mix fiction and reality; the latter in 1940 had announced on the radio an invasion of aliens. He thought that all listeners were able to decipher the ironic statement, but this was not the case—the listeners had not captured the "fictional signs" and projected this reality in the world of possibility. However, Eco realizes that this is not always the case and that postmodern literature has prepared the readers for "metanarrative perversion." This has happened with Sherlock Holmes, Madame Bovary, and Don Quixote, who the readers recognize as fictional characters. It can be argued that the extratextual life of the characters culminates in a cult phenomenon. That is why, Eco continues, *Gone with the Wind* becomes a *cult movie* and *Siddhartha* a *cult book*.

This same process is applicable to the creation of the American myth. According to Eco, narratives as well as reality are easily subjected to becoming misguided truths. The first impression of a reading can give an illusory sensation of the content of what you're trying to read, of its interior. The same danger was also advocated by Calvino and the neorealist writers. Eco attempts in "Travels in Hyperreality" to dissect the essence of the myths of American culture and contrast them with the efforts of European culture to incorporate in its structure the sense of modernity that America represents.

Like Calvino, Eco is fully aware that behind the facade and inside the container one is bound to find the Fortress of Solitude; nevertheless, Eco and Vattimo propose a postmodern reconciliation with the America paradoxes. Calvino never suggested a resolution to the paradoxical sides of the American myth; he leaves the reader with the paradox of the void within the facade. Eco, on the other hand, aims to take the criticism a step further, to construct from the paradox. As he says in his essay "On the Crisis of the Crisis of Reason":

> Let us consider something pleasant, like the crisis of representation. Even assuming that whoever speaks of it has a definition of representation (which is often not the case), if I rightly understand what they're saying—namely that we are unable to construct and exchange images of the world that are certainly apt to convey the form. . . . Those who rediscover the crisis of representation today seem to have charming vague ideas about the continuity of this discussion.[16]

Eco deals with the impact of American culture in a truly postmodern way, while Calvino is still linked to the neorealist frame. In analyzing the European museums, Eco recognizes that there is pragmatic solution to the American sense of modernity. He reflects on the positive properties of amusement in the American theme parks while warning of their symbolic threats:

> These places [Eco is referring to aquatic parks] are enjoyable. If they existed in Italian civilization of bird killers, they would represent praiseworthy didactic occasions; . . . I would say that the first, most immediate level of communication that these Wild Worlds achieve is positive; what disturbs us is the allegorical level superimposed on the literary one, the implied promise of a 1984 already achieved at the animal level. What disturbs us is not an evil plan; there is none. It is the symbolic threat.[17]

This same threat which Eco talks about is the threat of the fake, something with which he tries to come to terms. He states that the ideology that lies behind reproductions of European art can also be a positive preservation of a past, which Europeans take for granted. "It is the ideology of preservation, in the New World, of the treasure that the folly and negligence of the Old World are causing to disappear into the void."[18]

Gianni Vattimo expresses a similar necessity for tolerance for the new, while not concealing its paradoxes. In his books *The End of Modernity* and *The Transparent Society*, he states that in the postmodern era we are still looking for the "center of history" (a similar quest was presented by the deconstructionists). Reality has become so individualized by an immense proliferation of images, cultures, religions, and sexual orientations that the subject undergoes a sense of disorientation. Using Heidegger's and Nietzsche's philosophies, Vattimo shows that this experience of oscillation between different realities, which we are experiencing, is part of the postmodern reality; this new dimension offers us a new way of being. In *Transparent Society*, he asserts that everything in our society becomes an object of communication. This implies that the *facade* becomes the primary form of knowledge in today's world:

> But the fact remains that the very logic of the information "market" requires its continual expansion, and consequently demands that "everything" somehow become an object of communication. This giddy proliferation of communication as more and more subcultures "have their say" is the most obvious effect of the mass media. Together with the end, or at least radical transformation, of European imperialism, it is also the key to our society's shift towards post-modernity.[19]

Eco and Vattimo both look at postmodern society with disenchanted eyes and are able to read through the facade and interpret the ideology which lies behind it. Eco understands and acknowledges America's need to establish reassurance through representation and imitation of a historical past. Representation, as Vattimo has stated, has become a strong necessity for our society; this thought is underlined in *The Transparent Society*, where he engages in defining the most striking characteristic of the postmodern reality: the lack of a unified and universal historical truth. Society, according to Vattimo, is going through a phase of disorientation caused by the multiplicity of individual realities. As he states:

> We ourselves do not have a clear idea of its physiognomy and so have difficulty in seeing oscillation as freedom. Individually and collectively, we still have a deep-seated nostalgia for the reassuring, yet menacing closure of horizons. Nihilistic philosophers such as Nietzsche and Heiddeger (but also pragmatists like Dewey or Wittgenstein), in demonstrating that being does not necessarily coincide with what is stable, fixed and permanent, but has instead to do with the event, with consensus, dialogue and interpretation, are trying to show us how to take the experience of oscillation in the postmodern world as an opportunity of a new way of being (finally, perhaps) human.[20]

In the last sixty years, the impact that the American myth had on Italian intellectuals has significantly changed from a conservative position linked to the classical schemes of European culture to enthusiasm and admiration for the so-called *American way of life*. During the fifties, most of the culture and innovations coming from America were perceived as negative aspects of progress and modernity; nevertheless, for some, this brought not only modernization but also a flattening and standardization of the thought. Intellectuals such as Mario Soldati and Pier Paolo Pasolini regarded this as the sole responsibility of the dehumanization, solitude, and incommunicability of American society.

This never-ending dilemma for Italian writers between a positive and negative image of America even today characterizes the impact that the pacifist invasion of America had on Italian culture. In the course of the years, Italian intellectuals will still show attachment to European schemes and ideas, although opening their horizons to the changing of times. In particular, Calvino, Eco, and Vattimo have become the voices of the enlightened whose role is to indicate and understand all faces of reality, grasping the direction of contemporary history by remaining vigilant and critical. The works of these authors offer a kind of revival of the American myth, by fighting provincialism and showing an authentic enthusiasm for American society and its pragmatism and by expressing an appreciation of the American spirit and its tendency to innovate. Exploring the disposition that modern Italian writers had toward America has revealed the attitude toward modernity and progress.

Eco, Calvino, and Vattimo recognize the sense of fragmentation of one image of modernity where reality becomes realities, truths become signifiers, objects become processes. The myth, as emblem of modernity, is also subjected to weak thought; from a *centripetal* motion, it moves to a *centrifugal* one. The best way to end this investigation into the impact that the American myth has had on Italian contemporary novelists is to leave it with no conclusion, but with a postmodern openness of reinterpretation and critical thinking. America perceived as an icon of modernity or as a threat to humanity will be left for now as a work in progress.

Notes

1. Umberto Eco, *Travels in Hyperreality*, trans. from Italian by William Weaver (New York: Harcourt Brace Jovanovich, 1986), 5–7.

2. According to Mary Klages, the term *modernization* is often used to describe the economic and social development that took place along with the industrialization. On the other hand, *modernity*'s definition is linked to a group of political, philosophical, and cultural ideas which provided the basis for the aesthetic aspect of modernism.

3. Gentile Emilio, "Impending Modernity, Fascist and the Ambivalent Images of the United States," *Journal of Contemporary History* 28, no. 1 (January 1993): 15.

4. David Ellwood, "Expecting Growth," in *Rebuilding Europe* (London: Longman, 1993), 222.

5. Italo Calvino, *Una pietra sopra* (Torino: Einaudi, 1980), 11. I have completed the translations of the Italian quotations belonging to Calvino's works—*Una Pietra Sopra, Di-*

ario americano, and *The Cosmicomics* story "Daughters of Moon"—since at the time when this article was being written, they were not available in English translation.

6. Italo Calvino, *Eremita a Parigi* (Milano: Mondadori, 194), 29. Calvino at this point has already travelled through America for six months and has written his diary, in which he describes New York as his ideal city: "Since I left New York, I can't stop hearing bad things about it . . . but New York is probably the only place on earth where one feels in the center and not peripheral. . . . I prefer its horror to a beauty of privileges, slavery to freedom that is merely for few lucky ones and which do not constitute antithesis." In another part he says, "New York, a city with no roots, is the only place where I feel I may have my roots, and two months of traveling are sufficient, and New York is the only place where I can pretend to reside." Another significant comment: "Of course I travelled through the South and California, but I always felt as a Newyorker: my city is New York."

7. Calvino, *Eremita a Parigi,* 58.

8. Calvino, *Una pietra sopra,* 75.

9. It is significant to emphasize that Pavese and Vittorini had never travelled to America.

10. Calvino, *Le cosmicomiche* (Milano: Garzanti, 1984), 92.

11. Eco, *Travels,* 5–6.

12. Eco, *Travels,* 6.

13. Eco, *Travels,* 6.

14. Eco, *Travels,* 19.

15. Umberto Eco, *Sei passeggiate nei boschi narrativi* (Milano: Bompiani, 1994), 146. I have also translated the passage into English.

16. Eco, *Sei passeggiate,* 126–27.

17. Eco, *Sei passeggiate,* 52.

18. Eco, *Sei passeggiate,* 38.

19. Gianni Vattimo, *The Transparent Society,* trans. from Italian by William Webb (Baltimore: Johns Hopkins University, 1992), 6.

20. Vattimo, *The Transparent Society,* 11.

9

American Missionaries
to "Darkest" Europe

Rodney Stark

B ECAUSE MOST AMERICANS came from Europe and brought their religions with them, it often is assumed that the transmission of religious culture was a one-way process. Although most European intellectuals seem to cling to this view, millions of Americans know better because they have personally contributed funds to export American religious enthusiasm across the Atlantic, and tens of thousands of them have served as missionaries to Europe. Thus, while many Europeans express deep concerns about the "corruption" of language by the spread of American words, or about the cultural "devastation" inherent in McDonald's or Disneyland, nearly all European observers remain oblivious to the profound and rapidly growing significance of American religion for European culture.

For nearly two centuries, European visitors have been struck by the vitality of American religion. Thus, in 1818, the English traveller William Cobbett[1] wrote home to his neighbors in the town of Botley about the density of churches in America, how well supported they were, and the character of the clergy whose "piety, talent, and zeal" were unmatched in Europe. During his travels in the United States during 1830–31, Alexis de Tocqueville[2] had a similar response, noting that "there is not a country in the world where the Christian religion retains a greater influence over the souls of men than in America." At midcentury, the Swiss theologian Philip Schaff[3] observed that attendance at Lutheran churches was far higher in New York than in Berlin.

Meanwhile, as European visitors marvelled at American religiousness, Americans who travelled in Europe were shocked by the lack of religious participation they observed. Thus, Robert Baird,[4] the first major historian of American religion, reported after an eight-year sojourn on the Continent, that nowhere in Europe did church attendance come close to the level taken for granted by Americans. As concerns about the irreligiousness of Europe grew among Americans, Europeans began to worry about the threat of American interference in their religious affairs.

Conrad Dietrich Wyneken, a Lutheran pastor sent from Germany to Indiana in 1838 to serve immigrant parishes, was appalled at the large number of German Lutherans who had defected to the Methodists and Baptists. He sent many letters back to Germany appealing for help, asking that a large number of trained clergy, along with substantial funding, be sent immediately to enable the Lutherans to withstand these "dangerous enemies." For, if the battle were lost in America, soon it would be Germany that would be at the mercy of these diabolical sects: "The flood will soon enough flow across the Atlantic toward our German fatherland. . . . What is to stop them? Just observe the tremendous missionary efforts of the Baptists and Methodists."[5]

However, in the middle of the nineteenth century, when Wyneken expressed these fears, the Baptists and Methodists had their hands full Christianizing the rapidly expanding American frontier. So, it was left to a new American religion to be the first to send Americans to missionize Europe.

Mormons in Europe

In 1837, less than a decade after the world's first six Mormons founded the Church of Christ, soon to be known as the Church of Jesus Christ of Latter-day Saints, they began sending missionaries to Europe. Their first efforts were made in Great Britain and met with quite extraordinary success. It happened this way.

On 4 June 1837, Joseph Smith Jr. approached Heber Kimball in the Mormon Temple in Kirtland, Ohio, and told him that the Lord had revealed to him, "Let my servant Heber go to England and proclaim my gospel and open the door to salvation of that nation."[6] Thus, on 13 June 1837, Kimball and Orson Hyde, both members of the Council of Twelve (the Mormon governing body), along with Joseph Fielding and Willard Richards, left for Great Britain. Pausing in New York for a week to raise funds to pay their passage on the sailing ship *Garrick*, the Mormon missionary party landed in Liverpool after eighteen days at sea. They were immediately struck by the immense class distinctions. Kimball later wrote in his *Journal* (16 June), "[W]ealth and luxury, penuary and want abound. I there met the rich attired in the most costly dresses, and the next moment was saluted with the cries of the poor, without covering sufficient to screne them from the weather; such a distinction I never saw before." As soon as their baggage cleared customs (it took three days), the missionaries moved to Preston, a very rapidly growing mill town, and began public preaching in Vauxhall Chapel. They met with immediate success, and by the end of the year, they had recruited and baptized several hundred followers. The next year all but Fielding returned to America. Then, in January 1840, John Taylor and Wilford Woodruff, both members of the Council of Twelve, were sent to Great Britain. In April, Brigham Young, Heber Kimball, and Orson and Parley Pratt, also members of the council, accompanied by the young George Smith (Joseph's cousin), arrived to help missionize the British. And missionize they did. With half of the Council of Twelve traveling the country and preaching, the ranks of British Mormons swelled rapidly. By the end of 1840, they numbered 3,626; by the end of the decade, there were 30,747 Mormons in Britain.

What makes this total even more remarkable is that from the very start, large numbers of British converts departed for America. In 1840, emigration to the United States totalled 291 British Mormons. The next year 1,346 went—130 of them sailing from Liverpool on 21 April with Brigham Young as their group leader. As the decade passed, increasingly large numbers of British Mormons arrived in America. Despite these departures, the number of Mormons in Britain also grew rapidly. Indeed, by 1848, half of all Mormons lived in Britain, and by 1850, six of ten Mormons did so.

Why did the Mormons do so well in Britain? These were very stressful times there. The enclosure movement had driven millions from rural areas to lead lives of desperate poverty and misery in the polluted industrial cities. The majority of Britain's seventeen million people were extremely poor, lived in squalid, crowded tenements, or were homeless on the streets. Given these conditions, and the extraordinary class contrasts reported by Kimball, it is no surprise that there was increasingly bitter class antagonism. Moreover, a substantial amount of this antagonism was directed toward the conventional Churches. For the fact is that nearly all of them, including the "fundamentalist" sects, not only opposed the working class in terms of politics but charged pew rentals that were well beyond the means of most citizens. Of course, most denominations offered some free seats, but they were clearly set apart and most people found it degrading to use them. In contrast, all seats in Mormon meeting halls were free.[7]

Of even greater importance, however, Mormonism represented the "American Dream" in very tangible ways. For people who still lacked the vote, who had no realistic hope of ever owning property, and whose children would be lucky to attend school for even a year or two, America was a land of incredible plenty. Rich farm and ranch land was there for the taking. The income of the average American family was many times greater than that in any European nation. Even in remote wilderness areas, where there were settlers, there were schools—and even the poorest children attended. It is no surprise that many people joined the Mormon Church, given that they could expect to emigrate to America under Church auspices.

From the beginning, British Mormons crossed the Atlantic on ships chartered by the Church. In 1849, the Perpetual Emigrating Fund was established, not only to pay travel expenses but to advance sufficient funds to help the immigrants get started. Once they were established, the immigrants paid back their advance, thus restoring funds to be used by others to come over. As a result, a far higher proportion of residents of Utah than in any other state indicated on the 1990 U.S. Census that their ancestry was primarily "English." But an even more significant consequence is that the tide of emigration by English converts led to the collapse of the mission in Great Britain. As is well-known, conversion to new religions is a network phenomenon—people follow their relatives and friends into the movement. When converts departed for America, this ruptured their network ties in England, often before anyone followed them into the Mormon faith. Consequently, Mormon membership in Great Britain peaked at just above thirty-two thousand in 1851 and then began a long decline as departures for America took their toll. By 1860, at the start of the American Civil War, there were only about thirteen thousand Mormons in Great Britain, while more than thirty thousand had immigrated. By 1890, there were fewer than three thousand Mormons still in Great Britain, and almost ninety thousand had immigrated to Utah.

Similar patterns held for other Mormon missions in Europe—they enjoyed considerable success during the middle of the nineteenth century in Scandinavia and Switzerland, too. But, here again, converts were quickly sent to America, thus impeding the normal processes of conversion through networks.

Then, in the twentieth century, all American overseas missions were impeded by world events. In 1914, World War I broke out in Europe, and soon travel abroad was curtailed. Following the war, missionary efforts returned to prewar levels, only to be sharply reduced during the Great Depression. Then came World War II, and once again foreign travel was impossible, and the only Mormons going to Europe were in the armed forces. Finally, in the early 1950s, with wars and the depression behind them, the Mormons again launched missions to Europe. Since then, thousands of young Mormons have served two-year missionary tours in Europe (in 1999, there were more than fifty-six thousand full-time, unpaid, Mormon missionaries serving worldwide). And this time there was no emphasis on emigration, so local congregations have had a chance to grow. By 1980, there were more than 190,000 Mormons in Europe (90,000 of them in Great Britain). In 1998, there were more than 400,000 (173,000 in Great Britain). Although this is an impressive rate of growth, it is far lower than what Mormons have achieved on the other continents.[8] It also is far below that achieved by other American missionaries to Europe who are better able to claim to be fully within the Christian tradition.

Jehovah's Witnesses

Jehovah's Witnesses began sending missionaries to Europe shortly after World War I. Although the Witnesses rely mainly on individual members to serve as missionaries in their spare time, they often initiate mission work in a new society by sending full-time professionals. Thus, in 1920 they had forty-six missionaries from America serving in Great Britain—many of them equipped with a motorcycle having a sidecar.[9] That same year, they announced plans to launch missions to Europe, to be supervised from Berne, Switzerland. Thus, by 1925, they had eleven full-time missionaries in Poland, eight in Lithuania, six in the Ukraine, five in Greece, three in Italy, two in Hungary, two in Russia, two in Armenia, and one in

France. In Great Britain, the American missionaries had been joined by many recruited locally, and 167 were missionizing full-time, augmented by several hundred volunteers. The German mission had done so well that it had been made independent of supervision from Berne, and twenty-three full-time missionaries (most of them local) were at work.

Actual membership data for Europe are lacking for this era, but thousands often were reported to have attended public meetings in a given year—139,000 in Great Britain and more than a million in Germany. Of course, some people were counted many times as they attended various meetings, and many who attended a meeting did not return. Nonetheless, the Witnesses were undoubtedly growing rather successfully in Europe between the wars—their success in Germany was so sufficient that more than two thousand German Witnesses refused to recant and went as martyrs to the Nazi death camps.

After World War II, Witness missionaries combed Europe for their scattered members and quickly rebuilt their smashed Kingdom Halls. They were prevented from returning to Eastern Europe by Soviet repression, but by 1960, there were nearly 200,000 local Witness publishers in Western Europe—65,179 in West Germany and 43,650 in Great Britain. A publisher is a Witness who puts in about four hours a week as a missionary. Since Witness membership statistics are limited to publishers, they must be interpreted in light of this exacting definition of membership. In recent years, Witness statistics also report the total attendance at the annual Memorial Service (the closest thing they have to a holiday), and these are typically twice as large as the number of publishers.

Since 1960, Witness membership in Western Europe has increased by more than 400 percent in terms of the number of publishers, and Memorial Attendance for 1998 totalled almost two million. Meanwhile, of course, the Witnesses have joined the flood of missionaries to Eastern Europe. The Witnesses have long proved willing and able to operate underground in societies where they are prohibited. Hence, there were Witness congregations gathering in secret throughout the decades of Soviet repression, and some members were executed and many imprisoned for doing so. As soon as their activities became legal, the Witnesses surfaced and their initial reported memberships showed that they had long been at work. For example, in 1990 when the Witnesses first disclosed their USSR membership, they already had 39,306 publishers, and more than 100,000 attended the Memorial Service that year. In 1998, the Witnesses had 456,770 publishers in Eastern Europe, and more than a million attended the Memorial Service. Altogether, there were 1,412,895 European publishers in 1998.

Conventional Protestant Missions

Christian missionizing to the non-Christian world amounted to very little until the steamboat made travel safe, relatively fast, and affordable. From the start, it was mainly a Protestant undertaking, and the British and the Americans furnished the overwhelming majority of professional foreign missionaries. In 1880, there were 2,657 British and 1,440 American Protestant missionaries serving abroad, plus several hundred from northern European nations.[10] But the balance soon began to swing toward America. In 1900, there were 5,278 Americans and 5,656 British missionaries in the field. By 1923, when missions fully resumed following World War I, there were 13,463 serving missionaries from the United States and 8,408 from Britain.[11]

World War II and the postwar collapse of British and European colonialism turned the world Protestant mission effort into a virtual American monopoly. By 1960, there were more than thirty thousand full-time American missionaries abroad. In 1996, more than forty thousand American missionaries were serving commitments of more than one year.[12] In reality, the current American mission effort is far greater than even this total suggests. Earlier in the century, in far less affluent times and when travel was relatively far more expensive, most missionaries were sustained by denominational mission boards and societies that published full, reliable reports of their activities. But today there is a substantial (but unknown) number of self-supporting, self-appointed American missionaries serving abroad who do not show up in the published statistics. In addition, there are very many missionaries who are sponsored by a local congregation (both denominational and nondenominational), many of whom are not included in the statistics reported by any missionary agency. Moreover, there are many other large and well-tabulated omissions from this total.[13] Not included are 28,535 persons *fully supported* by American funds who are serving as full-time missionaries in their own country—more than ten thousand of them in India alone. An additional 1,791 foreign nationals are employed by American agencies as missionaries in countries not their own. Moreover, the 1996 total does not include the 63,995 American Protestants officially serving shorter-term foreign missions of a year or less.

So, how many American, or American-funded, foreign missionaries are out there? No one knows. But, if we limit the total to full-time professionals (serving tours of more than a year), there are more than seventy thousand, plus perhaps another fifteen thousand or more not reported to mission boards. Then factor in another hundred thousand volunteers doing tours of a year or less. That suggests that there currently are about 185,000 American Protestant missionaries abroad. And, of course, this total does not include Mormons or Jehovah's Witnesses.

When the subject of foreign missions is raised, most people think of Africa, Asia, and Latin America. But, in fact, Europe has become a very major American mission field. At the start of the twentieth century, some American mission officials began to discuss whether missions to Europe could be justified. Some argued that the lack of European religiousness was a disgrace and that they needed a Great Awakening. These suggestions aroused considerable antagonism in liberal denominational circles. Episcopalians were insulted at the idea that their Anglican colleagues were incapable of caring for the souls of England, and Presbyterians bristled at any suggestion that missionaries be sent to Scotland. Hence, all such notions were dismissed on grounds that these nations were fully Christian in their own way and in need of no outside interference. This view prevailed and Europe was placed off limits by the various mission boards except for minor efforts directed towards remote Catholic areas—in 1902, there were thirty-six American missionaries serving in "Papal Europe" (no more specific information was provided). In the 1920s, about two dozen American missionaries were in the Balkans.[14] But, when the Great Depression caused a serious reduction in American mission efforts, these minor efforts in Europe ceased.

The massive American military effort in Europe during and following World War II soon changed a lot of minds about the need for European missions. As American soldiers returned from service in Europe, especially service in the postwar European garrison forces, many of them enrolled in evangelical colleges and seminaries where they made it common knowledge that church attendance is extremely low and appreciation of basic Christian culture is largely lacking in much of Europe. Thus was interest in European missions rekindled.

Indicative of this growing concern, in his very influential textbook on Christian missions, J. Herbert Kane[15] quoted Hans Lilje, bishop of the German Evangelical Church and a president of the World Council of Churches, as admitting, "The era when Europe was a Christian continent lies behind us." Kane went on to note the very low levels of a church attendance in Europe; that on the entire continent there was only "one Christian radio station," and it was founded and supported by Americans; that it is impossible to purchase or obtain radio or television time (except for Radio Luxembourg); and that the state Churches supported these government restrictions. According to Kane, that is why "Europe came to be regarded as a mission field."

Of course, the liberal American denominations have been unwilling to accept this position. But their objections are of little importance since they have become essentially irrelevant to the American foreign mission effort. In 1880, the liberals—Congregationalists, Presbyterians, Methodists, and Episcopalians—provided more than nine missionaries out of every ten sent abroad from the United States. By 1935, the liberals supplied fewer than half of the American missionaries. In 1996, they sent out fewer than one out of twenty.

So it was that in the late 1950s and early 1960s, one after another of the major evangelical mission boards, such as the Southern Baptists, Assemblies of God, Seventh-day Adventists, and the Church of Nazarene, began to shift resources to European missions. By 1975, there were 2,363 American Protestant, full-time, long-term missionaries in Europe. By 1985, this total had grown to 3,898. Then the Berlin Wall came down and Communist prohibitions of mission activity collapsed, and American mission boards reacted. In 1996, there were nearly 5,000 missionaries in Western Europe and another 2,400 in the East. This total does not include many thousands of independents and short-term volunteers, who might number more than thirty thousand. Nor does it include thousands of Jehovah's Witnesses.

These massive efforts are having results. In many parts of northern Europe, on the average Sunday far more people attend evangelical and pentecostal congregations than go to services in the state churches. In Catholic nations, a new mission technique involves cooperating with the local parish rather than competing with it. A pentecostal missionary will arrive in a village in southern France, for example, and organize prayer and Bible study groups. But, rather than form participants into a Protestant congregation, with the official "blessing" of the local Catholic pastor, participants are urged to attend mass.

The official Catholic position on Europe as a mission field is perhaps reflected in the fact that in 1996 there were 181 members of American Catholic religious orders serving as missionaries in Europe—37 in Great Britain.[16]

What can missionaries from America really hope to accomplish, regardless of how many thousands of them take up the challenge to "Christianize Europe"? In time I think they might overcome the primary barrier to high levels of religious participation: *socialized* religion.

Free Markets versus Socialized Religion

The same European observers who marvelled at American religion in the nineteenth century also recognized why: that America was the first nation to sustain a highly competitive religious free market. In 1858, Karl T. Griesinger,[17] a militantly irreligious German, complained that the separation between Church and state fueled religious efforts:

> Clergymen in America [are] like other businessmen; they must meet competition and build up a trade, and it is their own fault if their income is not large enough. Now it is clear why heaven and hell are moved to drive the people to the churches, and why attendance is more common here than anywhere else in the world.

In 1837, Frances Grund, an Austrian journalist, made similar points, noting that establishment makes the clergy "indolent and lazy" because

> a person provided for cannot, by the rules of common sense, be supposed to work as hard as one who has to exert himself for a living. . . . Not only have Americans a greater number of clergymen than, in proportion to the population, can be found either on the Continent or in England; but they have not one idler amongst them; all of them are obliged to exert themselves for the spiritual welfare of their respective congregations. Americans, therefore, enjoy a threefold advantage: they have more preachers; they have more active preachers, and they have cheaper preachers than can be found in any part of Europe.[18]

Wittingly or not, these visitors echoed Adam Smith's[19] penetrating analysis of the weaknesses of established Churches which inevitably produce a clergy content to repose "themselves upon their benefices [while neglecting] to keep up the fervour of faith and the devotion in the great body of the people; and having given themselves up to indolence, were [to] become altogether incapable of making any vigorous exertion in defence even of their own establishment."

However, by the turn of the twentieth century, awareness of the invigorating consequences of religious competition was fading rapidly. Smith's work on religion was of so little interest that it was (and is) deleted from most editions of *The Wealth of Nations*. For the past century, the received wisdom was that pluralism harms religion because competing religious bodies undercut one another's credibility. Here social scientists uncritically accepted the old adage of comparative atheism that "each religion refutes each," which, ironically, was affirmed by monopoly churches which invariably have charged that should they be supplanted, religion will be dangerously weakened. Eventually these views were formulated into elegant sociology by Peter Berger,[20] who repeatedly argued that pluralism inevitably destroys the plausibility of all religions and only where one faith prevails can there exist a "sacred canopy" able to inspire universal confidence and assent.

It was not until the 1980s that anyone challenged Berger's claims.[21] Nevertheless, this view of the corrosive effects of pluralism was and is utterly inconsistent with the American experience. If competition erodes the plausibility of religions, why is the most pluralistic nation on Earth among the most religious? Because effort is rewarded and competition among religious group results in very energetic efforts to gain and to hold members.

Thus, having now had more than two centuries to develop under free-market conditions, the American religious economy surpasses Adam Smith's wildest dreams about the creative forces of a free market. There are more than 1,500 separate, religious "denominations," many of them very sizeable—Twenty-four have more than one million members each. Each of these bodies is entirely dependent on voluntary contributions, and American religious donations currently total more than $60 billion per year or more than $330 per person over age eighteen. These totals omit many contributions to church construction funds (new church construction amounted to $3 billion in 1993) as well as most donations to religious schools, hospitals, and foreign missions. In 1996, more than $2.3 billion was donated to support missionaries, and a significant amount of this was spent on missionaries to Europe.[22]

In contrast, in Europe rates of church attendance are low, and in most nations nobody donates to religious organizations, except indirectly though taxes. Even in Great Britain, where the established Anglican Church does not receive tax support, its funding is securely based on endowments amassed during the centuries of mandatory tithes.[23]

Just as socialized commercial economies destroy initiative, so does socialized religion. First, to an amazing extent the state imposes its religious views on state

Churches, sometimes to the point of imposing new "demythologized" translations of scripture as was done in Sweden.[24] Second, as Adam Smith warned, kept clergy are lazy. In Germany today the clergy are civil servants whose income is in no way dependent on member enthusiasm. In fact, their union contract with the government specifies that if fewer than eight people show up, the Sunday service may be cancelled and the flock directed elsewhere. Third, kept laity are lazy too, being trained to regard religion as free. This not only weakens commitment to the state Church but indirectly hinders all unsubsidized faiths as well.

Finally, despite claims of religious freedom, the reality is an unreliable religious toleration—the state often directly interferes with, and otherwise limits, potential competitors of the state Churches. In 1984, the European Parliament overwhelmingly passed a resolution allowing member states to curtail the "activity of certain new religious movements." Since then there has been an outbreak of religious persecutions all over northern Europe. The Germans have placed both Scientology and the Jehovah's Witnesses under secret service watch, and members of both faiths, along with a variety of evangelical and pentecostal Protestant groups, are prohibited from civil service employment. On 22 June 1998, the French Tax Authority placed a $50 million lien for back taxes on all property of the Jehovah's Witnesses on grounds that they were listed as a dangerous cult in an official French Parliament report on "Cults in France." Also listed in the report are 172 other evangelical Protestant groups—essentially all religious bodies that are not members of the left-leaning World Council of Churches. In 1997, the Belgian Parliament Commission on Cults issued a six hundred–page report in which 189 religious groups are denounced, including the Witnesses, Catholic Charismatic Renewal, Quakers, Hasidic Jews, the YWCA (but not the YMCA), Seventh-day Adventists, the Assemblies of God, the Amish, Plymouth Brethren, and Buddhists. And so it goes when socialized industries seek to prevent competition.

Energetic competition for the moribund established Churches is precisely what American missionaries see as the Christian hope for Europe. Some early returns suggest that the impact of religious competition will be as effective in Europe as it has been in America.[25] It also seems indicative that the immense progress made by evangelical Protestant groups in Latin America has not only substantially increased overall rates of church attendance but also invigorated Latin American Catholicism sufficiently to cause substantial increases in seminary enrollment.

Of course, most of my European colleagues will accept none of this, charging that American religiousness is nothing but an atavism caused by the social weakness of American intellectual elites. In contrast, they say, religion has been overcome once and for all in Europe. I find this nothing but whistling in the dark, given surveys that consistently show that overwhelming majorities in all parts of Europe say they are personally religious, that they pray, and that they believe in God. Hence, the so-called secularized and enlightened European is far better described as a "believing non-belonger," to use Grace Davie's[26] felicitous phrase. And it is a sense of belonging that the American missionaries are trying to bring about in Europe by creating energetic little groups prepared to challenge the lazy socialized Churches.

Notes

1. William Cobbett, *A Year's Residence in the United States of America* (Carbondale: Southern Illinois University Press, 1964), 233.

2. Alexis de Tocqueville, *Democracy in America*, 2 vols. (New York: Vintage, 1956), 314.

3. Philip Schaff, *America: A Sketch of Its Political, Social, and Religious Character* (Cambridge, Mass.: Belknap Press of Harvard University Press, [1855] 1961), 91.

4. Robert Baird, *Religion in America: Or, An Account of the Origin, Progress, Relation to the State, and Present Condition of the Evangelical Churches in the United States* (New York: Harper, 1844).

5. Friedrich Conrad Dietrich Wyneken, *The Distress of the German Lutherans in North America*, trans. S. Edgar Schmidt and ed. R. F. Rehmer (Fort Wayne, Ind.: Concordia Theological Seminary Press, [1843] 1982).

6. James B. Allen, Ronald K. Esplin, and David J. Whittaker, *Men with a Mission, 1837–1841: The Quorum of the Twelve Apostles in the British Isles* (Salt Lake City: Deseret, 1992), 23.

7. Rodney Stark, "The Basis of Mormon Success: A Theoretical Application," in *Latter-day Saint Social Life: Social Research on the LDS Church and Its Members*, ed. James T. Duke (Provo, Utah: Religious Studies Center, Brigham Young University, 1998), 29–70.

8. Stark, "The Basis of Mormon Success."

9. *Watch Tower*, 15 December 1920, 374.

10. William F. Bainbridge, *Along the Lines at the Front: A General Survey of Baptist Home and Foreign Missions* (Philadelphia: American Baptist Publication Society, 1882).

11. Harlan P. Beach, *A Geography and Atlas of Protestant Missions. Vol. 2: Statistics and Atlas* (New York: Student Volunteer Movement for Foreign Missions, 1903); and Harlan P. Beach and Charles H. Fahs, *World Missionary Atlas* (New York: Institute of Social and Religious Research, 1925).

12. John A. Siewert and Edna G. Valdez (eds. for MARC), *Mission Handbook: USA and Canadian Christian Ministries Overseas*, 17th ed. (Grand Rapids, Mich.: Zondervan, 1997).

13. Siewert and Valdez, *Mission Handbook*.

14. Beach and Fahs, *World Missionary Atlas*.

15. J. Herbert Kane, *A Global View of Christian Missions: From Pentecost to the Present* (Grand Rapids, Mich.: Baker Book House, 1971).

16. Siewert and Valdez, *Mission Handbook*.

17. Translated in Oscar Handlin, ed., *This Was America* (Cambridge, Mass.: Harvard University Press, 1949), 261.

18. Cited in Milton B. Powell, ed., *The Voluntary Church: Religious Life, 1740–1860, Seen through the Eyes of European Visitors* (New York: Macmillan, 1967), 77–80.

19. Adam Smith, *An Inquiry into the Nature and Causes of the Wealth of Nations*, 2 vols. (Indianapolis: Liberty Fund, [1776] 1981), 789.

20. Peter Berger, *The Heretical Imperative: Contemporary Possibilities of Religious Affiliation* (New York: Doubleday, 1979); and Peter Berger, *The Sacred Canopy* (New York: Doubleday, 1969).

21. Rodney Stark, "From Church-Sect to Religious Economies," in *The Sacred in a Post-Secular Age,* ed. Phillip E. Hammond (Berkeley: University of California Press, 1985), 139–49.

22. Siewert and Valdez, *Mission Handbook.*

23. J. F. Pickering, "Giving in the Church of England: An Econometric Analysis," *Applied Economics* 17 (1985): 619–32.

24. Christer Asberg, "The Swedish Bible Commission and Project NT 81", in *Bible Reading in Sweden,* ed. Gunnar Hansen (Uppsala: University of Uppsala Press, 1990), 15–22.

25. Rodney Stark and Roger Finke, *Acts of Faith: Explaining the Human Side of Religion* (Berkeley: University of California Press, 2000).

26. Grace Davie, *Religion in Britain since 1945: Believing without Belonging* (Oxford: Blackwell, 1994).

III
EASTERN EUROPE

10

Appropriation of the American Gangster Film and the Transition to Capitalism

Poland's *Dogs* and Russia's *Brother*

Herbert J. Eagle

TWO OF THE MOST POPULAR FILM HEROES to emerge in formerly Communist Eastern Europe in the 1990s were Franz Maurer (played by Bogusław Linda) in the Polish *Dogs* (1992) and Danila Bogrov (played by Sergei Bodrov Jr.) in the Russian *Brother* (1997). Both films were riding a popular wave of crime thrillers, imported from Hollywood and imitated, on the level of actions and visual icons (gun battles, car chases and crashes, explicit and graphic sex), in domestic productions. One might at first be tempted to attribute the popularity of such films primarily to the psychological attraction of depictions of aggressive and libidinous behavior, a vicarious indulgence in impulses which are repressed in civilized human behavior (and which were excluded, in their more visceral forms of expression, from the official socialist realist cinema of the Communist states). But that would be to ignore the narrative structures and the characterizations which make the better films in the crime genres significant from an intellectual standpoint as well, factors which render these works of art more complex reflections on culture, society, politics, and economics. Crime films, in particular, usually feature heroes who are struggling to succeed in a business (albeit an explicitly illegal and violent one), often in order to escape oppressive economic and social circumstances. The first popular cycle of American gangster films coincided in time with the beginning of the Great Depression of the 1930s; the films embodied both the opportunities and successes promised by American capitalism as well as the illusory and hypocritical nature of those promises. Although the genre evolved in various different ways in the subsequent decades, the nature of capitalism and the situation of the individual within that economic system remained at its heart. And what topic could be more relevant during the trying period of the transition to capitalism in Eastern Europe?

Before embarking on a specific discussion of what elements were appropriated from American crime genres in Russian and Polish films and how those elements are inflected, I should note some implicit hypotheses about popular cinema on which my analysis rests. Approaches to such mass-produced popular culture have oscillated between two poles: on the one hand, it is seen as designed and disseminated by the ruling group as a means of indoctrinating and controlling subordinate groups (the proletariat, ethnic minorities, women); on the other, subordinate groups are seen as having a hand in its creation and, even more important, as using it creatively to satisfy their own interests and desires.[1] For proponents of the latter view, advanced forcefully by John Fiske in the late 1980s, the internal structures of a mass-produced text do not constrain members of its audience from understanding the text in a manner congruent with their own interests. As Fiske puts it, "Popular discrimination's concern with relevance, then, separates it clearly from the universals of critical discrimination, for relevance is the interconnections between a text and the immediate social situation of its readers—it is therefore socially and historically specific and will change as a text moves through the social structure or through history."[2]

Popular cinema, it seems, shows ample evidence of the ideological effort to position the viewer through the internal structures of the text and resistance on the part of viewers who interpret a film in terms of their own experiences, even against the grain of some of the text's logic or explicit formulations. These two processes work in struggle with one another. Indeed, the financial backers of cinema as a relatively expensive industrial enterprise (whether Communist state bureaucrats or capitalist entrepreneurs) may seek to ensure that it encodes their ideology and encourages viewers to behave in a manner that supports the existing or developing economic and political system. However, these "ideological" backers do not create the film; it is the work of a series of creative artists (novelists, screenwriters, directors, cinematographers, actors, etc.) who instantiate the text. There are ample possibilities here for the expression of views subversive to the dominant system. Furthermore, reception of popular films depends on the willingness of audiences to view them. For the financial backers of the industry under capitalism (and even for its bureaucratic chiefs in Communist systems), audience attendance (box office) is a prime (or considerably important) consideration. Thus, there is to a greater or lesser extent a feedback mechanism between the audiences that watch films and the industry that produces them.

Films which are "popular" are reproduced; they form cycles and ultimately genres. In this way, audiences are not merely inert blotters for whatever messages a film industry produces in the interests of a ruling class; they "vote" with their tickets, and in this way they encourage the industry to incorporate messages which meet their needs and desires. Do we find that, in the final analysis, potentially subversive elements are appropriated, contained, and brought under control, as some cultural theorists have argued in applying Gramsci's concept of hegemony? Or are these texts some kind of Lévi-Straussian mediation, wherein elements which are logically opposite are brought together through an artistic sleight of hand? In the final analysis, there is usually considerable disagreement as to the "essential" meaning of popular genres. They typically contain contradictory and paradoxical elements. In this sense, they are not like messages but are more like specialized languages, well adapted for the examination of particular subjects. For the gangster genre that subject is capitalism and patriarchy.

The American gangster film and its recent transformations in Russian and Polish contexts provide an illuminating example of the flexibility of a genre's textual structures and their adaptability in the service of different kinds of messages. The American genre's meaning is hardly univalent, in the first place. The heroes of the most popular early American gangster films—Enrico ("Rico") Bandelo of *Little Caesar* (1930), Tommy Powers of *Public Enemy* (1931), and Tony Camonte of *Scarface* (1932)—are all young men from working-class families. Other gang members who are the heroes' friends, associates, or rivals in these narratives are also from immigrant families, Irish, Italian, or Jewish, as were the famous gangsters (Al Capone, Lucky Luciano, and Meyer Lansky) whose actual biographies provided some of the key incidents in the films. Furthermore, the soon-to-be-famous actors who played the heroes in these films were themselves Jewish (Edward G. Robinson as Rico Bandelo, Paul Muni as "Scarface" Tony Camonte) or Irish (James Cagney as Tommy Powers). All three actors were from Manhattan's Lower East Side, and Cagney and Muni re-created New York ethnic accents in realizing their roles. Thus, the films reached out, in terms of ethnic, class, and regional identification, to the urban, poor, working-class audience, and that audience received the films enthusiastically (so enthusiastically, as we shall discuss later, that pressures were successfully brought on the American film industry to alter the structures in these films which led to such a positive identification with ostensibly "criminal" heroes).

In very important ways, Rico, Tommy, and Scarface modelled successful behavior in a capitalist system (and, as several researchers have suggested, the rapid success of immigrants from the underclass, using these methods, may have been even more threatening to the white Anglo-Saxon elite than the criminal plots in and of themselves). All three characters want to achieve success in the form of status, material wealth, and power over others, and the crime business is for them simply the fastest and surest way to gain such success. Such aspirations are crucial to the functioning of a free-enterprise system—these are the goals which are believed to motivate workers to expend the fullest possible effort, to show initiative and take on responsibilities. Competitive spirit and even aggression are desirable in fueling market competition.

It is precisely these kinds of qualities that the gangster films of the period 1929–1933 celebrated. None of the aforementioned films dwell on their protagonists' decisions to become criminals—it is more or less a foregone conclusion that an immigrant must elect this sort of a "career" if he really wants to "get ahead." Tommy's career path is explicitly contrasted with the one taken by his honest older brother, Mike. Mike works as a streetcar conductor during the day and goes to school at night. Tommy continually derides his brother's efforts, suggesting that he has to steal nickels from his fares in order to get by and that his efforts at self-improvement amount to "learning how to be poor." And the path of the film's narrative in many respects confirms Tommy's opinion. Mike enlists in the Marines during World War I, as a patriot should; as "reward," he returns from the war shell-shocked and visibly weakened. He may lecture Tommy about proper values of citizenship, but his angry tirades carry no force—immediately afterward he collapses back into his chair like an invalid. The visual imagery suggests that the political and economic system has used him up and discarded him.

The gangster heroes, on the other hand, remain vibrant and dynamic almost to the very end of the narratives. They have enviable "capitalist" personality traits; they are all aggressive go-getters, ambitious, proud, and defiant. After robbing a gas station in his small hometown outside Chicago, Rico Bandelo reads a newspaper article about a big-time Chicago gangster, Diamond Pete Montana, and immediately decides that he can emulate him ("He don't have to waste his time on cheap gas stations. He's somebody. He's in the big time. I can do all the things that fellow does and more"). Boldness and toughness are what it takes in Rico's opinion ("Shoot first and argue afterward. This game ain't for guys that are soft"). In all three films, there is so much verbal and visual play with "hardness" versus "softness," and so many elongated props (machine guns, cigars, cars) that are extensions of the gangster's power that phallic associations are inevitable.

Initiative is the hallmark of these gangster heroes. All three immediately are inclined to go beyond the specific responsibilities and prerogatives given to them within their respective gangs. Rico first gets himself into Sam Vettori's Chicago gang by touting his toughness and skill; by the next sequence in the film, we see him planning a nightclub heist on his own. When Vettori tears up the plans ("I give all the orders"), Rico indicates bluntly that he intends to go ahead with the job anyway. Surprisingly, Rico does not suffer at all as a result of this insubordination; the other gangsters admire his guts. After the robbery, Rico informs Sam that he, Rico, is taking over as boss. Spontaneous aggressive behavior brings rewards for "Scarface" Tony Camonte as well. As in *Little Caesar*, Tony begins to question his boss Johnny Lovo's judgment. Tony wants to go after the rival "Northside" gang; Lovo insists that their gang is not strong enough yet for a full-scale war. Tony confides to his sidekick Rinaldo: "Some day I'm gonna run the whole works. In this business, there's only one law you got to follow to keep out of trouble: Do it first, do it yourself, and keep on doing it." Tony's motto, with its emphasis on initiative, self-reliance, and perseverance, could well belong to a captain of industry.

At the same time that these films valorize a virtually unbridled aggression on the part of the heroes, they also model more civil business behavior—organization, partnerships, alliances, and what might be termed company loyalty. Violence clearly has its costs, so it is prudent to reduce it via better planning and mutually profitable arrangements with other gangs. As Johnny Lovo tells his underlings,

"We're gonna get organized. It's gonna mean twice as much dough for everybody and half as much trouble. . . . It's a business and I'm gonna run it like a business."

Hierarchies, alliances, and organization are foregrounded in the early gangster films by adopting, in terms of language, settings, and props, the trappings of the "legitimate" business world. Gangsters in suits meet in offices, confer by telephone, smoke cigars, and celebrate their triumphs by frequenting fancy restaurants and nightclubs with their lavishly dressed wives and girlfriends. In *Little Caesar,* there is even a testimonial dinner at which gangsters and their "molls" gather to honor Rico and present him with a watch to commemorate his fine service. In many instances, the illegal dealings of the gangsters mimic or replicate the dealings of legitimate business. In *Public Enemy,* Paddy Ryan reaches an agreement with an established brewer, Leeman, whose business fortunes have, of course, plummeted with Prohibition. Now Leeman will provide his brewery for Ryan's illegal operation. In the gangster film, the boundaries between illegal rackets and legitimate business are entirely permeable.

Finally, just as for corporations, ingenuity and technological advances are key components of a gangland operation's success. Many heists involve precise timing and a clever utilization of available resources. Paddy Ryan's gang uses a fuel truck and fuel hose to disguise the fact that alcohol is being siphoned out of the barrels in a government warehouse; the placement of the hose has to be timed so as to avoid the policeman on his beat. When some of "Scarface" Tony Camonte's men are ambushed by the rival North Side gang, Tony seems unaffected by the bloodshed and the casualties; what fascinates him is the new technology being employed by his rivals ("Look at that. They've got machine guns you can carry"). Gangster heroes are interested in the same sort of advances which would make a corporation more competitive: better equipment, improved communication and transportation, and superior planning and design.

Because gangster "business" coincides with legal business in so many ways in these films, the clear implication is that *all* business participates in the process of skirting the law and in the use of intimidation and violence of some sort to increase and maintain profits. What drives the gangster to resort to immoral means to make more money? The psychological need for validation, for success, as exemplified by status (the admiration and respect one gets from others) and material wealth. The gangster hero engages in conspicuous consumption in an attempt to elevate himself in the eyes of his peers, moving from liquor and cigars to expensive suits, flashy jewelry, limousines, and beautiful women. Tony Camonte acquires a lavish apartment, furnishings, paintings, and so many shirts that he never has to wear one twice. After participating in his first big heist, Tommy Powers fairly glows as he is measured for a new suit. In the very next scene, he and his sidekick Matt drive up to a nightclub in a brand new car; both men sport hats and gloves. When they see two pretty young women at a nearby table, they have the women's dates thrown out of the club and then move in on the women. Tommy says to Kitty, "You're a swell dish . . . I think I'm going to adopt you." Matt (gesturing toward the other woman,

Mamie): "Look what I got measured for, Tom." The women do not protest their objectification; they seem happy to have been chosen by such "big" men.

Thus, these early gangster films represent the frequently coercive and immoral aspects of not only capitalism but also the patriarchy as well. The quest for power within a capitalist system is distinctly gendered. It is only men who compete for power in these films. Women are valued as nurturers or as possessions of the male hero. Romantic love is irrelevant or at best a distraction. Rico never shows any interest in women, and it is a romantic relationship that leads Rico's gangster pal, the dancer Joe Masara, to betray the gang. For Rico, both dancing and attracting women make a man "soft." Tommy Powers is happy with his girlfriend Kitty until she begins to express wishes of her own, at which point he dismissively mocks her ("I wish you was a wishin' well so that I could tie a bucket to you and sink you"). In a scene which has become virtually emblematic of the genre's misogyny, Tommy reacts to Kitty's further protests by picking up a half grapefruit from the breakfast table and smashing it into her face. The scene embodies an aspect of the culture encoded across classes, the subordination of women to men.

In most ways, the early gangster films are constructed in such a way as to draw admiration and sympathy for their heroes. Not only do these heroes succeed in their endeavors through bold and fearless actions, but they exhibit considerable ingenuity, and also have most of the witty lines in the dialogues. In spite of the fact that all three films' narratives contain the explicit message that crime is evil and the final moral "crime does not pay" (as voiced by police, newspaper editors, clergyman, and ordinary folks), as well as the ignominious deaths of the heroes (in facing death, they all are made to seem both cowardly and weak), audiences (particularly working-class and immigrant audiences) empathized far more with the criminal heroes than with the forces of social control, whose representation in the films is dry and pedantic (such scenes involve virtual lectures addressed to the audience). Underneath this monologic endorsement of the system's explicit civic values, there is a complex interplay between the hegemonic and subversive aspects of these texts. Depending on the viewer's approach, they might be seen as valorizing capitalist and patriarchal behavior or as critiquing the effects that the capitalist system has on the humanity, decency, and morality of human beings. The text supports both readings.

In spite of the fact that the early American gangster films would seem to endorse many of the values of capitalism and patriarchy which underpinned the culture's ideology, they were not received favorably by the institutions that were the ostensible guardians of the culture's "official" values. Those "official" values emphasized egalitarian democracy, the Protestant work ethic, and Christian religious principles and clearly masked the realities of economic life and gender power. Church and civic leaders battled to have the violent gangster films censored, and the industry's organizational arm, the Motion Picture Producers and Distributors of America (MPPDA), wishing to avoid adverse legislation, invoked its own code (known as the "Hays code," after Will Hays, a Republican politician who was head of the MPPDA) in forcing producers to declare a moratorium on the kinds of narratives which had made the genre such a rapid success. After 1935, gangster films continued to feature the battles that had been so popular, but the stars (Robinson, Cagney, and Muni) were now cast as crime fighters: undercover police officers, FBI agents, or G-men (in some films, they were former gangsters, now reformed). Nonetheless, their aggressive behavior, toughness, and entrepreneurial energy were retained in films like *Bordertown* (1935), *G-Men* (1935), and *Bullets or Ballots* (1936).[3]

American crime films underwent significant changes in the subsequent decades. In the film noir variant which developed in the 1940s and 1950s, the protagonists were not dominating figures but small-time operators (who often came from working-class backgrounds or were war veterans), pawns in the hands of large crime syndicates which used them and discarded them. The male hero was no longer necessarily a criminal, but if he was ostensibly a crime fighter (e.g., a private eye or an insurance investigator), he was one whose commitment to the legal establishment was not unconditional and that legal establishment was shown to be itself morally compromised. Though brash and tough, the so-called hardboiled detective usually fell victim to larger forces of evil which succeeded in manipulating him for their own ends. The criminal world was now much more explicitly a metaphor for the immorality of capitalism.

The gender politics of the patriarchy was also foreground to a much greater extent through the expanded role of a femme fatale in the narrative. Although this female character usually appeared to be herself trapped in a world of evil, frequently under the domination of an evil patriarch (such as a gangster boss), her motivations remained unclear within the narrative. Did she cooperate with evil because she was forced to? Or was she determined to liberate herself and achieve autonomous power at whatever cost? In either case, as in *The Big Sleep* (1945), the male protagonist must bring her under control or be destroyed by her. In one variant of the cycle, the private-eye figure succeeds in rescuing and rehabilitating the femme fatale, essentially marrying her at the end and thus taming her and putting her in her place within the patriarchal hierarchy. In what might be termed the tragic variant, the femme fatale is irredeemably evil and must be killed at the film's climax, the private eye not infrequently dying with her. From an ideological standpoint, the film noir cycle has been widely seen as an effort to contest the occupational and sexual independence which women in the United States had achieved during the Depression and World War II. As Jonathan Munby puts it, "The recasting of female independence in the form of the femme fatale (as home-breaking, avaricious, a sexual predator, and user of men) certainly played a role in the demonization of women's desires for autonomy."[4] In spite of this demonization, the femme fatale in American film noir was virtually the male protagonist's equal in terms of energy, cleverness, initiative, and her quest for power and status. This enabled a later generation of feminist scholars and theoreticians to give the genre a "subversive" reading, and see it as exhibiting a model of an independent and effective woman.[5]

Central European émigré directors were prominent in creating the film noir crime film, with such films as Billy Wilder's *Double Indemnity* (1944), Robert Siodmak's *The Killers* (1945) and *Criss Cross* (1949), and Fritz Lang's *Woman in the Window* (1945) and *The Big Heat* (1953). The émigré Polish director, Roman Polanski, captured the essence of the formula brilliantly in his *Chinatown* (1974). In that film, a private eye, Jake Gittis, struggles to unravel a vast and complex plot involving the murder of a government official in Los Angeles, Hollis Mulwray, head of the Water Department, and the scheme of his former partner, Noah Cross, to buy up acres of valuable land by creating an artificial drought. The femme fatale, Evelyn Mulwray, appears to Jake and the viewer to be implicated in both. In his zeal to bring the perpetrators to justice (and under his knowledge and control), Jake misapprehends what is really going on (leading the film's audience astray as well). Jake falls in love with Evelyn, but by the time he realizes that she is in every respect a victim (her father, Noah, raped her and desires as well to sexually possess his own eighteen-year-old daughter/granddaughter Catherine by this relationship), it is too late for him to prevent any of the looming disasters: Noah gets away with his landgrab, Evelyn is killed, and Catherine ends up in Noah's clutches. And Jake has unknowingly set up all of the prerequisites for this horrible denouement. Through the use of biblical visual imagery and names, Polanski created a truly apocalyptic vision of American capitalism and its relationship to patriarchy. When Jake asks Noah, who is already very wealthy, what more he could gain by his land scheme, Noah replies, "The future, Mr. Gittis, the future." He wants all of the power, all of the money, all of the women (his daughters to infinity), as it were.[6]

In the various appropriations of American crime film conventions by Polish and Russian directors in the past two decades, contradictory assessments of capitalist drives and their consequences are presented, just as in the American originals. The appearance of gangster heroes was in and of itself a significant development, since in the approved socialist realist cinema of Poland and the Soviet Union, it was crimes against the state (sabotage, espionage) which were the usual subject of crime thrillers, and the perpetrators were, obviously, villains. In liberal periods, for example the Khrushchev years in the Soviet Union and the period following the return of Władisław Gomułka to power in Poland in 1956, a rejection of the idealized treatments of contemporary reality prescribed by socialist realism did allow for a more realistic presentation of certain kinds of criminal activity (juvenile delinquency, prostitution, or even bureaucratic corruption), but films did not represent crime syndicates as powerful or successful, even when they occasionally surfaced in film plots. Criminal gangs were typically negative, as in Vasily Shukshin's *The Red Snowball Berry Bush* (1974), in which the good-hearted hero (played by Shukshin, a well-known writer of village prose) is an ex-convict who has returned to his village determined to lead a better and honest life, but he is tracked down and killed by his former gang. This gang is depicted in a manner typical for socialist realism—as disorganized, dirty, and alcoholic, a dissolute remnant, a "survival" of the dying capitalist past. Until later in the 1970s in Poland and the period of Gorbachev's glasnost in the mid-1980s in the Soviet Union, organized crime could not be acknowledged in the mass media as a significant factor in society, and the characteristics of gangs and gangsters could not be presented in a positive way.

In the years preceding and accompanying the rise of Solidarity in Poland (1975–1981), the most important films focused on the oppressive and immoral dimensions of three decades of Communist rule. Plots involving criminals emerged in this context as a way of critiquing the practices of the Polish police state, as in Marek Piwowski's *Pardon Me, Do They Beat You Here?* (1975). However, in Feliks Falks's *Master of Ceremonies* (1977, released 1979), corruption in the entertainment industry begins to be presented in the context of a free-enterprise mentality and with distinct gangsterish elements (although the main characters are not gangsters per se). The film's main protagonist, Danielak, is an up-and-coming young MC who is willing to betray everyone, including his best friend and his lover, in order to rise to the top. He and the already established MC's battle for status using graft and blackmail as tools; theft and fraud are rampant, and local government officials are clearly involved as well. What connects *Master of Ceremonies* to the American gangster genre is the fact that Danielak, in his energy, in his clever pursuit of his goal, and in his almost childlike need for power and status, is not an entirely unlikable personality. A capitalist ethos, driven by greed, already seems to permeate Polish society; its effects on society are for the most part censured in the film, but not without a certain degree of admiration for the nerve and audacity of the perpetrator, Danielak. The mediation is similar to what we find in the American gangster genre. The qualities needed for capitalist success are blatantly displayed, while at the same time the system's promotion of immorality is made clear.

This "positive" take on the gangster hero emerged much more strongly and explicitly in the films of Juliusz Machulski. In *Va Banque* (1983) and *Va Banque II* (1984), the gangsters' cleverness and ingenuity can be admired more unproblematically, since the films are set in the 1930s and the Communist system is not directly implicated. In the comedy *Deja Vu* (1989), made as Poland was on the verge of a much more extensive transition to free-market economics, Machulski's gangster heroes are juxtaposed directly with the bureaucrats of a Communist system. In unabashed homage to the American genre, *Deja Vu* begins in Prohibition-era Chicago, in 1925, where Mafia dons assemble at the home of the "godfather" Big Jim Cimino, whose mannerisms mimic those of Marlon Brando in Francis Ford Coppola's famous *Godfather* (1972). Furthermore, all of the other assembled Mafioso (Scorcese, Pacino, De Niro, Coppola, Stallone) bear the names of Italian American film directors or film stars associated with the gangster genre. The Mafia wants a gangster named Mick Nitsch killed at any cost, because he has dishonored the family by ratting on the mob to the police. Nitsch has fled to Odessa, in the Soviet Ukraine, so the mob decides to hire the celebrated Polish American hit man, Johnny Polack, to do the job; he speaks the language, and "Johnny's got the best reputation; he always makes his deliveries."

Polack is a clear embodiment of the early American gangster hero. When "Scorcese" and "Pacino" go to his home, the gangster's very Polish mother offers them a traditional cheesecake, explaining that Johnny is at the opera, since it is his day off. But a cut to Johnny at the opera shows us otherwise; he is in the midst of assassinating the lead tenor (for reasons unknown), shooting him at the opera's climax (a firing squad scene!), using a high-powered rifle built elegantly into an umbrella. Johnny is urbane, skilled, and efficient. He accepts the Mafia's assignment and proceeds to Odessa, where he is honored by the shipping trust, Russflot, as the first American passenger on the New York–Odessa line (he is posing as a professor of entomology, specializing in butterflies, en route to Sumatra, but stopping in Odessa to visit the grave of his father, a Pole who had been exiled by the czar). In spite of his protestations, Polack is settled in Odessa's fanciest hotel and turned over to an Intourist-style Soviet guide, determined to show him all the sights, including the "Potemkinites," as she refers to Sergei Eisenstein and his film crew, in the city to make the later world-famous "Odessa steps sequence" in the film *Battleship Potemkin*. The film's plot involves Polack's efforts to escape from his ardent Soviet hosts so that he can carry out his mission. Cleverness and ingenuity abound in the actions of Polack and of his gangster adversary Mick Nitsch, who in Odessa has reverted to a Ukrainian name, Mikita Niczyporuk. Niczyporuk rules a considerable gangster empire in Odessa. Using a bakery as a front, he borrows the old Chicago method of hiding bottles of bootleg liquor inside freshly baked loaves. Behind his bakery he has a gambling casino and nightclub which rival in their ostentatiousness and wildness the Chicago of the Roaring Twenties (e.g., the buxom cocktail waitresses are all bare breasted). As Niczyporuk's henchman proudly announces, this corporate operation has gone far beyond the days of Benya Krik.[7] Niczyporuk plans to ship his product to Chicago, New York, and Miami via Siberia and Alaska. His operation is a veritable celebration of capitalist ego and excess, and these qualities are displayed unproblematically throughout the film in the evocation of upper-class tourist life as well.

In their ongoing battle, the ingenuity and ruthlessness of both Polack and Niczyporuk are contrasted with the rigid, inefficient, and communal practices of the bureaucratized Soviet regime. Polack's "work" is delayed by a series of nonsensical Soviet devices and regulations: the hotel's mechanized luggage delivery system (designed to replace the exploitation of Negro bellhops), which damages Johnny's umbrella-gun; the hotel clerk, who assigns him two roommates, collective farmers from Ukraine and Uzbekistan (Russflot has booked only one place for Polack and the room has three beds; even though Johnny is willing to pay for the entire room, this is ideologically unacceptable); a porter who refuses him entry to his own hotel because he lacks the appropriate "pass"; clerks who refuse to send a telegram to Chicago unless he pays in rubles instead of dollars.

Even though both Polack and Niczyporuk are killers, the violence itself is so stylized and parodic as to be inoffensive. We are attracted by their flamboyance, nerve, ingenuity, and dedication to their profession. Polack hides guns in Bibles and bullets inside chocolates. When a group of Armenians mistake him for their countryman, Pollakian, he tries to resist getting drunk with them (as one of the Armenians says, "in America they can't keep their mind off their work"). In the film's most hilarious sequence, Polack, dressed as a White officer, is drafted by Eisenstein to lead the file of murderous troops down the Odessa steps, while Niczyporuk is hustled into the costume of the crippled beggar. As the magnificent Odessa-steps sequence is being filmed, Polack is *really* trying to shoot the cripple played by Niczyporuk, but he stumbles against a baby carriage and sends it rolling down the steps—"That's great!" shouts Eisenstein. In spite of all of the parody of Soviet life and culture, the film is given an "appropriate" socialist realist closure (albeit tongue-in-cheek). Niczyporuk is arrested by Soviet secret agents who, it turns out, have only been *posing* as hotel staff, collective farmer, cemetery watchman, and so on. "You're *all* in the police," exclaims Polack, in a hardly subtle reference to the Communist system's pervasive surveillance of its citizens. Polack's mission is, thus, finally foiled. A Young Pioneer tells him that the citizens of the United States must rise up in the fight against crime, because "your oligarchy is indifferent to gangsters." But this indictment of the complicity of capitalists in gangsterism is made to seem overblown, given that it is spoken by a child obviously repeating a propaganda slogan. Later Polish and Russian gangster films, set in the late 1980s and in the 1990s, take this particular indictment more seriously.

During the period of glasnost associated with Gorbachev's rule in the Soviet Union (1985–91), crime among youth, in particular, was depicted as a symptom of their alienation from a stodgy, repressive, and hypocritical society. Rock and roll, punk, and heavy metal music were the main vehicles which expressed young people's rebellion, but drugs, violence, and crime (realistically) accompanied these plots. Juris Podnieks's *Is It Easy to Be Young?* (1986) created a scandal when it showed Latvian young people trashing a train on the way home from a rock concert. In Valery Ogorodnikov's *The Burglar* (1987), the young hero Semeon steals a synthesizer to prevent his older rock-star brother from doing it to pay off a debt owed the leader of a punk motorcycle gang. That the real business of this gang might be drugs is only hinted at. A similar implication, that youth gangs are involved in illegal activities, is implied by the behavior of a secondary character, Tolya, in Vasily Pichul's *Little Vera* (1988). In Sergei Soloviev's *Assa* (1988) and in Rashid Nugmanov's *The Needle* (1989), the young heroes battle sinister evil criminal villains. Although crime as business enterprise is not the principal concern of these films, the main theme of conflict between youth values (freedom, creativity) and a rigidified bureaucratized older generation does echo the emergence of free-enterprise values.

Once Communist regimes collapsed in Poland and in the Soviet Union, and the accelerated transition to capitalism began in a "shock treatment" mode, the assessment of the capitalist system in gangster films became less laudatory and more critical. Appropriation of the conventions of the more pessimistic American crime film variants became more prominent. The main protagonists of Władysław Pasikowski's *Dogs* (1992) inhabit a post-Communist Polish milieu filled with a sense of entrapment and futility which echoes the American film noir crime film. Franciszek ("Franz") and Olo Zwirski are not gangsters at the beginning of the narrative, but members of the government's own "Firm," the secret police. But their situation couldn't be further from that of the G-men heroes who had battled organized crime in the American films of the late 1930s. The Firm is in the process of being liquidated by the anti-Communist democrats who have taken over the government of Poland. This does not initially seem to have diminished Franz and Olo's pride or their aggressive energy, however. They seem absolutely unafraid of danger and highly skilled with weapons. They are stars of their profession; they are merely in need of a new assignment, a new employer, or a new entrepreneurial venture.

In the film's opening sequence, Franz is being grilled by a governmental commission with regard to his shooting of a former secret police colleague, Captain Nowakowski, who had become a Solidarity activist. In describing how he shot Nowakowski, Franz reveals an ostensibly unassailable motivation: in his frustration, Nowakowski had gone berserk, killing his own wife and threatening to throw his daughter off the roof if his demands for a free labor union were not met. Franz regrets having to kill a man who was his friend but is proud of his marksmanship (he killed Nowakowski with a single shot, fired from a distance of 220 meters). We also learn from the remarks of the legislator who is heading the investigatory commission, Wencel, that Franz Maurer held a degree in law, had married the daughter of the vice minister of internal affairs, had received eighteen citations for bravery but also thirty-one reprimands, including three recommendations that he be dismissed (these, however, were cancelled, presumably on orders from unnamed politicians). To this point, Franz has clearly had a successful career as a police agent. After the hearing, Franz walks outside, past a pen of snarling police dogs; he snarls right back at them.[8] Franz is a tough man in a tough business.

However, the employment picture is not bright for Franz and his buddy Olo. They and other members of their unit have been reduced to burning files in large bonfires at night at a landfill; the implication is clear: the Firm has much compromising and incriminating evidence to destroy before their offices are inspected by the new political regime. At home, Franz also burns a picture of his wife and young son; his marriage has fallen apart, and they have emigrated to America. Later, his wife's legal representatives will appear on the scene to force him to sell his spacious house and his expensive car as part of the divorce settlement (the money in the marriage was apparently hers). Meanwhile, the secret police act like employees whose corporation has been bought out by a rival. Some hope that they will be able to keep their jobs ("Whom will they hire? Jesuits?"), while others are more realistic ("They'll hire their own people"). They joke about the seedy professions which will now be the only ones open to them: they could run sex shops or be weapons dealers. The most likely possibility is that they will be demoted to regular police, whom they have always looked down upon. And this is, in fact, what happens.

Franz and Olo are the closest of friends, but their reaction to their impending demotion is distinctly different. Olo laments the fact that he is about to lose his apartment, which he was given only because of his connections. When an officer newly assigned to their unit, a good cop named Wladek, turns out to be photographing the secret police's nightly bonfires (collecting evidence of the destruction of files), Olo catches him at this task, attacks him brutally, smashes his camera, and stands ready to shoot him (having reduced Wladek to this pathetic state, he shoots over his head). For this act, Olo is fired from the police entirely. The other former secret police are assigned to a regular crime-fighting unit headed by Major Bien, who is out to insult and humiliate his new charges as payback for their formerly elevated status, their misdeeds, and their arrogance.

In their first assigned operation, it turns out that the former secret service men (excepting Franz and Olo) lack the guts and the skill to be crime fighters. Staking out what they believe to be a car-smuggling operation, they are surprised by a gunman and his accomplice who unhesitatingly open fire on them, killing two of the police instantly and fatally wounding two others (Franz is not present during the attack because he had gone to a pay phone to deal with matters relating to his divorce). As the conversation which preceded this attack reveals, these former secret police are neither skilled nor experienced when it comes to fighting "real" criminals. They reminisce about the good old days when they terrorized dissidents and students and took advantage of young women. Such opponents, of course, offered no physical resistance. The first reaction of these men to being attacked is utter amazement that anyone would dare to shoot at them! They might be seen as representing, more broadly, a former Communist bureaucracy that is ill equipped to grapple with the dog-eat-dog realities of a genuinely competitive and aggressive free-enterprise system.

At the other extreme is Gross, the gunman who killed, maimed, and so utterly traumatized them. He, too, is a former secret police officer, a major from Lublin, who probably specialized in torture if we can judge by the cold-blooded sadism he exhibits in several of the film's scenes. Gross is now the leader of a gang involved in the drug trade and is anxious to expand its business by taking over the operations of a group run by former members of the Stasi, the East German secret police. It is one of these "Germans" that Gross had been in the process of torturing when he was surprised by the police, much to their misfortune.

That immorality and deceit are the order of the day in the emerging free-enterprise system worldwide is evidenced by Gross's foreign connections. Later, a leader of the Russian Mafia (code named "Rewizor," after the phony inspector general in Nikolai Gogol's famous play) arrives for negotiations with Gross; he is a part of an official Russian delegation, probably head of security for the

Russian leader who is greeted warmly at the airport by Polish democratic politician Wencel. The strong implication that not only former security men but also "legitimate" politicians are involved in crime and graft is strengthened as we begin to see more of Gross's organization. He has in his employ in Poland not only members of the police but also government prosecutors and judges. As vile and brutal as Gross is in some scenes, he dresses impeccably (even when killing), and conducts his business negotiations in the best hotels and restaurants, apparently with no fear of apprehension. A toast which Gross and Olo ironically exchange underscores the widespread cynicism about those in power both before and after the fall of Communism: "To hell with the Blacks!" "To hell with the Blacks and the Reds!"

Olo's motivations after he is fired from the police, as he begins, seemingly, to work for Gross, remain somewhat unclear until the film's finale. Gross first contacts Olo as he is about to lose his apartment, offering him enough money for a new spacious apartment and a new car. Olo accepts, but with Franz he implies that he is working for the gangsters only so as to infiltrate their organization and expose them. Finally, it becomes necessary for Olo also to "buy" some favors from Franz. A defining conversation ensues. Olo: "Have you ever thought about money? Big money. A million bucks, say." Franz: "If we don't stop those sons of bitches, it means we really are waste material and our place is on the garbage dump." Olo: "What are we good at anyway?" Franz: "If we won't be policemen, we won't be anything." Where Olo takes for granted the need for capitalism's rewards (money, material goods, power), Franz, who here (and earlier) refers to himself as a saint, remains steadfast in his dedication to order and justice. Franz never seems to reflect on the sources of a reigning definition of order; his outlook is simple and naive: there is evil in the world and it needs to be controlled.

Deeply enmeshed in the cycle of betrayals in the narrative is a teenage femme fatale named Angelika, who is either a nymphomaniac or a woman who has absolutely no compunction about using her body to gain material advantages (perhaps she is both). Franz takes custody of Angelika from a girls' home where she has been placed because of an alleged sexual relationship with a priest who is also her father (this is one of the cases that Franz and Olo have been ordered to bring to a conclusion). At the home, we see a beefy teacher/guard in suspenders who runs his classroom by hazing his young female charges. In rescuing Angelika from this situation, Franz sees himself as a parental figure; he ends up allowing her to live with him. Her thinking and intentions are suggested in the first conversation they have, after Franz takes her from the school and buys her lunch (Angelika: "OK. I'm full. You can fuck me now. . . . Why did you take me out?" Franz: "Maybe I didn't want that butcher in suspenders to fuck you." Angelika: "In that case, you're too late"). For a while, Franz manages to play the parent role in spite of Angelika's sexual advances, but finally, devastated by the deaths of his friends (and accused of dereliction of duty in making a personal phone call while the attack occurred), he seeks release in sex with Angelika and ends up falling in love with her.

In the end, material wealth is the determining motivation for both Olo and Angelika. As the convoluted plot unfolds, we realize that Olo is deceiving both Franz and Gross, apparently in an effort to take over the lucrative drug operation himself. As Franz's economic status falls (Angelika cries when they have to move from his large house to a bare apartment, as Franz, romantically, muses, "We will live here as in heaven") and Olo's visibly rises, Angelika leaves Franz and shacks up with Olo (there is perhaps a hint that she believes she must do this to protect Franz, but her motivations remain mysterious and undefined). The stronger meaning is that in a world defined by money and power, these two are willing to do whatever it takes to get that. Franz, in spite of an increasingly devastating series of financial, professional, and personal setbacks, never wavers in his forceful and courageous pursuit of the criminals. His commitment to order, "sainthood," and a knightly tradition (he doesn't use this metaphor, but his actions fit it) carry him to a final confrontation in which he succeeds in killing both Gross and Olo. By this time, Franz has already been dismissed from the police, so he ends up imprisoned for these murders. Angelika visits him in prison in the film's last scene, offering her affection once again. Franz stoically refuses.

Thus, although *Dogs* displays in its two main protagonists the ruthless energy, initiative, and fortitude demanded by the new conditions of free-enterprise "business," the film, to a much greater degree than American gangster films, places its emphasis on the attendant brutality, exploitation, and immorality. The film does not imply that the Communist system was any better, but it presents scant hope for positive changes under the new economic and political circumstances. What it offers as the only saving grace are the nation's historic commitment to justice and to religious values (these latter play no explicit role in the film's plot, but they are implied by Franz's repeated references to himself as a saint). These values are represented not only by Franz but also by Waldek (the young police recruit who had earlier sought to expose the secret police's illegal burning of files); Franz and Waldek join forces in the latter part of the film to battle evil. The film thus suggests that the principles of morality and a just order must be defended, even if the campaign has no immediate prospects for victory. Although there is no better political and economic system in sight, the film affirms the need for justice and morality.

If the above aspect of *Dogs* might be deemed as progressive in some religious or spiritual sense, such a claim cannot be made as far as issues of gender equality are concerned. Like the early American gangster film genre it copies in many of its structures, *Dogs* is unremittingly patriarchal and misogynistic. Aside from a few prostitutes who appear very briefly in the sequences involving police raids and Gross's wife and daughters (who appear for a few seconds to show us how normal and how refined his home life is), the deceitful and disturbed Angelika is the only female character in the film. Women's only role in the free-enterprise struggle for power is, in this film's view, exploitative and parasitic. The presumption of the narrative is that women can be only sexual objects and wives, in either case the property of men, serving the interests of men. Angelika does not exhibit the independence, energy, creativeness, or intelligence of the American film noir heroine of the late 1940s and after.

Capitalism and gender relations also play a very significant role in Krzysztof Kieslowski's *White* (1994), although it is not a gangster film per se. The film's hero Karol Karol is divorced by his French wife Dominique because of the sudden onset of impotence right after his marriage. This condition coincides with Karol's diminished economic potency in France: he doesn't speak the language well, and all of the finances for their hairdressing salon are in his wife's name. After the divorce, Dominique (who has the personality of a femme fatale) takes everything. Karol manages to return to Poland hidden in a suitcase, which is stolen by corrupt baggage handlers who beat Karol when they discover that he is its only contents. Tossed out onto a snow-covered garbage dump, Karol murmurs, "Home, at last." The color white marks Karol's descent into destitution, and his remarks link his fate to Poland's as the country entered free-market Europe after the collapse of Communism.

After this ignominious start, however, white becomes the color of Karol's recovery of male potency and economic power. Employed as a bodyguard by gangsters, he learns of their scheme to buy land cheap from peasants and then sell it at a huge profit. He outsmarts the gangsters and buys the land himself, insuring himself against retaliation by willing all of his assets to the church. The gangsters have to buy from him at ten times what he paid. Karol's continuing march to capitalist success involves a predominance of white—the land maps, his entirely white corporate office space, his white company warehouses. The color suggests the essential sterility of Karol's campaign. Although he succeeds in luring Dominique back to Poland, taking away her power, bringing her to sexual climax, and regaining her love, the film's color symbolism puts all of his triumphs under a question mark. Is what Karol has gained through deceit and the reassertion of male power really something of essential value? What is the ultimate value of sexual or economic potency?

In Russia, Aleksei Balabanov's popular cycle of gangster films *Brother* (1997) and *Brother, 2* (1999) also raises questions as to the ultimate value of capitalist acquisitiveness, even as the films' protagonist Danila Bogrov retains many of the positive personal characteristics and qualities of the American gangster hero of the 1930s. Danila is clearly a member of the impoverished lower class, hailing from a small northern Russian town and probably from a family of peasant origin. As the narrative unfolds, we learn that he is a veteran of the war in Chechnya, and we see that his service in that war has evidently gotten him nowhere in terms of either social or economic status. In spite of his friendly, charming, naïve, and seemingly kindly demeanor, he turns out to be absolutely fearless and extremely proficient in all manner of fighting—from martial arts to guns and homemade explosives. He is creative in devising operations and determined, resolute, and efficient in carrying them out. In both films, he succeeds in winning virtually every battle, even when he is outnumbered ten to one. He continually devises highly lethal guns and explosives, making them out of everyday materials such as wood, nails, and the phosphorus match tips. In an American gangster film, his skills, determination, and initiative would bring him wealth and power as he moved up the corporate ladder of gangsterdom.

But Danila Bogrov, although he enjoys doing what he does well, is uninterested in capitalist wealth and power. The first shot in *Brother* is of a quintessentially Russian pastoral landscape: a river, woods, a birch tree, an ancient stone wall. It is out of this environment that Danila emerges, as the camera pans to the left to reveal a platinum blonde young woman stripping off a sleek black dress, with her back to us. Thus, in its first move, the camera contrasts traditional Russia with the new Westernized Russia of the 1990s. It turns out that Danila has unknowingly wandered onto the set of a music video that is being filmed. Danila has ruined the shot and the director is furious. He orders one of his security guards to remove Danila from the set—the screen fades to black as we hear the noise of a fight. In a subsequent scene at the local police station, we learn that Danila acquitted himself well in an unequal fight; although his face is battered, he broke the security man's arm and almost knocked his eye out. Learning that Danila has just left the army, the chief offers him a job with the local police. Danila declines.

In the next scene, Danila's mother nags him about his easygoing nature and his lack of ambition ("You'd rather chop wood than stick your neck out") and sings the praises of her older son Viktor, a "big man" in St. Petersburg. She tells Danila that he must go to Viktor, because Viktor has been like a father to him and will help him find his way in life. The Viktor we meet in the very next shot *is* a gangster in the classic American mold. We watch as he bargains with a higher gangster boss, "Roundface," over his fee for assassinating "the Chechen," the leader of a rival gang that has taken over the protection racket at a local market. Because the Chechen is under the protection of an even higher gangster, Roundface needs an anonymous method of having him killed. Offered $15,000 for the job, Viktor demands $20,000 and gets it, with $10,000 paid up front (as we learn in the next sequence, Roundface intends to have Viktor killed anyway, as soon as he accomplishes his task). This is the business into which Danila travels to St. Petersburg to be initiated, although there is no initial indication that he would want such work.

Watching Danila proceed to St. Petersburg and look for his brother there, we do not get the impression that making a fortune is of any concern to him. His one prized possession is his Sony Discman portable CD player, and he would like to buy CDs of his favorite performers, like Nautilus, but he doesn't have enough money. When he does finally find Viktor, the latter offers him $2,000 (only) to kill the Chechen. Viktor is behaving as an opportunistic capitalist businessman would, taking a huge profit for acting as a middleman, even though it is his own brother whom he is exploiting. After Danila successfully carries out the murder, Viktor suggests that they start a firm, "Bogrov Brothers." "What will we do?" asks Danila. "Business," replies Viktor. So the metaphor of the gang as a business (also, unfortunately, a literal reality in Russia) is firmly in place, as in the American genre. With the money he is paid, Danila gets himself some more stylish clothes, buys himself some CDs and concert tickets, and also obtains a small amount of drugs for recreational use from a young hippie woman, named Kat, whom he has met outside McDonald's. But these material possessions do not represent any significant wealth or status. Viktor is the ambitious and deceitful gangster as businessman; Danila is his opposite, not only indifferent to success in a material sense but to status as well. When asked what he did during the war, he replies sheepishly that he sat out the fighting as a clerk at headquarters, but his skill in the technology of guns and explosives, and his coolness under fire, suggest otherwise.

If money and success do not drive Danila, what does? The answer to this question is not immediately apparent, but we get a clue in his first visit to the market, before he has even reconnected with his older brother. A shabbily dressed man is selling watches and other small items on the sidewalk; a thug in a leather jacket comes up to him and demands money for "protection." When the poor man protests that he has not even managed to sell anything yet, the thug begins to confiscate his meager array of "goods." Danila, who has been watching these events unfold, intervenes. He knocks the thug out with a single blow and rescues the man, who turns out to be a Russian of German descent, named Goffman. Understanding that Danila is a good person, Goffman warns him about being corrupted by the norms of city life ("The city is a terrible force. It sucks you in").

As Danila proceeds with his clever plan to assassinate the Chechen (he disguises himself as a student and uses some decoy explosives to distract the crime king's bodyguards) and subsequently foils or repels repeated efforts by Roundface's henchmen to kill him, he also goes out of his way to help others in need (and those he helps reciprocate). Danila shares the homemade food his mother has sent (for brother Viktor) with Goffman and other seemingly homeless folks who find shelter in a shed at the old Lutheran cemetery. He comes to the aid of a tram conductor who is trying to collect fares from two recalcitrant passengers of non-Russian (perhaps Chechen) ethnicity. He befriends Sveta, a trolley driver who aids him in his escape from Roundface's gang and takes it upon himself to protect her from her drunken husband who beats her. Goffman and Sveta, in their turn, help Danila. Goffman aids him in finding an apartment and later helps him by burying a couple of gangsters whom Danila has killed. Sveta provides Danila with comfort and love when he is wounded and lies to Roundface about Danila's whereabouts (for which she is later beaten and raped by thugs as revenge).

Rather than being an entrepreneur striving to carve out a successful position for himself in Russia's new capitalist society, Danila selflessly takes the side of ordinary Russians who are the economic losers in the new Russia. When Danila, at the film's end, rescues his brother Viktor from Roundface's clutches, he exacts no revenge for Viktor's betrayals (by this time, Viktor has knowingly set up Danila to be killed). Instead, he reminds Viktor of his love for him ("You're my brother. . . . You took Dad's place. I even called you 'Papa'") and tells him that he should return to their hometown, take a job with the local police, and be of assistance to their mother. Although he is every bit as tough as the American gangster hero, Danila represents not egoism and narcissism, but a commitment to decent, honest, family, and communal behavior. Such love of community is expressed as well when Danila wanders accidentally into a party at the apartment of one of his singing idols, Viacheslav Butusov. Danila seems spellbound by the warm romantic sentiments reflected in the music, and enchanted by the air of congeniality which abounds. It isn't fame and fortune that Danila seeks but simply a pleasant, friendly, and humane life with good people. There is no explicit connection of any of this with Communism as an ideology, but it does vaguely suggest Russian nineteenth-century Slavophile beliefs about Russia as a community.

There is a further link to the Slavophile tradition in the fact that Danila's sense of community is distinctly Russian and not multiethnic. When Goffman introduces himself as a German, Danila says that he has nothing against Germans, although he doesn't care for Jews. He is willing to accept the ethnic Germans who are centuries-long inhabitants of St. Petersburg and are thoroughly Russified, but he is particularly antipathetic to people from the Caucasus region or Central Asia (he called the men who refused to pay their fare on the trolley "black-assed worms"), always referring to them in pejorative terms. In fact, Viktor successfully recruits Danila to assassinate "the Chechen" by appealing to his Russian ethnic loyalty ("He knows we're weak, so he is strangling us. So now it's them or us, brother"). Danila is anti-American as well; at a dance he says to a Frenchman he mistakes for an American: "Your American music is shit and you yourselves are, too" (this in spite of the fact that the folk rock that Danila favors is strongly influenced by American models). In this sense, Danila's loyal and protective behavior toward others and his spectacular efficiency as a hit man take on a distinctly chauvinistic cast.

The film's endorsement of Russian chauvinism is complemented by its commitment to traditional patriarchy. Women in the film act exclusively in the service of men. Danila's mother is devoted to her boys. Kat, the young hippie, is willing to provide Danila with both drugs and sex, as long as he has the money to pay for a good time. Although he is not driven by a need for either of these things, he accepts them, albeit with some reluctance. He more willingly accepts the affectionate sex that comes his way from Sveta. Neither of these women stays with him in the end, and he is gracious in accepting this. He gives Kat money when he leaves St. Petersburg; he wants Sveta to go with him, but she feels she must stay with her husband, who is so helpless without her (especially after Danila shoots him in the leg after he returns to his wife in a drunk and abusive state). Sveta tells Danila, "Don't come by anymore. I don't love you." He places a CD that he has brought her on the table and leaves quietly. Danila is not a brute, and he does not force himself upon women; nonetheless, the film's major women characters please him of their own accord and do not act in the film except in relation to men and their needs.

These basic patterns are continued in the sequel, *Brother, 2* (Balabanov, 1999). The business nature of the gangster activities in this film are now globalized, international, and corporate. There are two allied gangster syndicates, whose leaders (Belkin in Russia and Manis in the United States) live in mansions and conduct their affairs in vast corporate office buildings. Modern business communication and information systems abound—even at the lower levels where Danila, his brother Viktor (once more in the fold), and his war veteran buddy Ilya operate, computers and cell phones are in constant use. Another of Danila's war buddies, Kostya Gromov, is double-crossed and killed by Belkin's gang, and Danila and Viktor fly to the United States to the defense of Kostya's brother, who is playing professional hockey in Chicago. Of course, they foil the villains, after many gun battles, and also rescue a Russian prostitute Dasha (a.k.a. Marilyn) who is being exploited by an African American pimp. The most violent and bloody scenes involve Danila's assault on the members of the pimp's gang. The level of racist sentiment in the film is high, with African Americans the main target in other sequences as well. Danila does become good friends with an American truck driver, Ben Johnson, but he is white (like the German, Goffman, in *Brother*). Just as disturbing are scenes back in Russia where Danila and Viktor buy guns and artillery from an arms dealer nicknamed "Fascist," who wears a Nazi uniform and whose premises are decorated with swastikas.

Danila's relationships with women are quite similar to those in *Brother*. In the early Russian sequences of the film, he easily strikes up a romantic liaison with the Russian pop singer Irina Saltykova and maintains contact with her via cell phone throughout his American adventures. In Chicago, he just as easily beds an African American television newscaster, Lisa Jeffries, when she takes him to her home after accidentally running into him with her car. Finally there is Dasha, the Russian prostitute whom he rescues and brings back to Russia with him in the film's final sequence. All of these women are in the narrative only to be charmed by Danila and to help him, although, in Dasha's case, he is also her rescuer.

Thus, in both *Brother* and *Brother, 2,* the emphases on entrepreneurial skills and on capitalist goals are displaced or mediated by values of a different sort. Foremost among these is a principle of community and solidarity with the people at the very lowest end of the economic ladder (the wealthy and successful gangsters in both films are Danila's enemies; he seeks not to replace them but to eliminate them so that they cannot continue to exploit others). Another value represented positively is, unfortunately, Russian racism: the ordinary people to be defended in these films are for the most part Russians, and there is strong antipathy to "others" who threaten Russians (these others are people of color in both films). Finally, traditional patriarchal stereotypes around gender and sexuality are steadfastly maintained in both films, as they were in the early American gangster film.

In conclusion, we can note that the two most popular heroes of the past decade's Polish and Russian crime films conform to the patterns established by the American genre with regard to the personal qualities of their protagonists. Both

Franz Maurer and Danila Bogrov exhibit the qualities necessary for success in a capitalist economy: toughness, determination, initiative, ingenuity, technical proficiency. Both characters defeat their enemies by acting, unhesitatingly, beyond the bounds of the law; capitalist legality is viewed only as a cover for ruthless economic competition—there is no real distinction between gangsters and "legitimate" businessmen. Finally, both films assert patriarchal prerogatives, with the heroes wanting to protect and possess the women they desire (in both cases, the protagonists represent a benevolent rather than a rapacious patriarchy).

But Franz and Danila differ markedly from the American crime film hero in their seeming indifference to success and material wealth. Self-interest is condemned in both films. Franz, the self-proclaimed "saint," fights to the end for an abstract principle of order and justice. It is never defined, but it may point in the direction of the ideal values of Poland's Catholic tradition, values clearly at odds with capitalist goals on the material level. Danila's dedication to the well-being of the Russian community as a whole also takes on a vaguely religious cast in its echoes of Slavophile ideals, along with an unmistakable national chauvinism. The films are symptomatic of a thorough-going skepticism in both societies as to the ultimate worth of the capitalist system, particularly against the background of deep-seated cultural, religious, and ethnic values.

Notes

1. The broad dimensions of this debate are described, for example, in Joanne Hollows and Mark Jancovich, eds., *Approaches to Popular Film* (Manchester: Manchester University Press, 1995).

2. John Fiske, "Popular Discrimination," in *Modernity and Mass Culture*, ed. James Naremore and Patrick Brantlinger (Bloomington: Indiana University Press, 1991), 104. Fiske's views on the creativity of popular responses to "mass" culture were elaborated in two concurrent books, *Understanding Popular Culture* (Boston: Unwin Hyman, 1989) and *Reading the Popular* (Boston: Unwin Hyman, 1989).

3. For an excellent discussion of the efforts to control and alter the content of the gangster film, see Jonathan Munby, *Public Enemies, Public Heroes: Screening the Gangster from Little Caesar to Touch of Evil* (Chicago: University of Chicago Press, 1999), 83–114.

4. Munby, *Public Enemies*, 193.

5. See, in particular, the collection of essays in *Women in Film Noir*, ed. E. Anne Kaplan (London: British Film Institute, 1978).

6. For a more complete analysis of Polanski's *Chinatown*, see Herbert Eagle, "Polanski," in *Five Filmmakers: Tarkovsky, Forman, Polanski, Szabo, Makavejev*, ed. Daniel Goulding (Bloomington: Indiana University Press, 1994), 143–55.

7. Benya Krik was the Jewish gangster hero who appeared in several of the Russian writer Isaac Babel's celebrated "Odessa Tales."

8. This is the first of many visual and verbal references to dogs in connection with the secret police, the regime's hunting dogs, as it were. To retain this association, the film's English distribution title was changed to *Pigs*.

11

Two Cheers for the Red, White, and Blue

Hungarian Assessments
of American Popular Culture

handwritten note: "the displays (local tradition) values but culture"

ARTICLES IN THE U.S. PRESS on the expansion of American popular culture into
East Central Europe suggest that there is no resistance, that, like
Pinocchio in Fantasyland, Hungarians and other East Central Europeans have
gone on a pleasure binge of eating cheeseburgers, watching *Wheel of Fortune,* and
playing Nintendo. Thus, for example, a *New York Times* article quotes an official
at Hungary's Home Box Office as saying that while the government wants a television system which serves the people, "that's not what the people want. They
want to be stimulated, they want to be entertained."[1] Even more polemically, a
Hungarian correspondent for *The Nation* asserted that "Hungarians, Czechoslo-
vaks, and Bulgarians try to imitate everything that is American—and I mean
everything."[2]

Obviously, the author is exaggerating. But his stylistic flourish raises interesting
questions: What *does* the red, white, and blue label mean to Hungarians? What
significance do they attach to the expansion of American culture and its growing
influence in Hungary? Even scholars who argue against notions of cultural imperialism concede that the U.S. exerts a strong influence around the world, but they
deny that drinking Coca-Cola or smoking Marlboros profoundly transforms local
cultures. In Claude-Jean Bertrand's words, "Jeans worn by a Russian youth do not
Americanize him."[3] Thus, another question which arises is whether Hungarians
are concerned about the displacement of local traditions and values by imported
culture.

These questions were the focus of a pilot project conducted by the American
Studies seminar at Janus Pannonius University in Pécs during the spring of 1993.
In order to explore the reception of American culture by Hungarians, we designed
a study based on the ethnographic approach to media audiences established by

David Morley.[4] Following this research tradition, we conceptualized Hungarian audiences as socially situated subjects for whom the consumption of popular culture is an active process of making meaning and an integral part of larger cultural patterns. In an effort to capture some of the complexity of their encounter with American culture, the investigation was based on unstructured interviews.

Thirteen people, whose ages ranged from nineteen to fifty-three, were interviewed. While we assumed that certain demographic traits such as class position were powerful determinants of attitudes toward imported popular culture, sample limitations in the study did not allow us to examine such correlations. Most of our respondents were members of a highly educated class which was unrepresentative of Hungarian society. (Five were professionals, five were university students, and three were clerks.) We collected data on the occupation, education, age, and family status of respondents as a basis for further investigations. In addition, we made it a point to locate respondents who belonged to each of three major "taste cultures"—people who preferred popular entertainment, people who preferred the fine arts, and people who regularly participated in folk music or dancing. Of course, these categories are not discrete. But the idea was to include representatives of a spectrum of musical tastes.

An interview schedule guided the questioning and enabled us to spot common trends in the responses, but the interviews were loosely structured and informants were encouraged to respond freely to open-ended questions. The interviews lasted about thirty to forty minutes. Conducted in Hungarian, they were tape-recorded and later transcribed and translated into English. The analysis of the transcripts involved searching for patterns in the responses. In interpreting and reporting the results, we have noted some points of divergence as well as convergence in the responses. The extended use of direct quotes in the report is intended to allow respondents to tell their stories in their own words. Their names have been changed to ensure anonymity.

Before I discuss the results, a short description of the status of American culture in Pécs is in order. A city of 170,000 at the time, Pécs is the seat of Baranya county and an ancient center of culture and learning (the university was founded in 1367). About 80 percent of the films shown in its three movie theaters at the time were American, according to the managers. In a random week in March 1993, the lineup included one German-French production (Wenders's *Sky over Berlin*), and one film from Great Britain (Greenaway's *The Cook, the Thief, His Wife, and Her Lover*). The rest were American: *Thelma and Louise, Mo' Money, Of Mice and Men, She Devil, Frankie and Johnnie,* and *Steel Dawn*. In addition, video rentals have been popular; in 1993, there were more than twenty rental shops in the city. A clerk in a typical shop estimated that about 1,000 of the shop's tapes were American.

Studies show that Hungarians have relatively little leisure time, and that television is the major source of entertainment and relaxation. In Baranya county, people spent an average of just under two hours per day watching television.[5] In addition to several Hungarian channels, cable television was already offering news and entertainment channels from Britain, Germany, Italy, France, Croatia, and Serbia. The local cable systems were already delivering the European edition of MTV, Eurosport, and programs of the Hungarian affiliate of HBO. The last mentioned carries mainly American films and dramatic series dubbed into Hungarian. American action series, situation comedies, soap operas, miniseries, and other genres have also been available in a variety of languages.

As far as English-language programming is concerned, the British entertainment channels, Sky One and the Super Channel, carry programs ranging from *Star Trek* to *The Simpsons* to *Saturday Night Live*. But because of the language barrier for most Hungarians, of more importance to this study is American programming dubbed into Hungarian. The two major Hungarian channels, Magyar TV 1 and 2, broadcast Disney cartoons, *Sesame Street,* some American films, and a handful of American dramatic and action series.

Finally, we should note the high visibility of a limited but expanding range of American products, services, and franchises. Pepsi Cola is bottled at the local beer factory. Nike, Levi's, and Lee's apparel were on sale in specialty shops. And Dairy Queen opened its doors to business at one end of the town center.

I shall begin this report of our findings with a discussion of the general attitude of Hungarians toward America and a review of the process of cultural importation. This will be followed by a closer look at what they admired and what they disliked about the products of American culture and the values those products embodied. I shall then address the question of whether the Hungarians sampled in 1993 believed that American culture influences local behavior, styles, and values. Finally, I shall consider whether Hungarians viewed American culture as a threat to the local culture.

Importing Images

The image Hungarians carried of the United States was a mixture of the popular and fine arts, man-made and natural wonders, and mythic episodes in the nation's history. For Ildikó, a fifty-year-old physician, the word "America" means

> Walt Disney, country music and jazz, the Empire State Building and the Grand Canyon, Indians and settlers, the beat generation, and the big city of New York. . . . "American culture" means different things, like the New York Philharmonic, the films of Sidney Pollack or Chaplin, the works of Updike, Hemingway, Norman Mailer or James Jones; . . . actors such as Paul Newman, Robert Redford, Jane Fonda, Dustin Hoffman, Spencer Tracy, or Gregory Peck.

The geographic location of Hungary has placed it at the crossroads, or even within the confines, of various civilizations over the centuries. Today, traces of Roman, Turkish, and Austrian influence are plainly visible in Pécs. Nor has cul-

tural exchange been a one-way process. The borders of Hungary have been noto-
riously fluid, and it has left its linguistic and cultural imprint in neighboring
countries. Perhaps for geographic and historical reasons, then, cultural synthesis
is accepted as an inevitable process. In talking about imported cultural products,
a number of our respondents insisted that *origin* is not important, but rather
quality. Ferenc, a twenty-year-old student of ethnography, put it like this:

> If we are talking about American culture we have to distinguish. What I am afraid of
> is not that culture which can be hallmarked by Truman Capote or Leonard Bernstein
> or Woody Allen. . . . American culture includes not only Batman and McDonald's.
> Being an "American something" doesn't say a word about the thing's quality. It can be
> valuable or worthless.

The insignificance of national origin as a determinant of a product's quality
was raised repeatedly in discussions of film. The comments of Gábor, a twenty-
one-year-old medical student, are representative:

> I like good films, for example, *All that Jazz.* I don't think only American films can be
> good, or because a film is American it doesn't automatically mean it's good. There are
> very good Hungarian movies, for example, *Indul a Bakterhaz, Mert Kell egy Csapat,*
> *Sose Halunk Meg,* [and] *?-álom.* Good films are not connected to specific nations. I
> like Czech movies, too. My favorite actor is Jean-Paul Belmondo, who is French. . . . I
> don't watch a movie just because it's American. It can be a good Lithuanian film and
> I'll go [and] watch it.

The problem many of our respondents see is that most of the films imported
from the U.S. have little aesthetic value. Zoltán, a fifty-three-year-old journalist,
voiced this opinion: "I would say that the films broadcast in Hungary are of extremely low quality, with of course some exceptions. They are mainly action films
with plenty of blood and murders."

In addition, in the case of films, it is hard to overlook the dominance of American products in the Hungarian market or to ignore the consequences for domestic production. A number of respondents voiced regret about the paucity of Hungarian films, or at least their inaccessibility to mass audiences. Edit, a
twenty-year-old travel agent, said, "Only a few Hungarian films are advertised.
There may be more, but they are unknown to the average person." Several interviewees blamed Hollywood. Zoltán stated that the heavy importation of foreign
films posed a danger to local production. He explained, "It's the same as the
dumping of goods. They come to Hungary in such large quantities and at such
cheap prices that the cost of renting American films may be one-thousandth of
the cost of making a single Hungarian film."

In the case of other cultural products, where local artists and industries are not
directly threatened by American monopolization, cultural importation is met
with fewer reservations. For instance, most respondents said that Western fast

food franchises are not likely to drive local restaurants out of business, because they are not so plentiful and because they serve different clienteles. Indeed, imported products are highly valued for adding variety to Hungarian life, for presenting choices to suit consumers' moods and tastes. Gabriella, a thirty-year-old clerk in a florist's shop, stated that McDonald's, Dairy Queen, and Kentucky Fried Chicken have "introduced new flavors into the Hungarian cuisine."

This variety is particularly attractive in light of the fact that products from the West, especially the United States, were not widely available in the past. Eszter, a thirty-eight-year-old lawyer, explains that American brands are attractive

> because we couldn't get Western goods for so long. . . . Everybody thought we should buy them rather than use homemade products. But this feeling is changing as a lot of people have experiences with these "famous" Western products. More and more people are learning that packaging is less important than the contents.

Thus, American products are attractive in part because they are still a little exotic. As such, some of their current popularity is likely to wane as they lose the luster of novelty.

Ferenc summed up the prevailing attitude toward the general process of cultural importation when he told us, "One thing's for sure. It's fundamental for a culture to come into contact with other cultures. This is the only and most effective way for development to take place."

Attitudes toward American Culture and Products

Situated at a busy intersection in the middle of a city, the Dairy Queen is the most visible symbol of American culture in Pécs. It is thus a good place to begin discussing what Hungarians specifically like and dislike about American life as it is stamped into the nation's exports. In addition to ice cream and soft drinks, the local Dairy Queen serves burgers and fries. Its interior is similar to a McDonald's in the United States. The lighting, the tile floors and plastic counters, and the clean lines of the furniture lend a pleasing sense of space. Touches of Americana include a salad bar, a youthful staff sporting red, white, and blue uniforms, and a wall-sized television monitor perpetually tuned to MTV.

The quality of the food served at the Dairy Queen is clearly of less salience than the symbolism attached to the act of patronizing a Western-style, fast-food restaurant. (Comments about the taste of the hamburgers ranged from "terrible" to "pretty good.") For young people, fast-food outlets represented "a slice of America," a fashionable spot to see and be seen. Several parents reported taking their children to the Dairy Queen to celebrate birthdays or other special occasions. Gabriella, a single mother, sometimes treated her nine-year-old son to a hamburger and cola as a reward when he would achieve high marks in school. For teens and young adults, fast-food restaurants serve as a social space for hanging out with friends. Several adults described this function of fast-food restaurants in positive terms, explaining that when they were young, teens had no place to go.

Most of our respondents found the atmosphere of the Dairy Queen inviting, and several women praised the décor—the soft colors, the harmony, the design of the furniture. But, for some people, the uniformity of food, décor, and service amounted to an alien intrusion of American standards. Miklós, a twenty-eight-year-old physician, expressed this criticism in terms of the excessive sterility of the Dairy Queen: "I find it irritating that when somebody drops a piece of food on the floor, one of the staff is there right away and cleans it up immediately. This exaggerated precision is annoying to a Hungarian. . . . I don't like to eat in a place which resembles an operating room."

The standardized nature of mass culture was criticized in terms of global fads in fashion as well as in food. Miklós extended his critique of fast-food outlets to the predictability of internationally marketed clothing: "It's not just Dairy Queen. It's the same with jeans stores. What bothers me is that you know exactly what you're going to get, what the product looks like. A pair of Levi's 501s is the same all over the world." But American industry and the mass production of consumer products were applauded by others for delivering high quality goods at reasonable prices. Zoltán cited cars as an example, stating that the American system of manufacturing resulted in cars which are comfortable and not too harmful to the environment.

Because of the multiple modes of viewing films—going to the cinema, watching rented videos at home or in a dormitory lounge, watching movies on cable television—distinctions between film and television tended to blur in the interviews. Most respondents said they go to the movies or watch television in order to relax and be entertained, functions in which American products excel. Ákos, a twenty-two-year-old student majoring in social work, believed that the escapist quality of American productions accounted for their popularity. While he himself preferred Hungarian films, he said, "They stink of life, of reality. Hungarian audiences can't relax, can't step out of reality as they can when they watch an American movie."

Given the fact that many Hungarians held second or even third jobs in order to make ends meet, the value placed on escape made sense. But it was not universal—Pál, the local leader of a political party, liked to watch political programs and nature films—and the form escapism might take was varied. Peter, a nineteen-year-old clerk in a video store, liked to watch MTV. Jozsef, a twenty-seven-year-old student of Hungarian music and folk culture, liked the film *Cotton Club* for the tap dancing. Ildikó enjoyed light television comedies such as *Family Ties* or *Full House*.

But within this variety of preferences, a couple of common patterns emerged. First, most people expressed a strong distaste for violent television programs and films. They often cited the *Rambo* or *Terminator* series as examples of American dramas in which flimsy plots served as vehicles for grotesque forms and levels of violence. Zoltán raised these objections: "I can think of a very popular film which is mainly admired by kids, *The Terminator.* I can easily tell you why I didn't like it. It presents as a hero to the audience a man we ought to condemn. Such films glorify the power of the physical body, not that of the intellect, and they present it as behavior to be emulated."

But the prevalence of such films in Hungarian theaters in the early 1990s attested to their popularity and suggests that demographic characteristics need to be taken into account in evaluating the acceptance of American culture. While this study does not allow us to establish correlations between socioeconomic class and cultural tastes, it is suggestive that one of our few working class interviewees, Gabriella, was fond of action films and counted Charles Bronson and Sylvester Stallone among her favorite actors. And once again, as with fast food, parenthood made a difference in the willingness of Hungarians to tolerate certain products of American culture. Eszter, who had a thirteen-year-old son and a six-year-old daughter, said she did not personally like the characters played by Arnold Schwarzenegger. But she admitted that she watched his films with her children, who enjoyed the action.

A second recurring them involved disdain for the false pictures of wealth presented in American cultural productions—the constant parade of luxurious cars, palatial homes, and gorgeously dressed people. As Zoltán put it, American films and television programs present an image of the United States as a paradise where "even the fences are made of sausage." Several respondents leveled this charge against the highly popular television program *Dallas.* Miklós said, "I cannot bear *Dallas.* This is the falsest picture of America ever. It shows only the happy life of the upper class."

This criticism emerged indirectly in a discussion of music as well. Virtually all of our respondents detested rap music for the monotony of the rhythm. One exception was Ákos. Although he didn't speak English, he had seen translations of rap lyrics and found them compelling. He explained why: "They give a very precise picture of the American underclass. Rap artists have managed to call the world's attention to what is behind the American glitter, to show the other side of the coin."

The distaste Hungarians expressed for the false appearances presented in film and television spilled over into disdain for the superficiality of American values. Gábor expressed it like this: "The American people seem to be empty. They have appearance and nothing else, though they're not aware of it and don't seem to care about it. Personality means outward appearance for them: clothes, perfect looks, makeup. For us Hungarians, personality is inside." But if Americans are shallow and their goals materialistic, there was still great admiration for the determination of Americans to achieve those goals, and for a system which makes their realization attainable. Gábor continued, "In America, and this is what I like the most, if you have an aim, an idea, and if you're even a little bit ambitious, you can achieve anything you want, you can make your dreams come true."

Hungarians also admire the optimism and cheerfulness of Americans. Gabriella watched the Clinton inauguration on HBO. To her, the behavior and demeanor of the nation's new leaders and their families, the performers, and the guests suggested that Americans were patriotic, upbeat, carefree, and believe deeply in their system.

U.S. Popular Culture: A Threat?

Let us turn now to the question of whether Hungarians believe American culture influences the behavior, style, and values of Hungarians. Most of our respondents believed that the influence was mainly on young people, and that for the young, this influence was direct, immediate, and annoying, if not harmful. Zoltán described the effects of American culture on the behavior of youngsters in these words: "That certain movement when they put their feet on the table as in American films, or the constant chewing of gum everywhere, even in church or in restaurants. Then the half-mad youths who ride around town on their motorcycles, frightening the passersby. Or those who wear jackets studded with nails." Several interviewees provided examples of the actual modelling of the style of celebrities or their fictitious characters as evidence. For example, Edit told about a classmate in her hotel management and tourism course who modeled herself after *Dallas*'s Pamela. But respondents disagreed about whether the adoption of the trappings of American culture involved shifts in values as well. Asked whether she believed her classmate adopted Pamela's values, Edit responded, "Does it influence internal values as well? I can't imagine that it does. It's only the external look." Zoltán disagrees:

> If someone dresses in a certain way, it shows that he is apt to behave in a certain way. A person's values change even if that person does not want them to. If I think of bomber jackets, which are not new even in America but are part of some nostalgic cult of war, if they spread, then a certain aggressive, power-loving behavior will also spread.

As for mature adults, respondents denied that there were any direct effects on behavior. Ildikó, for example, said that American culture did not affect her way of life at all. She added, "I'm not interested at all in junk food, printed T-shirts, or chewing gum, if you know what I mean." But while respondents denied any immediate influence, they admitted the likelihood of subtle behavioral and attitudinal influences. For instance, Eszter stated, "You hear how fit American women are and how much they care about their health, so you do the same. You are influenced indirectly." As for deeply rooted values, once again, respondents stated that the effects are subtle and the sources of influence are complex. Gábor said, "America has an influence on us, not only through films, but unconsciously. . . . I have a complex picture in my mind about America. I have it from films, from people who are Americans or once lived in the States. All these unconsciously influence my *Weltanschauung.*"

Finally, asked for their thoughts about whether American products threaten local culture, our respondents were generally unconcerned. A variety of reasons surfaced. The most common argument was that in a market economy, people are free to choose as they wish. A majority of people will always shun literature and the fine arts in favor of mass entertainment, and it doesn't particularly matter where this is produced. The comments of Béla, a twenty-one-year-old student majoring in Hungarian literature and linguistics, reflected this sentiment. Béla said he is not opposed to American culture because if American mass media were not available, most people would simply select Hungarian "trash": "You can't do anything to stop this process. . . . [The Hungarian writer] Kazinczy was right when he said that sophisticated culture is not for the masses but for a chosen few."

A second common explanation for the lack of concern had to do with the domestic economy of the average Hungarian household. Budgetary constraints narrowly limit the ability of most Hungarians to purchase expensive imported goods. Gabriella said, "In their clothes or home furnishings, people can't afford to follow American fashions because they don't have enough money." And virtually all of our respondents noted that fast-food outlets were prohibitively expensive, at the time, for most Hungarians. Ákos compared their prices to the cost of preparing the same food at home: "They are extremely expensive. I cannot afford them. A hamburger in Dairy Queen costs nearly 100 forints, but you can buy the ingredients for a similar one in a store for about 30 forints." In addition, the holding of multiple jobs left little time for entertainment and limited exposure to foreign works. Most respondents reported that they seldom went to the movies or even watched much television, and that, as a result, their traditional living habits were not disrupted very much by the intrusion of American media.

At the time, there were no legal restrictions on the importation of films or television programs into the country. Legislation had been drafted, however, to place quotas on television programs broadcast over Hungarian channels, but would not limit cable or satellite delivery of foreign channels. The responses of several of our interviewees suggested that a third reason for the lack of concern about American imports was an erroneous assumption that the Hungarian government vigorously protected local culture against foreign influences. Eszter, a lawyer, stated: "The values and traditions of a country can't be changed so easily by popular culture. This process is checked by the leaders of the country." (The assumption of government intervention into the economy seems to be a vestige of the old system. Béla said that he resented the fact that fast-food outlets were permitted into Hungary after studies elsewhere had revealed that their food is not nutritious. He did not say who should have stopped them or how.)

Several people found comfort in the fact that Hungarian culture is grounded in broader European traditions. For Ildikó, the strength of this tradition protected

Hungary against the intrusion of images and ideas from the United States. She said, "I don't think American culture can threaten the Hungarian one, because our culture is part of European culture, which is much older than the American one. It is the classical one, and in spite of the fact that Hungary is considered to be an East European country, its culture is definitely European." Other people noted that the United States and Hungary share a common West European heritage, and that American contributions to Hungarian culture are, thus, not entirely alien.

In conclusion, the investigation revealed a great deal of sensitivity among Hungarians to issues of cultural influence. Cultural synthesis was seen as a healthy process, and there was a general tolerance for foreign ideas, practices, and products. Among young people, there was a fascination with the emblems of American culture. But many people were uneasy about the consequences of an unrestricted expansion of foreign culture, and concerned specifically about the quality of media products imported from the United States. Hungarians certainly realize that the stakes are high. Ferenc put it best: "Culture means everything. If you have lost your culture or it has become highly standardized, you have lost your identity. That cannot happen here."

Notes

First published in *Journal of Popular Culture* 29, no. 2 (Fall 1995). Reprinted by kind permission of the author and the editor of *Journal of Popular Culture*.

1. *New York Times* (27 December 1992), p. 16.

2. Miklós Vámos, "Hungary for American Pop," in *The Nation* (25 March 1991), p. 375.

3. Claude-Jean Bertrand, "American Cultural Imperialism—A Myth?" in *American Studies International,* Vol. 25, No. 1 (1987), p. 58.

4. See David Morley, *The Nationwide Audience* (London: British Film Institute, 1980); and David Morley, *Family Television* (London: Comedia, 1986).

5. *Helyzetkép Baranya Lakossaganak Idö felhasználásáról* (Pécs: A Kozponti Statisztikai Hivatal, Baranya Megyei Igazgatosaga, 1989), p. 31.

12

Have a Nice Day: From the Balkan War to the American Dream and the Things That Shape the Way We See Each Other

Gordana P. Crnković

The Importance of Being Esther

IN *HEJ BABU-RIBA*, a film set in Yugoslavia in the 1950s, the nickname of the main female character is uncharacteristically foreign—"Ester." The real name of this girl, the heartthrob of all the young men in the story, is actually Mirjana, but she gets the nickname Ester in reference to American swimmer and actress Esther Williams, whose films were shown all over Yugoslavia in the fifties and whose popularity at the time was immense.

As Croatian writer Dubravka Ugrešić remarks, Esther Williams and Hollywood films were among the main allies in the Yugoslav struggle against Soviet ideology and culture after the famous Tito–Stalin break of 1948. After 1948, Yugoslavia attempted to create its own unique politics which included being a socialist country with its own non-Soviet mode of socialism (marked by attempts of worker self-management), refusing to belong to the Warsaw Pact bloc or to take its orders from the USSR, opening borders to the West without being in NATO, and founding the nonaligned movement (together with Egypt and India). The creation of an independent politics was followed by attempts to create a unique culture, one that included rather than excluded a variety of international influences in its own national space. The "mixture" included historically prominent Germanic, Italian, French, and Russian cultures, newly established ties with countries and cultures of the Third World (through, for example, students who came to Yugoslavia from a variety of Asian, African, and Latin American countries, as well as through newly formed economic connections with those countries), and, very prominently, American culture and the increasingly popular English language. Though postwar U.S. politics was often severely criticized (e.g., the war in Vietnam), American films, rock music, and later television serials (e.g., *Peyton Place, Bonanza, Dynasty,* and *Dallas*) have existed more or less peacefully and influentially in the Yugoslav cultural space. American writers like Theodore Dreiser, Jack London, and later J. D. Salinger were popular and frequently translated.

Speaking in general terms, one could say that the United States was for many people a contradiction. On the one hand, the perception of the United States was greatly shaped by the official discourses of politics and Marxist education (even when these discourses were opposed), which saw this country as the embodiment of the worst type of capitalism, marked by worker exploitation, interpersonal alienation, imperialist politics, and the demonization of communism as well as socialism. In a country like the former Yugoslavia, with general medical insurance and free education, for example, an average person would cringe in disbelief upon hearing "American" stories about people not getting proper medical treatment or not being admitted to a good school just because they were poor. On the other hand, American popular culture was a strong force in setting the norms of various aspects of everyday life, including things such as bodily beauty, desirable objects (cars, houses, clothes, furniture), or romantic affairs. When the British actor Richard Burton played the role of Josip Broz Tito in the Yugoslav film *Neretva*, he and his wife, American actress Elizabeth Taylor, visited Yugoslav president Tito in his residence on the island of Brioni. All the loves of Elizabeth Taylor were themselves a subject of great interest in the Yugoslav tabloid press, but it was a disappointment to bystanders when the actress visited the Croatian resort city of Opatija and was found to be much less attractive in person than on screen.

American culture has been a source of continuous interest, a fact illustrated by the accounts of Yugoslavs who travelled to or lived in the United States and tried to interpret or translate American culture to domestic audiences. This chapter involves one such account, written by Dubravka Ugrešić, entitled *Have a Nice Day: From the Balkan War to the American Dream* and relating to the author's 1992 stay in Middletown, Connecticut, and New York City.

After I delivered a paper about this book to the 1994 American Association of Teachers of Slavic and East European Languages, (AATSEEL) Convention, I was asked questions about the ways in which Ugrešić's national, ethnic, gender, class, and sexual locations and identities affected her views of the United States and the American culture. Questions were also posed about the effects which the political situation at the time of the book's composition (the onset of the violence in the former Yugoslavia and the U.S. stand on it) had on Ugrešić's perception of America. I attempted to answer these questions as well as I could, but I felt that these were the "wrong questions" to the extent that they focused the understanding of this text within a list of already established categories of discursive analysis (including ethnicity, nationality, gender, etc.), instead of trying to find different and currently not so prominent notions which might better explain both this text and its understanding and presentation of American culture. In response to such an approach, this chapter intends to show the importance of the often disregarded individual aesthetic sensibility and personal poetics (regardless of whether one is a professional writer like Dubravka Ugrešić or an "amateur" deciding to write his or her experiences of another culture), in the shaping of mutual cultural perceptions and presentations between the United States and Europe.

A Chosen Literary Technique: "The Baring of Devices"

So I sit down at the typewriter and start thinking about writing just such a story. . . . Choice of technique, then? I think I've made it.[1]

"How about adding a chapter to describe Steffie Speck's married life? They have a nice, normal wedding, and she has her first child—a girl say. . . . Then she has a second child and, of course, starts to let herself go. So he finds himself a mistress, some young student, and she—Steffie—finds out and is quite devastated. . . ."

"We've seen it all hundreds of times, in films!" Aunt Sissy was becoming increasingly furious.

. . . I was about to say that wasn't a bad idea, but my mother, ignoring Greta's suggestion, forestalled me: "All right," she said, "if you think the marriage is impossible then let them part! The life of a divorced woman and all the difficulties that entails is also interesting!"

"But we've seen it hundreds of times. . . !" said Aunt Sissy, annoyed.[2]

These two quotations are taken from Ugrešić's novel *Steffie Speck in the Jaws of Life* (1981); the first appears at the very beginning of the narrative, when the narrator deliberates on the technique she will use in telling her story and finally decides that she will make a "patchwork" text "sewn" of various fragments. The second appears toward the end of the novel and is part of a conversation which the narrator has with her mother and elderly neighbors, in which they discuss the possible new episodes of the story of Steffie Speck.

These two fragments can serve as a sample of many similar ones spread throughout Ugrešić's fictional opus, in which the narrator talks about her writing of a story, and about all the numerous poetic and thematic choices she has to make along the way. Although the narrator's discussion of her literary procedures should, of course, not be taken at face value (because the narrator is also only one of the characters of the story and not the "real author"), this discussion participates (along with some other literary procedures) in constantly making visible and self-conscious the particular ways of constructing a narrative, such as choice of genre, creation of plot, or making of a character. In the short novel *Steffie Speck in the Jaws of Life*, for instance, the narrator and the narrative reveal that the subjectivity of the main character, the shy and slightly overweight young typist Steffie Speck, is constructed as a mélange of various popular culture discourses which shape femininity, including gossip, sentimental love novels, and practical advice from women's magazines. It is repeatedly emphasized that this and other characters are not some "real" people about whom we happen to read but rather fictional creations which are fully a product of the author's making and choice.

A dominant aspect of Ugrešić's fiction is precisely this ongoing and often humorous reflection on the very creation of a narrative, which involves a playful and self-reflexive writing about writing. Being continuously shown as calculable products of identifiable literary devices, cultural clichés, and authorial choices, the plots and characters in Ugrešić's fiction become—and this is precisely the desired effect—"flattened," inhabiting more the realm of literary parody, grotesque, and caricature rather than that of literary realism, and also more the realm of predictable stories and characters defined in advance rather than the one of seemingly endless possibilities.

By focusing on given forms of the creation of a particular narrative (e.g., on clichés of a "romance" and a "woman's story" in *Love Story* and *Steffie Speck*), Ugrešić's works point at, emphasize, and play with what we can call the morphological frames of literature, or the underlying rules and molds of storytelling. It is precisely these frames that can be seen as the major theme of Ugrešić's fiction. This fiction can thus be seen as liberating in its subversion of a still strong "realistic" narrative, marked by erasure of the traces of its own making. On the other hand, this fiction can also be seen as decidedly "nonliberating" in its emphasis on morphology over contingency or in its emphasis on underlying rules (which govern the making of a plot or characterization) over any possibility of narrative freedom.[3] Once we know the formative system, everything else can be derived from it, and plots and characters become solely its predictable results, without having any potential to deviate or be(come) free.

I have discussed poetic features of Ugrešić's fiction at some length because the literary, aesthetic, and philosophical consciousness which shapes this fiction is also crucially instrumental in the creation of her "ethnographic" nonfictional (or semifictional) work *Have a Nice Day: From the Balkan War to the American Dream*, a collection of texts that comment on and attempt to explain some of the elements and aspects of contemporary U.S. culture to the European reader. The specific aesthetic and literary sensibility which informs Ugrešić's fictional writing also shapes her perception of and writing about the United States, and it is important to keep in mind this originating aesthetics in order to see how it affects the view of "America" present in *Have a Nice Day*.

Looking at Them Looking at Us: American "Eastern Europe"

Originally written as a series of weekly columns entitled "My American Dictionary" for the Dutch paper *NRC Handelsblad*, *Have a Nice Day: From the Balkan War to the American Dream* was assembled and published in the Croatian language in Zagreb in 1993, under the title *Američki fikcionar* (American Fictionary). The book takes the form of a loose dictionary of American culture, with entries such as *shrink, manual, couch-potato, body, personality,* and *contact* receiving separate short chapters as their descriptive definitions. Each of these texts combines anecdotes from the author's life in the United States which exemplify a given cultural phenomenon and which are rhetorically presented as authentic "real-life" anecdotes rather than invented ones, essayistic reflections that elaborate on the same phenomenon, and also some fictional elements such as the fantastic endings of some chapters. Given that the first-person narrator is rhetorically equated with the author herself, the book comes across as the author's reflexive diary of her stay in the United States.

Throughout the book, the author mentally intertwines fragments of "Americana" before her eyes with scenes of violence happening simultaneously across the ocean in the former Yugoslavia, site of the worst European carnage since World War II. This juxtaposition of these two spaces cannot fail to shed an ominous light on the elements of the American culture being described. For instance, writing about the concept of an "organizer" (everything from a time schedule to organizers of clothes), which the author sees as ubiquitous in American everyday culture, Ugrešić compares organizers with the army that destroyed the Croatian city of Vukovar, stating simply, "Organizers. Kill—cleanse—organize."[4] In a similar way, while writing about the term *shrink*, Ugrešić recounts how her own appointment with a New York psychologist ended unsuccessfully, the reason being her focus on the war in Yugoslavia instead of "her own concerns," or rather her inability to separate her own personality from the "problems" in her country, an inability which the American psychologist is shown as incapable of comprehending.

Ever alert to the given frames of making of a story, Ugrešić recurrently deals with the constructions of "Eastern Europe," the current war in the former Yugoslavia, and the "Balkans" in the American cultural space. Through satirical retelling of her encounters with Americans "interested in 'Eastern Europe'" or with editors of publishing houses, Ugrešić shows how these American presentations (or constructions) of the East European "others" often get shaped by nothing more planned than sheer ignorance, on one hand ("Oh, you are from that country where there is a war going on?"), and forces of the market economy, on the other.

"The American market is saturated with East European writers," an editor in one publishing house told me.

"Oh?" I said.

"I personally don't intend to publish a single one," he said.

"But what has that got to do with my books?" I said, stressing the word books.

"You are an East European writer," he replied, stressing every word. (140–41)

"It's a real shame you're not a Cuban writer," the editor of another publishing house told me, with feeling.

"Oh?"

"At present, the American market is open to ethnicities, particularly Cubans, Puerto-Ricans, Central America in general.

"Interesting," I said.

"Have you any connection with China?"

"No."

"Pity. That would have helped too. The Chinese immigrant novel, that's fashionable now." (141)

Ugrešić also writes about the enforcement of the cultural stereotype of the "Balkans" through which Americans perceived the war in that area, convenient because it helped specific policies of the United States in the early 1990s with regard to the violence in the Balkans.

> Unpredictable reality continues its game with myths. From here I observe the media reinforcement of the Balkan Myth as it is gradually built up from newspaper photographs and television reports. The television shots of desperate, wretched, disheveled people with wild eyes absolutely coincide with the Balkan stereotype. And no one asks how it is that many of these desperate people have a decent command of the English language. (110)

Ugrešić does not take as her theme only what she calls the "American" discursive production of the former Yugoslavia and the war there.[5] By recounting meetings with American publishers, editors, academics, and journalists, she maps a web of pressures put on the writer from *any* East European country with the goal of having him or her construct his or her identity and work according to the stereotypical American categories of seeing Eastern Europe at the time (the beginning of the 1990s). In Ugrešić's experience, the East European writer is literally "pushed" into upholding, and adjusting to, these established discourses of his or her homeland.

> As soon as I crossed the border, the customs officers of culture began roughly sticking identity labels on me: *communism, Eastern Europe, censorship, repression, Iron Curtain, nationalism* (Serb or Croat?)—the very labels from which I had succeeded in protecting my writing in my own country.
>
> "What do you think about communism?" an American journalist asked me. "I know it was terrible," she said emotionally, screwing up her face, "but in a transitional period the phenomenon itself seeks re-articulation. . . ."
>
> I listened to her, not believing my ears. How did she know it was *terrible*, and how easily all those words: communism, transition, postcommunism tripped off her tongue.
>
> "I'm not a politician, I'm a writer," I said.
>
> "I'm asking you because you're a writer, an intellectual, the representative of a postcommunist country. . . ."
>
> God, I thought, if she only knew that in my country writers, taking on the role of politicians, were as responsible for the war as the generals, because when they were asked the same questions they were only too eager to answer.
>
> "We're talking about literature," I said.
>
> "Let's leave boring questions about literature to Western writers. As an East European writer and intellectual you surely have far more interesting things to talk about than literature." (139)

Have a Nice Day points at the mechanisms by which American publishing, media, and academia shape and change the self-presentation of an "authentic" East European writer so that it corresponds to established preconceptions. In the view of this book, East European writers do not challenge so much these stereotypes with an assertion of their own and different knowledge of themselves and their homelands. On the contrary, they gradually come to accept (consciously or not) the others' notions about themselves and, as Ugrešić puts it, do not know any more "how much is true, and what is a newly acquired image" (140).

> At gatherings here I sometimes come across colleagues of mine, "Easterners," EEWs (East European Writers), and see how they have adapted in advance to the given stereotype, how readily they chatter about censorship (although they've had no experience of it themselves). I hear them babbling on about postcommunism, about the everyday life of their sad Eastern Europe . . . eagerly accepting identity tags, wearing them like badges. . . .
>
> I sometimes come across my fellow-countrymen here as well, and watch them chattering about ex-Yugoslavia, about the war and its causes . . . making personal statements, becoming *the voice of the people*, accepting the role . . . I watch them adapting, modeling their own biographies, no longer knowing how much is true, and what is a newly acquired image. (140)

Writers adapt (*prilagodjavaju*) themselves to the stereotype and accept (*prihvaćaju*) the given role. They tell only what is already "known," expected and proclaimed as "authentic." Therefore, they do not really say anything but rather merely "blab" (onomatopoeic *trtljaju, brbljaju*) meaninglessly. As one of Ugrešić's friends from the former Yugoslavia, a journalist-turned-emigrant, says:

> And I'll sell garbage from the communist store-room, says the journalist. I'll give them the expected picture of the world, stereotypes of life behind "the iron curtain," stereotypes about gray, alienated Eastern Europe standing in line for sour cabbage.
>
> But we never stood in line for sour cabbage, we observe. (67)

Ugrešić refuses to write about herself as an "authentic" East European and about the Yugoslav war in the prescribed ways, about her presumed past oppressions and current (already equally "well-known") victimization. Her refusal lies precisely in the baring of American mechanisms of the creation of "authentic" East European texts, in writing about the market demands and established discourses which are forced on East European writers. *Have a Nice Day* also attempts to shatter stereotypical American views about the people in the former Yugoslavia by including letters and dialogues of some of the author's friends, materials that show these people as interesting, thoughtful, educated and peaceful, and not the wild-eyed and wretched beings they are supposed to be.[6]

The Kitsch of American Self-making

And I thought something to the effect that everything was a cliché, including life it-self . . . that the kitsch microbes are the most vigorous organisms.[7]

As I mentioned earlier, Ugrešić's fiction points out clichés—or what she calls "kitsch"—in the making of narratives such as, for example, a "woman's story" and/or a "love story." In *Have a Nice Day*, Ugrešić writes about American kitsch in the presentation of Eastern Europe and the war in former Yugoslavia. Construct-ing the violence in the Balkans as an unavoidable outcome of "thousand-year-old" hatreds in the "land of demons" justifies policies very different from those which could have been created in relation to some more accurate and less "kitschy" dis-cursive construction of this violence. Lie replaces truth, and stereotypes are asked for and rewarded in place of an exploration of unfamiliar realms different from preconceived ideas.

Have a Nice Day, however, looks for stereotypes not only in the American con-struction of the East European "Other" but also in the individual Americans' construction of themselves, their identities, and their lives. Aside from expecting East Europeans to approximate the given notions of what they are, Americans themselves, as this book sees them, relentlessly try to approximate the given ideal type of themselves. These ideal types of a desirable personality, body, or career are defined and disseminated by the centers of cultural influence such as the mass media, and they are in general unquestionably accepted—or so we read. Imitat-ing these types as well as they can or, in other words, merely executing the role given to them by someone else, Americans in Ugrešić's prose acquire a strangely mechanical quality. They become all alike, and while performing prescribed roles, they "do not wonder about their meaning, they simply—behave" (156).

American television, like a great brain-washing machine, produces a type of behav-ior, forms taste, emotions, introduces new topics into circulations. In the flood of new American sensibility, undisguised sentimentality, a new, "better quality" attitude to life, I clearly observe the way the television model is reflected in everyday life and be-comes (for me, at least) unbearable kitsch. In Middletown there is a shop run by Ital-ians. The owner is called Romeo. And everything is as it ought to be, everything is in real-life the way it is in serials about a warm, friendly neighborhood where there is a mixture of various ethnicities. And as I wait in line for my mozzarella I couldn't say whether it is this life that has inspired the television serials or whether life has been inspired by the television serials. Everything, as I say, is as it ought to be. The Italian has an impudent, swarthy manner, gruff and curt. The customers in front of me in-quire in simpering, friendly voices what the salad is like today, then tell me, Romeo, should one add basil to mozzarella, if so, then tell me, Romeo . . . . (182)

Writing about her New York friend's use of the phrase "strong personality," Ugrešić says, "[S]he, my American acquaintance, doesn't know that I've heard this same phrase, spoken with the same intonation, at least fifty times since I've been here" (122). This "American acquaintance" is shown as thinking herself highly original and successful yet in fact participating in very unoriginal (and used by many) conceptualization and verbalization of the world around her and her own "unique" place in it. Ugrešić proceeds with a discussion of how the enforcement of the well-defined general idea of a "strong personality" destroys the possibility of an individual's unique creation of this "strong personality" in his or her particular case. Namely, when the idea of a strong personality becomes thoroughly defined by the influential personality industry (including psychiatric and ego-building manuals and the media), then the actual peculiarity of a person loses out, because its numerous original appearances—always happening for the first time—simply cannot be recognized and experienced as such.

Americans produce an abundance of autobiographies, confessions, and memoirs, trying to celebrate and make sense of their individual lives, but all these texts, in the view of this book, look alike, written according to given rules. Thus, Ugrešić asks, "Will Americans soon begin to wonder how it is that they—who have believed their whole lives in ideologemes about individualism, individual choice, personalness—are so terribly like their immediate neighbors?" (149). And she states, "Americans today make public confessions of their personal experience—to order" (147).

Reproducing the Problem

This somewhat extensive account of the several main themes in *Have a Nice Day* should suffice to make the following point: A reader of this volume might find it hard to avoid being increasingly uneasy about this book's own perpetuation of stereotypes about the United States. While pointing out conventional and problematic American constructions of both Eastern Europe and itself, *Have a Nice Day* nevertheless replicates the same mechanisms of simplification and "falsity" in its own presentation of the American "Other."

At the beginning of the book, sentences starting with the phrase "every American" or "no American" sound fresh and humorous: "[n]o American with an iota of self-respect knows who he or she is: That's why every American has a shrink" (51). However, this kind of formulation loses its potency after repeated use and gradually becomes literal and referential rather than ironic and playful. "Whoever follows the instructions, must reach the desired aim. No one can shake an American's fundamental belief in that truth" (48). "For the American body does not communicate with anyone and does not serve any purpose" (125). "America has imposed the dictatorship of happiness" (74). "*Contact, network, networking* are words which are part of American etiquette, automatic American behavior" (156).

The Americans in *Have a Nice Day* are satirically portrayed as individuals who fully inhabit their own ideal types (the American student, the American academic, the American businessman, the American salesperson) and are therefore rarely

named by their proper names. The only individual American who keeps reap-
pearing in this narrative is "my American friend Norman," who is mostly referred
to with precisely this same phrase, "my American friend Norman," much less often
as "my friend Norman" or simply "Norman." Such qualification and the stories
about Norman tend to imply that he is a friend only as much as an American can
be a friend, or else that he is a friend in a peculiarly "American" way that is seen as
limited and wanting. Norman is also seen as a "typical" American, a kind of American Everyman; the sporadic record of his behavior reduces him to a caricature
lacking the ability to sympathize, understand, or truly communicate. (Norman's
Croatian is poor; he uses masculine verb endings with the female subject Madeline. The translator shows this by using masculine pronouns to refer to Madeline.)

The phone rings, it's my American friend Norman.
"Madeline loves me, he told me today," he says cheerfully.
"Oh?" I say.
"It was silly of me to say I'd kill myself. Madeline wants me. Did you hear?"
"I heard."
"So why are you sad?"
"Dubrovnik has been bombed."
"Oh? I'm sorry, I'm really sorry," he says, genuinely upset. We say nothing for a
while, and then my American friend asks cautiously, "What do you think, did Made-
line really mean it when he said he loved me?" (50).[8]

A little while ago my American friend Norman invited me to the cinema. Accustomed
to going Dutch, I waved my wallet like a sword.
"No, there's no need. I invited you out," said Norman generously and bought the
tickets.
We saw *Fried Green Tomatoes at the Whistlestop Café*, a new, sophisticated product
of American soap. We cried like little kids. Norman sniffed on my shoulder, thinking
of his mother Edith in Detroit and his grandmother Ellen in an old people's home. I
howled as well. When we came out of cinema, Norman looked at me sadly and said
in a plaintive voice:
"By the way, you owe me seven dollars for the ticket."
Instead of the handkerchief I badly needed, I obediently took the money out of my
purse. And I didn't need a handkerchief any more. I was shaking with laughter. (184)

If *Have a Nice Day* were more of a straightforwardly autobiographical work,
these episodes would be read in a different way. But the larger part of this volume
consists of cultural commentary and analysis; in conjunction with that kind of
discourse, these anecdotes read not so much as parts of a unique narrative of the
author's stay in the United States but rather as typical examples of "American
ways" which complement ethnographic parts of the text such as the following
short essay on networking:

Contact, network, networking are words which are part of American etiquette, automatic American behavior. Americans do not wonder about their meaning, they simply—behave. They collect visiting cards in their organizers, write down addresses,

telephone, write thank you letters, although there is nothing to be thankful for, take your telephone number and do not telephone, warmly invite you to a party, without giving you the address, fall over themselves to come to your party, without forgetting to take your address. In the little dictionary of etiquette, words stick to one another like magnets. The words contact and networking are joined by another two: image and schedule. It is almost impossible to network without an image or a schedule. In the great idea of the image, the fundamental notion is that in the world of media everything is just a picture; in the world of pictures, everything is, of course, an impression. American socializing ideology offers numerous suggestions as to how to design and redesign your own image, how to create a favorable impression, how to increase your personal social rating. The image is a small step on the path to eternity, to myth. And myth is also, we know, only a picture.

The schedule is the organizer: the daily, monthly, yearly or even several-yearly timetable Americans introduce into their work, their life and the network of their contacts. Even if he is dying of boredom, even if there has not been a human being on his horizon for days, an American will not leap at the first invitation, but will say: Hmm . . . let me look at my schedule. Americans are long-lived. It now seems to me that this is not the result of a general, panic-stricken anxiety about health, but of the simple word schedule. When death knocks at an American's door, I imagine that he will say: Hmm . . . let me look at my schedule. (157)

There is a distinct shift toward more literal writing during the course of the book, a shift which places increasing emphasis on the nonfictional and analytical elements of the text. The beginning chapters, for instance, are often characterized by dominance of a story, fantastic elements in the narrative, mediation of the author's reflections by these literary devices, and by being written in the form of self-contained paragraphs rather than one continuous text, thus precluding the rhetorical self-presentation of the text as *the* authoritative explanation of this or that aspect of American culture, and showing it instead as a collage of separate and potentially even contradictory impressions and thoughts on the United States. In the early chapter entitled "Missing," for example, the author reads old Croatian newspapers and finds out that "30,000 missing persons have been registered in Croatia" (43). The chapter ends with the author hearing the doorbell, opening the door of her Connecticut apartment, and having "unknown people spill into my flat. They pour in uncontrollably, like a flood, women, children, old men, wounded people, soldiers. . . . And I understand, here they are, all 30,000" (43). The chapters "Shrink" and "Jogging" revolve around stories (e.g., the author's visit to a counselor) and also have fantastic endings. In "Jogging," the author joins the seductive quiet jogger and the two of them run into the sky, echoing the famous scene of Pontius Pilate and Jesus strolling onto the beam of moonlight at the end of Bulgakov's novel *Master and Margarita.*

The later chapters of *Have a Nice Day*, however, contain less storytelling or fantastic elements. They are characterized by an increasingly theoretical discourse which transforms the author persona from writer to cultural critic. The text no longer consists of fragments but rather of systematic elaborations on American cultural characteristics. The chapter "Body" thus discusses at length the American ideology of the body (with the help of Russian literary theorist Mikhail Bakhtin's concept of "carnivalesque body"), unambiguously making assertions such as these:

> In its ideology of the body, America deprives the body of the right to its carnival-grotesque ambivalence. (122)

> In its ideology of the unambiguous body America has decisively removed all its opposites: illness, aging, death, ugliness, physical decay. As a deeply infantile culture, America builds its ideology of the body on infantile mechanisms. . . . This collective American body is like a baby that feeds, burps, shits, pees, takes its first steps—and receives the enthusiastic acclaim of its surroundings. (123)

> For the American body does not communicate with anyone and does not serve any purpose. That is to say, the American ideology of the body has deprived this alluring body of its right to association, to its sexual function, it has deprived this sexually attractive body of its right to sexual attraction. (125)

The pervading tone of the writing also becomes increasingly literal and assertive, and it loses the playful ambiguity characterizing the earlier chapters; the text simply starts saying "how the things are."

> It seems that America does not produce anything other than the genre of collective autobiography. Americans appear to swarm unconsciously toward a large police (or psychiatrist's) interviewing room where they will confess their lives. (147)

> [An] American will not deny himself the right to tell you his whole life's story at the first possible opportunity. (148)

The Importance of Poetic Forms

On her return flight from the United States, in the plane from New York to Amsterdam and on her way to Zagreb, Ugrešić "tremble[s] at the thought of [her] homeland":

> I tremble at the thought of the misery pouring into me concentrated in newspaper articles, in television pictures, in newspaper photographs, I tremble at the thought of the sorrows that have crept towards me along telephone lines, the smell of which has reached me in letters. I tremble at the thought of my old homeland in which I have become a stranger, which in fact no longer exists, I tremble at the thought of its ghost, I tremble at the thought of the new one in which I shall be a stranger, whose citizenship I have yet to apply for, having lost citizenship of the first, I shall have to prove that I was born there, although I was, that I speak its language, although it is my mother tongue, I tremble at the thought of that old-new homeland for which I shall have to fight in order to live there as—a permanent émigré. (224)

My heart is small and receptive. How many other people's sorrows will fit into one heart? How elastic is the average human heart? How much can fit in it without it bursting? Or does the heart after a certain time turn into a little blunt bellows blindly throbbing out its rhythm? (225)

As the author approaches her home and the text gets close to its end, *Have a Nice Day* changes from distanced and preconceptualized observation of Americans into engaged exploration of the author's attempts to deal with her vastly altered "home." The book actually appears to be arriving to its real subject and to concerns which have obviously been foremost throughout the volume—the war in the Balkans, the situation in a newly independent Croatia (which is both war ravaged and increasingly chauvinistic, conservative, and nondemocratic), and Ugrešić's own encounter with this new Croatia. Preoccupation with these issues during the author's stay in the United States may account for the lack of genuine interest and attention toward her new environment.

This predicament might have promoted an easy transferal of fictional poetics of Ugrešić's works into nonfictional writing about the American culture. As mentioned at the beginning of this chapter, the main feature of Ugrešić's fictional poetics is pointing at the literary or cultural clichés which shape any narrative and dominate over any possibility of narrative contingency or, in other words, over the possibility of a story and its characters going in a different direction from the one already known. *Have a Nice Day* points at given clichés which the American cultural context prescribes for East European writers, discursive constructions of the "Balkans," and individual Americans themselves, and it shows these things as fully a product of such clichés. East European writers in the United States, as well as the author's American acquaintances, are types in the same way in which Ugrešić's fictional characters—Emancipated Ella, the Driver, the Hulk, and the Intellectual from *Steffie Speck in the Jaws of Life*, or the Czech or Yugoslav writers from *Fording the Stream of Consciousness*—are types, parodistically embodying this or that cultural characteristic or pretensions.[9]

The poetics of "always already knowing" the stories and characters, prevalent in Ugrešić's fiction, shapes decisively *Have a Nice Day* and limits its ability to really engage with the American culture. Things that are unique, different, and free, contingent and nontypical, are left out; things belonging to the "other" America of people who are not egocentric, artistically and culturally insensitive, blindly pursuing the proscribed ideals of their own "culture," and the instances of Americans desperately trying to struggle against their own culture. Left out is also a presentation of the genuine desire and efforts of many ordinary American citizens to help the victims of the atrocities in the former Yugoslavia, as well as acknowledgment of dissenting voices in American public space—and there were many—on this war. Being the good writer that she is, Ugrešić cannot avoid making a lively text that vividly conveys first impressions of the United States and its culture and people to European readers. Her book paints in broad strokes some elements of the American cultural landscape and has informational value for a European reader unfamiliar with the United States. But the potential of this work to really see "America" is diminished by a transferal of a specific fictional poetics into non-fictional, ethnographic, and essayistic writing about the others.

Much of recent cultural studies sees politics as the ultimate source of discursive production and of cross-cultural presentation that forms a part of discursive production. For example, a lot of work has focused on analyzing the mechanisms by which the various centers of power discursively construct their objects in the ways that correspond to their political goals and practice (so assorted discourses of colonial powers, for instance, often describe peoples of the colonized nations as infantile and incapable of ruling themselves), and discursive practice of those who are politically inferior or subjugated is correspondingly seen as primarily opposing or subverting the practice of the powerful ones.

Literary, aesthetic, or poetic conventions and sensibilities are often put into the background and deemed less important. But *Have a Nice Day* could show us that particular individual or group aesthetics can be as important (or even more important) as politics in cultural understanding and representation of others, not only in the case of this specific "European representation of the U.S." but also more broadly. Aesthetic and literary sensibility is a crucial part of one's identity. This sensibility shapes decisively one's perception and representation of another place, and it should be taken into account when assessing any cross-cultural understanding in general, including the American–European one in particular.

Notes

An earlier version of this chapter was presented at the annual American Association of Teachers of Slavic and East European Languages (AATSEEL) convention in 1994 in San Diego, under the title "Dubravka Ugrešić's *American Fictionary* and the Non-Marketable Refusal to Conform."

1. Dubravka Ugrešić, "Steffie Speck in the Jaws of Life," in *In the Jaws of Life and Other Stories*, trans. Celia Hawkesworth (Evanston, Ill.: Northwestern University Press, 1993), 6.

2. Ugrešić, "Steffie Speck in the Jaws of Life," 74.

3. The opposition of "morphological necessity" versus "narrative contingency" is theorized in a seminal book by Ernesto Laclau and Chantal Mouffe, *Hegemony and Socialist Strategy* (London: Verso, 1985). The work of Gary Saul Morson (especially his book, *Narrative and Freedom: The Shadows of Time* [New Haven & London: Yale University Press, 1994]) also devotes much attention to an opposition between what he calls structural givens and narrative freedom.

4. Dubravka Ugrešić, *Have a Nice Day: From the Balkan War to the American Dream*, trans. Celia Hawkesworth (New York: Viking-Penguin, 1995), 38. Future references to this text will be made by the page number next to the quote.

5. As Professor Sibelan Forrester of Swarthmore College has pointed out, the use of the term *America* solely for the United States might rightly anger Canadians, given the implied

conflation of America with the United States, common to both many U.S. citizens and Europeans. The translation in British English also emphasizes this European perspective. While agreeing with this point, I would also add that the term *America* in the former Yugoslavia and its successor states has customarily meant only the United States (which has "America" in its name) and never the whole North American continent (when referring to a continent, one says "North America"). Ugrešić thus only participates here in one established linguistic (and political) convention of her home country.

6. See especially the chapters "Mailbox" and "Yugo-Americana."

7. Ugrešić, "Steffie Speck in the Jaws of Life," 80.

8. It might also be noted here that the Croatian original of *Have a Nice Day* does not have the following somewhat assuaging interjection (relating to Norman) of the quoted text, which appears in the English translation: ". . . genuinely upset. We say nothing for a while, and then my American friend asks cautiously. . . ." Instead, the original reads, "he says, and then adds with a darker tone in his voice: 'What do you think . . .'" ("*kaže, a zatim dodaje s tamnijom bojom u glasu . . .*"). Dubravka Ugrešić, *Američki fikcionar* (Zagreb: Durieux, 1993), 41.

9. "Indeed each writer of the conference paradistically embodies a national type. Mark Stenheim, the American, lists his numerous educational degrees from various universities, from writing programs, and even from deep sea fishing school, obsessed with the fear that he will not be considered sufficiently intellectual. For his part, the Czech writer, Jan Zdrazila, is tormented by guilt as he works for years on his lengthy and unpublishable 'masterpiece,' while earning his living by censoring the works of other writers. Yugoslav writers are not spared irony either." Tanja Pavlović, "Demystifying Nationalism: Dubravka Ugrešić and the Situation of the Writer in (Ex-) Yugoslavia," unpublished paper, 5.

13

Shake, Rattle, and Self-Management

Rock Music and Politics in Socialist Yugoslavia, and After

Sabrina P. Ramet

ROCK MUSIC, ignored at first by social scientists, became the object of increasingly frequent scholarly analysis, beginning in the late 1970s. There are a number of general studies of a sociological nature,[1] complemented more recently by a small literature on rock music in the East European area.[2] As John Orman has noted, rock is a political phenomenon both because rock artists sometimes take positions on controversial issues (or on the elites themselves) in their songs or through their stage presentation, and because political elites may use legislative or coercive force to suppress, inhibit, or regulate rock performers, regardless of the political intent or content of their songs.[3] At least two regimes—the Hoxha regime in Albania and the Taliban regime in Afghanistan—attempted to ban rock music altogether, viewing the medium as socially subversive.

Rock is also political insofar as it is part of a cultural or subcultural milieu which may exalt specific social values. In the late 1960s and early 1970s, rock music was closely linked with the hippie culture, which propounded a leisure ethic in opposition to the Protestant work ethic.[4] Indeed, one observer writing in 1971 concluded that "the only really new feature in the lives of the young is the intensity and resolution of their devotion to pleasure, a commitment to enjoyment and consumption."[5] And beginning in the 1980s, especially in the United States, much of rock music has celebrated dance, love, and the pursuit of ephemeral pleasure—values which, when contrasted with the protest rock of 1967–1971, seem to encourage political apathy and resignation, or, perhaps, the selfish pursuit of one's own material gratification. By the end of the 1980s, a new kind of rock had appeared—rap music. This new strain, characterized by an emphatically monotonous tone, fast pace, and lyrics laced with ill-focused and unpoliticized (and therefore ultimately impotent) anger, had established itself in some of the mainstream mediums, such as MTV, by the end of the century.

From the very beginning, the impact of American rock music abroad has been very powerful—initially above all in Europe, but ultimately globally as well. Whether one watches rock videos from Turkey, from Africa, from Serbia, or from South America, the global character of rock music is unmistakable, even if local accents remain. But where rock music is concerned, one may speak, more accurately, of a common Anglo-American culture which is exerting influence worldwide. Groups such as Britain's Beatles and Rolling Stones, and Australia's Men at Work have had at least as much impact worldwide as most American rock groups. That the genesis of rock music owes much to African-American blues and southern "hillbilly" music is well known. Less well-known is the fact that some of "the seeds of pop music . . . had already been planted in the soil of inner America by European immigrants, principally from the Celtic countries."[6]

Rock music in Yugoslavia started as a purely imitative celebration of the better-known Anglo-American rock bands, and rock music in the successor states of Yugoslavia continues to reflect rock trends worldwide. But there have also been some characteristics peculiar to the Yugoslav context, characteristics which became more important once the Yugoslavs found their own "voice" as it were. In musical terms, the folk traditions from which Yugoslav rock musicians have drawn inspiration are, of course, very different from, say, those of the United States and Britain. Moreover, in terms of the audience, whereas a study published in 1972 found that American youngsters at that time did not take lyrics too seriously and more often than not either had only the vaguest notion about what a song's message was or completely misconstrued the message,[7] Yugoslav youngsters have tended to take the lyrics very seriously and in any case listen more attentively.

And finally, in political terms, American authorities banned songs and harassed rock performers in the early years (1955–70) essentially because of their personal disgust with the rhythmic sensuality of the music or because of language they found obscene.[8] In 1985, there were congressional hearings concerning the putative desirability of introducing warning labels on recordings of rock songs with lyrics which some might find offensive. Later, in the 1990s, American authorities were still concerned about obscenity, as shown in the October 1990 trial of the rap music group 2 Live Crew in Fort Lauderdale, Florida, for example, and in accusations in 1992 that the rap songs "Cop Killer" and "Apocalypse Now" had inspired fans to kill police.[9] Nor should one forget that the Pennsylvania House of Representatives passed a bill in 1990 which requires "parental warning" labels on certain records offering "lewd" or "provocative" lyrics.[10] Just two years later, the State of Washington passed a law banning the sale of recordings with "erotic" lyrics to minors, though the law was later found to be unconstitutional.[11] In this context, Allan Bloom's claim, in his 1987 book, *The Closing of the American Mind,* that "nobody thought to control it [rock], and now it is too late,"[12] sounds laughable. In communist Yugoslavia, by contrast, rock performers had to deal not only with a parallel reaction from their own parents and elders[13] but also with problems of specifically political censorship.

Originally highly imitative of American trends, Yugoslav rock came of age in the late 1970s and, by the early 1980s, boasted a broad range of styles—protest rock, punk, new wave, rockabilly, orthodox rock, and various kinds of revivals and syntheses. The "golden age" of Yugoslav rock was the period from about 1974 to 1991, when the country broke up. The Yugo-rock scene at this time was characterized by stylistic and musical heterogeneity. There were, for example, groups like Bora Djordjević's Fish Stew (Riblja ćorba), which saw themselves as social critics (as Bora still does) and accordingly were regularly attacked in the party press. Other groups were bored with politics and sang of romance almost exclusively—as was the case with the Zagreb-based hard rock band, Steamroller (Parni valjak), until the outbreak of war between Serbia and Croatia in 1991.[14] Still others, like the highly talented Belgrade combo of Vlada Divljan and Saša Šandorov, were experimenting with "noninstrumental music," putting household items to work in the production of new musical effects. From heavy metal to hard-core to soul to breakdancing to rap,[15] all the genres known in the West appeared in Yugoslavia, sometimes with local variations. There was even a group in Ljubljana in the 1980s (Borghesia) whose members incorporated elements of sadomasochism into their songs and attire. There was also a specifically home-grown genre called "šogor rock,"[16] which developed in Hungary and in the Hungarian community in the Yugoslav province of Vojvodina and which generously blended local folk music with rock.

Yugoslav rock groups borrowed from the West but produced their own blend, often crossing genres and blending elements not previously blended. In fact, there was so much experimentation and borrowing that the boundaries between genres and subgenres became fuzzy. Some of the music of the Macedonian rock group Bread and Salt (Leb i Sol) illustrates this, blending rhythmic patterns of the Turkish Orient with rock melodies and interspersing country sounds straight out of Nashville.[17] The Slovenian group Bastards (Pankrti), which enjoyed popularity in the 1980s, blended elements of punk with more mainstream rock, while Tonny Montano, a kind of latter-day Elvis Presley who sang of terrorism and drugs, the Mafia, and comic-book fantasies, talked to me (in 1987) of infusing the rhythms of the late 1950s with the energy of punk.[18]

Rock music remains, in a certain sense, a phenomenon of the cities. The major rock clubs are naturally in the larger cities—in the late 1980s these included Kulušić, Lapidarija, and Jabuka in Zagreb, Akademija and the Drugi Novi Klub in Belgrade, and in an earlier day (1982–85) the F.V. Club in Ljubljana.[19] Later, with the closure of the F.V. Club, the Ljubljana alternative scene moved to the Disco Amerikanec, in the Old Town. New wave, hard rock, and alternative music find their supporters in the cities. Heavy metal, however, developed rather as a phenomenon of the smaller towns. Novi Sad, a quiet town with a provincial atmosphere, became one of the big centers for heavy metal in the mid-1980s, with several heavy metal clubs and Yugoslavia's only heavy metal magazine.[20]

More generally, there have long been some important regional differences in musical trends, differences which may be accentuated now that the country has fragmented. In the years prior to the Serbian Insurrectionary War, which broke out in June 1991, the major centers for "Yugo-rock" were Belgrade (in Serbia), Ljubljana (in Slovenia), and Sarajevo (in Bosnia). But with the virtual destruction of Sarajevo in the course of months-long bombardment beginning in 1992, many of Sarajevo's top rock performers fled (Goran Bregović of White Button fleeing to Paris, Nele Karajlić of Smoking Forbidden (Zabranjeno pušenje) fleeing to Belgrade, and Gino Jevdjević fleeing to Seattle, for example), and its once lively rock scene came to a virtual end (Elvis J. Kurtović was among a handful of rock musicians to remain in Sarajevo). Aside from these three cities, Zagreb (in Croatia) and to some extent Skopje (in Macedonia) have also been important, the latter chiefly because of the accomplished group Bread and Salt, with smaller rock scenes in Rijeka, Split, Novi Sad, and elsewhere. But musical tastes differ widely. In Serbia, for example, folk music remained more popular than rock music even among the young, and even before Milošević took power and began to use the resources of the state to promote "turbo-folk," rock had to compete for its share of the market.

Serbian rock groups have tended to be orthodox (or perhaps better, purist) in their approach to rock, giving the rise of "turbo-folk" the character of a cultural threat. In Bosnia-Herzegovina, in contrast, White Button (Bijelo dugme), long the most popular and most influential rock group in socialist Yugoslavia ("the Yugoslav Beatles" as one music critic put it,[21] but a casualty of the war), sometimes used folk music as an introduction to its songs; another Sarajevo group, Blue Orchestra (Plavi orkestar), built its reputation by fashioning its own successful mix of folk and rock. Folk music is part of the old Slavic soul, and the temptation to draw upon it is very strong. Fiery Kiss (Vatreni poljubac, 1977–87) also brought folk elements into its music and favored a syncopation which is native to Balkan folk music, not to rock.[22]

Again, Slovenia, the most developed and most Western of Yugoslavia's republics and long renowned for its more liberal political and social attitudes, saw the sprouting of Yugoslavia's only important hard-core punk scene in the early 1980s. Bands like Demolition Group, Epidemic, UBR, Tožibabe, the Third Category, and the Trash of Civilization all played during the heyday of punk in the early 1980s.[23]

As Marshal Tito and his comrades looked on, rock music spread to every corner of Yugoslavia—even to economically and socially underdeveloped Kosovo, where the social separation of Serbs and Albanians was reflected, from early on, in the emergence of two parallel rock scenes divided by language, ethnicity, and, of course, politics. Serbian groups in Kosovo sang in Serbian for local Serbs, while Albanian rock groups sang in Albanian for local Albanians.[24] When Tito passed away, the Rijeka-based group Paraf struck an ostensibly patriotic note, singing,

"Long live Yugoslavia,/Long live the LCY . . . /We love the [party] line—/Long live Yugoslavia!"[25]

Influences from the West

Almost all rock musicians in the "Yugoslav" region speak English, as they always have. The reason is very simple: Yugo-rock grew and developed under the influence of American and British rock, and no other country has ever come close in influence. English remains, in this sense, the language of rock (even if the Slovenian group Laibach opted, for rather specific reasons, to sing many of its songs in German). Asked (in 1987) which Western rock performers impressed them the most, the rock musicians I met in Yugoslavia repeatedly mentioned Deep Purple, Billy Idol, Bryan Adams, Bruce Springsteen, Lou Reed, the Rolling Stones, the Kinks, and U2. Also mentioned—though less frequently—were the Beatles, Cream, Frank Zappa, Led Zeppelin, and Van Halen.

Of course, the Beatles' impact on Yugoslav rock musicians was both direct and indirect. The Beatles' distillation and "reinvention" of the genre had an enormous impact on American rock music,[26] so that the Beatles' influence could enter Yugoslavia also "covertly" as it were. This cross-fertilization resulted, over time, in the emergence of a global rock culture, with local accents and permutations to be sure, but global and even, at least where Anglo-American rock is concerned, *cosmopolitan*. In this way, as Mel van Elteren has noted, rock liberated itself from connection to a sense of place and became associated rather with social networks and particular lifestyles.[27] To be a "rocker" came to be equivalent to being "sophisticated," "cosmopolitan," even "cultured," in the eyes of the rockers, and among rockers themselves, a hierarchy was established, with acid rockers, for example, looking down their noses at those who, in the 1970s and 1980s, frequented disco joints.

Much the same thing happened in Belgrade, Zagreb, Ljubljana, and Sarajevo—the "Big Four" among socialist Yugoslavia's urban centers. In these cities, being a "rocker" established a claim to *sophistication,* and an "entitlement" to view the fans of "narodna muzika" (folk music) with contempt. As one Belgrade rocker put it, at the height of the "turbo-folk" ascendancy,

> Now the culture is gone, there is nothing but this garbage (*šund*). But our generation, we listened to rock and roll. That was the normal music then, it was what you heard in the *kafane,* over the radio. It was our music—not because it was American music but because it was international music.[28]

At least part of the reason for the rockers' self-satisfaction has been their consciousness of being part of a global mass culture, a global culture dominated, incidentally, by American artists and American media. As for the "turbo-folkers," they reciprocated this contempt, and, where the rockers revelled in American culture, the "turbo-folkers" reviled American culture. Miroslav Ilić, a turbo-folk performer, played up his love of Serbia and his disinterest in America specifically:

> America, a big country
> But one meter of my village is [worth]
> all of America.[29]

Most Yugoslav rock groups either have performed in the West or dream of doing so. Bora Djordjević boasts, among other things, of having had a video aired on MTV, and Goran Bregović, the leader of the famed White Button, was interviewed at one time on MTV.

But where Russia is concerned—whether Soviet or post-Soviet—disinterest has been widespread. Russian rock records are nowhere to be found. No one in the area listens to Russian rock music, and most rock aficionados in the area are unable to name a single Russian rock group. In fact, aside from the special relationship between Hungarian rock and Hungarian-language rock in Vojvodina, essentially the only foreign countries whose rock performers have exerted any influence on the Yugoslav (and post-Yugoslav) rock scenes are the United States, Britain, and Ireland.

Origins and Growth: The Art of Imitation

As was the case everywhere, when rock 'n' roll first came to Yugoslavia, it was considered impossible to sing in any language other than English. Yugoslavia's first genuine rock star, Karlo Metikoš, not only sang exclusively in English and French but also took the stage name "Matt Collins" in order to seem less local. He recorded various records for Philips under this name from 1960 to 1963, spent a few years touring Hilton hotels in Athens, Tehran, and Africa, and then, toward the end of the 1960s, retired from performing to write his own songs.[30]

In the 1960s, rock music was, by definition, "alternative" culture. Zagreb was an early center for rock culture in Yugoslavia. Many Zagreb groups would listen to the top twenty on Radio Luxemburg on Saturday night and by Monday be playing the songs locally. Some Croatian groups specialized in soul (such as We from Šibenik and Robots from Zagreb). In fact, soul music was quite big in Yugoslavia in the 1960s, with Wilson Pickett, Otis Redding, and Aretha Franklin among the favorites. Yugoslav soul bands would sing in English, trying to copy the style of the original. Later they started to write their own soul, singing it in Croatian, but by and large this was not successful.[31]

Yugoslavia had its "Woodstock" in the mid-1960s, when Belgrade played host to the country's first rock festival. Fifteen thousand young people turned out to hear the bands—which was more than anyone had believed possible until then.[32] Rock music had come of age in Yugoslavia. The year 1967 registered another important watershed when Index became the first Yugoslav group to play its own songs. After that, gradually more and more groups started writing their own material and singing it in Serbo-Croatian, Slovenian, or any of the other languages of this multiethnic country.

Gradually rock took hold in Yugoslavia and gained access to the media. A string of specialty magazines started to cater to the new taste—first *Ritam* in Novi Sad, then *Džuboks* and *Pop ekspres* in Zagreb, *ITD* in Belgrade, and in 1982, Belgrade's *Rock* magazine. All of these early endeavors are now defunct.

Yugoslav Rock Comes of Age

In 1974, a new group was created in Sarajevo, the aforementioned Bijelo Dugme (White Button), led by Goran Bregović. The group would in time establish itself as the number one rock group in the country. White Button changed the rules of the game, singing eloquently about the issues and problems confronting Yugoslavs and looking to local, Bosnian traditions for inspiration. In both lyrics and music, White Button was "Yugoslavicizing" rock music. At one point, White Button was subjected to a series of attacks in the weekly magazine *NIN*. But the group ignored the attacks and the affair blew over.[33]

The decade of the 1970s was a time of consolidation in the Yugoslav rock scene, in which a handful of groups established themselves as the leading rock voices of the day. Aside from White Button, three other major rock groups were founded at the end of the 1970s: Bora Djordjević's Fish Stew (in Belgrade) and the Macedonian group Bread and Salt (in Skopje)—both of them in 1978, and Vlada Divljan's group Idols (Idoli), whose best-loved album, *Odbrana i poslednji dani* (Defense and the Last Days) would be issued in 1982.[34] Together with White Button, these three groups shared center stage with Azra (a Zagreb group which folded at the end of the 1980s) and Index. The hitherto renowned Belgrade group Korni Group folded in 1974. Aside from these groups, the Slovenian group Bulldozer (Buldožer) won a large audience by taking up political themes and singing in Serbo-Croatian.

The 1970s were also the years of the Boom rock festivals in Yugoslavia, which attracted thousands of fans to annual spectacles held variously in Ljubljana, Novi Sad, and finally Belgrade. The end of the 1970s brought new trends to Yugoslavia, when new wave (*Novi val* or *Novi talas*) and punk arrived, almost simultaneously. Punk had its center in Slovenia; among its purveyors there were Papa Kinjal, a punk band led by a Ph.D. student at the Philosophy Faculty, the Bitches, a band based in Idrija, and Petar Lovšin's Bastards, a Ljubljana band.[35] Several popular groups were formed toward the end of the 1970s—among them: the highly melodic Galija, based in Niš, which first emerged in 1975; Pekinska Patka (Peking Duck), formed in Novi Sad in 1978; the Belgrade band Laki pingvini (Easy Penguins), established at the end of 1979; and the imaginative combo Atomsko sklonište (Atomic Shelter) formed in 1977 in Pula, which would issue such albums as "Mental Hygiene" (1982), "Space Generation" (1983), "This Space Ship" (1987), and the satirical "East Europe Man" (1992).

Rock was flourishing. In 1982, *Rock* magazine tried to come up with a tally of how many rock groups were playing in Yugoslavia and asked the groups to inform the magazine of their existence; some 2,874 professional and amateur groups responded. Petar Popović, an international label manager for RTB PGP Records in Belgrade, estimated (in 1987) that there were, at that time, thirty to fifty professional rock groups in Yugoslavia and perhaps 5,000 amateur groups. There were by then more than 200 amateur groups in Belgrade alone.

Several important new groups were formed in Yugoslavia in the 1980s: Ljubljana's Laibach (formed in 1980), Belgrade's Bajaga and the Instructors (formed in 1984), and Ljubljana's Falcons (Sokoli, formed in summer 1989, after the dissolution of the Bastards). These groups, together with the Belgrade groups Fish Stew and Yu-Group, Skopje's Bread and Salt, Maribor's Center za dehumanizacijo (still going strong twenty years later), Ljubljana's Miladojka You Need (formed in 1985), and Zagreb's long-lasting bands Steamroller and Haustor (briefly enjoying a reincarnation as the satirical Dee Dee Mellow in 1988 before returning to a more "serious" presentation once again as Haustor) dominated the Yugoslav rock scene in the late 1980s.[36] Jasenko Houra's Dirty Theater (Prljavo kazalište) gradually built its reputation as a strong band, and by 1990–91 it was widely considered Zagreb's top rock band. It still holds that title today, having achieved an essentially legendary status among Croats, for both musical and political reasons.[37] In 1982, on an initiative by Dražen Vrdjoljak, Zagreb got its first bluegrass band, appropriately named Plava Trava Zaborava (Blue Grass Forgets).

Belgrade's brassy Discipline of the Spine (Disciplina kičme) offered musical fare vaguely inspired by the American group Chicago and had a loyal but local following in Serbia, while Blue Orchestra[38] and Red Apple (Crvena jabuka) offered a lighter fare for young teens. Other prominent bands of the 1980s included Belgrade's Electric Orgasm (Električni orgazam), which disappeared from public view in 1988, Partibrejkers (another Belgrade band),[39] Indeksi (of Sarajevo), the legendary group Šarlo akrobata (of Belgrade), Kud Idijoti (of Pula), Idoli (the aforementioned Belgrade band, which folded in the early 1980s), and the lesser known Peking Duck, as well as two all-female acts: Cacadou Look (Opatija) and Boye (Novi Sad).[40] In Croatia, the 1980s also saw the birth of the hard-rock Rijeka band, Dr. Steel, the Split group Eighth Traveler (Osmi Putnik), which drew inspiration from the American hard-rocker David Lee Roth, the neo-romantic Zagreb band La Fortunjeros, and the legendary Satan Panonski, which rose from the grave of the Vinkovci group Pogreb X in 1985.[40a] The only well-known band to sing in Macedonian was Mizar, which wove Byzantine liturgical elements into its music.[41] The top female soloists as of 1992 were Snežana Mišković Viktorija (in Belgrade) and a new entrant, Kasandra (in Zagreb).[42] The top male vocalists as of 1992 were the erratically original Rambo Amadeus (in Belgrade) and Oliver Mandić (also in Belgrade), though Peter Lovšin and Zoran Predin were rapidly establishing themselves as Slovenia's most popular male vocalists in rock music (with Vlado Kreslin occupying a rather unique niche in the Slovenian musical scene). Among Yugoslav rock figures living in emigration, the most important were, and are, Vlada Divljan (who lived in Australia from August 1991 until March 1999, and who has been living in Vienna since then) and Goran Bregović (who moved to Paris at the beginning of the war in Bosnia-Herzegovina[43] and now leads his own fifty-member orchestra).

Coexisting with the Authorities

Rock music came to the attention of the authorities very soon, and, as rock journalist Dušan Vesić has revealed, Tito and Kardelj personally discussed this genre in order to decide what posture to adopt toward it. In contrast to the other communist elites of Eastern Europe, Tito and Kardelj opted for a policy of toleration.[44] Tito was sensitive to rock's potential for rebelliousness but hoped that by showing toleration he could win the rock scene over to a supportive stance. His gamble paid off, and the 1960s in particular saw a rash of panegyric rock ballads praising him and his program of self-management.[45]

Yugoslav rock musicians would sometimes say that the communist authorities never banned a rock song in their country. That was not entirely true. Release of an album by the Sarajevo rock group Smoking Forbidden, for example, was held up in spring 1987 because of official disapproval of one of the songs included on the album.[46] The group was criticized for singing of people wanting to leave the country, and although the incriminated song remained on the album, the record directors decided to cover up the offending section of text on the record jacket and had grey ink printed over the passage in question.[47] The problem was that the lyrics could quite easily be read through the "censor's" ink, which looked rather more like highlighting than like an attempt at obliteration.[48] But it is clear that the political atmosphere was fairly relaxed when it came to rock when one considers that the market saw songs comparing the Yugoslav Communist Party to the Mafia, portraying Naziism in an ambiguous and hence possibly favorable light, and blasting East and West, and, of course, highly pessimistic and cynical songs—none of which were banned.

Even so, rock groups occasionally encountered roadblocks. For instance, whenever a record was being taped, the group always had to submit in advance its song texts and its proposed jacket design to the recording company for approval. But when difficulties arose, there was usually a way to get around them—Yugoslav style. Fish Stew, for example, had recorded its sixth album with the Zagreb company Jugoton, but when it submitted the texts for its seventh album, Jugoton grumbled. So Fish Stew left Jugoton and went back to its earlier recording company and recorded the original texts without alteration.[49] The Slovenian group, The Bastards, had a similar experience. In 1982, the group wanted to call its second album "The

Bastards in Collaboration with the State" and to adorn the cover with a photo of a band member (Gregor Tomc) kissing a memorial to the partisan struggle. This was too much for the company, whose managers advised the group that the state did not enter into "collaboration" with rock groups. The group was advised to come up with an alternative. So the Bastards submitted a nearly identical photo using a monument from World War I and suggested the transparently sarcastic title, "Lovers of the State." It passed. And between songs dealing with sexual relations between the state apparatus and the individual citizen, the listener can hear excerpts from a speech by Stalin.[50] But I heard few such stories, and there was a not so fine line over which it was impossible to tread.

A classic case involved singer Esad Babačić-Car, whose 1981 song "Proletarian" seemed to train its guns on the self-proclaimed protectors of the proletariat:

> Where are you now, proletarian?
> Where's your gun now?
> Where are your fists now,
> proletarian?
> We're raising our flags
> in honor of your fight,
> lead us now, proletarian!
> Never mind blood,
> never mind lives,
> our thoughts will be with you,
> proletarian!
> Proletarian, proletarian,
> you're just an idol hewn in stone,
> proletarian![51]

The song was banned.

All the performers with whom I talked agreed that in Yugoslavia the lyrics were more important than the music, and some Yugoslav singers—Slovenia's Jani Kovačič, for instance—owed their popularity almost exclusively to their ability to verbalize the concerns and preoccupations of the current generation. Many of the groups were willing to tackle political subjects. For example, Hungry Frank (Lačni franc), a popular band from the provincial town of Maribor, satirized one-candidate elections.[52] Or again, Azra, a mainstream rock group active in the 1970s and 1980s, took up an even more sensitive subject in a 1982 song titled "Weekly Commentary." In the song, the group called attention to the media practice of attacking people with different political ideas and alluded to the Yugoslav presumption to be "the center of the world" in some usually ill-defined sense.[53]

The general, pervasive disillusionment with the Communist Party was reflected in other songs, too. Bora Djordjević, for example, in his 1987 song, "Member of the Mafia," compared the party to the Mafia. Against a Harry Belafonte–style calypso rhythm, he sang:

> I don't want to be a member of the mafia.
> It's the wrong step.
> I don't need a piece of paper
> where it's written that I am a member
> of the mafia.
> Even if they put me in jail,
> I don't want to be a member.[54]

Nor were religious themes taboo in communist Yugoslavia. The Bosnian group Blue Orchestra, in its 1986 album, *Death to Fascism* (Smrt fašizmu!), evoked the spirit of a revival in the song "That's the Shock." The song dealt with the alleged appearances of the Madonna at Medjugorje.[55]

Domination and the Libido (in Slovenia)

Domination has, one might say, compelling power, and that power, as psychologists know, has libidinal connections.[56] Two Slovenian groups which gained notoriety in the 1980s played on that connection between domination and the libido to tap into the energy and intensity experienced in "the psychic space where the libido comes into contact with the superego."[57] But whereas Laibach, a pop totalitarian band created in 1980, has explored what we might call "social domination," staging totalitarian-style pageants and singing music which derived as much from fascist traditions as it did from industrial rock trends, Borghesia, the Ljubljana group which folded in 1988, preferred the "private domination" of S&M. Both bands had trouble booking performances and marketing their videos domestically. But both have targeted primarily the foreign market, producing their records in Britain, Belgium, and Germany, and marketing them in the United States through Wax Trax Records of Chicago and Play It Again Sam Records.

Laibach was created in Trbovlje around 1 June 1980, coinciding with the anniversary of the town's antifascist uprising in 1924. An industrial town of 20,000 inhabitants, located about 60 kilometers (36 miles) from Ljubljana, Trbovlje has a strong revolutionary tradition, which fed and nurtured Laibach. The first exhibition-concert by the new group was planned for 27 September 1980, but the authorities did not appreciate the group's posters and quashed the concert.[58] The group's posters stirred trouble again in 1983, when Dušan Mandić produced a poster showing a heterosexual couple who looked like they had been wrenched out of an Annette Funicello movie. The male wore a suspicious-looking armband with the "approved" star and the words "Disko FV," while the woman had two badges on her dress, with the inscriptions "Crazy Governments" and "Nazi Punks Fuck Off."[59] The authorities did not like the poster if only because one of the badges depicted had been banned and had already put Laibach collaborator Igor Vidmar in jail for its alleged fascist overtones. But Laibach seemed to relish in provocation and advertised its satirical attitude with the declaration, "Our freedom is the freedom of those who think alike."[60] Some years later, asked if the group was doing what it did from a sense of humor, Laibach spokesman Ivan Novak responded, "We only appreciate the kind of humor that is not a joke."[61] Laibach's supposed advocacy of totalitarianism was always rather transparent. Where real Nazis would claim that the New Order they sought to consolidate would overcome all alienation, for example, in the case of Laibach's members, as Slavoj Žižek has pointed out, "their fundamental cry was 'We want more alienation.'"[62]

In 1983, Laibach was banned from appearing publicly under its name. It responded by forming a mock political superstructure, calling it Neue Slowenische Kunst (New Slovenian Art, but always referred to either in the German or by the initials NSK). It passed "statutes" for NSK, requiring that "a[n] NSK member must be diligent, respectful towards the tradition and history of the NSK, obedient and cooperative in carrying out common decisions and irreproachable in living up to the universal and secret, legal and moral norms of the NSK."[63] In a later manifesto, "Ten Points of the Convent" (1983), Laibach declared, under Point One: "Laibach works as a team (team spirit), in the fashion of industrial production and totalitarianism, which means the individual does not speak out—the organization does. Our work is industrial, our language political."[64]

Aside from Laibach, there were three other component parts of NSK: the New Collectivism (its "propaganda" division), the Irwin Painting Group, which did the artwork for the band, and the Theater of the Sisters of Scipio Našica, which developed the stage presentations of Laibach rock pageants. The artwork and stage presentations followed the music in drawing inspiration from Nazi art and totalitarian art in general. The Irwin group, for its part, took to ironic mimicry of the paintings of old socialist realism (the official art form decreed by Stalin in the Soviet Union in the 1930s). The group worked underground during these years, from 1983 to 1987: Its 1984 concert in Ljubljana, for example, was announced only by a wordless poster marked with the familiar Laibach cross by Malevich and the date. Laibach would be restored to legal status only in 1987, with its concert, Birds of a Feather, staged in the Festival Hall in Ljubljana.

Laibach quickly stirred controversy across socialist Yugoslavia. Some people felt that Laibach sympathized with Naziism, others thought the members were suggesting that communism was the same as Naziism, and still others thought they were using Nazi imagery as an energized medium in which to communicate their ideas about culture and politics. People in the Communist Party were nervous and unable to shake the suspicion that the group was equating them with the Nazis. NSK members were always rather tight-lipped about their intentions. One member told me, for instance, only that "art has to be frightening. It cannot be comfortable," and he offered that what Laibach was doing was waging "psychological terror" on its listeners.[65]

Communists concerned about Laibach's political tendencies could have obtained some clarification by reviewing the voluminous texts issued by the group. Thus, for example, no group which declared that "All art is subject to political manipulation except that which speaks the language of the same manipulation"[66] could be operating in anything other than a satirical, humorous mode. In fact, Laibach has, from the start, been fiercely antitotalitarian—but that is not the only point being made by the group. Fascism, thanks to the persistent drumbeating of the communist press, had remained a part of the political mythology of Yugoslavia, and the communists never stopped recalling their days of glory in the struggle against fascism in World War II. Thus, although the fascist motif would be an energized medium in any society, it acquired additional energies in the Yugoslav context. Laibach's "official" thinking about individualism and individual rights/needs was captured in a 1988 exchange between *Rockpool* and one of Laibach's members:

"What is your definition of an individual?"
"A multititude of one million divided by one million."[67]

Every concert which Laibach staged became the vehicle for political provocation. A 1989 concert in Slobodan Milošević's Belgrade was no exception. In this concert, Laibach showed *The Bombing of Belgrade*, a documentary German propaganda film from 1941, together with a section of a later (Tito-era) film entitled *First Official Meeting of the Nonaligned Countries in Belgrade*, in which the political leaders of the nonaligned states were shown dancing with their wives. Before the concert began, Laibach members read a text, mixing Serbian and German, with the intention of warning Serbs of the totalitarian proclivities of Serbian party boss Slobodan Milošević. In a prescient warning, the text read, "Brother Serbs, we are not going to let anyone rape you any more. We understand your problems." This was an allusion to Milošević's later-broken promise (of early 1987) that he would not let anyone "beat you any more."

By contrast with Laibach, Borghesia makes a rather different impression. This can be gathered already from the text of its 1988 song, "Am I?":

> Am I a man machine?
> Am I a sex machine?
> Am I a fuck machine?
> Am I a dream machine?
> Am I a killing machine? . . .
> Am I . . . am I . . . am I . . .[68]

Borghesia's music was industrial, making use of many noninstrumental sounds, and its videos featured everything from S&M scenes to film clips of the Partisan struggle to shots of Tito. The S&M motif recurs in the group's art, as indicated by the album, *Surveillance and Punishment*,[69] and song titles such as "Discipline! (Punish Them)" and "Disciple."[70] In the 1988 song, "Beat and Scream," Borghesia sings,

> I care for my slave
> sometimes I even feed him

would you?
Yes . . . captain
that's a good boy
please, sir
master I worship you.
I love your boots
yes, stomp and kick . . .
you, wonderful boots
yes, you can beat me and whip me
beat me!
beat me!
beat me! . . .
let me serve you, master . . .
why screaming? . . .
screams?
just a part of me to use
and command.[71]

At times, as in the case of Laibach, Borghesia turned its sights toward social criticism, as in the song, "Police Hour":

Everything is under control
Streets are empty
Night is cold
Headhunt!
Patrols are everywhere
Special divisions
and civil agents
Rhythm of metal drum
Broken windows
Smashed cars
Everything is under control
There is no matinee today.[72]

Borghesia had been even more explicit in its 1986 record *Their Laws, Our Lives,* which showed a well-armed "lawman" against a backdrop of number 133 written over and over again. Article 133 of the federal penal code provided for legal penalties for "verbal offenses."

Borghesia had links to the gay, lesbian, and pacifist movements in Slovenia, and its members gave firm support to all forms of sexual liberation. Goran Lisica, rock critic and manager of the Ljubljana group Videosex, offered that Borghesia systematically pursued the "subversion of traditional sexuality by negation of the classical family, in order to have a clean slate on which to reexamine the nature of sensuality, formulate new meanings and establish the reasons of sexual deviation."[73]

Laibach and Borghesia both inspired cult followings within Yugoslavia and the West, and Laibach conducted very successful tours of a number of U.S. cities in

1989 and 1993. Inevitably, musical clones appeared, especially of Laibach, such as the groups Children of Socialism, Ciao, Cunts, O! Cult, and Abbildungen Variete, all of which played at the New Rock festivals of 1982 and 1983.[74] In Osijek (Slavonia), an eclectic band was formed in 1991, taking the satirical name, Noise Slawonische Kunst.

Rock and the War

In my *Balkan Babel*, I have sketched out the multivarious connections between Yugoslav rock and the famed "national question," which was ultimately manipulated to tear the country apart.[75] These connections made it clear that the bands were in a position to comment on, reflect, and even to some extent affect interethnic behavior, especially at local levels.

As the political tensions boiled over into war, rock bands in the republics of what was once Yugoslavia took differing positions on whether and how to respond to the new situation. Some favored advocacy, such as Zagreb's Psihomodo pop, whose 1991 album, *Maxi Single za Gardiste*, featured four "patriotic" songs, including the strident "Croatia Must Win."[76] On the Serbian side, rock stars Simonida Stanković and Oliver Mandić lent their support to the campaign, touring the front lines and serenading the troops. Stanković even sang a panegyric to international bank robber and cut-throat Željko "Arkan" Ražnjatović.[77] Within Serbia, state sponsorship of "turbo-folk" made Ceca Ražnjatović, Arkan's wife, the reigning queen of Serbian popular culture. Milošević eventually withdrew his sponsorship of "turbo-folk," with its militant presentation and in January 2000, Arkan was gunned down in a Belgrade restaurant. But Ceca Ražnjatović continued her career, singing to Turkish-sounding pop having roots in the syncopations of southern Serbia and issuing a new CD, *Ceca 2000*, toward the end of the year.[78] Certain Croatian punk groups began singing obscene anti-Milošević lyrics in early 1992. Others, such as Belgrade's Rimtutituki (a composite band), urged pacifism, as in this group's song "Peace."[79] The town of Zaječar, for example, played host to rock groups from across the war-torn former SFRY republics, 29–31 August 1991. Bands from Belgrade, Pula (in Croatia), Skopje, Zagreb, and Sarajevo played to a crowd of 20,000 fans, promoting the old Beatles' message, "All you need is love."[80] About a month later (on 4 October), several pacifist-minded bands got together for a Rock for Peace festival in Ljubljana. The participating groups were Peter Lovsin's Falcons, Steamroller, Hungry Frank, Martinka Krpan (Ljubljana), Šank Rock (Velenja, Slovenia), and Automobili (Gorica).[81] Belgrade likewise saw its own Peace Concert, on 22 April 1992, with a crowd of some 50,000 people. Among the groups and artists singing for peace in Belgrade were Boye, Colored Program (Obojeni program), Rambo Amadeus, Ekaterina Velika, Electric Orgasm, Rimtutituki, Rade Šerbedžija, and Mira Karanović.[82] Yet another peace concert, this one dedicated to the city of Dubrovnik, was held in

Pula on 22 August 1992. Artists from Croatia, Slovenia, and Bosnia-Herzegovina performed at this event, with some 6,000 fans in attendance.[83]

In 1992, the rock group Atomic Shelter, with its lead singer Bruno Langer, issued an album entitled *East Europe Man,* with a political message: the only escape from fratricidal nationalism and bigotry is to free people from ideology and the manipulation by nationalist-oriented politicians. The album included the song "Chinese Bike," with words of hope:

> Hey, do you know where I come from
> A beautiful country, you're never alone, . . .
> Ask me what I believe,
> Hope is alive in our dream.[84]

Some artists, such as Belgrade's self-styled "anarcho-rocker" Rambo Amadeus, declared themselves to be in "opposition."[85] Belgrade's rock bard Bora Djordjević actually registered a political party, half in jest, calling it the Party of Ordinary Drinkers (Partija običnih pijanaca, or POP). Soon he had recruited 1,100 members; so he decided to run as his party's candidate for the Federal Assembly. He finished second in his district.[86] Djordjević, an early supporter of Milošević, had in fact turned against Milošević before the end of 1991, because of the Serbian leader's decision to go to war. In any case, he would seem incongruous in any role other than permanent rebel. On 6 October 2000, Djordjevic took his band, Fish Stew, to Milošević's home town of Požarevac, interrupting his concert to announce, "I came to free Požarevac after ten years and it is I who [have] the honor to let you know that Milošević has admitted that he lost."[87]

For some musicians, such as Nele Karajlić, who saw the dangers of war three or more years before it finally broke out, the start of the war meant only a new phase in their activism for peace.[88]

The war gutted Bosnia altogether and obliterated its indigenous culture. Many of the republic's best-known rock stars fled abroad. But rock music has continued unabated, both in Bosnia and elsewhere in the post-Yugoslav region. In Croatia, in particular, a number of new groups were formed between 1990 and 1992.[89]

A New Generation

Some of the classic Yugoslav groups of yesteryear have disappeared or reconfigured. Sarajevo's White Button, Zagreb's Dee Dee Mellow and Haustor, Ljubljana's Bastards and Falcons (both groups headed by the talented Peter Lovšin), Skopje's Mizar, and Belgrade's Ekaterina Velika and Electric Orgasm have long since vanished from the stage, while Nele Karajlić's Smoking Forbidden, which had been based in Sarajevo in the late 1970s and 1980s, has reemerged in two rival incarnations: the original players, minus Karajlić, teamed up with the comic genius Elvis J. Kurtović to issue an album under the name "Smoking Forbidden" in 1997,[90] with Nele Karajlić recruiting a new team in Belgrade to issue an album of his own under the same name also in 1997.[91] The Sarajevo incarnation decorated its album with elements of Arabic script and reissued a song first released in 1988 by the Elvis J. Kurtović Band, "Hajle Selasije." Nominally dedicated to Ethiopia's longtime emperor, the song's seemingly sweet claim, "He was an amazing man, / loved by the masses, / wise like Gandhi, / and as handsome as Nasser,"[92] referred in fact to Yugoslavia's President Tito and had come across as tongue-in-cheek and satirical in 1988. But nine years later, the same lyrics seemed wistful and nostalgic for an earlier era.

Rock dynamo Rambo Amadeus, who had spoofed "turbo-folk" fans by making some appearances under the more "folkish" name *Ranko* Amadeus,[93] was hauled over the coals by rock critics after the issuance of his album *Titanic*,[94] but his next album, *Collected Works, Vol. 2*—the title itself a mockery of the old "collected works" of Marx & Engels, Lenin, Tito, and others—found an enthusiastic reception among critics.[95] Adorned with pictures of Mao, Castro, Che Guevara, and Rambo himself, the album included a telling spoof of the pseudo-solemn Slovenian group Laibach.[96]

Among newer artists one should mention Belgrade bands Sunshine (Sanšajn) and Pan Bend, and Croatia's all-female group Witches (Vještice)[97] and Montaž stroj, whose 1994 album *Better Dead than Red* incorporated the voice of V. I. Lenin into one of its tracks.[98] In Slovenia, newer arrivals on the rock scene have included the soft rock soloist Magnifico and the hard rock group Strelnikoff (formed in Celje in 1988 and named for a character in Boris Pasternak's *Dr. Zhivago*), alongside the charmingly silly sextet, Agropop, whose 1997 album, *We Are Happy Slovenes*, included a "Ballad for Janez," leaving it unclear whether Prime Minister Janez Drnošek or Social Democratic leader Janez Janša was being "celebrated."[99] Magnifico struck a chord with his song "I Think," with its reflections on excesses of nationalism and hints about endless unsatisfying negotiations (but in Bosnia? in Slovenia? about what?—Magnifico takes advantage of artistic license to remain ambiguously silent).[100]

But by far the most controversial rock group at the end of the century was Strelnikoff, even if the controversy it generated has been limited to Slovenia. In post-communist Slovenia, one of the noisiest debates has concerned the constitutional guarantee of a woman's right to obtain an abortion. The Catholic Church has set its sights on this provision, finding allies in those parties on the right side of the political spectrum. Strelnikoff leaped into the fray in February 1998 with the release of its album, *Bitchcraft*, which featured an "altered" picture of Slovenia's most famous painting of the Blessed Virgin Mary, the so-called "Madonna of Brezje." The alteration involved the replacement of the Christ-child with a giant rat. The album's five tracks are listed as follows:

Bitchcraft (Radio Vatikan edit)
Bitchcraft (Satan Himmelfahrt remix)

Bitchcraft (Torquemada remix)
Bitchcraft (Ali Agca remix)
Bitchcraft (Endlösung remix).[101]

The first of these features the transparently sarcastic lyrics

> Why did you kill your unborn baby?
> Why did you flush foetus down the drain?
> Where did you hide your knitting needle?
> You are the poison in our nation's vein!
> Bitchcraft! Bitchcraft! Bitchcraft!
> Someone's gotta stop it!
> Don't you know that the life is sacred? . . .
> We will stop your fuckin bitchcraft!
> We will teach you right from wrong![102]

Archbishop Franc Rode was furious and publicly denounced the CD. A special mass was celebrated, attended by 7,000 people, to pray for forgiveness from the Virgin Mary. Petitions were circulated in the churches, demanding criminal prosecution of the band members.[103] But all the clamor only achieved the opposite of what the Church wanted, turning the CD into an overnight commercial success and rallying those citizens with anti-clerical sympathies.

In Belgrade, on the other hand, rock musicians have been playing for higher stakes, alternatively performing as part of a protest against the country's just-introduced restrictive law on information (in November 1998),[104] lending encouragement to the Serb "national cause" during the NATO aerial campaign in spring 1999,[105] and joining the anti-regime student group Otpor (Resistance) to stage a protest concert in November 1999, as part of an effort to mobilize support to oust Serbian dictator Slobodan Milošević.[106]

There have been apocalyptic forebodings in Belgrade for years now—indeed since soon after Milošević's seizure of power in 1987. These forebodings were aptly captured by the irrepressible rock dinosaur Bora Djordjević in a 1997 concert, in which the singer referred to Mirjana Marković, Milošević's wife and head of the Yugoslav United Left (JUL), as Grandma Jula (JULa). "On to chaos and disintegration," the forty-four-year-old rocker sang, acknowledging in which direction the country had been heading. "We are led by Grandma Jula, who uses us all. We dance in a vampire ball, run by our decrepit Grandma Jula."[107] The general malaise associated with the Milošević years may even be read in the names of the rock groups which emerged during his thirteen years in power. These included: the Belgrade groups Baal, Belgrade Ghetto, Dead Idea (known, among other things, for its 1992 album, *Welcome to the Abyss*), Clinically Dead (Klinički mrtav, formed in 1991), Urgh!, and Who is the Best; Eva Braun, a group based in Becej; and the Novi Sad group, Generation without a Future (Generacija bez budućnosti). By contrast, the would-be Scots of the Belgrade band, Orthodox Celts, offered a

Balkan version of Celtic music for those with more exotic (or more escapist) tastes.[108]

Conclusion

In the 1950s and early 1960s, Yugoslav rock was highly imitative of the West, which is to say of American and British rock trends and fashions. If Western groups featured three guitars and percussion, then Yugoslav groups wanted the same combination. If Western groups sang of love, then Yugoslav groups did likewise. If soul gained a following in the West, then a local variant of soul gained popularity also in Yugoslavia. For Yugoslav rockers in the 1950s and early 1960s, America and England set the standard for what was "correct" in rock music.

But from the beginning there were local influences and local dynamics as well; "panegyric rock" is a good example of this. But by the mid-1970s, Yugoslav rock was increasingly freeing itself of its Western tutelage, though not shutting itself off from Western models altogether. Paul Simon's 1986 album, *Graceland,* making use of South African musicians had a tangible impact on Yugoslav musicians, for example, giving encouragement, in the process, to the incorporation of local musical traditions into rock. By the 1980s, Yugoslav rock musicians were increasingly looking to local culture and audiences more than to Western models, and developing their own styles and accents. Since 1980, further, local politics and controversies have claimed the attention of rock performers in Serbia, Croatia, Bosnia-Herzegovina, Slovenia, and elsewhere in the Yugoslav and post-Yugoslav region. In the process, Yugoslav and post-Yugoslav rock performers have played a role in reflecting the concerns and values of the society, as well as in shaping those concerns and values. As Simon Frith has pointed out,

> Rock culture is not confined to ceremonial occasions, but enters people's lives without aura, taking on a meaning there independent of the intentions of its original creators. The rock audience is not a passive mass, consuming records like cornflakes, but an active community, making music into a symbol of solidarity and an inspiration for action [even if only an inspiration to dance]. . . . The rock audience is not always manipulated but can make real choices; the music doesn't always impose an ideology but can, in [Greil] Marcus's phrase, "absorb events," absorb its listeners' concerns and values.[109]

Notes

This chapter is a revised and updated version of the author's "Shake, Rattle, and Self-Management: Making the Scene in Yugoslavia," which was published in Sabrina P. Ramet, ed., *Rocking the State: Rock Music and Politics in Eastern Europe and Russia* (Boulder, Colo.: Westview, 1994), which, in turn, was a revised and updated version of the author's "The Rock Scene in

Yugoslavia," originally published in *Eastern European Politics and Societies* 2, no. 2 (Spring 1988). Reprinted by permission of Westview Press and of the University of California Press.

1. Dieter Baacke, *Jugend und Subkultur* (Munich: Juventa Verlag, 1972); Simon Frith, *The Sociology of Rock* (London: Constable, 1978); Tibor Kneif, *Einführung und Unterlagen für Studium und Unterricht* (Wilhelmshaven: Heinrichshofen's Verlag, 1979); John Orman, *The Politics of Rock Music* (Chicago: Nelson-Hall, 1984); William S. Fox and James D. Williams, "Political Orientation and Music Preferences among College Students," in *Public Opinion Quarterly*, Vol. 38, No. 3 (Autumn 1974); Philip Lamy and Jack Levin, "Punk and Middle-Class Values: A Content Analysis," in *Youth and Society*, Vol. 17, No. 2 (December 1985); James J. Leming, "Rock Music and the Socialization of Moral Values in Early Adolescence," in *Youth and Society*, Vol. 18, No. 4 (June 1987); Harold G. Levin and Steven H. Stumpf, "Statements of Fear through Cultural Symbols: Punk Rock as a Reflective Subculture," in *Youth and Society*, Vol. 14, No. 4 (June 1983); Karen Beth Mashkin and Thomas J. Volgy, "Socio-political Attitudes and Musical Preferences," in *Social Science Quarterly*, Vol. 56, No. 3 (December 1975); Lorraine E. Prinsky and Jill Leslie Rosenbaum, "'Leer-ics' or Lyrics: Teenage Impressions of Rock 'n' Roll," in *Youth and Society*, Vol. 18, No. 4 (June 1987); S. Lee Seaton and Karen Ann Watson, "Counterculture and Rock: A Cantometric Analysis of Re-tribalization," in *Youth and Society*, Vol. 4, No. 1 (September 1972); John Stratton, "What is 'Popular Music'?" in *Sociological Review*, Vol. 31, No. 2 (May 1983); Simon Frith, *Sound Effects: Youth, Leisure, and the Politics of Rock 'n' Roll* (New York: Pantheon Books, 1981); Hannelore Wass, M. David Miller, and Robert G. Stevenson, "Factors Affecting Adolescents' Behavior and Attitudes toward Destructive Rock Lyrics," in *Death Studies*, Vol. 13, No. 3 (May–June 1989); Janet S. St. Laurence and Doris J. Joyner, "The Effects of Sexually Violent Rock Music on Males' Acceptance of Violence Against Women," in *Psychology of Women Quarterly*, Vol. 15, No. 1 (March 1991); Christine Hall Hansen and Ranald D. Hansen, "Constructing Personality and Social Reality through Music: Individual Differences among Fans of Punk and Heavy Metal Music," in *Journal of Broadcasting & Electronic Media*, Vol. 35, No. 3 (Summer 1991); Simon Frith, *Rock and Popular Music: Politics, Policies, Instruments* (London: Routledge, 1993); Thomas C. Shevory, "Bleached Resistance: The Politics of Grunge," in *Popular Music and Society*, Vol. 19, No. 2 (Summer 1995); Michael Bernard-Donals, "Jazz, Rock 'n' Roll, Rap, and Politics," in *Journal of Popular Culture*, Vol. 28, No. 2 (Fall 1994); Charles Fairchild, "'Alternative' Music and the Politics of Cultural Autonomy: The Case of Fugazi and the D.C. Scene," in *Popular Music and Society*, Vol. 19, No. 1 (Spring 1995); Simon Frith, *Performing Rites: On the Value of Popular Music* (Cambridge, Mass.: Harvard University Press, 1996); J. D. Considine, "Violence in Popular Music," in *Neiman Reports*, Vol. 50, No. 4 (Winter 1996); and Martin Cloonan and John Street, "Politics and Popular Music: from Policing to Packaging," in *Parliamentary Affairs*, Vol. 50, No. 2 (April 1997).

2. Christoph Dieckmann, "'Rock 'n Roll's Here to Stay'—Jugendkultur in der DDR," in *Kirche im Sozialismus*, Vol. 12, No. 3 (June 1986); Rainer Erd, "Musikalische Praxis und sozialer Protest: Überlegungen zur Funktion von Rock and Roll, Jazz und Oper," in *German Politics and Society*, No. 18 (Fall 1989); Volker Gransow, "The Political Culture of Pop-Music in the GDR," in *GDR Monitor*, No. 17 (Summer 1987); Y. H., "Rock-and-Roll in Hungary," in *Cross Currents*, Vol. 7 (1988); Zsolt Krokovay, "Politics and Punk [in Hungary]," in *Index on Censorship*, Vol. 14, No. 2 (April 1985); Olaf Leitner, *Rockszene DDR: Aspekte einer Massenkultur im Sozialismus* (Hamburg: Rowohlt Verlag, 1983); Günter Mayer, "Popular Music in the GDR," in *Journal of Popular Culture*, Vol. 18, No. 3 (Winter 1984); Sabrina P. Ramet, *Social Currents in Eastern Europe: The Sources and Consequences of the*

Great Transformation, 2nd ed. (Durham, N.C.: Duke University Press, 1995), chap. 10 ("Rock Music and Counterculture"); Sabrina P. Ramet, *Balkan Babel: The Disintegration of Yugoslavia from the Death of Tito to the Fall of Milosevic*, 4th ed. (Boulder, Colo.: Westview Press, 2002), chap. 7 ("Rock Music"); Timothy W. Ryback, *Rock around the Bloc* (Oxford: Oxford University Press, 1990); S. Frederick Starr, "The Rock Inundation [in the USSR]," in *Wilson Quarterly*, Vol. 7, No. 4 (Autumn 1983); Anna Szemere, "Pop Music in Hungary," in *Communication Research*, Vol. 12, No. 3 (July 1985); Anna Szemere, "Some Institutional Aspects of Pop and Rock in Hungary," in *Popular Music*, Vol. 3 (1983); Artemy Troitsky, *Back in the USSR: The True Story of Rock in Russia* (Boston: Faber & Faber, 1987); Peter Wicke, *Anatomie des Rock* (Leipzig: VEB Deutscher Verlag für Musik, 1987); Peter Wicke, *Rockmusik* (Leipzig: Verlag Philipp Reclam Jun., 1987); Peter Wicke, "Young People and Popular Music in East Germany: Focus on a Scene," in *Communications Research*, Vol. 12, No. 3 (July 1985); "Pop im Prager Untergrund: Brief eines Fans," in *Kontinent*, Special issue (1976); Ekaterina Dobrotvorskaja, "Soviet Teens of the 1970s: Rock Generation, Rock Refusal, Rock Context," in *Journal of Popular Culture*, Vol. 26, No. 3 (Winter 1992); Tony Mitchell, "Mixing Pop and Politics: Rock Music in Czechoslovakia before and after the Velvet Revolution," in *Popular Music*, Vol. 11, No. 2 (May 1992); Jolanta Pekacz, "Did Rock Smash the Wall? The Role of Rock in Political Transition," in *Popular Culture*, Vol. 13, No. 1 (January 1994); Sabrina P. Ramet (ed.), *Rocking the State: Rock Music and Politics in Eastern Europe and Russia* (Boulder, Colo.: Westview Press, 1994); Uta G. Poiger, "Rock 'n' Roll, Female Sexuality, and the Cold War Battle over German Identities," in *Journal of Modern History*, Vol. 68, No. 3 (September 1996); and Georg Maas and Harmut Reszel, "Whatever Happened to . . . : The Decline and Renaissance of Rock in the Former GDR," in *Popular Music*, Vol. 17, No. 3 (October 1998).

3. Orman, *The Politics of Rock*, p. x.

4. Frith, *Sociology of Rock*, p. 54; also Loyd Grossman, *A Social History of Rock Music* (New York: David McKay, 1976).

5. Jeremy Seabrook, *City Close-up* (London, 1971), as quoted in Frith, *The Sociology of Rock*, p. 20.

6. Michael Watts, "The Call and Response of Popular Music: The Impact of American Pop Music in Europe," in C. W. E. Bigsby (ed.), *Superculture: American Popular Culture and Europe* (Bowling Green, Ohio: Bowling Green University Popular Press, 1975), p. 124.

7. R. Serge Denisoff, in *Sing a Song of Social Significance* (Bowling Green, Ohio: Bowling Greeen State University Popular Press, 1972) reported a study he had conducted among 180 students when a pessimistic, nihilistic song titled "Eve of Destruction" was the number one record. Only 36 percent of those surveyed understood the lyrics as the composer had intended, and 23 percent completely misconstrued them. Denisoff concluded that "the protest song is primarily seen as an entertainment item rather than one of political significance." Quoted in Orman, *The Politics of Rock Music*, p. 150.

8. For example, in the mid-1950s, the Juvenile Delinquency and Crime Commission of Houston, Texas, banned more than fifty rock 'n' roll songs within the space of a single week. This and other cases are discussed in Orman, *The Politics of Rock Music*, pp. 3–8. Regarding censorship of the Sex Pistols and of Elvis Presley, see Greil Marcus, *Lipstick Traces: A Secret History of the Twentieth Century* (Cambridge, Mass.: Harvard University Press, 1989), pp. 10, 75, 148. See also Trent Hill, "The Enemy Within: Censorship in Rock Music in the 1950s," in Anthony DeCurtis (ed.), *Present Tense: Rock & Roll and Culture* (Durham, N.C.: Duke University Press, 1992); Michael Goldberg, "Crackdown on 'Obscene' Shows: New

San Antonio Law Aimed at Rock & Roll Concerts," in *Rolling Stone* (30 January 1986); Henry Schipper, "Rock Censorship Debate Rages," in *Variety* (8 April 1989); Dennis Wharton, "FCC Warns Rock Shockcasters to Clean 'Disgustingly Obscene' Broadcasts or Face the Music," in *Variety* (22 April 1987); David Koen, "Fear of Music," in *Harper's* (August 1990); and Edward I. Volz, "You Can't Play That: A Selective Chronology of Banned Music, 1850–1991," in *School Library Journal*, Vol. 37, No. 7 (July 1991).

9. *New York Times* (17 October 1990), pp. A1–A11; and *Neue Zürcher Zeitung* (22 September 1992), p. 5. Regarding issues of censorship in the 1990s, see Jonathan L. Crane, "The Long Arm of the Law and the Big Beat," in *Popular Music and Society*, Vol. 16, No. 3 (Fall 1992); and Eric Boehler, "Culture Skirmishes: Rock, Rap and Country Musicians across the Nation," in *Rolling Stone* (21 August 1997).

10. *New York Times* (5 February 1990), p. A15.

11. Theodore Gracyk, *Rhythm and Noise: An Aesthetic of Rock* (Durham, N.C.: Duke University Press, 1996), p. 126.

12. Quoted in the *Seattle Post-Intelligencer* (1 November 1987), p. F-1. See also the *New York Times* (18 October 1987), p. 30.

13. *Vjesnik* (Zagreb), 8 December 1984, p. 11, called Bora Djordjević's album *The Truth* "ethically unacceptable."

14. Interview with Husein Hasanefendić, member of Steamroller, Zagreb, 24 June 1987.

15. Such as the Croatian rap group Ugly Leaders. See *Mladina* (Ljubljana), 17 March 1992, p. 40.

16. Literally "brother-in-law rock" but probably best understood as a homegrown equivalent of country rock.

17. See, in particular, the album *Zvučni zid: musika za teatar, film i TV,* JUGOTON LSY-63249 (1986).

18. Interview with Tonny Montano, Zagreb, 24 June 1987. See also Snežana Golubović, "Čovek koji je ubio i taličnog tema" [interview with Tonny Montano], *Rock* (Belgrade), July 1987, pp. 26–28.

19. See Dragan Ambrozić, "FV založba," in *Rock* (August 1987), p. 48; also *Novi Vjesnik* (Zagreb) 5 October 1992, p. 24C.

20. Interview with Petar Popović, International Label Manager for RTB PGP and founder of *Rock* magazine, Belgrade, 16 June 1987. See also Jadranka Janković, "Ja sam običan mali lajava" [interview with Zlatan Stipišic-Džibo of the heavy metal group Osmi putnik], in *Rock* (June 1987), pp. 26–27. For a discussion of this era, together with sample rock lyrics, see *Drugom stranam: Almanak novog talasa u SFRJ* (Belgrade: SSO Srbije, 1983).

21. Interview with Petar Popović. The definitive study of White Button is Darko Glavan and Dražen Vrdoljak, *Ništa mudro—Bijelo dugme: Autorizirana biografija* (Zagreb: Polet Rock, 1981).

22. Interview with Mimo Hajrić, former member of Fiery Kiss (Vatreni poljubac), Sarajevo, 15 September 1989.

23. Interview with Zemira Alajbegović, manager of Borghesia, Ljubljana, 3 July 1987.

24. The Kosovo rock scene is discussed in Darko Hudelist, *Kosovo: Bitka bez iluzija* (Zagreb: Dnevnik, 1989), pp. 109–129.

25. Text from Paraf, "Živjela Jugoslavija" (from *A dan je tako lijepo počeo*, 1980), at ftp.yurope.com/pub/books/yu_rock/37-juga1.xyu.

26. For discussion, see David P. Szatmary, *Rockin' in Time: A Social History of Rock-and-Roll*, 4th ed. (Upper Saddle River, N.J.: Prentice Hall, 2000), chap. 6.

27. Mel van Elteren, "Rocking and Rapping in the Dutch Welfare State," in John Dean and Jean-Paul Gabilliet (eds.), *European Readings of American Popular Culture* (Westport, Conn.: Greenwood Press, 1996), p. 65.

28. Quoted in Eric D. Gordy, *The Culture of Power in Serbia: Nationalism and the Destruction of Alternatives* (University Park: Pennsylvania State University Press, 1999), p. 143.

29. Quoted in Gordy, *The Culture of Power in Serbia*, p. 128.

30. Interview with Dražen Vrdoljak, music director of Radio Zagreb, Zagreb, 22 June 1987.

31. For an excellent account of the early years of Yugoslav rock, see Ljuba Trifunović, *Vibracije* (Belgrade: SSO Srbije, 1986).

32. Interview with Aleksandar Tijanić, *NIN* music critic, Belgrade, 18 June 1987. Tijanić later served as Minister of Information in Belgrade.

33. As reported in Dušan Vesić, "Dvadeset taktova za Tita," in *ITD* (Belgrade), 18 June 1987.

34. "Idoli," at www.vladadivljan.com/Idoli-diskografija.htm [accessed on 20 December 2000]. See also Darko Hudelist, "Vlada Divljan: 'Dogadjanje naroda' bilo je oličenje svega protiv čega su se Idoli borili" [An interview with Vlada Divljan], in *Globus* (Zagreb), no. 495 (2 June 2000).

35. Mark Thompson, *A Paper House: The Ending of Yugoslavia* (London: Random House, 1992), p. 39. For a detailed analysis and documentation of this trend, see *Punk pod Slovenci* (Ljubljana: Univerzitetna Konferenca, ZSMS, 1985).

36. Regarding these groups, see Petar Janjatović, *Ilustrovana ex-Yu Rock enciklopedija 1960–2000,* Dopunjeno izdanje (Novi Sad: Prometej, 2001), pp. 19–21, 41–42, 89–90, 114–116, 117–119, 132–133, 146–147, 168–175, 188.

37. See Darko Glavan and Hrvoje Horvat, *Prljavo kazalište—Sve je lako kad si mlad: Autorizirana biografija* (Zagreb: Minerva, 2001).

38. For a recent article about the group, see Nedzad Haznadar, "Saša Losić: Koncerti, intervjui i promocije za mene su previše . . ." [An interview with Saša Losić], in *Globus,* no. 482 (3 March 2000), pp. 90–93.

39. See "Partibrejkers biografija" at members.lycos.co.uk/partibrejkers/biog.htm.

40. On these groups, see Janjatovic, *Ilustrovana ex-Yu rock,* pp. 35–36, 41, 43–45, 57–59, 72–74, 93–94, 110–111, 147–149, 149–150, 154–156, 195–196.

40a. Siniša Radaković (ed.), *Mala enciklopedija Hrvatske pop i rock glazbe* (Rijeka: Nema problema, 1994), pp. 85, 119, 142–143, 170–171.

41. See Janjatović, *Ilustrovana ex-YU rock,* pp. 134–135.

42. Regarding Viktorija, see *Pop Rock* (Belgrade), 3 May 1989, p. 20; regarding Kasandra, see *Novi Vjesnik* (Zagreb), 27 September 1992, p. 16B, and *Vreme* (Belgrade), 16 March 1992, p. 52.

43. Goran Bakić, "Bregović: Svjetska karijera bivšeg rockera" [An interview with Goran Bregović], in *Globus,* no. 453 (13 August 1999), p. 68.

44. Dušan Vesić, "Novi prilozi za istoriju Jugoslovenskog rock'n rolla": Part 1, "Josip Broz i rock'n roll," in *Pop Rock* (10 May 1990), p. 2.

45. For details, see Ramet, *Balkan Babel,* 4th ed., p. 131.

46. *Danas* (Zagreb), as cited in *Bulletin* of the Democratic International Committee to Aid Democratic Dissidents in Yugoslavia (New York), July 1987, p. 18.

47. Aleksandra Marković, "Tragično smo odrasli" [interview with Nele Karajlić of "Zabranjeno pušenje"], in *ITD* (June 1987), p. 5; and interview with Nele Karajlić, leader of Smoking Forbidden, Sarajevo, 14 September 1989.

48. Song "Dan Republike" ("Republic Day") on Zabranjeno pušenje, *Pozdrav iz zemlje Safari,* DISKOTON LP-8248 (1987). See also the report in *Glas istre* (28 June 1987), p. 17.

49. Interview with Bora Djordjević, lead singer of Fish Stew, Belgrade, 18 June 1987.

50. Interview with Peter Lovšin, lead singer of the Bastards, Ljubljana, 30 June 1987.

51. Song "Proletarian" by Esad Babačić-Car, banned, quoted in Aleš Erjavec and Marina Gržinic (eds.), *Ljubljana: The Eighties in Slovene Art and Culture* (Ljubjlana: Mladinska knjiga, 1991), p. 43.

52. Interview with Zoran Predin, lead singer of Hungry Frank, Ljubljana, 1987.

53. Song, "Poljubi me," on Azra, *Ravno do dna,* JUGOTON LSY-61661/2/3 (1982).

54. Song "Član mafije," on Riblja čorba, *Ujed za dušu,* RTB PGP 2320436 (1987).

55. Song "To je šok," on Plavi orkestar, *Smrt fašizmu!* JUGOTON LSY-63262 (1986).

56. See, for example, Robert J. Stoller, *Pain and Passion: A Psychoanalyst Explores the World of S&M* (New York: Plenum Press, 1991).

57. As I put it in my *Social Currents,* 2nd ed., p. 251.

58. Interview with Ivan Novak, member of Laibach, Ljubljana, 21–22 March 1992. This interview was conducted in the hotel lobby of the Hotel Slon, between 2 and 4 a.m.

59. The poster is reproduced in Erjavec and Gržinić, *Ljubljana: The Eighties,* p. 58.

60. Quoted in ibid., p. 88.

61. Quoted in *The Times* (London), 29 November 1994, on *Lexis-Nexis Academic Universe.*

62. Quoted in Thompson, *A PaperHouse,* p. 43.

63. Quoted in Erjavec and Gržinic, *Ljubljana: The Eighties,* p. 89.

64. Quoted in ibid., p. 89.

65. Interview with Ivan Novak.

66. Laibach (1984), as quoted in Michael Benson, "Neue Slowenische Kunst: The 'State in Time'" (Spring 1996, posted 20 October 1999), at www.tO.or.at/˝micz/threadder/messages/148.htm [accessed on 27 February 2001].

67. From material assembled by NSK for its project, *NSK Embassy Moscow,* in 1992.

68. Song "Am I" [text in English], on Borghesia, *Escorts and Models,* PLAY IT AGAIN SAM RECORDS BIUS-1014 (1988).

69. Borghesia, *Surveillance and Punishment,* PLAY IT AGAIN SAM RECORDS BIUS-3023 (n.d.).

70. Both featured on the album *Surveillance and Punishment.*

71. Song "Beat and Scream" [text in English], on Borghesia, *Escorts and Models.*

72. Song "Police Hour," on Borghesia, *Resistance,* PLAY IT AGAIN SAM RECORDS BIUS-1038 (n.d.).

73. Quoted in Erjavec and Gržinić, *Ljubljana: The Eighties,* p. 47.

74. Regarding the Slovenian rock scene more broadly, see Gregor Tomc, *Druga Slovenija* (Ljubljana: Krt, 1989), especially pp. 116–123.

75. Ramet, *Balkan Babel,* 4th ed., chapter 7, especially pp. 134–136.

76. Song "Hrvatska mora pobijediti," on Psihomodo pop, *Maxi Single za Gardiste,* CROATIA RECORDS MS-D 2 035553 3 (1991).

77. Text in Ramet, *Social Currents,* 2nd ed., p. 261.

78. *The Guardian* (London), 1 December 2000, p. 10, on *Nexis.*

79. *Politika—International Weekly* (Belgrade), 18–24 April 1992, p. 16. See song text, "Slušaj vamo!" at www.yurope.com/people/sen/The.Book.Of.Home/pesmarica/ekv/pesme/slusajvamo.html.

80. *Bosanski pogledi* (Sarajevo), 5 September 1991, p. 22.

81. Interview with Peter Lovšin, leader of the Falcons, Ljubljana, 26 March 1992.

82. *Vreme* (27 April 1992), p. 19. See also Igor Kolovrat, "Rambo Amadeus: Moji nastupi u Hrvatskoj neće izazvati skandal" [An interview with Rambo Amadeus], in *Globus*, no. 479 (11 February 2000), pp. 88–91.

83. *Novi Vjesnik* (23 August 1992), p. 7A.

84. Text from Atomic Shelter, "Chinese Bike" (from *East Europe Man*, 1992), at ftp.yurope.com/pub/books/yu_rock/65-antiw.x.xyu.

85. Miha Štamcar and Jani Sever, "Mitingaš v Sloveniji" [interview with Rambo Amadeus], in *Mladina* (Ljubljana), 17 March 1992, p. 29. Regarding Rambo Amadeus, see also *NIN* (5 June 1992), p. 34.

86. *Politika ekspres* (Belgrade), 16 June 1992, p. 17.

87. Quoted in *Agence France Presse* (7 October 2000), on *Nexis*.

88. In addition to being a rock musician, Karajlić was also a comedian with his own show on Sarajevo Television. In September 1989, he devoted an entire show to warning, albeit through comedy, of the risks of ethnic hostilities, partition of the country, and war. Regarding Karajlić, see also *Politika ekspres* (10 May 1992), p. 12.

89. Such as the popular group Overflow (from Koprivnica). See the report in *Heavy Metal World: Novine za ljubitelje heavy metala* (October 1992), p. 8.

90. Zabranjeno pušenje, *Fildžan viška*, Dallas CD 130 (1997). See also Ahmed Burić, "Nemam želju raditi s Neletom" [An interview with Elvis J. Kurtovich], in *Dani* (Sarajevo), no. 117 (27 August 1999), pp. 48–49.

91. Zabranjeno pušenje, *Ja nisam odavlje*, Komuna CD 155 (1997).

92. See fuller text in Ramet, *Balkan Babel*, 4th ed., p. 142.

93. Gordy, *The Culture of Power in Serbia*, pp. 116–119.

94. Rambo Amadeus, *Titanik*, Komuna Records, CD-147 (N.D.).

95. Rambo Amadeus, *Zabrana dela 2*, Manja Records, VM CD 010 (1998).

96. "Samit u burekdinici Laibach," on ibid.

97. See, for example, Vještice, *Djevojke u ljetnim haljinama*, CBS, CD 116 (1995).

98. Montaž stroj, *Better Dead Than Red—Post-Communism*, Croatia Records, CD SG D 5 048121 (1994). The voice of Lenin was taken from the album "Words of V. I. Lenin 1919," issued by Melodiya Records (Moscow).

99. Agropop, *Srečni smo Slovencki*, Sazas, 104077 (1997).

100. Magnifico, *Kolo je Cefur*, MCD, 005 (N.D.).

101. Strelnikoff, *Bitchcraft*, Law & Auder Records, 001 (1998).

102. Ibid.

103. "Slovenia's Holy Civil War: Rock Group Strelnikoff and [the] Virgin Mary," on *Telepolis* (9 April 1998), at ftp.heise.de/tp/english/inhalt/te/1440/1.html.

104. *Beta news agency* (Belgrade), 3 November 1998, trans. in *BBC Monitoring Europe—Political* (3 November 1998), on *Lexis-Nexis Academic Universe*.

105. See, for example, *New York Times* (24 May 1999), p. 1, on *Lexis-Nexis Academic Universe*.

106. *Agence France Presse* (22 November 1999), on *Lexis-Nexis Academic Universe*; and *Beta news agency* (22 November 1999), trans. in *BBC Summary of World Broadcasts* (24 November 1999), on *Lexis-Nexis Academic Universe*.

107. Quoted in *International Herald Tribune* (Neuilly-sur-Seine), 18 January 1997, p. 5, on *Lexis-Nexis Academic Universe*.

108. Janjatović, *Ilustrovana ex-Yu rock*, pp. 223–250.

109. Frith, *The Sociology of Rock*, p. 198.

14

UFOs over Russia and Eastern Europe

Sabrina P. Ramet

Start here. Our home is Upsilon Boötes, which is a double star. We live on the sixth planet of seven, counting outward from the sun, which is the larger of the two. Our sixth planet has one moon. Our fourth planet has three. Our first and third planets each have one. Our probe is in the position of Arcturus, known in our maps.

—Alleged message of an unmanned probe allegedly placed in orbit around our moon between 15,000 and 13,000 years ago by the inhabitants of another planet and allegedly translated by British astronomer Duncan Lunan in 1974[1]

SINCE THE LATE 1940s, there have been increasing numbers of reports of UFOs in Russia and Eastern Europe. Worldwide, the first known sighting of a UFO occurred on 8 December 1733, when a Dorset man allegedly saw a shiny silver disc in the sky.[2] In Russia, the Tunguska meteorite (1908) has sometimes been counted as a UFO sighting, but more properly, one should date the first recorded UFO sighting in Russia to 4 May 1910, when a Dr. I. Plemely, a professor mathematics in the town of Cirnovti, saw a bright celestial body approaching from the south at a high speed.[3] In the East European area, among the earliest sightings were those in Transylvania in 1904, in Sofia, Bulgaria, in 1908, at the Struma Valley prison (in Bulgaria) in 1912, and in Moravia in 1913.[4] A particularly spectacular sighting was reported in Colun Judetul Sibiu (Romania) in 1926, when a hovering illuminated object "the size of the moon" allegedly made a loud whistling noise and lit up the entire district.[5] Other sightings were reported in the Polish province of Jelenia Gora in 1938 (a crashed UFO),[6] over Budapest on 10 July 1947,[7] in Gdynia on 21 January 1959,[8] and over Lake Onega in the USSR on 28 April 1961 (in what was reported as a "near crash landing ... making a tremendous noise and causing considerable damage before regaining forward motion and disappearing from sight").[9] Since 1989, particularly after a well-publicized "sighting" in the Russian

Basic UFO Vocabulary

UFO = literally *unidentified flying object*, but generally understood to refer to a space vehicle manufactured on another planet and designed for interplanetary travel.

UOV = *unknown orbiting vehicle*. Such vehicles are sometimes thought to have been placed in orbit around the earth by the inhabitants of other planets.

sighting = any report of a mysterious light or mysterious flying object which is given an extraterrestrial or other non-natural explanation.

abduction = a temporary kidnapping of a person or group of persons, allegedly by space aliens, for the purpose of conducting physical examinations, impregnating fertile women, extracting sperm from males, altering the brain, or implanting devices in humans (also called *Close Encounters of the Fourth Kind*).

T.I.I. = *temporary involuntary invisibility*, generally induced—so it is said—by space aliens using higher technology.

implant = a small metal implant, generally inserted into a person's nose, allegedly designed to permit space aliens to track an abductee from childhood to adulthood.

hybrids = alleged offspring of aliens and humans, with human eggs fertilized or human sperm extracted, during abduction episodes. Some sources estimate that there may be as many as 2 million "hybrids" on the earth.

Roswell Incident = the alleged crash of a UFO near Roswell Army Air Base in New Mexico in 1947. In its initial statement concerning the incident, the army referred to the recovery of a flying disc; later, it claimed that only the wreckage of a weather balloon was concerned.

crop circles = complex designs produced in crop fields by bending the crops, usually associated with dramatic changes in levels of radioactivity and generally attributed, by believers, to extraterrestrials.

contactees = persons who claim to have had an encounter with extraterrestrial beings or non-human but highly intelligent beings living in remote parts of the earth (such as beneath the South Pole).

temporal lobe seizure = an affliction affecting the temporal lobe of the brain, induced by certain frequencies of light, which is said to cause the victim to experience visions of beings grabbing and pulling them, in essence triggering the beginning of an abduction "experience."

city of Voronezh, the number of sightings in the region has sky-rocketed. Many ufologists have noted that the dramatic upsurge in UFO sightings in the region coincided closely with the fall of communism, though few,[10] as far as I am aware, have speculated on any putative connection between the two. More usefully, we may note that the increase in the number of UFO sightings coincides with the recently accelerating development of secret and advanced military technology, and that many UFO sightings occur in the vicinity of top-secret military installations.

UFO phenomena occur worldwide even without reinforcement from American cultural artifacts. But American cinematic and television culture has clearly reinforced and shaped local expectations, perceptions, and interpretations in a specific direction. In this regard, the American television series *X-Files* has played an identifiable role.

Literally speaking, UFO means *unidentified flying object*. If, at a certain distance, one cannot tell if a certain object is a plane or a missile or a helicopter, for example, then it would seem to qualify as "unidentified"—at least for the poor observer on the ground who is wondering what it is. In 1972, Carl Sagan defined a UFO as "a moving aerial or celestial phenomenon, detected visually or by radar, but whose nature is not immediately understood."[11] But in practice, the expression is not usually employed in so modest or literal-minded a way. In practice, the acronym *UFO* is taken to refer to a flying vehicle of extraterrestrial origin. The University of Colorado UFO Project provided a working practical definition of "UFO" in 1969, equating it with

> the stimulus for a report made by one or more individuals of something seen in the sky (or an object thought to be capable of flight but seen when landed on the Earth) *which the observer could not identify as having an ordinary natural origin*, and which seemed to him sufficiently puzzling that he undertook to make a report of it to [the] police, to government officials, to the press, or perhaps to a representative of a private organization devoted to the study of such objects.[12]

The fascination that the UFO phenomenon holds lies precisely in those cases where a completely satisfactory explanation cannot be provided, for whatever reason. By virtue of the lack of some "normal" explanation, the door is opened to interpretation or even to fantasy, whether of a benevolent or of a nightmarish kind.

Communism and UFOs

The communist governments of the Soviet bloc displayed an ambivalence concerning UFOs. On the one hand, they treated stories concerning UFOs as "bourgeois propaganda"—the Hungarian government claiming (not entirely honestly), in 1954, that all reports concerning UFOs had originated in capitalist countries.[13] On the other hand, the higher echelons were clearly interested in such reports, and sought to obtain reliable information and interpretations of them. Thus, for example, as early as 1948, Soviet dictator Iosif Vissarionovich Stalin invited Valery Burdakov, a Soviet scientist, to review top secret materials (relayed by Soviet operatives in New Mexico) concerning the crash of an alleged extraterrestrial space vehicle near Roswell Army Air Base the previous year.[14] By 1955, Dr. Felix Zigel, a professor at the Moscow Aviation Institute, began to collect information concerning UFOs, and in 1967, formed an unofficial grouping of top Soviet scientists and cosmonauts, who shared a common interest in UFOs.[15]

Meanwhile, in 1959, there were two dramatic sightings—one in Poland and one in the Soviet Union. The Polish sighting, considered to be of dubious reliability by UFO researchers themselves, concerns aforementioned claims that a UFO crashed into Gdynia harbor on 21 January 1959. Reports differ as to what happened next. According to one report, a small humanoid was subsequently picked up on the waterfront where he had been wandering around "in a confused state." The alien is said to have been taken to a clinic but to have died in the course of medical procedures. According to reports, the alien's body was subsequently transferred to a research institute in Moscow.[16] But another report, dated May/June 1998, holds that possibly two EBEs (Extraterrestrial Biological Entities) "were found and recovered by soldiers of the Border Guard or the Navy. These were next transported under tight security to the Soviet Union, where they remain to this day."[17]

The second report from 1959 originated in Sverdlovsk, headquarters of a tactical missile command. UFOs were allegedly seen by ground personnel in spring of that year, hovering and circling over command headquarters for more than twenty-four hours. Eventually, the base commander ordered pilots to take to the skies and chase away the intruders.[18]

Some of the alleged sightings in the USSR seemed, rather transparently, to have been concocted to cover up local incompetence or negligence. Two examples may serve here. The first dates from 1961 when an explosion reduced a factory manufacturing heavily armoured tanks to rubble. At first, Soviet authorities blamed the explosion on U.S. operatives, but later, local witnesses promulgated a UFO theory, blaming the explosion on a supposed "ball of fire" which allegedly hovered above the scene for a few minutes to make sure that its mission had been accomplished. That the UFO story could protect factory workers from charges of gross negligence, while avoiding unnecessary provocation to the United States, seems rather obvious.

The second story dates from the Andropov era. On 26 August 1983, or so the story has it, Soviet radar picked up the presence of an undeclared aircraft in the vicinity of their top secret submarine base at Ventspills, on the Latvian coast. Six fighter aircraft with heat-seeking missiles were dispatched with orders to destroy the intruding craft. The intruder was flying at an altitude of 9,000 feet, according to reports, and the Soviet aircraft now fired their missiles. But, according to Russian UFO researcher Dr. Eduard Naumov, the missiles exploded the instant they were launched, thereby destroying the planes which had fired them. Five of the six Soviet aircraft were lost in the operation, with only Second Lt. Mikhail Anisimov returning alive. That the UFO story could have served (a) to protect Lt. Anisimov from a court-martial for treasonous action, or (b) to protect field maintenance personnel whose responsibility it was to keep the firing systems in good working order, again is quite clear. But interestingly enough, soon after the story broke, officials revised the story, now attributing the disaster to ball lightning. One is entitled to speculate that this may have been a double cover-up, with the ball lightning story designed to cover up the UFO story, which had in turn been concocted to cover up either incompetence or treason. Needless to say, two cover-ups are better than one, insofar as the second cover story makes the first cover more believable.[19]

Other stories dating from this time remain inconclusive. The premature return of the Soviet spacecraft Voskhod I, on 12 October 1964, after remaining only twenty-four hours aloft, in what had been billed as "a prolonged flight," immediately raised questions. One answer was supplied by S. R. Oilinger, writing for a German newspaper, who recounted that his sources in Moscow had attributed the abortion of the mission to "extremely fast-flying discs which struck the craft violent, shattering blows with their powerful magnetic fields."[20] A similar encounter awaited Voskhod II which, on 19 March 1965, allegedly sighted an unmanned satellite. There were persistent rumors that this "satellite" was, in fact, an extraterrestrial craft and that it harassed the Russian spacecraft, resulting in complications during its return to earth.[21] Could the United States or some other power have been involved in these incidents? Or should the difficulties experienced in these episodes be traced to natural phenomena? The verdict remains inconclusive.

The foregoing examples all come from military-related operations or spacecraft. But some sightings in the communist era were reported by ordinary civilians. One such sighting involved an eleven-year-old girl in Poland who, in July 1954, had an alien encounter while on holiday at Wegierska Gorka. Invited on board the alien craft, she claimed to have seen several "entities" who looked essentially like humans except for the presence of "humps" on their backs.[22] Like many such stories from private individuals, it did not serve any exculpatory function for her; indeed, as in many cases involving non-military persons, she did not remember anything of this episode until much later (in 1986, in her case).

A similar encounter was reported by Polish farmer Jan Wolski on 19 May 1978. Driving his horses and cart near Emilcin, he claimed that he was stopped by "entities" with slanting eyes, taken aboard an alien craft, stripped naked, and given a medical exam. There is no indication as to whether he somehow lost his horse and cart, but assuming that they were not lost and that he was not inexcusably late in getting home to his family, then his UFO story would seem not to have served any particular purpose for Wolski (except, perhaps, for getting some attention).[23] But the lack of a complete context makes any final judgment on the matter of Wolski impossible.

Perhaps the most provocative UFO story from the communist era dates from 1969 and relates to the American landing on the moon. According to three Russian scientists (Dr. Vladimir Azhazha, Prof. Aleksandr Kazantsev, and Dr. Sergei Bozhich), Soviet intelligence monitoring the event discovered that two extraterrestrial craft were on hand to observe the landing of the Apollo 11 lunar module on 20 July 1969. Soviet intelligence reports allegedly claim that astronaut Neil Armstrong informed Mission Control in Houston about the alien craft, and that his companion Buzz Aldrin took pictures of the alien craft from inside the module. Steiger and Steiger write that "the three Russian scientists charge that NASA censored Armstrong's verbal report of the two UFOs on the moon's surface and immediately placed Aldrin's motion picture film in a top-secret repository after the astronauts returned to Earth on July 24."[24] Bozhich allegedly speculated that the extraterrestrials were present as a "back-up", just in case the Americans should run into any difficulties.

James Oberg, author of *Red Star in Orbit* and a renowned specialist in the Soviet space program, believes that "most, if not all, of the more sensational UFO incidents to emerge from behind the Iron Curtain in past decades, can be rationally explained" without reference to notions of space aliens.[25] For example, on 20 September 1977, TASS reported the presence of a huge glowing object along the Finnish border which "moved slowly toward Petrozavodsk and, spreading out over it in the form of a jellyfish, hung there, showering the city with a multitude of very fine rays which created an image of pouring rain."[26] Azhazha, already one of the leading Russian ufologists, who would go on to establish an interdisciplinary network of UFO societies in 1990, immediately embraced an extraterrestrial explanation, affirming that the object was "either a UFO, a carrier of high intelligence with crew, and passengers, or it was a field of energy created by such a UFO."[27] Soviet science-fiction writer Aleksandr Kazantsev shared this view, declaring that the object sighted over Petrozavodsk was "a spaceship from outer space, carrying out reconnaisance."[28] In actuality, the mysterious object was apparently a secret rocket fired from a military space installation at Plesetsk. The "jellyfish" and "shower" phenomena were the result of a severe malfunction. But clearly it was less embarrassing to Soviet authorities to have locals blame the unusual event on extraterrestrials.

For a brief period in the mid-1960s, the communist authorities of the pre-Gorbachev Soviet Union were willing to allow researchers to discuss UFO phenomena frankly. This brief interlude was probably triggered by a wave of UFO sightings in 1966, across Eastern Europe, the USSR, and China. Be that as it may, on 18 October 1967, a UFO research division was created at the Moscow House of Aviation and Aeronautics, chaired by Major General Porfiri Stolyanov. Although Stolyanov was assisted by Felix Zigel, a research scientist with considerable prestige, the division soon encountered roadblocks as it found itself denied access to official documents.[29] In spite of this, Moscow scientific journals organized a meeting at the Central Journalism House on 5 February 1968, providing an occasion for a frank discussion of UFOs. But shortly after the meeting, the UFO research division was closed down, and on 29 February 1968, *Pravda* published a blistering attack on ufology. From then until 1989, UFO sightings could be mentioned in the Soviet media only to debunk them. Soviet citizens were forbidden to study UFOs or to publish concerning the subject.[30] The result was the spawning of a UFO underground. In Voronezh in 1978, amateur ufologists defied officialdom by organizing a Group for the Study of UFOs. The following year a similar group formed in Gorky, and other groups sprang up in other cities. Only in 1982 was the Voronezh group officially registered, and even then only under a euphemism.[31]

1989: Sightings in Vologda and Voronezh

In ufology, as in politics, 1989 was a turning point in the communist bloc. Where the Soviet Union had hitherto enforced strict secrecy where reports of UFOs were concerned, *glasnost* dictated a new openness. The first UFO story to be publicized in the Soviet Union as a result of *glasnost* involved Vologda, in the heart of European Russia, where schoolchildren reported seeing a space vehicle land and an ostensibly headless being emerge and walk around the meadow.[32]

But Vologda was only a kind of preparation. The big UFO story of 1989 involved Voronezh, a city with 860,000 inhabitants, located about 300 miles southeast of Moscow. On 9 October 1989, TASS released an unprecedented story. The release is worth quoting:

> *Voronezh, October 9.* Scientists have confirmed that an unidentified flying object recently landed in a park in the Russian city of Voronezh. They have also identified the landing site and found traces of aliens who made a short promenade about the park.
>
> "Aliens visited the place after dark, at least three times, locals report. A large shining ball or disk was seen hovering above the park. It then landed, a hatch opened, and one, two, or three creatures similar to humans and a small robot came out.
>
> "The aliens were three or even four meters high, but with very small heads, witnesses say. . . ."[33]

In a follow-up report the following day, TASS added some details, reporting that the sighting had occurred on 27 September, and that the alien was three-meters tall, "had three eyes, was clad in silvery overalls and 'boots' the color of bronze, and had a disk on its chest."[34] TASS also reported that when a sixteen-year-old boy started screaming, he was first rendered silent by the alien and then disappeared as a result of a beam from the alien's ray gun. The boy was said to have reappeared immediately after the alien craft had departed.

The TASS reports provoked a rash of ufo-humor across Russia. For example, *Krasnaia zvezda*, the Soviet Army newspaper, editorialized, with mock outrage, "We are disappointed and offended (also). Why did the UFO not select Moscow for landing instead of a provincial town?"[35] The paper added, "There are several good airports around Moscow. There is place enough to land. We shall welcome them at any time."[36] Subsequently, *Komsomol'skaia pravda*, the news organ of the communist youth organization, reported what it claimed was an encounter between its journalist, Pavel Mukhortov, and the extraterrestrials. The encounter was said to have taken place in Perm, where, a few months earlier, a milkmaid had reported an alien encounter.[37] The paper even provided a transcript of the alleged conversation:

"Where are you from?" journalist Pavel Mukhortov was said to have asked the aliens, who glowed in the dark and were reportedly six to thirteen feet tall.

"The constellation Libra, Red Star, our homeland," replied the creatures, communicating in the form of illuminated letters in the Siberian night.

"Your goal?"

"It depends on the center. We are directed by a central system."

"Can you take me to your planet?"

"There would be no return for you and it would be dangerous for us."

"Why would it be dangerous?"

"You might bring thought bacteria."[38]

Translate "thought bacteria" into "ideological pollution" and you have the vestiges of communist-style thinking.

But not everyone made jokes about the sightings. Amateur ufology groups began multiplying rapidly and before the end of 1989, there were reportedly some fifty such groups across the USSR.[39] It was, moreover, in the wake of the alleged incident at Voronezh that Azhazha, Russia's most vocal UFO enthusiast, organized the aforementioned UFO network (initially called SOYUZUFOTSENTR). Moreover, Soviet sightings themselves multiplied like rabbits. Already on 10 October, the day after its initial report concerning Voronezh, TASS reported that a flying saucer had been sighted over Sakhalin.[40] Later, in the village of Kostenki, a mysterious hole about one hundred-mm. wide, five-meters deep, and inclined at a seventy-degree angle, appeared in one resident's garden. Scientists examining the hole found that their magnetometer would not function in the vicinity of the hole, and could not find any stray dirt from the hole anywhere close. When a neighbor offered that she had seen "a huge fireball" the night before, ufologists inferred that space aliens might have taken a sample of dirt for evaluation.[41] And even as these new reports came in, alien visits to Voronezh continued, at least if one takes O. Stolyarov at his word. According to Stolyarov, local schoolchildren even had the opportunity to play soccer with the extraterrestrials.[42]

A Proliferation of Sightings

Since 1989, the region has been witness to a proliferation of sightings, as well as of crop circles. Indeed, this has been a general European phenomenon, with Russia, Hungary, Britain, and Belgium figuring as the sites for some of the more spectacular (and more persistent) reports. On 1 December 1993, Tullio Regge, an Italian socialist and an eminent physicist, even brought before the European Parliament a report which sought to account for the sharp increase in the number of sightings, by alleging that "people should not rule out the theory 'that [space] aliens have established a base in the asteroid belt.'"[43] But Regge disputed claims by Russian Professor Silanov to have communicated with the aliens in Voronezh by means of mental telepathy.[44]

A surge of Hungarian sightings began in late October 1989, when Hungarian Air Force pilots claimed to have been followed, during training flights in the vicinity of Kecskemet, in southern Hungary, by "a 'strange, spherical, orange-colored' flying object which did not show up on radar."[45] *Nepszabadsag* reported, at about the same time, that a farmer in southeastern Gyomaendrod claimed to have seen greenish beings with long ears. "The man tried to hit them with his shovel, but they paralysed him with an unknown power and disappeared," *Nepszabadsag* reported matter-of-factly.[46] Soldiers on duty at Kecskemet's military airport also reported seeing a greenish figure, whom they described as four-ft. tall and fluorescent and who, according to the soldiers, "beamed himself up into space."[47] As the rash of sightings continued, Hungary's Urania Observatory, located in the city of Eger, set up a UFO Data Collection Center.

Meanwhile, there were other sightings reported: in the Croatian hamlet of Bobanci, and to an entire Hungarian army unit in Tarnaszentmaria, in 1990; in Bucharest, the Hungarian village of Szecsenyfelfalu, and again near Kecskemet in 1991; over central Serbia in 1992; over Sniezka, the highest peak of Poland's Karkonosze mountain range, and over Szolnok (in Hungary) and Zadar (Croatia) in 1994; over the Jaslovske Bohunice nuclear power plant in Slovakia, over the Albanian beach at Durrës, and around Hungary's Lake Balaton in 1995; over Vilnius, Galati, and the Croatian village of Bregana Pisarovinska (near Zagreb) in 1996; over Russia's Dagestan region in mid-November 2000; over the village of Arda in the region of Shoikovsko in December 2000; over Barnaul airport in southern Siberia in January 2001; and over the Yaroslavl highway in Moscow in July 2001.[48] Not all of these sightings were innocent. In the aforementioned Zadar case, Alan Roberts, spokesperson for UNPROFOR Sector South, told a regularly scheduled press conference on 10 August 1994 that the UN observation posts had been under attack by UFOs.[49] Evidently Roberts felt that he could safely rule out the possibility that one of the three warring forces in the region might have been responsible for the attack.

Colonel Gyorgy Keleti, appointed Hungarian defense minister in summer 1994, takes these reports seriously. Keleti had earlier written several articles on UFO sightings by members of the Hungarian Armed Forces, for the monthly *Ufo-magazin*. One such article bore the ominous title, "We Don't Stand a Chance in a UFO Invasion."[50] And in 1995, a commission of Hungarian scientists investigating UFOs requested international assistance in verifying sightings of so-called "intelligent plasma balls."[51]

Not all local governments have been understanding, however. In 1992, Vladimir Azhazha, vice president of the All-Union Ufological Association in Moscow, "responded to the Russian Ministry of Justice's threat to outlaw the Association for financial irregularities by warning that this would severely jeopardize Russia's security and leave its inhabitants exposed to extraterrestrial attacks."[52] In an effort to drive home the "urgency" of the situation, Azhazha used the occasion of an interview with *Kommersant* to warn that "each year extraterrestrials abduct 5,000 people from CIS territory and kill cattle with laser."[53] Incidentally, Azhazha's figure is a compilation of the total number of "missing persons" in areas in which UFO activity had been reported.[54] Azhazha himself is nothing if not colorful. In a 1995 interview with *Unsolved UFO Sightings*, for instance, Azhazha recounted,

Once I took part in a contact with an invisible entity. It was interesting . . . I left a meeting which I was conducting when I was told that a representative of a higher intelligence would like to speak to me. I left and took Sochevanov and Varlamov as witnesses, two extra-sensors, two people who understand *their* language. Three chairs were placed for the invisible visitors. I did not know how to behave—it is a breakthrough, I never took part in anything like this (before). And there was a conversation around and around for two hours. There was no concrete proposal. I did not hear any voices. . . . And I left (thinking) "why was I invited?"[55]

UFOs have entered into popular culture and everyday reality in the Russian/East European area, just as they have in the United States and much of Western Europe. Thus one finds the establishment, in Poland, of a religious cult around an alleged extraterrestrial named Antrovis,[56] the revelation by Kiki, Plovdiv's advice-dispensing space alien, that Bulgarian is the intergalactic language of choice,[57] rumors that extraterrestrials visiting Germany were eager to learn the Saxonian dialect and local customs in Saxony,[58] and claims by three fortune-tellers in Bulgaria that aliens from the Planet Krissi would land in Schtaklevo and give away eight trillion leva, so that Bulgaria's national debt would be wiped clean and its people elevated, overnight, to prosperity. Incidentally, the Schtaklevo landing, scheduled to occur in September 1995, never took place, and police had to rescue the fortune-tellers from an angry crowd of 1,500 people.[59]

With all of this activity in the sky (and on the ground), it came as no surprise to UFO watchers that crop circles began to proliferate—in the Czech Republic, Slovakia, Hungary, Croatia, Bulgaria, Poland, and Russia.[60] In Germany, crop circles in a cornfield near Hildesheim, south of Hannover, ominously assumed the shape of the communist hammer and sickle. But if the inspiration was socialist, the fallout was capitalist: the field's owner recognized opportunity when he saw it, and quickly began charging an entrance fee to visitors wishing to inspect his field more closely.[61]

Possible Explanations

Most unidentified flying objects, once identified, turn out to be natural phenomena. A luminous object seen in the Budapest skies the evening of 18 January 1991, for example, was later said to have been a meteor.[62] The object seen over Vilnius and mentioned above may have been ball lightning or some other lightning-related phenomenon; the sound that accompanied it was said to resemble electricity crackling. Or again, the scorched earth reported in July 1989 by the Soviet newspaper *Sotsialisticheskaia industriia* was originally attributed by that paper to the blast from a space alien vehicle. It was later revealed that the burned ground had been produced by a haystack fire.[63] Or again, a UFO reported in the Lublin region in early 1999 turned out to have been a visual anomaly produced by the conjunction, in the line of vision, of Venus and Jupiter.[64]

The second most likely explanation for any given sighting is that the craft being viewed is a man-made aircraft, possibly even a secret military aircraft (this latter explanation would be more likely in the vicinity of certain top-secret military bases). The "jellyfish" incident at Petrozavodsk in 1977 is one example. The famous 1989 incident at Voronezh also took place near a Soviet military installation, as did a sighting in Khabaravosk krai in May 1995.[65] In a non-military example of what proved to be a man-made craft, stories circulated toward the end of the 1980s of an alleged space alien vehicle thought to have been shot down by Soviet armed forces over the Stolovaia mountain range in Ordjonikidze on 5 March 1983. Russian UFO researcher Marina Popovich made strong claims on behalf of the authenticity of this "find" at a Munich conference organized by German researcher Michael Hesemann in June 1990. Four years later, Polish UFO researcher Jerzy Sniezawski came upon these allegations and revealed that the alleged UFO was an inoperable stage prop which he had designed for use in a Polish film, *On Silver Globe*, which had been premiered in Wrocław in 1977.[66]

Third in the order of likelihood is dreaming. Many alleged abduction experiences occur during sleep. Most people have had the experience of having a dream so vivid that they are momentarily unsure whether it was reality or a dream. Under the spell of hypnosis, retrieved memories of forgotten dreams may come to be confused with reality. The frequency of such dreams may, of course, be stimulated by the media. The power of suggestion was amply demonstrated when, in the wake of the release of Steven Spielberg's film, *Close Encounters of the Third Kind*, the number of sightings and abduction experiences increased exponentially worldwide.[67] Professor Michael Persinger, a Canadian researcher, has simulated abduction experiences in the laboratory and, based on his experiments, attributes the experiences to physically induced temporal lobe seizures. Persinger cautions, however, that the way in which the brain interprets the sensations of light, grey presences, and strange pains may be affected, to a large extent, by *cultural* factors, such as the aforementioned film by Steven Spielberg.[68] The role of cultural preconditioning is suggested in the following account ascribed to documents from Elizabethan England:

> The flying dragon is
> when a flame kindled apeereth
> bended, sand is in the middle
> wrythed like the belly of a dragon,

> but in the fore part,
> for the narrownesse,
> it representeth the figure of the neck,
> from whence the sparkes are breathed
> or forced forth with the same breathing.[69]

In addition, sexual deprivation may be a factor influencing who is likely to have such dreams. As Robert Sheaffer points out, "a number of [reported] abductees indicate that their only sex life takes place on board the flying saucers or in their dreams about aliens."[70]

Fourth most likely is fakery. People may engage in hoaxes for any of a number of reasons, including monetary profit (the most likely motivation for the creation of the alleged documentary film, *Alien Autopsy*, which is now generally regarded as a counterfeit[71]). Some of the crop circles, for example in Bohemia,[72] have been exposed as forgeries, even if others continue to perplex and mystify researchers.

Arguably fifth most likely is the misinterpretation of mundane phenomena. In summer 1996, for example, residents of Hurbanovo, in southern Slovakia, reported strange lights which they ascribed to the work of space aliens. Authorities investigating these reports were able to trace the "strange" lights to the laser lights at a local disco.[73]

Sixth most likely is disinformation whether generated by government officials or promulgated outside the government. Such disinformation could serve to cover up more embarrassing or damaging information; examples of this were provided earlier in the text. Possibly related in nature is the mindless caution cited by *Komsomol'skaia pravda* and attributed to "the staff" of Khankala Airfield, in Chechnya, during Russia's war with that republic, to the effect that the region was a common haunt of UFOs and that "it just could be that some inexperienced Chechen pilot might mistake an encounter with a flying saucer for a 'hostile act of a neighboring state.'"[74] Better to let ten Russian bombers pass unhindered than to risk offending the pilots of even one space alien vehicle!

Beyond these six explanations one enters controversial territory, and most, if not all, of the remaining available explanations will probably strike most people as paranoid. But tastes differ, and people make choices based on widely different experiences. Thus, the BBC World Service did not consider it paranoid to suggest that Russian UFO reports tended to come from areas where salt and sugar were in short supply, thereby inferring that such reports could take people's minds off their economic difficulties.[75] Mark Rodeghier, director of the Center for UFO Studies in Chicago, disputes this interpretation, considering UFO stories unlikely to distract people from problems as basic as nutrition and financial solvency.[76]

An alternative explanation, which at first sight seems very plausible, but which, on second glance, reveals some features of the paranoid was offered by Cosmonaut Pavel Popovich, chair of the (Soviet) Ufological Commission, in 1990. In conversation with *Trud*, Popovich suggested that "many experts tend to agree that the 'contacts with aliens' occur not in reality, but in human consciousness—under the influence of unknown natural factors. *These 'visions' are caused by something which carries definite information,* and this can only be done by Reason. Which means that we have to seek contact with this Reason."[77] Rather than actual UFO sightings, Popovich offers us a notion of "alien-induced" hallucinations. The ubiquitous Azhazha, who was also present for the talks with *Trud,* offered this gloss on Popovich's comments:

> It is necessary to find out who is the real master on this planet—we, the humans, or the "intelligent medium" that, entering into contact with us, has been displaying not just a simple curiosity, but also aggressiveness.[78]

From the way in which Azhazha phrased this challenge, it is clear on which side of the ledger he believes the answer can be found.

That American and possibly also Russian engineers have experimented with flying saucers developed from German designs is well-known.[79] The supposition that flying saucers must necessarily come from other planets depends upon the entirely unwarranted assumption that the U.S. and Russian governments keep their citizens fully informed about all technological developments, experimental programs, new weapons systems, and special forces operations—an assumption which most would agree qualifies as naive in the extreme. On the other hand, the utility of this explanation in addressing sightings of mysterious craft flying directly over large population centers is at best limited. But it may not be entirely without its uses. When, for example, Russian researchers discovered, at two alleged UFO landing sites in Siberia, microscopic worms in soil content which were common to Mexico but not occurring naturally in the USSR, it appeared conceivable, assuming the accuracy of the representations concerning the worms, that an American espionage flight might have been involved which, it would follow, made a landing in Mexico before continuing on to Siberia.[80]

There are at least four remaining conceivable explanations, any of which would require a leap of faith. For those inclined to suspicion of the government, UFO mania could be construed as a U.S. government plot to condition people to believe in space aliens so that, at some future point in time, it may use the cover of an "alien invasion" to establish a world totalitarian state ruled from the Pentagon. Those inclined to this interpretation would then interpret so-called "alien abductions" as abductions by Pentagon personnel masquerading as aliens. (Something along these lines was suggested on at least one episode of the popular television series *The X-Files.*)

For those inclined to believe in mass hallucinations, it would be possible to speculate about the discharge of hallucinatory drugs into the environment as part of a government program for perfecting mind control or for testing collective behavior in conditions of hallucination. This "explanation" has the advantage of providing an accounting as to why most sightings in Russia, the United States, and Britain have been far from major urban centers (Voronezh being an exception of sorts) and, in the most spectacular instances, conveniently close to military installations (Voronezh following the rule here). This explanation has at least two disadvantages: first, it requires that one believe that hallucinogens will, under specified conditions, induce identical hallucinations in all exposed persons; and second, it is overtly paranoid in the extreme.

For those who consider that time travel would be technologically more feasible than intergalactic travel (with its phenomenal fuel and speed requirements), one could *imagine* an "explanation" that what is involved in UFO sightings are human craft from the future, visiting our time zone for reasons best known to future generations. Although I have not come across any ufologist who embraced this theory, it would appear to be compatible with the argumentation of philosopher David Lewis, who has defended the possibility of time travel.[81]

And finally, there are explanations which associate UFOs with space aliens. For some, especially those who have had experiences for which they lack any other explanation they find acceptable, especially if experiences of a frightening or of a harmful nature, the belief that space aliens are visiting the planet assumes something of a religious quality, which is to say, it becomes a matter of faith to which no challenge is brooked.

Not all ufologists adopt a "religious" orientation, of course. Some scientists are skilled researchers who are serious about their work, engage in it with a certain amount of skepticism, but, fascinated by the data, are unwilling to shrug it off with a gasp of "impossible!" But ufology has also attracted its share of, let us say, *enthusiasts.* Take, for example, Bulgarian-born physicist Vladimir Tereziski, a UFO specialist, who allegedly has argued that Hitler's scientists landed a man on the moon in 1942 and, in collaboration with the Japanese, sent a mission to Mars. Tereziski also reportedly believes that some two million people inhabit an underground colony at the South Pole and have been perfecting space travel.[82]

The overwhelming majority of "sightings" turn out to be easily explainable in terms of natural phenomena or man-made craft—or sometimes in terms of local discos—as professional ufologists themselves readily point out. But there are those troubling incidents, for which the "less paranoid" explanations seem entirely inadequate, and some of these incidents have led some serious researchers to speculate about visitors from other galaxies. There is, to date, no case for which there is public information sufficient to "prove" the extraterrestrial nature of any given craft. However, as any UFO enthusiast can tell you, it would take only one authentic (or perhaps, authenticated) sighting of a space alien visitation to radically change the way in which we view ourselves, and with the arrival of the millennium, a certain sector of the public seems increasingly prepared to embrace just such a change of worldview.

Americanization or Global Culture?

Anyone taking the trouble to peruse East European UFO magazines or to check East European UFO sites is struck immediately by the broad similarities with UFO culture in America. In Eastern Europe as in America, extraterrestrials are generally thought to be short (by human standards), grey, and hairless, with large, dark (possibly insect-like) eyes, their craft are usually silent[83] and often glow in ways unfamiliar to earthlings, and they seem to have a mastery of all known languages (though, according to one report, their mastery of Croatian is far from perfect[84]). As in the United States, East Europeans report that extraterrestrials enjoy taking soil samples, creating mysterious-looking crop circles, and conducting medical exams on ostensibly unwilling human subjects. As in the United States, extraterrestrial visitors are generally thought to be of a higher intelligence—not just in technological terms but biologically as well.[85] And, as in the United States, there is a fascination with apparent similarities between geographic formations on Mars and the remnants of ancient civilizations on earth,[86] as well as with the widely disparaged film *Alien Autopsy*.[87]

If one is a believer (as are 62 percent of Czechs, according to a poll conducted in August 2000[88]), then the explanation for these similarities is that one is talking about real phenomena which exist in a specific form and which have known manifestations and artifacts. But if one is not a believer, then the commonality of perceptions and interpretations, of representations and accounts, reflects cultural diffusion and the influence of specific (human) cultural artifacts. And in this latter case, the proliferation of the UFO subculture in Central and Eastern Europe is a classic example of the evolution of what was originally an *American* subculture into a (sometimes commercially driven) global subculture. And in the course of this evolution, reports which deviate from the established cultural norms (such as the reports at Voronezh that the soccer-loving aliens were three to four meters tall with three eyes) are marginalized, while those which reinforce the dominant cultural paradigm are mainstreamed.

Mirroring a pattern already seen in the United States and England, UFO clubs and societies have sprouted throughout the region since 1989, not just in Russia,[89] but also in the Ukraine,[90] Lithuania,[91] Poland,[92] the Czech Republic,[93] Slovakia,[94] Hungary,[95] Slovenia,[96] Croatia,[97] Romania,[98] and Bulgaria.[99] In Romania, military echelons have recently become interested in reports about UFOs, while Hungary allegedly boasts Europe's first official UFO landing site.[100] Meanwhile, in Serbia, a 1999 issue of *Dosije X* carried an interview with Dr. Todor Jovanović, who warned the magazine's readers that extraterrestrials had recently taken control of the brains of U.S. President Bill Clinton, British Prime Minister Tony Blair, NATO Secretary-General Javier Solana, and other Western leaders.[101] That seemed as good an explanation as any, in Jovanović's mind, for NATO's seventy-eight-day aerial campaign against the Federal Republic of Yugoslavia earlier that year.

According to recent survey data, 20 percent of Germans believe that extraterrestrials have been visiting earth, while 40 percent of Czechs consider it at least probable that there is *intelligent* life on other planets.[102] The level of belief in Bulgaria may be comparable since a Sofia insurance company announced in 1995 that it would offer insurance to compensate for "physical and psychic damage" resulting from "alien abductions."[103]

In the years 1993–1996 alone, international UFO conferences were held in Kosice, Budapest (twice), and Debrecen (twice).[104] There has also been a proliferation of popular magazines devoted to extraterrestrials, such as Croatia's *Dossier UFO*, which bears the subtitle *Misterij letećih tanjura [The Mystery of the Flying Saucers]*, Slovenia's *Revija X*, and Serbia's *Zona šumraka [The Twilight Zone]*, *Dosije X [The X-Files]*, and *Treće oko [The Third Eye]*. The film *Alien Autopsy* was shown in Prague to sellout crowds.[105] And Polish ufologists showed off their own UFO film in a screening in Łodz on New Year's Eve 1995/96.[106]

Conclusion

UFOs obviously have the power to tantalize, but this power resides precisely in the fact that no one has been able either to completely disprove the existence of space aliens (and it is not clear what kind of "proof" could accomplish that task) or to provide much by way of descriptive information of a definitive nature concerning what must still be called *alleged* space aliens. If either of these conditions were satisfied, much of the interest in this topic might subside. For if the existence of space aliens could be definitely excluded, then they could scarcely hold more interest than tales of leprechauns and hobgoblins and fairy queens. And if an exhaustive and definitive accounting could be provided, they would merely be added to the list of known species. And who knows, they might even end up on a list of "endangered species"!

Ufology uses scientific instruments. Is it therefore a science? Or should it be classed with pseudosciences such as alchemy and astrology which use scientific instruments for nonscientific purposes? For now at least, these, like other questions on this subject, remain open questions, and further, questions upon which the politics of government secrets may turn. Meanwhile, as the Russian/East European area is proving fertile ground for the publishing of UFO magazines and the activity of UFO clubs, local popular culture increasingly partakes in a global popular culture to which American society makes a disproportionate contribution.

Notes

This chapter is reprinted, with revisions, from *Journal of Popular Culture* 32, no. 3 (Winter 1998). Permission for reuse is gratefully acknowledged.

   1. As quoted in Brad Steiger and Sherry Hansen Steiger, *The Rainbow Conspiracy* (New York: Pinnacle Books, 1994), p. 152.

2. *Press Association Newsfile* (8 December 1999), on *Lexis-Nexis Academic Universe.*

3. "USSR UFO History, Vol. 1, Part 4: 1900–1942 Sightings," at www.wufoc.com /ufofiles/english/issue_3/ussr4.htm.

4. Ibid.

5. Ibid.

6. "Polish UFO crashes," from *Graham Birdsall's UFO Magazine* (May/June 1998), at www.cseti.org/crashes/197_198_199.htm.

7. "'Silver Balls' over Budapest, Hungary, 10 July 1947" (4 September 1997), at ufomind.com/misc/1997/sep/d04-001.html.

8. "Polish UFO crashes."

9. "1961 28 April. 2 am. Lake Onega USSR nr Finland," at www.cseti.org/crashes /033.htm.

10. The only example of such speculation which I have found is "Auch Piloten der Luft-waffe bestätigen UFO-Alarm in Ungarn," in *OÖNachrichten* (27 November 1989), p. 4, at www1.oon.at/public/wrap.

11. Quoted in John Spencer (ed.), *The UFO Encyclopedia* (New York: Avon Books, 1991), p. 301.

12. Quoted in ibid., p. 301, my emphasis.

13. Ibid., p. 153.

14. Graham W. Birdsall, "Beyond the Wall," in *UFO Magazine* (January/February 1996), p. 16. See also "USSR UFO History, Vol. 1, Part 5: May 1946—the modern UFO-era begins for USSR" (2/8/88), at www.wufoc.com/ufofiles/english/issue_3/ussr5.htm.

15. Steiger and Steiger, *Rainbow Conspiracy,* p. 93.

16. Spencer (ed.), *UFO Encyclopedia,* p. 125.

17. "Polish UFO crashes."

18. Steiger and Steiger, *Rainbow Conspiracy,* pp. 98–99.

19. Both of these stories are taken from Steiger and Steiger, *Rainbow Conspiracy,* pp. 97–100. In their account, however, the information is presented in such a way as to take it for granted that space aliens were involved. The interpretation I have presented in the text is my own.

20. Quoted in ibid., p. 140.

21. Ibid., pp. 140–141.

22. Spencer (ed.), *UFO Encyclopedia,* p. 320.

23. Ibid., p. 326. The absence of any indication concerning his schedule or whether he "lost" his horse and cart is regrettable. Certainly, if Wolski had indulged in wanton behavior, then a UFO story might have provided a logical, if desperate, cover.

24. Steiger and Steiger, *Rainbow Conspiracy,* p. 145.

25. Birdsall, "Beyond the Wall," p. 13.

26. TASS dispatch, as quoted in ibid., p. 13.

27. As quoted in Birdsall, "Beyond the Wall," p. 13.

28. As quoted in ibid., p. 13.

29. Paul Stonehill, "UFOs in Russia: A History of Sightings," in *UFO,* Vol. 7, No. 2 (March/April 1992), p. 31; and Spencer (ed.), *UFO Encyclopedia,* p. 287.

30. *Moscow Times* (5 September 1998), on *Lexis-Nexis Academic Universe* (hereafter, *Nexis*).

31. Stonehill, "UFOs in Russia," pp. 31–32.

32. *Financial Times* (5 August 1989), p. 3.

33. TASS (9 October 1989), on *Nexis.*

34. TASS (10 October 1989), on *Nexis.*

35. Quoted in UPI (13 October 1989), on *Nexis.* I have changed "provincial towns" to "a provincial town," since only Voronezh is indicated.

36. Ibid.

37. Concerning the milkmaid, see *Los Angeles Times* (10 October 1989), p. 10.

38. *Washington Post* (13 October 1989), p. C1.

39. Ibid.

40. TASS, as summarized in *BBC Summary of World Broadcasts* (11 October 1989), on *Nexis.*

41. TASS (18 April 1990), on *Nexis.*

42. *Vozdushny Transport* (1991), no. 45, trans. in *Russian Press Digest* (13 November 1991), on *Nexis.* Regarding Soviet military encounters with UFOs near Hanoi (1965) and in Turkmenistan (1990), see "Croatian Media Carries Russian UFO Report," at www.qtm .net/~geibdan/newse/sep/rus.html; and "Russian Journalist Reports Military Clash with UFO," from *CNI News,* reprinted in *UFO Folklore Center,* at www.qtm.net/~geibdan /newsc/rus2.html. Regarding a Soviet civilian sighting over Zaostrovka (1989), see Nikolay Subbotin, "Russian Roswell?" in *UFO Folklore Center,* at www.qtm.net/~geibdan /a1998/jan/rusros.html. Regarding an encounter involving a Soviet spacecraft returning to earth (9 October 1991), see Nikolai Lebedev, "Important Developments in the Former Soviet Union," in *UFO Folklore Center,* at www.qtm.net/~geibdan/newsc/rus.html.

43. *The Guardian* (Manchester), 2 December 1993, p. 11.

44. *Calgary Herald* (3 December 1993), p. C13.

45. *Reuter News Service* (13 November 1989), quoting *Del-Kelet,* on *Nexis.*

46. Quoted in *Reuter News Service* (13 November 1989), on *Nexis.*

47. *Reuter News Service* (8 August 1990), on *Nexis.*

48. Re. Bobanci, Tanjug (21 September 1990), trans. in *BBC Summary of World Broadcasts* (25 September 1990); re. Tarnaszentmaria, *The Times* (London), 16 August 1991, on *Nexis;* re. Bucharest, *Agence France Presse* (31 May 1991), on *Nexis;* re. Szecsenyfelfalu, *Reuter News Service* (30 September 1991), on *Nexis;* re. Kecskemet, *Reuter News Service* (21 January 1991), on *Nexis;* re. central Serbia, TASS (3 May 1992), on *Nexis;* re. Szolnok, *The Times* (28 December 1994), on *Nexis;* re. Zadar, Croatian TV satellite service (10 August 1994), trans. in *BBC Monitoring Service: Eastern Europe* (12 August 1994); re. Jaslovske Bohunice, *CTK National News Wire* (10 August 1995), on *Nexis;* re. Durrës, *Gazeta Shqiptare,* summarized in *Reuter News Service* (11 August 1995), on *Nexis;* re. Lake Balaton, "Our Hubcap Is Missing: Close Encounters with Aliens of Four Kinds," in *Pozor* (Prague), No. 12 (December 1996/January 1997), p. 88; re. Vilnius, TASS (26 June 1996), on *Nexis;* re. Galati, *Curierul National,* summarized in *Reuter News Service* (12 July 1996), on *Nexis;* re. Bregana Pisarovinska, *Vecernji list,* summarized in *Reuter News Service* (22 October 1996), on *Nexis;* re. Dagestan, TASS (14 November 2000), on *Nexis;* re. Arda, Global News Wire (22 December 2000), on *Nexis;* re. Barnaul airport, *Western Daily Press* 31 January 2991), p. 2, on *Nexis;* and re. Yaroslavl highway, *RusData Dialine—Russian Press Digest* (2 July 2001), on *Nexis.*

49. Croatian TV satellite service (10 August 1994), trans. in *BBC Monitoring Service: Eastern Europe* (12 August 1994), on *Nexis.*

50. *Daily Telegraph* (London), 29 July 1994, p. 10. See also *Reuter News Service* (27 July 1994), on *Nexis;* and J. Antonio Huneuus, "Hungary's Minister of Defense Proclaims: Aliens Are Mapping Our World!" in *UFO Universe,* Vol. 6, No. 2 (Summer 1996), pp. 30–37.

51. *Reuter News Service* (2 October 1995), on *Nexis*.

52. *Russian Press Digest* (31 August 1992), on *Nexis*.

53. Quoted in ibid.

54. Birdsall, "Beyond the Wall," p. 14.

55. Antonio Huneuus, "*UFO Universe*' s Roundtable with Russia's Leading Ufologists," in *Unsolved UFO Sightings*, Vol. 3, No. 2 (Summer 1995), p. 69.

56. *The Warsaw Voice* (3 October 1993), on *Nexis*. For details concerning this cult, see Sabrina P. Ramet, *Nihil Obstat: Religion, Politics, and Social Change in East-Central Europe and Russia* (Durham, N.C.: Duke University Press, 1998). After being pressured by the press to declare its self-dissolution in 1994, the Antrovis cult has recently reemerged with a vengeance. See TV Polonia (Warsaw), 7 November 2000, trans. in *BBC Monitoring Europe – Political* (7 November 2000), on *Nexis*.

57. *The Independent* (London), 17 August 1990, p. 8.

58. *Dresdener Morgenpost,* summarized in *Reuter German News Service* (5 January 1995), on *Nexis*.

59. *Evening Standard* (13 September 1995), p. 19.

60. Re: the Czech Republic, *CTK National News Wire* (11 July 1995), on *Nexis; CTK National News Wire* (19 July 1995), on *Nexis; CTK National News Wire* (21 July 1995), on *Nexis;* and *CTK National News Wire* (18 July 1996), on *Nexis*. Re: Slovakia, Bill Donovan, Jr., "Reality Check," in *Pozor* (Prague), September 1996, p. 50. Re: Hungary, *MTI Econews* (23 August 1996), on *Nexis;* and "Crop Circle Appears on a Farm in Hungary," in *UFO Roundup*, Vol. 3, No. 32, at www.ufoinfo.com/roundup/v03/rnd03_32.html. Re: Croatia, "UFO Leaves Crop Circles in Northern Croatia," in *UFO Roundup*, Vol. 2, No. 17 (27 April 1997), at www.ufoinfo.com/roundup/v02/rnd02_17.shtml. Re: Bulgaria, *The Sunday Times* (London), 19 August 1990, on *Nexis*. For full-color photos of crop circles in the Czech Republic, see Petr Novak and Marie Lowova, trans. by Alice Brabcova, "Czech Crop Circles," in *UFO Reality,* Issue #5 (December 1996/January 1997), pp. 38–39. Re: Poland, *Deutsche Presse Agentur* (26 July 2000), on *Nexis*. Re: Russia's first crop circle (in 2000), see *Sunday Times* (London), 17 June 2001, on *Nexis*.

61. *Daily Telegraph* (26 July 1991), p. 9.

62. *MTI Econews* (22 January 1991), on *Nexis*.

63. *New York Times* (10 October 1989), p. A1; and *Newsday* (10 October 1989), p. 2.

64. TV Polonia satellite service (Warsaw), 23 February 1999, on *BBC Monitoring Service—Political* (24 February 1999), on *Lexis-Nexis Academic Universe*.

65. "Inside the KGB UFO Files," pp. 39–40.

66. Birdsall, "Beyond the Wall," p. 15.

67. *The Guardian* (23 May 1995), p. 3.

68. "Where Are All the UFOs?," televised broadcast on the Arts & Entertainment Channel, 22 February 1998.

69. "Inside the KBG UFO Files," in *From Beyond: Investigating Alien Phenomena,* Vol.. No. 8 (1997), p. 43.

70. Robert Sheaffer, "Close Encounters of the Fourth Kind," in *Scientific American,* Vol. 273, No. 5 (November 1995), p. 84.

71. See *Focus* (Munich), 6 November 1995, pp. 256, 258.

72. *CTK National News Wire* (1 August 1996), on *Nexis*.

73. *CTK National News Wire* (8 July 1996), on *Nexis*.

74. *Russian Press Digest* (23 January 1992), on *Nexis*.

75. Spencer (ed.), *UFO Encyclopedia,* p. 153.

76. Mark Rodeghier, "Sociologist's Viewpoint: Soviets Mine UFO Motherlode," in *UFO,* Vol. 5, No. 1 (January/February 1990), p. 30.

77. *Trud* (9 July 1990), p. 4, my emphasis.

78. Ibid.

79. "Saucer Kraut: Inside the German Research Project," Henry Stevens in interview with D. Guide, in *paranoia: the conspiracy reader,* Issue #15 (Winter 1996/97), p. 41. See also *Daily Mail* (London), 31 March 2000, p. 11, on *Nexis.*

80. On this case, see Birdsall, "Beyond the Wall," p. 56.

81. David Lewis, "The Paradoxes of Time Travel," in Robin Le Poidevin and Murray MacBeath (eds.), *The Philosophy of Time* (Oxford: Oxford University Press, 1993).

82. *The Guardian* (11 January 1993), p. 7.

83. See, for example, "Soviet KGB Files on UFOs," transcript from ABC News Prime Time (5 October 1995), at www.qtm.net/~geibdan/newsc/kgb.html.

84. "Aliens Land in Croatia," in *UFO Roundup,* ed. by Joseph Trainor, Vol. 3, No. 3 (18 January 1998), at www.ufoinfo.com/roundup/v03/rnd03_03.shtml.

85. See, for example, the report in "Top Russian Ufologist Ponders 'Cosmic Psychology,'" from *CNI News,* at www.qtm.net/~geibdan/newse/may/r2.html.

86. See "Zvezdno mesto na Marsu," in *Revija X* (Ljubjlana), Vol. 1, No. 11 (November 1999), p. 14.

87. See the photo stills in "Trupla nezemljanov," in *Revija X,* Vol. 1, No. 11 (November 1999), p. 27.

88. *CTK National News Wire* (18 August 2000), on *Nexis.*

89. For example, Russian UFO Research Station, P. O. Box 6303, Perm 614010, Russia, phone/fax = 7-3422-450184. See "Russkie anomal'nye saity I resursy" (2/9/88), at www.geocities.com/Pentagon/3000/site_r.html.

90. For example, the Research Institute on Anomalous Phenomena (RIAP), P. O. Box 4684, 310022 Kharkov 22, Ukraine, email = riap77@chat.ru, also www.geocities.com /Area51/Starship/1527/.

91. For example, Global Lithuanian Net: san-taka station, email = san-taka@lithuanian.net, also www.nso.lt/scriptur/vaimanika.htm. See also "East Meets West," in *UFO Magazine,* Vol. 18, No. 2 (July/August 1999).

92. Regarding Poland, see *PAP News Wire* (2 February 1996), on *Nexis.*

93. For example, UFO Klub Záblesk, email = cerny@cernyseed.cz. See "UFO Club Záblesk—Home Page," at freeweb.coco.cz/klub.zablesk/vstupte.htm.

94. For example, Asociacia UFO Badatelov, Waldemar Urminsky, Komoca 259, 941 21 Nove Zamky, Slovak Republic, email = aufob@mailbox.sk; and SUFOR (Slovak UFO Research), Grosslingova 52, 811 09 Bratislava, Slovak Republic, tel. = 00421-7-905-269-102, fax = 00421-7-326-429, also www.geocities.com/area51/dimension/50221.

95. See *MTI Econews* (2 November 1992), on *Nexis;* and *The Times* (28 December 1994), on *Nexis.*

96. Alien Research Group, Polanska 133, Si-2311 Hoce, Slovenia, Phone/fax = 011-386-41-66-84-31, email = alex.mohar@siol.net, also www.angelfire.com/mo/ARB/.

97. For discussion and details, see Giuliano Marinkovic, "A Short Review of Ufology in Croatia" (29 September 1998), at ufoinfo.com/news/croatia.html.

98. For example, Asociatia pentru Studiul Fenomenolar Aerospatiale Neidentificate (ASFAN), Observatorul Astronomic Municipal, Bd. Lascar Catargiu 21, Bucharest, Romania.

Tel. = 650-34-75, or 310-25-63, fax = 310-25-73; and Romanian UFOnetwork, OP8-CP22, cod 5500, Bacau, Romania, Tel. = 011-40-92-643-640, email = rufon@ufon.org, also www.ufon .org/rufon/. See also *Rompres* (25 August 1998), on *BBC Monitoring Europe—Political* (25 August 1998), on *Nexis.*

99. See Ergosfera UFO&PARA Bulgaria, Evgeni Alexiev, 76/b Exarch Jossif str., Sofia 1000, Bulgaria, Tel. = 011-359-2-431-292, email = ergosfera_bg_1@hotmail.com, also www.homestead.com/ergosfera/index.html.

100. Regarding Hungary, see *The Times* (30 May 1998), on *Nexis.*

101. *The Independent* (London), 8 August 1999, p. 19, on *Nexis.*

102. Regarding Germans, *Focus* (6 November 1995), p. 250; regarding Czechs, *CTK National News Wire* (16 December 1996), on *Nexis.*

103. *Financial Times* (28 October 1995), p. XXII.

104. *MTI Econews* (5 November 1993), *CTK National News Wire* (26 November 1993), *MTI Econews* (28 September 1994), *MTI Econews* (1 October 1994), *MTI Econews* (16 November 1994), and *MTI Econews* (29 September 1996)—all on *Nexis.*

105. *CTK National News Wire* (7 October 1995), on *Nexis.*

106. *PAP News Wire* (2 February 1996), on *Nexis.*

15

Émigré-zation

Russian Artists and
American Children's Picture Books

Beth Holmgren

A S ITS TITLE ONOMATOPOEICALLY WARNS, this volume of essays largely assesses the
impact—if not the outright damage—of the juggernaut of American commercial culture on diverse European communities. Exported brand-name products and formulaically designed franchises and theme parks do present monoliths
of American vulgarization and obvious targets for European disdain and critical
dissection. Proprietary labels and enfranchisements are by no means exclusively
American phenomena, but European consumers are perhaps most rankled by the
protectively homogenized product or experience many American companies in-
sistently purvey.

Yet it would be a serious mistake to presume that homogeneity for all American
cultural exports and to prolong what Richard Pells describes as a "conversation between the United States and Europe . . . characterized more by an exchange of
metaphors than by a sharing of information."[1] Any analysis of U.S.-European cultural interactions should acknowledge and explore the ethnic hybridity of American
culture—a hybridity which, until the very late twentieth century, especially privileged
European contributions. Just as deftly commercialized American exports have been
said to substitute for a pan-European culture today, so modern American culture
could be defined as the continuous co-production of its immigrants from all over the
world. The nationalist, racist, classist policy of Americanization in the first decades of
the last century at best compartmentalized and at worst degraded, but never erased,
the "foreign" influences and subjects of transplanted cultures. As the turbulent twentieth century advanced from one "world" conflict to the next, subsiding in a long
Cold War, American attitudes toward European immigrant and/or refugee artists
vacillated between insecure isolationism and high-minded cosmopolitanism, commercial demands and campaigns for edifying culture. The twentieth century marked

the emergence of the United States as a political and economic superpower, but American culture remained at once awed by and audaciously exploitative of the "superior" cultures of Europe. Indeed, some of the cultural exports most clearly tagged as American courted and featured European talent, as Hollywood's film production even prior to World War II clearly demonstrates.[2]

The complex interdependency between American cultural production and European talent has been especially far-reaching in American children's literature, for this publishing industry, separately cultivated only since the 1920s, wed the popular market with an educational agenda, reprising the classic combination of American commercial savvy with a distinctly European insistence on cultural cultivation.[3] The American children's book industry to some degree approximated a nationalized enterprise in an otherwise free-market system. Professional educators and invested parents zealously monitored and often shaped its development, and their supervision yielded higher quality and more self-consciously worldly products. Moreover, the mass production of the picture book, a development of the late 1920s, lured all manner of artists into the business, for writing and illustrating mass-marketed picture books ensured them steady money and widespread visibility.

In consequence, twentieth-century American children's literature proffers an extraordinary showcase of American–European cultural interaction, begun between the world wars and booming after 1945 with the growth of huge postwar markets and a globally ascendant, refugee-absorbing United States. It is this rather sophisticated and exploitative collaboration that I propose to examine by concentrating on the experience and production of Russian émigré artists in America. More than any other European émigré group, the Russians tried out the American cultural extremes of commercial standardization and quirky creative refuge, and the exchange haphazardly benefited both sides.

A Coincidence of Cultural Interests

The American children's book industry truly coalesced between the world wars, manifest in the increase of children's rooms in public libraries; the new popularity of specialty bookstores such as Bertha Mahony's trendsetting Boston-based Bookshop for Boys and Girls; the institution of recommended book lists, children's literature awards, and new specialty journals in children's literature such as *The Horn Book Magazine* and *The Elementary English Review*; and the influence of progressive schools that urged book production according to posited patterns of children's development.[4] In its multipli-vetted quest to educate, the industry aimed for thorough geographical and cultural coverage. However isolationist the political climate in the United States following World War I, the world, appropriately narrated and depicted, was deemed important for America's children to know. An avid market recruited both world travelers and self-styled experts to tell children's stories—very often diluted historical romances—about foreign lands, and even Russia and East Europe presented exotic subjects for insipid processing. The prolific author Eric P. Kelly, for example, exulted in the "rainbow radiancy" of Poland in his Newbery Medal–winning *The Trumpeter of Krakow* (1928) and hinted at the "thousand secrets" of Vilnius in his *Blacksmith of Vilno*.[5] A relatively unknown Californian named Monica Shannon dreamed up the surprising bestseller *Dobry* about a Bulgarian boy aspiring to be an artist.[6] In this naive experimental era, it sufficed for a noted travelling author to sail "down the Volga on peasant boats, singing to her own *taropatch* and *balalaika*" to acquire the prerequisite credentials for lecturing and composing children's books about Mother Russia.[7]

At roughly the same time, educators and merchandisers alike sought out the more integrated, sophisticated *look* of European picture books, collecting samples for public consumption and display. Anne Carroll Moore, the formidable head of the Children's Room at the New York Public Library, began exhibiting foreign picture books "on equal terms with American and English picture books" a number of years before World War I.[8] The New York Public's display initiated a nationwide trend in children's rooms and over the years expanded its collection to feature books from Norway, Sweden, France, Italy, Germany, Czechoslovakia, and Russia. Indeed, the New York Public's Russian holdings encompassed both "the old Russian picture books illustrated by Ivan Bilibin" and "modern Russian picture books" donated by a Russian teacher of library science.[9] These imports on exhibit served to cultivate what one illustrator dubbed "eye appetite" in the American public—the desire for fresh color, innovative layout, and new types of line drawing.[10] The challenge lay in satisfying that appetite at home and at a reasonable cost, for the American children's book industry was suffering "a shortage of trained, experienced personnel" in color printing and engraving.[11]

Enter the cheap, skilled labor required, "the direct transfusion of much of the best of living European talent" and the *émigré-zation* of a growth industry.[12] The immigrant artists who fled a politically troubled, economically depressed Europe in the interwar period and immediately after World War II exerted a major impact on American picture books. Among these illustrators, Russians have figured prominently in number and accomplishment, with an impressive list including Boris Artzybasheff, Andrei Avinoff, Vladimir Bobritsky (Bobri), Vera Bock, Nicolas Mordvinoff, Theodore Nadejen, Fedor Rojankovsky, Nicolas Sidjakov, and Esphyra Slobodkina. It is crucial to note that these Russians were refugees of a newly Bolshevized Russia and did not belong to the huge pre–World War I immigration of Russian and East European peasants and Jews. By virtue of their small number (an estimated sixty-three thousand), better education, and anticommunist pedigree, they largely eluded the humiliating "Americanization" prescribed for poor immigrants. A few made directly for the States in the early 1920s, but most spent the interwar years in Europe or the large Russian colony in the Manchurian city of Harbin until World War II drove them to America. All hailed from educated, upper- to middle-class families forced to improvise their survival as political refugees; very few came to America as affluent expatriates. The fact of their political exile did abet their admission into the States, but asylum did not guarantee them a livelihood, and, given the dispersed character of their immigration (especially after the extensive émigré diaspora in Europe and Harbin), their greatest challenges lay in forging their own supportive associations and surviving individually in a market-driven, culturally fragmented America.

Ironically, the homeland they had had to abandon was soon furnishing artists lifelong institutionalized support, albeit at the high cost of political censorship. These émigré artists had known a vibrant arts scene that seemed only temporarily in abeyance due to the Russian revolutions and the civil war. The so-called Silver Age in Russian culture commenced in the last decades of the nineteenth century, fomented by the pan-European movements of neo-Romanticism and Art Nouveau, rich native folk arts, concentrated Russian talent, and savvy new merchant patrons and collectors. The Silver Age engendered the stunning paintings and designs of Alexander Benois, Leo Bakst, Marc Chagall, Vasily Kandinsky, and many others and inspired such master collaborations as Sergey Diaghilev's *Ballet-Russe* and *The World of Art* society, with its attendant exhibitions and journal. Coming of age in this heady atmosphere, young Russian artists felt charged to transform and/or transcend the world with their art, working in a wide variety of venues (public buildings, set design, private residences, even advertisements).[13] Consequently, the Silver Age sparked interest in such "lesser" artistic venues as the illustrated children's book, a genre technically pioneered by Abramtsevo Circle artist Elena Polenova and cultivated on a grand scale by Viktor Vasnetsov and, most famously, Ivan Bilibin.[14] Children's book illustration also flourished in the new "artistic clans" of the Benois, Dobuzhinsky, and Roerich families:

> [These clans] not only dedicated books to their children, sketching their children in these books, but also ventured to exhibit their own juvenile drawings alongside these sketches, as was the case in early 1908 at the fifth exhibition of Petersburg's "New Artists' Society," where both Benois and his daughters displayed their work.[15]

Thus, well-schooled heirs of Russia's Silver Age stumbled onto an American growth industry in many ways prepared to receive them. Children's picture book publishers were open to artistic experiment, eager for innovative artists and skilled technicians, and, in a striking number of cases, willing to underwrite the high culture production these Russians had been primed to pursue. The émigré artists were welcome, within the bounds of a somewhat elastic bottom line, to make their imported high-quality mark on books for American children.

Negotiating American Commercial Culture

The experience of two prominent Russian émigré artists demonstrates in detail how American culture variously impacted on their work. Fedor Rojankovsky (1891–1970) and Esphyra Slobodkina (1908–) proved to be the most prolific, successful, and critically acclaimed book illustrators among their Russian peers. Their production peaked after World War II (Rojankovky only arrived in the States in 1941) and several of their books—Rojankovsky's *The Cabin Faced West, Over in the Meadow,* and *Frog Went A'Courtin'* and Slobodkina's *Sleepy ABC* and *Caps for Sale: A Tale of a Peddler, Some Monkeys and Their Monkey Business*—remain in print and popular today. These two successful artists contrast, nonetheless, in their negotiation of what was for them the most problematic aspect of their host culture—its insistence on commercial value and mass production.

Fedor Rojankovsky most enjoyed and suffered the career of the accomplished commercial artist. He first departed Russia for Central Europe, lingering in Poland where he survived by sketching for fashion magazines, illustrating books, and designing opera sets; proceeding on to Danzig and Berlin; and settling hopefully in Paris where he masterminded his debut as an "international" illustrator. Due to his subsequent steady employment for the French Père Castor (Father Beaver) series of animal histories, Rojankovsky's way to America in 1941 was paid on rather onerous terms. The Castor series producer, Georges Duplaix, who joined Simon and Schuster's new wartime venture of Little Golden Books, held "exclusive use of Rojankovsky's services for ten years," and the Russian artist in consequence churned out thirty illustrated books over the next decade.[16]

Rojankovsky's exploitation by Little Golden Books resulted in a stale standardization of his art, an overuse of his trademark "soft-textured" animal figures. Yet at the outset of his "American" career, he had lobbied effectively not to forfeit fine craftsmanship for quick profits. Rojankovsky already had acquired several years of experience as a high-end catalogue artist in Paris when he encountered two enterprising American women, Esther Averill and Lila Stanley, and persuaded them to issue an American edition of a children's book he had made in Poland:

> Rojankovsky came to see us not once but several times with the little Polish ABC under his arm. And in the end we told him that if he would illustrate a new book for children, we would finance its printing in Paris, where color processes seemed superior to those in America, and that afterwards we would try to place the book with an American publisher. I do not know what else we could have said, longing, as we did, to see for once a series of Rojankovsky's designs adequately reproduced.[17]

Rojankovsky's commissioned work, the book *Daniel Boone* in lieu of an animal ABC, stunned discerning American and French consumers with its lavish layout and brilliant colors, recalling the impact made by the *Ballet Russe* some twenty years before, "when its bright colors outraged the retina of eyes used to pallid tones."[18] A book born out of Rojankovsky's laborious initiation into lithographic engraving (a process in which an artist must redraw illustrations on lithographic stones), *Daniel Boone* showcased illustration at the expense of text, resembling the deluxe catalogues the Russian artist expertly produced. His subsequent illustrations for Averill and Stanley's Americans abroad Domino Press (*The Voyages of Jacques Cartier, Powder: The Story of a Colt, a Duchess and the Circus,* and *Flash*) entrenched his reputation as a superb colorist and a master of dramatic, bold, clean design.

What proved more marketable in Rojankovsky's art, however, was his facility, routinized in the French Pere Castor series, for drawing animals with naturalistic texture and human emotiveness. It was this skill that attracted the editors at Little Golden Books, although apart from his illustrations for *The Three Bears* (1948), Rojankovsky's finest animal drawings appeared in books by other, less-cost-cutting American firms—for example, his illustrations for Mikhail Prishvin's translated *Treasure Trove of the Sun* (Viking Press, 1952). Rojankovsky's animal illustrations eventually won him the prestigious Caldecott Medal for his 1955 *Frog Went A'Courtin'*, a book that has undergone repeated reprints. In the case of this émigré artist, a standardized signature art resulted in institutional recognition.

Almost twenty years Rojankovsky's junior, Esphyra Slobodkina was still an art student when she came to America in 1928. Her cultivated, financially comfortable Jewish family had settled in Siberia before the revolution, and then emigrated to Harbin and on to New York where she, her mother, and sister worked as seamstresses for their support. When a meeting was arranged for her with the legendary Margaret Wise Brown, author of over eighty children's books, Slobodkina cleverly manufactured a sample book portfolio, pioneering with it the paper-doll collage technique that would win her repeated acclaim.[19] Slobodkina later remarked that Brown, a girl raised to be well married, "was a much better businesswoman than I could ever hope to be," but the Russian artist's correspondence with publishers, editors, and art directors reveals her to be a tough negotiator and relentless perfectionist.[20] She especially honed her business skills in her tempestuous relationship with her first publisher, William R. Scott, Inc., a firm run by wealthy dilettantes who epitomized the industry's high-culture aspirations.[21]

Both because and in spite of her early association with Young Scott Books, Slobodkina also invented distinctive illustrating and printing techniques. Dedicated to the progressive education principles of 69 Bank Street, a New York school and teacher-training institute, Young Scott Books pursued innovations in text, design, and packaging and developed books in consultation with children themselves. Slobodkina won tremendous artistic license with the first breathtaking books she made for Scott in collaboration with Margaret Wise Brown, but she later had to resist the firm's tampering with what they perceived as her work's child-disapproved features. Throughout her long career she fought vehemently for quality control in her work's reproduction, demanding respect for the *art* of children's book illustration.

Slobodkina's pictorial style varied over the decades, commencing with the modernist primitive collage of *The Little Fireman* and concluding with the realistic pencil drawing of her 1980 *Billy, the Condominium Cat* (see figure 15.1 from *The Little Fireman*). But her children's books are most distinguished by their importation of abstract art. Through the mentoring and contacts of her first husband, the émigré painter Ilya Bolotowsky, Slobodkina helped to found the American Abstract Artists' Group in 1937, and exhibited her work with various circles of cubists and abstractionists through the early 1980s.[22] Her attraction to vibrant colors, her fascination with mechanical elements and functions, her play with biomorphic and geometric shapes all resurface in her picture books, from the boldly intersecting planes and cutout figures of *The Little Fireman* to the geometrically fragmented page layout of such later books as *The Clock* and *The Little Dinghy*. Unlike Rojankovsky, who reproduced familiar images to order, Slobodkina consistently approached her illustrations as a serious mutable extension of her art and pitched her books to consumers as a form of aesthetic education and "a work of art which they are likely to keep for many years to come."[23]

FIGURE 15.1.
An illustration from *The Little Fireman*.
Reproduced from *The Little Fireman* (1938) by permission of Esphyr Slobodkina.

Illustrating Ethnicity

Just as Rojankovsky and Slobodkina differently negotiated the American commercial market, either accommodating mass circulation publishing houses with
standardized products or successfully defending their "superior" art in uneasy collaboration with small quality presses, so they differently ventured "ethnic" content
and style in their work. The children's book industry identified and valued both
as desired European experts, as highly skilled, committed craftsmen. Although
Slobodkina continued her studies and expanded her creative purview in the
States, both had emigrated as formed, educated Russian subjects, psychologically
and professionally equipped to survive as bicultural or, in Rojankovsky's case,
multicultural artists abroad.

The post-1945 climate in the United States soon became charged with anti-
communist paranoia, witch hunts for "anti-Americans," and Cold War prepara-
tions, but American popular culture nonetheless retained and recycled certain
Russian and East European ethnic stereotypes in genres ranging from animated
cartoons to quality children's books. In the postwar period a Russian émigré artist
could resort safely to the market-adaptive tactics of his or her predecessors, exploiting folkloric or prerevolutionary Russian themes and imitating the known
styles of such popular Russian illustrators as Ivan Bilibin and Viktor Vasnetsov.
Boris Artzybasheff (1899–1965), a children's book artist who soon "graduated" to
magazine illustration, shrewdly pursued this strategy when he first immigrated in
the 1920s: "He went back to Russian folklore motifs for murals in Russian restaurants and, like other Russians in foreign lands, conformed to the concepts of Russians and Russia fostered by the peoples of those lands."[24]

The émigrés, however, not only played it safe in terms of approved Russian
themes and styles but also manipulated and "corrected" their hybrid host culture.
When Slobodkina at last embarked on a Russian topic in 1964, she ceded illustration of *Boris and His Balalaika* to another émigré artist, Vladimir Bobritsky
(Bobri), and herself assumed control of the text. As author, Slobodkina argued extensively with her editor over the authenticity of various "Americanized" story elements—over renaming peasants "farmers," rephrasing the indirect way Russians
scold their children, and even recalibrating the temperature of the Russian taiga.[25]
Her serious investment in and vehement defense of her Russian expertise stand
out strongly in her correspondence.

Slobodkina, moreover, wrote and illustrated *non*-Russian ethnicity with much
the same authoritative attitude. When a reader for Rand McNally questioned
some of the details in what would become her 1969 picture book about China,
The Flame, the Breeze and the Shadow, the author replied that a Chinese house servant had told her this tale during her childhood in Manchuria.[26] A subsequent
critical review provoked her insistence that the book's admittedly "incorrect" elements nonetheless "would have pleased most of my Chinese friends of old."[27] Yet
Slobodkina's most popular effort, *Caps for Sale* (1940, 1947, 1968, 1985, 1987,

1988, 1999, 2000), proved to be a highly successful feat of "authored" folk art, read and cheaply imitated as a vaguely mittel-Europa folktale rather than her own creative effort. When the firm Grosset and Dunlap plagiarized *Caps* for their cheap knockoff, *Monkey See Monkey Do*, they justified doing so on the grounds that Slobodkina was simply retelling an "old tale."[28]

More artistically impressive, given her prolificacy during America's staid, self-absorbed 1950s, was Slobodkina's stunning picture book *Americana*. After twenty-five years in the States, the Russian émigré waxed nostalgic about her American experience by combining conventional American subjects with her own distinctive illustrations. Her ambitious *Clock* (1956) and *Little Dinghy* (1958) poach on the New England territory made popular in American children's literature by Robert McCloskey, but these also evoke the author's past summer vacations and particularly her visits to Margaret Wise Brown's rustic island retreat off the Maine coast. In both, Yankee images and plots about self-reliance are stripped down to abstracted forms and very simple story lines—an old steeple clock in a Vermont town that rusts to a halt and must be fixed, a little dinghy beached by a storm and lovingly restored by a local boy. The visual effects are revelatory, filtering conventional American icons through Slobodkina's vividly colored, geometrically skewed abstractions (figure 15.2).

Rojankovsky, unlike Slobodkina, never dared authorship, but his illustrations likewise demonstrate skillful ethnic impersonations. His French pigs in *Gaston and Josephine* sport about convincingly in a world of French signs and shops; the Russian children in *Treasure Trove of the Sun* dress like authentic Russian peasants and subsist in a hut with appropriate wooden carvings. Rojankovsky's first America, sight unseen and painstakingly lithographed in Paris, was reconstructed from his own childhood books and games.[29] His *Voyages of Jacques Cartier* replicate log forts and noble, buckskin-attired Native Americans. His depicture of Daniel Boone and "the hunters' paradise" of Kentucky convey a cultured artist's fascination with the primitive and the exotic, a Russian Gauguin painting a Kentuckian Tahiti.

Rojankovsky's work also illustrates the problems of national attribution for an endlessly aggregate American culture. A talented shockworker[30] for Little Golden Books, this émigré artist resembles, in some startling ways, the Soviet heirs of Russia's Silver Age. With the loss of a private arts market and the increasing political regimentation of Soviet culture, Soviet artists resorted to children's book illustration for a relatively safe livelihood, cultivating in the process new modes of printing and graphic design.[31] The government embraced the picture book, in turn, as a means of improving literacy and education; consequently, it financed the mass production of cheap, colorful, informational varieties:

> To advance the program, offset printing in two to five flat colors was perfected; books could be designed freely, with their pictures and text merged, and, eyecatching and un-forbidding, they could be produced in large quantities at low cost. What technology

FIGURE 15.2.
An illustration from *The Little Dinghy*.
Reproduced from *The Little Dinghy* (1958) by permission of Esphyr Slobodkina.

facilitated, policy fostered: editions of fifty thousand are recorded in 1930, of a million or more in 1934, selling most commonly at ten cents (this when the average American printing was twenty-five hundred, the average price two dollars).[32]

These mass-produced pamphlet books, with "their fresh good looks and success in conveying information," created an exceptional stir on the Western publishing scene, and they were credited with inspiring the production of the Puffin Picture Books in Great Britain, the Story Book series in the United States, and, interestingly enough, the Père Castor series in France.[33] To a great extent, nevertheless, their appearance did not cause but coincided with similar, if smaller-scale, educational efforts in the States. Lucy Sprague Mitchell, the organizational genius behind 69 Bank Street, had already launched her informational "Here and Now" series for children, and, as Margaret Wise Brown and Mary Phelps could assert proudly in 1937, "especially the Russians acknowledge her leadership in education and children's literature."[34] The mass production of Soviet picture books seemed not so much a national peculiarity as fulfillment of a globalized wish.

Rojankovsky's illustrations in exile—for the Père Castor series and Little Golden Books—curiously parallelled the mass-produced work of his Soviet peers. Several scholars have remarked on the connection, pointing to the contributions of both Rojankovsky and his fellow émigré Nathalie Parain to Père Castor, and implying that Russian style is a quantifiable essence automatically achieved by shared training and sensibilities.[35] The parallel also struck visitors to the Children's Room of the New York Public Library, who noted the resemblance of Rojankovsky's drawing for Little Golden Books' 1948 *Three Bears* to Iurii Vasnetsov's 1935 Soviet illustration of the same tale[36] (figure 15.3).

Rojankovsky's work, then, incarnates a recurring conundrum in hybrid American culture—the difficulty of national attribution. Did he become an American or remain a Russian artist? Do his accessible images reflect the requirements of commercial standardization or conscientious concerns for mass accessibility and education? Into whose cultural history should he be written? Rojankovsky's illustrations, as well as those of Slobodkina and other émigré artists, constitute as much a trajectory from Russia's Silver Age as the Soviet-sponsored picture books of the 1920s—indeed, a vital line of descent given the subsequent Stalinist repression of many promising illustrators.[37] Has the time come for their "national" reclamation, for a different kind of "émigré-zation" of *Russian* culture? To which country should their "impact" be ascribed?

Émigré-zation/Americanization

For much of the twentieth century, American culture profitted from the European refugee artists it presumed to protect from physical persecution and artistic censorship in their native lands. The experiences of two Russian émigré artists, Rojankovsky

FIGURE 15.3.
An illustration from *The Three Bears*.
From *The Three Bears* by Feodor Rojankovsky, copyright © 1948, renewed 1976 by Golden Books, a division of Random House, Inc. Used by permission of Golden Books, a division of Random House, Inc.

and Slobodkina, example the features of this exploitative and productive exchange—the asylum granted poor political refugees and their recruitment as inexpensive and expert talent; the émigré's relative freedom from overt political interference and desperate dependence on the market; the incessant tug of war between ambitious émigré illustrator and cost-conscious American firm, technical innovator and standardized industry; and the émigré's assumption of his or her American peers' self-styled expertise in successfully portraying and enhancing a variety of ethnic stereotypes. Of course, most émigré illustrators did not achieve Slobodkina's and Rojankovsky's degree of fame and satisfaction, for reasons ranging from lack of opportunity to distaste for applied art and market demands. Still, the gradual globalization of the children's book industry and the serious educational import Americans exceptionally accorded children's books rendered illustration more acceptable to European émigré artists than other kinds of popular culture production.

Perhaps most striking about these émigrés' treatment is how readily and completely American culture has engulfed them. Once these artists came to the United States, their ethnic identity, already muddied in American eyes by their different stations of exile, proved to be of very limited professional use. At first they figured as better-trained Europeans, but soon their identity derived mainly from their work. The publishing industry expediently individuated their value. For a buyer of children's books, the name Rojankovsky signals no more (and no less) than that of a classic illustrator, a guarantee of a quality purchase. American mass culture pioneered the levelling of national/political distinctions in calculated deference to name-brand products and celebrities. But although these and other European émigré artists have been blended into the American mix, their biographies reveal their tough negotiations and ingenious adaptations, and their technically sophisticated, richly distinctive art influences from within a general American inheritance, not only paving the way for other émigré contributions (see the recent work of Vladimir Radunskii and Gennadii Spirin) but also inspiring native-born American artists to emulate their experimentation with ethnic styles. In this sense, émigré-become-American artists cultivated other American artists as cosmopolitans, as artists schooled in "foreign" sensibilities and adept at visually reproducing other cultures. As the Russian artists themselves demonstrated, cultural hybridity need not reflect different cultural experience but great creative imagination and imitative skill.

And cultural hybridity, however derived, may become desirable fashion. Whether it affects the techniques and styles of book illustration or filmmaking or food preparation, émigré-zation in the American culture industry very often infuses American products with sophistication, quality, exotic allure. In tentative conclusion, we might construe this cosmopolitanizing process as a move toward genuine multiculturalism, a subtle internationalizing of consumer tastes. Or we might add a final "gulp!" to our sound-effect rendering of American cultural impact, heeding this absorption of émigré contributions as advance warning of a new Americanization that would appropriate and commodify an entire world of distinctive artists and their work.

Notes

The author thanks Esphyr Slobodkina for her kind permission to quote from her letters contained in the Esphyr Slobodkina Papers (no. DG0905) held in the de Grummond Children's Literature Collection, University of Southern Mississippi. Thanks also go to Dee Jones, curator, and the staff of the de Grummond Collection for their expert help.

1. Richard Pells, *Not Like Us: How Europeans Have Loved, Hated, and Transformed American Culture since World War II* (New York: Basic Books, 1997), 2.

2. See, for example, John Russell Taylor's *Strangers in Paradise: The Hollywood Émigrés, 1933–1950* (New York: Holt, Rinehart & Winston, 1983); also Pells, *Not Like Us*, 18.

3. Anne Scott MacLeod, *American Childhood: Essays on Children's Literature of the Nineteenth and Twentieth Centuries* (Athens: University of Georgia Press, 1994), 122–25; Mary Lystad, *At Home in America as Seen through Its Books for Children* (Cambridge, Mass.: Schenkmen, 1984), 9.

4. Sharyl G. Smith, "Maud and Miska Petersham: Their Work in American Children's Book Publishing, 1920–1939," Ph.D. diss., Columbia University, 1985, pp. 2–5; Barbara Bader, *American Picturebooks from Noah's Ark to the Beast Within* (New York: Macmillan, 1976), 12; Bertha E. Mahony's introduction to Maria Cimino's "Foreign Books in a Children's Library," *Illustrators of Children's Books, 1744–1945,* comp. Bertha E. Mahony, Louise Payson Latimer, and Beulah Formsbee (Boston: Horn, 1947), 125.

5. Eric P. Kelly, "The City That Sings," *Horn Book* 5, no. 1 (February 1929): 27; and "The City of a Thousand Secrets," *Horn Book* 6, no. 1 (February 1930): 37.

6. See the profile of Monica Shannon by another expert dilettante, Elizabeth Cleveland Miller (author of a children's book about Albania), in *Horn Book* 9, no. 2 (March–April 1935): 73–81.

7. Louise Seaman, "From California to the Volga with Fjeril Hess," *Horn Book* 10, no. 6 (November–December 1934): 386–87.

8. Mahony's introduction to Cimino's "Foreign Picture Books in a Children's Library," 125.

9. Mahony's introduction to Cimino's "Foreign Picture Books in a Children's Library," 129, 131.

10. Lynd Ward, "The Book Artist: Yesterday and Tomorrow," in *Illustrators of Children's Books,* 254.

11. Smith, "Maud and Miska Petersham," 162.

12. Ward, "The Book Artist," 255.

13. For good surveys of this period in Russian art history, see Camilla Gray's *The Russian Experiment in Art, 1863–1922,* rev. and enlarged by Marian Burleigh-Motley (London: Thames & Hudson, 1986), and John E. Bowlt's *The Silver Age: Russian Art of the Early Twentieth Century and the "World of Art" Group* (Newtonville, Mass.: Oriental Research Partners, 1979).

14. See Robert Greenall's overview of a Valerii Blinov's children's book collection, "A Collector's Passion," *Russian Life* 469 (February/March 1999): 55.

15. Iurii Molok, ed., *Staraia detskaia knizhka: 1900–30-e gody iz sobraniia professora Marka Ratsa* (Moscow: n.p., 1997), vii–viii.

16. Bader, *American Picturebooks,* 277, 296–97.

17. Esther Averill, "A Publisher's Odyssey," *Horn Book* 14, no. 5 (September–October 1938): 275–81.

18. Averill, "A Publisher's Odyssey," 281.

19. Gail Stavitsky and Elizabeth Wylie, *The Life and Art of Esphyra Slobodkina* (Medford, Mass.: Tufts University Gallery, 1992), 21–22.

20. Esphyra Slobodkina, *Notes for a Biographer*, vol. 2: (privately printed by Urquhart-Slobodkina, 1976), 491.

21. Bader, *American Picturebooks*, 214–21; Leonard Marcus, *Margaret Wise Brown: Awakened by the Moon* (Boston: Beacon, 1992), 88–107. On account of Scott's bungled second printing of *The Little Fireman*, Slobodkina's signature collaboration with Wise Brown, she demanded her name's removal from its cover: "Modest as it is, my career as an artist has been rather satisfactory and my slowly built reputation is worth, in my opinion, being maintained." Quoted from her 2 March 1948 letter to William Scott. Correspondence held in box 3, Slobodkina papers, de Grummond Collection, University of Southern Mississippi.

22. Stavitsky and Wylie, *The Life and Art of Esphyra Slobodkina*, 16–28.

23. Quoted from Slobodkina's 14 March 1966 letter to Miss Loretta Epstein's class in Brooklin and her 14 April 1966 letter to Miss Epstein herself. Slobodkina papers, box 3, de Grummond Collection.

24. Bruce Lockwood, "Boris Artzybasheff," *Creative Art* (January 1933): 16.

25. See her correspondence with Frances Schwartz, children's book editor at Abelard-Schuman Limited, from 28 February to 22 March 1963, box 1, Slobodkina papers, de Grummond collection.

26. Slobodkina's 13 November and 10 December 1967 letters to Lillian Lustig McClintock, children's book editor at Rand McNally, box 2, Slobodkina papers, de Grummond collection.

27. Slobodkina's 30 April 1974 letter to Dorothea Scott, box 2, Slobodkina papers, de Grummond collection.

28. The title page of *Monkey See Monkey Do* noted that it was "based on the old tale *Caps for Sale*." Slobodkina threatened to sue and won compensation.

29. Averill remarks that Rojankovsky had read James Fenimore Cooper in his childhood and had played cowboys and Indians in far-off Mitava. "A Publisher's Odyssey," 277.

30. The term derives from Stalinist culture and refers to workers who, in response to Communist Party exhortation, overfulfilled their work plans/production norms.

31. Babette Deutsch, "Children's Books in Russia," *Creative Art* (September 1931): 223.

32. Bader, *American Picturebooks*, 88.

33. Bader, *American Picturebooks*, 88; Smith, "Maud and Miska Petersham," 147; Cimino, "Foreign Picture Books in a Children's Library," 142.

34. Mary Phelps and Margaret Wise Brown, "Lucy Sprague Mitchell," *Horn Book* 12, no. 3 (May–June 1937): 161.

35. Bader, *American Picturebooks*, 88; Joyce Irene Whalley and Tessa Rose Chester, *A History of Children's Book Illustration* (London: Murray with the Victoria and Albert Museum, 1988), 197; Bettina Hurlimann, *Three Centuries of Children's Books in Europe*, trans. and ed. Bryan W. Alderson (Cleveland: World, 1959), 225.

36. Bader, *American Picturebooks*, 297–98.

37. Molok lists all the illustrators killed, imprisoned, and outcast by the Soviet regime (xxv).

Afterword

Uta G. Poiger

THE TITLE FOR THIS VOLUME—*Kazaaam! Splat! Ploof!*—highlights the fact that American culture has had considerable impact on Europe since World War II. At the same time, this ironic borrowing from a Disney cartoon opens the question as to what the meanings of this impact have been. Destructive? Benign? Transformative? Liberating? After reading the fourteen chapters united here, can we draw any definitive conclusions? And can we ask new questions?

Three major themes emerge from this volume: First, American culture has been an important reference point in cultural, intellectual, and social developments in Eastern and Western Europe. This is true for both the Cold War era and the years since. Second, as these chapters reveal, the American cultural impact in Europe manifests itself in a great variety of forms and genres, ranging from Disneyland, to Hollywood movies, to religious sects, to rock music, to fast food, and to images of UFOs. Moreover, these influences are visible in a great variety of political contexts, from the reconstruction years in postwar Germany, to 1950s Cold War Britain, to socialist Yugoslavia, to post–Cold War Hungary, and to war-torn Croatia, Bosnia, and Serbia, just to name a few. Third, the interpretations of the American cultural impact on Europe are almost as diverse as the products and political contexts they discuss. In this volume, they cluster around several notions: a leveling or displacement of European culture, a Europe in the grip of U.S. cultural imperialism, and creative adaptations of U.S. imports in Europe.

Since the turn of the century, European anti-Americanism has often been more eloquent and pervasive than positive assessments of the impact of U.S. culture abroad. European critics have pointed to American culture as shallow and standardized with stultifying effects on consumers at home and abroad. Voicing fears, for example, about allegedly overly powerful and overly sexual American women or racial transgressions in American music and movies, this anti-Americanism has labelled American cultural influences a threat to European nations, a danger, say, to proper "Frenchness" or "Germanness."[1] The tropes of this anti-Americanism, which has cut across political divides of Left and Right, and of the Cold War, resonate among the Europeans portrayed in this volume: they include the assertions about the "loneliness," the "fakeness," and the "lack of history" of American culture made by postwar Italian theorists as well as the more recent assessment by Hungarians that Americans are "shallow." They also resonate in the analyses of the U.S. cultural impact which some of the authors bring forward.

From the 1960s to the 1980s, the concept of cultural imperialism, which overlaps with the long tradition of anti-Americanism, was particularly important for critiques of cultural Americanization. The notion first proliferated east of the iron curtain with the advent of the Cold War. It gained currency in the West only during the late 1960s. In the wake of the Vietnam War, leftists and members of the countercultures in the United States and abroad began to criticize U.S. foreign policy and pointed to American culture as one of its imperialist tools. The cultural imperialism paradigm assumes that cultural exports directly serve U.S. foreign political and economic interests; it tells a story of manipulation and decline, and it mourns the disappearance of cultural diversity.[2]

In this collection, Laura E. Cooper and B. Lee Cooper invoke the term *cultural imperialism* explicitly as an analytical tool, when they trace a back and forth of U.S. and British cultural imperialism in the changing fortunes of U.S. rock 'n' roll in Britain and the "British invasion" of 1960s rock into the United States. Their contribution highlights that cultural flows have not constituted a one-way street for the United States and that influences from abroad have at times had considerable impact in the United States. But given the asymmetrical power relations between the United States and societies abroad exposed to U.S. culture, is a "mutual cultural imperialism" really possible?

The cultural imperialism paradigm was in part a response to a much more benign view of American culture encapsulated in the modernization paradigm. The modernization paradigm, another Cold War construct, links American culture to economic development and political democratization and presents Americanization as a process by which the United States, through its political, economic, and cultural preeminence, encourages the development of liberal democracies, market economies, and consumer cultures abroad. Constructed in the post–World War II period, under the impact of the Marshall Plan and the Cold War, this paradigm builds on a firm belief in the American superiority over totalitarianism, over both the fascist losers of World War II and Cold War enemies. The experiences of postwar Western European countries and especially the democratization and growing wealth of West Germany seem to confirm that U.S. power applied abroad brings peace, progress, and prosperity. Crudely put, this paradigm, which has shaped much sociological and historical scholarship on post–World War II Europe, posits the existence of an American culture which reflects and transports a uniform, democratic American value system.[3]

Over the past decade, both the modernization and the cultural imperialism paradigm have lost much of their appeal in scholarship, as scholars have reassessed the relationship between American culture and political systems. One important impetus for these reassessments has come from careful investigations of the cultures of fascist regimes by historians and film scholars. Over twenty years ago, Charles S. Maier pointed out that American production methods such as Taylorism were taken up by various political groups and ultimately by states ranging from liberal democracies in France or Great Britain to fascist regimes in Italy and Germany to the Communist Soviet Union.[4] Along similar lines, Guilia Guarnieri mentions in her chapter for this volume that Italian fascists found U.S. culture both fascinating and threatening. Indeed, a number of scholars have shown that, in spite of intense anti-American rhetoric and autarchic policies, fascist regimes were in conscious competition with American cultural models and often adapted them.[5] Victoria de Grazia, for example, has analyzed how Italian fascists responded to "the aesthetic disorder aggravated by the proliferation of American movies, advertising plates and commercial displays" in the interwar years. In spite of official campaigns that sought to promote images of nubile rural women and devoted mothers, "Americanized images of female beauty" proliferated in Italy— for example, in 1930s beauty contests. Fascist regimes were unable to dominate the meanings of commercial culture. Yet de Grazia warns against exaggerating the power of the "resistance" that Americanized commercial culture enabled.[6] Investigations such as hers have revealed the complex ways in which American culture has assumed varying, and often unintended, meanings.

For National Socialism, scholars have likewise pointed to continuities with American consumer culture. Linda Schulte-Sasse and Rick Rentschler have demonstrated the similarities between Nazi commercial film and classical Hollywood cinema. And Hans Dieter Schäfer has reminded us that in 1930s Berlin, advertisements for that quintessentially American product, Coke, urged visitors to the *Sportpalast*, where Goebbels gave many of his racist speeches, to drink "Coca-Cola ice-cold."[7] Thus, scholarship on fascist Italy and Nazi Germany has shown that Americanization cannot be attached to any one political system.[8]

This volume supports that conclusion, from a different angle. One of its major contributions is that it pays attention to American culture in Yugoslavia and in areas formerly east of the iron curtain. These areas have long been neglected, yet they contribute to a complex picture of cultural Americanization. As my own work shows, East German authorities permitted jazz as a proletarian music from the 1950s onward, even though they were largely hostile toward U.S. culture. And by the 1970s, they allowed homegrown rock as a youthful diversion, in an effort to make their state attractive for young people. For Yugoslavia, Sabrina P. Ramet shows that authorities used U.S. cultural imports to bolster their legitimacy within the country. By demonstrating how U.S. culture is deployed by states in domestic projects and international politics, such examples reveal that generalizations about U.S. culture as a tool for democratization or U.S. imperialism are questionable.

Ethnographic studies likewise have been important in making this point by tracing the complex and varying responses that audiences abroad have had to U.S. culture.[9] As the authors of *Golden Arches East* have shown for East Asian countries, even highly standardized products and environments such as those of McDonald's are constantly remade by the local reception.[10] In Beverly James's chapter in this volume, the confidence of the Hungarian interviewees of the 1990s is striking: they claim that the long tradition of Hungarian culture makes them immune to being seriously overrun by U.S. culture, in spite of the strong presence of U.S. movies or fast-food restaurants since the fall of communism.

In recent years, scholars have also begun to debate the relationship of globalization and Americanization. For some, globalization signifies a decrease in American power and the significance of U.S. culture in Europe and worldwide, while others see continued U.S. domination. Conclusions drawn about the increasingly negative impact of global uniformity, whether generated by U.S. power or global capitalism, owe much to the earlier cultural imperialism paradigm, just as celebrations of the progress which globalization allegedly brings partially echo the modernization paradigm. But here, too, many scholars urge careful investigations that explore the interplay of greater homogeneity and greater heterogeneity as a result of global transformations; they also seek to examine U.S. dominance in a global world while acknowledging the complex webs of transnational interactions that don't always run through the United States. Americanization thus is not eclipsed by globalization and remains an important subject for the study of past and present.[11]

Americanization should not be seen as a phenomenon in which nations unambiguously follow an American model. Scholars are increasingly realizing that in order to assess the American impact abroad, including the successes and failures of American policies and culture, they need to pay close attention to social, economic, and political conditions within recipient nations.[12]

Such work also requires that culture be understood as a productive force, as an always present yet always changing series of sites in the formation of international relations. By contrast, both the cultural imperialism paradigm and the modernization paradigm have interpreted culture largely as reflective of and subordinate to political and economic developments at home, while reinforcing political and economic developments abroad. Culture, in these visions, has been defined in relation to allegedly universal criteria. Instead, culture needs to be seen as a constitutive element in the formation of identities and in the shaping of interactions between foreign countries; cultural products transform relations of power within as well as between nations. What constitutes culture is constantly negotiated, and these negotiations, which happen often in the context of uneven power relations, need to be traced.[13]

A related point on which Beth Holmgren's chapter ends this volume is worth reiterating: U.S. culture in fact relies constantly on adaptations from abroad. Holmgren shows this through the concrete example of Russian creators of children's books who have worked in the United States. As she correctly observes, "[a]ny analysis of U.S.-European cultural interactions should acknowledge and explore the ethnic hybridity of American culture." And the diverse chapters in this volume underline just how multifaceted U.S. culture is, in origin, form, and content.

If U.S. culture is multifaceted, so is the U.S. political landscape. The U.S. government and exporters of U.S. culture have frequently been at odds. As studies on American cultural influences abroad in the 1950s have shown, the American government sometimes worried that the American entertainment industry spread undesirable exports which could reinforce the impression that the United States lacked culture.[14] Nor do the religious missionaries whom various American churches have sent to Europe (examined in Rodney Stark's chapter) necessarily promote the interests of the U.S. government.

Even as the U.S. influence on Western Europe reached new heights with the Cold War (and as *consensus* became a key term), neither the United States nor the "receiving" nations were simply unified. European governments and elites in the 1950s were worried about the taste for imports such as jazz, rock 'n' roll, or westerns among younger generations. Some forms of American culture could provide alternative modes of identification along the lines of gender, generation, or class for Europeans. For example, young people who consumed rock 'n' roll or jeans exposed the upper-class and high-cultural character of much of what was deemed authentically "British," "German," or "French." Criticisms of these adolescents also reveal that many Europeans continued to link respectability to "whiteness."[15]

The issues of ethnicity and race further complicate an assessment of European interactions with American culture. In encountering American soldiers, who come from various racial groups, as in encountering diverse strands of American culture, Europeans have confronted their own notions of racial hierarchies. Investigations of these questions are just emerging.[16] After 1945, desegregation quickly became a "Cold War imperative" for the United States, but this push for desegregation was accompanied by a push for homogenization, a denial of differences between ethnic groups, and a celebration of an America where male breadwinners of all races and classes provided for wives and children. It was not until 1956, under the impact of an emerging civil rights movements and many requests from abroad, that the United States Information Agency sent African American musician Dizzy Gillespie and his band abroad to play jazz—now promoted as "high" American culture with "universal" appeal.[17] Since then diversity has increasingly become something that the United States government uses in its self-presentation at home and abroad.[18]

Young people especially have adopted some U.S. imports with great enthusiasm at certain moments: Sabrina P. Ramet reports on the heterogeneous styles of Yugoslav rock musicians in the 1970s and 1980s. Some of them designed their music as a form of social criticism against the party line. East and West German youth of the 1950s used rock 'n' roll music and dancing to challenge dominant sexual mores. The meaning of such changes for young German women was ambiguous. On the one hand, open sexual expression became more acceptable for them; on the other hand, being sexy created new, often misogynist expectations. Thus, European encounters with U.S. culture have often been gender specific. Moreover, the uses and adaptations of U.S. imports mean that we need to question celebrations of "traditional" cultures which existed prior to an American onslaught.

Marianne Debouzy, for example, rejects the label cultural imperialism but is deeply concerned about the way in which EuroDisney displaces local celebrations and traditional French culture. She correctly points to Disney's disturbing labor practices in France and elucidates the French debates on Disney's cultural impact. Nonetheless, one wonders whether changes in European leisure time behavior, including the disappearance of local fairs, have primarily American roots. In this era of multinational television, media, and publishing giants, some of them German, Japanese, or French owned (e.g., Bertelsmann, Sony, and Vivendi), accusations leveled by European intellectuals or politicians against U.S. culture often run the risk of romanticizing allegedly original European national cultures. Pan-European efforts to fend off U.S. culture can also be problematic. Most recently, the attempts of the European Union to create a European core culture based apparently largely on sports events (mentioned by Anthony Giffard in his chapter on European measures to keep Hollywood at bay) make such pan-European alternatives seem rather uninspiring.

This volume opens up several issues which deserve further scrutiny in future scholarship on U.S. cultural imports in Europe. As Gordana P. Crnković points out, we need to pay more attention to form when we analyze the U.S. impact abroad. Surely there is a big difference between the songs of Ella Fitzgerald and McDonald's hamburgers, and we need to ask what kind of horizons of interpretation specific products open. Crnković also reminds us that the formal conventions of European responses—for example, in travel journals—have shaped debates on Americanization. In short, we need to pay more attention to the form of the import as well as to the form of the response.

If cultural imperialism seems too crude a concept to most scholars in this volume, they nonetheless rightly struggle with the question of U.S. cultural domination. Indeed, the United States exports vastly more movies, television shows, and popular music than it imports. It remains important to ask how specific cultural products support, or at times undermine, U.S. policies both with the United States and abroad, and how they create desires for new social or political visions. Melani McAlister in her timely study of U.S. representations of the Middle East in movies, news reports, or museum exhibits, has shown how cultural products relate to both the domestic politics of race and U.S. foreign policy.[19] Many of the products McAlister covers—for example, *The Ten Commandments* or *Die Hard*—were exported to Europe (and elsewhere) and elicited different reactions. Sustained comparisons between the meanings of cultural products within the United States and abroad are still rare and require new collaborations. They will have much to tell us about the dynamics of U.S. power. In the changing environment after 11 September 2001, it seems likely that in the United States the value of U.S. cultural exports will be measured not just by their market value but increasingly again by their alleged strategic value.

The relationship between U.S. culture and politics at home and abroad is highly complex, and, as Steinar Bryn reminds us in this volume, anti-Americanism and critiques of U.S. policies can be compatible with a desire for specific American goods or attraction to American myths (e.g., those about the Wild West). Even if we conclude that over the past fifty years Europe has become more like the United States, we might ask additional questions about how U.S. cultural influences relate to changing stratifications of European societies—for example, along the lines of generation, gender, class, ethnicity, or citizenship.

In the future, we will also have to grapple further with the complexity of Europeans' position in the twentieth century, versus the United States and the Soviet Union, on the one hand, and versus other, often subordinate countries, on the other.[20] Europeans have often understood Americanization as a form of colonization, all the while ignoring their own histories as expansionist, imperialist, or fascist powers and their relations with postcolonial nations. The Cold War made such a one-dimensional focus on Americanization possible, but scholarship is now going in new directions.

For studies of cultural influences and consumption, this means that we need to put American imports into much broader frameworks. We need a wider understanding of how the politics of consumption and of culture have related to the understanding and obscuring of international relations. For example, European consumption—prior, during, and since the Cold War—has to be located in trade relations and understandings of the exotic that have extended well beyond the United States. In this context, the relationships among European colonialism, Americanization, and globalization need further investigation. In the end, the difficulties of assessing the U.S. cultural impact on Europe point to the urgent need to read culture in relation to business decisions and to policies. Readers might thus want to put the chapters united here in direct conversation with the other volume in this set (*Coming in from the Cold War,* edited by Sabrina P. Ramet and Christine Ingebritsen, 2002). Attention to these various factors will no doubt further complicate our assessments of the United States cultural impact in Europe by exploring the interconnections among culture, domestic politics, foreign relations, and international trade.

Notes

For helpful comments on this afterword, I thank Madeleine Yue Dong, Priti Ramamurthy, Lynn Thomas, and Alys Weinbaum.

1. On the history of European anti-Americanism, see especially Dan Diner, *America in the Eyes of the Germans: An Essay on Anti-Americanism,* trans. Allison Brown (Princeton,

N.J.: Wiener, 1996); Rob Kroes and Maarten van Rossem, eds., *Anti-Americanism in Europe* (Amsterdam: Free University Press, 1986); Richard F. Kuisel, *Seducing the French: The Dilemma of Americanization* (Berkeley: University of California Press, 1993); and Richard H. Pells, *Not Like Us: How Europeans Have Loved, Hated, and Transformed American Culture since World War II* (New York: Basic Books, 1997).

2. On the concept of American cultural imperialism east of the iron curtain, see, for example, Uta G. Poiger, *Jazz, Rock, and Rebels: Cold War Battles over Gender, Race, and Nation* (Berkeley: University of California Press, 2000); S. Frederick Starr, *Red and Hot: The Fate of Jazz in the Soviet Union, 1917–1980* (New York: Oxford University Press, 1983). On the history of the paradigm in the West, see John Tomlinson, *Cultural Imperialism: A Critical Introduction* (London: Continuum, 1991), and Jessica Gienow-Hecht, "Shame on US? Academics, Cultural Transfer and the Cold War—A Critical Review," *Diplomatic History* 24 (Summer 2000): 465–94. Examples of scholarship shaped by this notion include Armand Mattelart, Xavier Delcourt, and Michelle Mattelart, *International Image Markets: In Search of an Alternative Perspective* (London: Comedia, 1984); Herbert I. Schiller, *Mass Communications and American Empire,* 2d ed. (Boulder, Colo.: Westview, 1992); and Jeremy Tunstall, *The Media Are American: Anglo-American Media in the World* (London: Constable, 1977). My treatment of these paradigms, and challenges to them, is adapted from Heide Fehrenbach and Uta G. Poiger, "Americanization Reconsidered," in *Transactions, Transgressions, Transformations: American Culture in Western Europe and Japan,* ed. Heide Fehrenbach and Uta G. Poiger (New York: Berghahn, 2000), xiii–xl.

3. Examples include L. H. Gann and Peter Duignan, *The Rebirth of the West: The Americanization of the Democratic World, 1945–1958* (Cambridge, Mass.: Blackwell, 1992); Alfred Grosser, *Germany in Our Time: A Political History of the Postwar Years* (New York: Praeger, 1971); and Dennis L. Bark and David R. Gress, *A History of West Germany,* 2 vols. (Oxford: Blackwell, 1989).

4. Charles S. Maier, "Between Taylorism and Technocracy: European Ideologies and the Vision of Industrial Productivity in the 1920s," *Journal of Contemporary History* 5, no. 2 (1970): 27–61. See also Mary Nolan, *American Business and the Modernization of Germany* (New York: Oxford University Press, 1994).

5. Ruth Ben-Ghiat, "Envisioning Modernity: Desire and Discipline in the Italian Fascist Film," *Critical Inquiry* 23 (Autumn 1996): 109–44; Victoria de Grazia, "Mass Culture and Sovereignty: The American Challenge to European Cinemas, 1920–1960," *Journal of Modern History* 61 (March 1989): 53–87; Philipp Gassert, *Amerika im Dritten Reich: Ideologie, Propaganda und Volksmeinung, 1933–1945* (Stuttgart: Steiner, 1997); Michael H. Kater, *Different Drummers: Jazz in the Culture of Nazi Germany* (New York: Oxford University Press, 1992); Detlev Peukert, *Inside Nazi Germany: Conformity, Opposition, and Racism in Everyday Life,* trans. Richard Deveson (New Haven, Conn.: Yale University Press, 1987); Eric Rentschler, *The Ministry of Illusion: Nazi Cinema and Its Afterlife* (Cambridge, Mass.: Harvard University Press, 1996); Thomas J. Saunders, *Hollywood in Berlin: American Cinema and Weimar Germany* (Berkeley: University of California Press, 1994); and Linda Schulte-Sasse, *Entertaining the Third Reich: Illusions of Wholeness in Nazi Cinema* (Durham, N.C.: Duke University Press, 1996).

6. Victoria de Grazia, "Nationalizing Women: The Competition between Fascist and Commercial Cultural Models in Mussolini's Italy," in *The Sex of Things: Gender and Consumption in Historical Perspective,* ed. Victoria de Grazia (Berkeley: University of California Press, 1996), 337–58.

7. Hans Dieter Schäfer, "Amerikanismus im Dritten Reich," in *Nationalsozialismus und Modernisierung*, ed. Michael Prinz and Rainer Zitelmann (Darmstadt: Wissenschaftliche Buchgesellschaft, 1991), 199–215; and Gassert, *Amerika im Dritten Reich*, passim.

8. On this point, see also Detlev Peukert, *The Weimar Republic: The Crisis of Classical Modernity* (New York: Hill & Wang, 1987); J. Victor Koschmann, "The Nationalism of Cultural Uniqueness," and Mary Nolan, "Against Exceptionalisms," both in *American Historical Review* 102 (June 1997): 758–68, 769–74, respectively.

9. See, for example, Ien Ang, *Watching Dallas: Soap Opera and the Melodramatic Imagination*, trans. Della Couling (London: Methuen, 1985); Tamar Liebes and Elihu Katz, *The Export of Meaning: Cross Cultural Readings of Dallas* (New York: Oxford University Press, 1990); and Jackie Stacey, *Star Gazing: Hollywood Cinema and Female Spectatorship* (New York: Routledge, 1994).

10. James L. Watson, ed., *Golden Arches East: McDonald's in East Asia* (Stanford, Calif.: Stanford University Press, 1997).

11. For debates on the relationship of Americanization and globalization, see, for example, Hecht, "*Shame on US?*"; Thomas L. Friedman, *The Lexus and the Olive Tree: Understanding Globalization* (New York: Farrar, Straus & Giroux, 1999); Frederic Jameson and Masao Miyoshi, *The Cultures of Globalization* (Durham, N.C.: Duke University Press, 1998).

12. See Volker R. Berghahn, *The Americanization of West German Industry, 1945–1973* (New York: Oxford University Press, 1986); John Dean and Jean-Paul Gabilliet, eds., *European Readings of American Popular Culture* (Westport, Conn.: Greenwood, 1996); David W. Ellwood, Rob Kroes, and Brunetta Gian Piero, eds., *Hollywood in Europe: Experiences of a Cultural Hegemony* (Amsterdam: VU University Press, 1994); Fehrenbach and Poiger, eds., *Transactions*, passim; Heide Fehrenbach, *Cinema in Democratizing Germany: Reconstructing National Identity after Hitler* (Chapel Hill: University of North Carolina Press, 1995); Konrad Jarausch and Hannes Siegrist, eds., *Amerikanisierung und Sowjetisierung in Deutschland* (Frankfurt-am-Main: Campus, 1997); Kuisel, *Seducing the French*, passim; Alf Lüdtke, Inge Marßolek, and Adelheid von Saldern, eds., *Amerikanisierung: Traum und Alptraum im Deutschland des 20. Jahrhunderts* (Stuttgart: Steiner, 1996); Kaspar Maase, *Bravo Amerika: Erkundungen zur Jugendkultur der Bundesrepublik in den fünfziger Jahren* (Hamburg: Junius, 1992); David Morley and Kevin Robins, *Spaces of Identity: Global Media, Electronic Landscapes, and Cultural Boundaries* (New York: Routledge, 1995); Pells, *Not Like Us*, passim; Reinhold Wagnleitner, *Coca-Colonization and the Cold War: The Cultural Mission of the United States in Austria after the Second World War*, trans. Diana M. Wolf (Chapel Hill: University of North Carolina Press, 1994); Reinhold Wagnleitner and Elaine Tyler May, eds., *Here, There, and Everywhere: The Foreign Politics of American Popular Culture* (Hanover, N.H.: University Press of New England, 2000).

13. See, for example, Benedict Anderson, *Imagined Communities: Reflections on the Origin and Spread of Nationalism*, rev. ed. (New York: Verso, 1991), and Stuart Hall's many interventions, including "Cultural Studies and Its Theoretical Legacies," in *Stuart Hall: Critical Dialogues in Cultural Studies*, ed. David Morley and Kuan-Hsing Chen (New York: Routledge, 1996), 262–75.

14. See for example, Poiger, *Jazz, Rock, and Rebels*, chap. 1; and Volker R. Berghahn, *America and the Intellectual Cold Wars in Europe: Shepard Stone between Philanthropy, Academy, and Diplomacy* (Princeton, N.J.: Princeton University Press, 2001).

15. On youth and Americanization in the 1950s, see especially Dick Hebdige, "Toward a Cartography of Taste," in Hebdige, *Hiding in the Light: On Images and Things* (London:

Comedia, 1987), 45–75; Maase, *Bravo Amerika,* passim; Poiger, *Jazz, Rock, and Rebels,* passim; and Wagnleitner, *Coca-Colonization,* passim.

16. On the significance of race in encounters with American culture, see John G. Blair, "Blackface Minstrels and *Buffalo Bill's Wild West:* Nineteenth Century Entertainment Forms as Cultural Exports," in *European Readings of American Popular Culture,* ed. Dean and Gabillet, 3–12; Paul Gilroy, *The Black Atlantic: Modernity and Double Consciousness* (Cambridge, Mass.: Harvard University Press, 1993); and Morley and Robins, *Spaces of Identity,* passim.

17. Mary Dudziak, *Cold War Civil Rights: Race and the Image of American Democracy* (Princeton, N.J.: Princeton University Press, 2000); "Symposium: African Americans and U.S. Foreign Relations," *Diplomatic History* 20 (Fall 1996): 531–650; Charles A. Thomson and Walter H. C. Laves, *Cultural Relations and U.S. Foreign Policy* (Bloomington: Indiana University Press, 1963); and Poiger, *Jazz, Rock, and Rebels,* passim.

18. Amy Kaplan and Donald E. Pease, eds., *Cultures of United States Imperialism* (Durham, N.C.: Duke University Press, 1993).

19. Melani McAlister, *Epic Encounters: Culture, Media, and U.S. Interests in the Middle East, 1945–2000* (Berkeley: University of California Press, 2001).

20. On this point, see Kristin Ross, *Fast Cars, Clean Bodies: Decolonization and the Reordering of French Bodies* (Cambridge, Mass.: MIT Press, 1995), 7–9; and Morley and Robins, *Spaces of Identity,* passim.

Index

Subject Index

About the Editors and Contributors

Sabrina P. Ramet is professor of political science at the Norwegian University of Science & Technology (NTNU) in Trondheim, Norway. She is the author of seven books, among which one has gone into an expanded fourth edition (*Balkan Babel: The Disintegration of Yugoslavia from the Death of Tito to the Fall of Milosevic,* Westview, 2002), while two others have gone into expanded second editions. She is also the editor or coeditor of fifteen books and translator (from German) of Viktor Meier's *Yugoslavia: A History of Its Demise* (Routledge, 1999). Her articles have appeared in *Foreign Affairs, World Politics, Orbis, Political Science Quarterly, Problems of Post-Communism, Slavic Review,* and other journals. Born in London, she lived for extended periods of time in Britain, Austria, Germany, Yugoslavia, Japan, and the United States, before moving to Norway in August 2001. She received her A.B. in philosophy from Stanford University in 1971, her M.A. in international relations from the University of Arkansas in 1974, and her Ph.D. in political science from University of California–Los Angeles in 1981. She is currently finishing a book entitled *The Three Yugoslavias: The Dual Challenge of State-Building and Legitimation among the Yugoslavs, 1918–2001.*

Gordana P. Crnković is an associate professor of Slavic languages and literature at the University of Washington, Seattle. She received her Ph.D. in the Program of Modern Thought and Literature from Stanford University in 1993. She is the author of *Imagined Dialogues: East European Literature in Conversation with English and American Literature* (Northwestern University Press, 2000). She contributed two chapters to *Gender Politics in the Western Balkans: Women and Society in Yugoslavia and the Yugoslav Successor States* (Penn State Press, 1999), edited by Sabrina P. Ramet. Her articles have appeared in *Film Quarterly, Vanishing Point, Feminist Issues, Stanford Humanities Review,* and other journals.

Steinar Bryn is a professor at Nansen Skole in Norway. He is the author of *Norske Amerika-bilete: om amerikanisiering av norsk kultur* (Det Norske Samlaget, 1992) and coauthor (with Rolf Lundén and Erik Åsard) of *Networks of Americanization: Aspects of the American Influence in Sweden* (Almqvist & Wiksell International, 1992).

B. Lee Cooper is professor of history and American culture and vice president for academic affairs/dean of the College at Reinhardt College in Waleska, Georgia. He is the author of twelve books, including *A Resource Guide to Themes in Contemporary American Song Lyrics, 1950–1985* (Greenwood, 1986), *Popular Music Perspectives: Ideas, Themes, and Patterns in Contemporary Lyrics* (Bowling Green State University Popular Press, 1991), *Baseball and American Culture* (with Donald E. Walker, McFarland, 1995), and *Rock Music in American Popular Culture*, 3 vols. (with Wayne S. Haney, Haworth, 1995, 1997, 1999). His articles have appeared in the *Journal of American Culture, Rock and Blues News, Popular Music and Society, Social Education,* the *Drexel Library Quarterly,* the *ARSC Journal,* and *Social Studies.* He received his B.S. in English and history from Bowling Green State University in 1964, his M.A. in history from Michigan State University in 1965, and a Ph.D. in history and humanities education from Ohio State University in 1971.

Laura E. Cooper is compensation specialist at Republic Bank in Lansing, Michigan. Her articles have appeared in the *Journal of Popular Culture,* the *International Journal of Instructional Media,* and *Popular Culture in Libraries.* She earned a bachelor's degree in history from Michigan State University in 1991 and continues to read and research in the fields of art, African American history, and women's studies.

Marianne Debouzy is professor emerita of American social history at the University of Paris–8. Her articles have appeared in *in Le mouvement Social à Cahiers Internationaux de Sociologie* and *Reviews in American History, History and Anthropology.* Her books include *Travail et Travailleurs aux États-Unis* (1984; 2d ed., 1990). She is also the editor of *In the Shadow of the Statue of Liberty: Immigrants, Workers and Citizens in the American Republic, 1880–1920* (University of Illinois Press, 1992) and contributed a chapter to *European Readings of American Popular Culture* (Greenwood, 1996), edited by John Dean and Jean-Paul Gabilliet, among other works.

C. Anthony Giffard is a professor of communications and director of the School of Communications at the University of Washington, Seattle. He has also taught and worked as a journalist in Africa and Europe. His books include *UNESCO and the Media* (Longman, 1989) and *The Press under Apartheid: Censorship and Repression in South Africa* (with William A. Hachten, University of Wisconsin Press, 1984). He is a consultant for various UN agencies and international nongovernmental organizations. Recent research concerns include media coverage of global issues.

Giulia Guarnieri is a Ph.D. candidate in the Department of Romance Languages at the University of Washington, Seattle. Previously she received her master's degree at the University of Bologna in 1993. Her articles have appeared in *Via, Babel, Arcade,* and *Italian Quarterly.* Fluent in English, French, and Spanish, as well as in her native Italian, Guarnieri played a crucial role in the establishment of an exchange program between the University of Washington and the University of Bologna.

Herbert J. Eagle is an associate professor of Slavic languages and literatures at the University of Michigan, where he teaches courses on Russian and East European film. His works on cinema include *Russian Formalist Film Theory* (University of Michigan Press, 1981) and articles on filmmakers Dusan Makavejev, Jiří Menzel, Vera Chytilová, Andrzej Wajda, Roman Polanski, Peter Gothar, Sergei Eisenstein, Alexei German, Karen Shakhnazarov, Vasily Pichul, and Pavel Lungin in journals such as *Film Studies Annual, Wide Angle, Michigan Quarterly Review,* and *Cross Currents,* as well as in anthologies such as Daniel Goulding's *Five Filmmakers: Tarkovsky, Forman, Polanski, Szabo, Makavejev* (Indiana University Press, 1994) and Sabrina P. Ramet's *Eastern Europe: Politics, Culture, and Society since 1939* (Indiana University Press, 1998). He also has translated texts published in *Russian Futurism through Its Manifestoes, 1912–1928,* edited by Anna Lawton (Cornell University Press, 1988).

Beth Holmgren is a professor of Slavic languages and literatures at the University of North Carolina at Chapel Hill. Her books—*Women's Works in Stalin's Time: On Lidiia Chukovskaia and Nadezhda Mandelstam* (Indiana University Press, 1993), *Russia, Women, Culture* (coedited with Helena Goscilo, Indiana University Press, 1996), and *Rewriting Capitalism: Literature and Market in Late Tsarist Russia and the Kingdom of Poland* (University of Pittsburgh Press, 1998)—reflect her interests in women's studies and cultural studies. Her cotranslation, with Helena Goscilo, of Anastasya Verbitskaya's fin-de-siècle blockbuster, *Keys to Happiness,* was published by Indiana University Press in April 1999.

Beverly James is an associate professor in the Department of Communications at the University of New Hampshire. Her research on cultural transformations in postcommunist Hungary has appeared in *Media, Culture & Society, Critical Studies in Mass Communication,* and *Javnost/The Public,* as well as the *Journal of Popular Culture.* She is currently writing a book about the formation of postcommunist identities and ideologies through an investigation of monuments, museum exhibits, holiday rituals, and films related to the 1956 Hungarian Revolution.

Uta G. Poiger is associate professor of history at the University of Washington, Seattle. She is the author of *Jazz, Rock, and Rebels: Cold War Politics and American Culture in a Divided Germany* (University of California Press, 2000) and coeditor (with Heide Fehrenbach) of *Transactions, Transgressions, Transformations: American Culture in Western Europe and Japan* (Berghahn, 2000). Among her scholarly articles are "Rock 'n' Roll, Female Sexuality, and the Cold War Battle over German Identities," in *Journal of Modern History* 68, no. 3 (September 1996), and "A New 'Western' Hero? Reconstructing German Masculinity in the 1950s," in *Signs* 24, no. 1 (Autumn 1998).

Rodney Stark lives in New Mexico. Until 2000 he was a professor of sociology at the University of Washington, Seattle. He is the author of *The Rise of Christianity: A Sociologist Reconsiders History* (Princeton University Press, 1996) and coauthor of *Religion and Society in Tension* (Rand McNally, 1965), *Patterns of Religious Commitment* (University of California Press, 1968), *The Future of Religion: Secularization, Revival, and Cult Formation* (University of California Press, 1985), *The Churching of America, 1776–1990: Winners and Losers in Our Religious Economy* (Rutgers University Press, 1992), *A Theory of Religion* (Rutgers University Press, 1996), and *Religion, Deviance, and Social Control* (Routledge, 1997).